Why the Sister in Black Works Hardest

African-American Women as Labor in the Novels of Toni Morrison, Alice Walker and Gloria Naylor

Madhumita Purkayastha

ATLANTIC

PUBLISHERS & DISTRIBUTORS (P) LTD

Published by

ATLANTIC

PUBLISHERS & DISTRIBUTORS (P) LTD

7/22, Ansari Road, Darya Ganj, New Delhi-110002
Phones : +91-11-40775252, 40775214, 23273880, 23275880
Fax: +91-11-23285873
Web: www.atlanticbooks.com
E-mail: orders@atlanticbooks.com

Branch Office: Chennai
Phones : +91-44-48531784, 28291383
E-mail: chennai@atlanticbooks.com

Printed & bound in India by Atlantic Print Services

Dedication

In memory of my beloved father Dilip Kumar Purkayastha,
whose cherished wish was to see the completion
and publication of this work. A friend, philosopher and
guide to me in his life time, his indomitable spirit
has ever guided me, and his blessings have
always been with me even when
death took him away.
Baba this is for you.

Acknowledgements

I am indebted to my supervisor Professor Aparna Mahanta whose able guidance has made the completion of this work possible. I am deeply grateful to Dr. Dipankar Purkayastha for encouraging me to take up the study, and to late Prof. K.N. Phukan for the invaluable advice and support he offered me. I would like to thank Dr. B.K. Danta for the ready help he extended whenever I approached him. My sincere gratitude is extended to Prof K. Saikia, Dept. of Economics for his kind help.

I wish to express my thanks to the authorities of D.H.S.K. College, Dibrugarh for allowing me to avail of the study leave, which enabled me to complete my work. I gratefully acknowledge the financial assistance received from the U.G.C. through Dibrugarh University. I am also thankful to the teachers and staff of the Department of English, Dibrugarh University for their co-operation and help. I owe my thanks to the authorities of I.A.C.I.S. library of Hyderabad and the authorities of U.S.I.S. library of Calcutta for providing me with necessary materials. I also thank the authorities and staff of Dibrugarh University library, especially late Mr. Nilim Chaudhury for allowing me to use the journals and books.

I am grateful to my mother Manjulika Purkayastha for her encouragement and support. My husband Partha Ganguli merits special mention, without whose untiring help and unwavering conviction in my abilities, the completion of this work would have been impossible.

I am grateful to the Atlantic Publishers and Distributors Pvt. Ltd., New Delhi for the interest evinced in publishing this book.

Madhumita Purkayastha

Preface

I had always felt that I should publish my maiden research as a book because of two primary reasons. First—the research undertaken on three key African-American women novelists—Nobel laureate Toni Morrison, noted "womanist" writer Alice Walker and the American Book Award winner Gloria Naylor—spanning 14 novels would be a pioneering work in this part of the world where African-American fiction has been critically approached, but not as exhaustively, or using the triple filter of race, class and gender. I have not attempted to edit the original work in terms of thematic or structural content as I wished to retain the detailed critical analysis from the stated perspective, which I believe shall be of use to present researchers insofar as it offers a deep critical comprehension of intersecting issues of ethnicity, identity, self-identification and literary representations in the tangled web of existential experience of the African-American diaspora. The "Categories" evolved with the purpose of bringing within the fold of close reading an exhaustive stream of characters and as an inclusionist strategy remain as flexible parameters to facilitate an enhanced appreciation of the intricate mesh and complexities of African-American women's existence and experience.

The second reason was my conviction that the feminist interpretation and understanding of the term labor coupled with the black feminist standpoint incorporated in the present study would have unique and groundbreaking implications in examining the "labor of love, labor of sorrow" of the African-American women in America, who have been treated as "the mules of the world". I sincerely hope that this study shall contribute meaningfully and add new dimensions to the existing plethora of information on African-American women fiction writers.

A third reason that evolved in course of my continuous engagement with literary research was the possibility of a cross-cultural study on tea garden laborers' representations in the mainstream fictional texts of Assam, given the backdrop of tea plantations where during British colonial rule, an enforced diaspora of mingled tribal origins from Bengal, Bihar and Orissa had been co-erced to settle. Subsequently, stereotypes of the tea garden labor women emerged in the mainstream psyche of Assam that are strikingly similar to the stereotypes of African American women represented in American literature. Marginalised groups throughout the world have always had to invent liberating and empowering strategies of self-expression while resisting oppression from dominant groups to cast them into social and cultural stereotypes through misrepresentation in cultural/literary texts as disempowering and undermining strategies with the agenda of perpetuating subjugation and oppression. I believe that in drawing parallels between the African American women laborers and tea garden laborers of Assam, the critical insights gained from the one would enrich an interrogation of the other. Publishing this work would be a stepping stone to further innovative literary research, which I look forward to eagerly.

Madhumita Purkayastha

Contents

List of Abbreviations

The titles of the novels selected for the study are abbreviated as follows:

Novels by Toni Morrison

The Bluest Eye	*TBE*
Sula	*S*
Song of Solomon	*SOS*
Tar Baby	*TB*
Beloved	*B*
Jazz	*J*

Novels by Alice Walker

The Third Life of Grange Copeland	*TLGC*
Meridian	*M*
The Color Purple	*TCP*
The Temple of My Familiar	*TMF*

Novels by Gloria Naylor

The Women of Brewster Place	*WBP*
Linden Hills	*LH*
Mama Day	*MD*
Bailey's Cafe	*BC*

Introduction

1

Why the Sister in Black[1] Works Hardest

Know how it happened? After God got thru makin' de world and de varmints and de folks, he made up a great big bundle and let it down in de middle of de road. It laid dere for thousands of years, then Ole Missus said to Ole Massa: "Go pick up dat box, Ah want to see whut's in it." Ole Massa look at de box and it look so heavy dat he says to de nigger, "Go fetch me dat big ole box out dere in de road." De nigger been stumblin over de box a long time so he tell his wife:

> "Oman, go git dat box." So de nigger 'Oman she runned to git de box.

She says:

> "Ah always lak to open up a big box 'cause there's nearly always something good in great big boxes." So she run and grabbed a-hold of de box and opened it up and it was full of hard work.

Dat's de reason de sister in black works harder than anybody else in de world. De white man tells de nigger to work and he takes and tells his wife.[2]

I

The quotation from Zora Neale Hurston strikes the keynote of the present study in more ways than one. The purpose of the study is to probe into the literary representations of the roles of African-American women as labor in the novels of Toni Morrison, Alice Walker and Gloria Naylor—African-American women writers who have emerged as three of the most sensitive novelists in African-American literature in the last two decades. The question posed in the title of the popular African tribal folk tale is an ironical pointer to a fact that has been generally accepted and taken for granted by the American society and that condenses in itself a host of historical, sociological and cultural realities of the African-American woman's existence in America. It is also a reminder that the role of the "sister in black" has centrally been that of a laborer in America, both in the context of the Anglo-American and African-American societies. Through a humour tinged with the typically fatalistic resignation of an oppressed group, the folk tale conveys the moving reality of the African-American women's existence—that the big box of burden and responsibilities has been handed down to her in a game of "passing the parcel" because she was not in a positon to give orders to any one or no one to pass the parcel on to in the world. So the "ole Missus"—the pampered southern white lady ordered her spouse "ole Massa"—the white slave master, to get the box for her which she thought contained untold treasures. "Ole Massa" promptly passed the command to the "nigger" who in his turn, shifted the onus of toting the huge and heavy-looking box on his wife "de nigger woman". She was active, inquisitive and hopeful and there was no 'other' to transfer her burden to. So she hoisted the heavy burden, which upon inspection, turned out to be a box load of worries, cares, tiresome work and toil—the lot that fell as a curse on "the sister in black". The simple folk tale revolves round a network of related socio-historical truths and stems from a collective group experience of the African Americans in America.

Significantly, with an inverted humour, the story ostensibly lays the blame of the African-American woman's wretched lot on her own foolishness and acquisitiveness while subtly hinting at the identity of the real oppressors—the white woman, the white man and the African American man who have been accomplices in making the Arican-American woman the "mule of the world"[3]—the beast of burden.

Taking the cue from the folk tale quoted here, the study proposes to focus on the hitherto unemphasized aspect of the fictional representation of the roles of African-American women as labor within and outside the family in the novels of the three afore-mentioned authors. By delving into the socio-economic and historical background of the real life situations of African-American women in America and exploring their situation and locating them in the said perspective, the study aims to place the fictional representation of these women against the backdrop of the struggles of their real life counterparts. It would therefore be within the scope of the study to briefly analyse the socio-economic and cultural melieu that has been instrumental in shaping the African-American experience in America and as depicted in the novels of Toni Morrison, Alice Walker and Gloria Naylor. The influence of these factors is perceived as being pivotal in conditioning the roles of African-American women (real and literary) as wage earners, which in turn influences their roles as mothers, sisters, wives, lovers, daughters or mistresses.

The examination of the socio-economic background is of considerable importance because it is these specific conditions which are responsible for fostering the complex nature of work relationships of African-American women in the first place. Any attempt to understand such relationships would require the proper perspective without which such a study would be lopsided. However, since this study proposes to concentrate on the representations of the roles of women as labor in totality, viz. not only as wage-earners but also as family members and partners of emotional and sexual relationships, therefore their labor in exchange of money as well as their labor for love, the fruitfulness or futility of their work in the outside world and domestic arena likewise would come within it's scope.

The study proposes to investigate the dilemma of the African-American women enmeshed in a multiplicity of work-roles and problems peculiar to them. It aims to shed new light on questions of contemporary feminist issues by taking up the novels of three representative writers whose works have been pioneering in the field of literature and have been internationally acclaimed. Using a novel angle of exploration, this work proposes to examine and concentrate on the treatment and presentation of the African-American women characters in these novels through a process of artistic transformation as against the possibility of their being taken as faithful social chronicles echoing authentic social and economic data of discrimination.

As African-American women writers of the same generation, Toni Morrison, Alice Walker and Gloria Naylor share a common interest and a natural empathy with Black women in particular. The unenviable reality of being both black and female works as a common bond for these writers and contributes largely in their sensitive rendering of African-American women's roles as labor and the multiple responsibilities entailed therewith in their novels. The attitudinal similarity or difference leading to similarity or difference of treatment and presentation is to be explored and brought out in the subsequent chapters of this thesis. Undeniably, the works of these authors point to an unavoidable truth that black women play a major role in their novels which consequently leads to the question—how do these women contribute to the raising of the economic status of the family, or, how pivotal are their roles in ensuring the economic solvency of the family. This would in turn lead to the key question—the actual and/or perceived position of the black women in the context of the family, in the wider socio-economic context, and most importantly, in the context of the specific novel in question, in the determining of the inter-character relationships.

An understanding of the term 'labor' is of crucial importance at this stage and both it's socio-economic implications and the resultant consequent significance in relation to this study must therefore be made clear. The generally accepted broad definition of labor is that it is human factor of production. It refers to the application of human efforts and energy to the process of production. In other words, labor refers to that man's work or exertion, physical or mental, whose object is not to yield pleasure for himself, but to create utilities for others and to earn a living. However, even productive services which are rendered free of charge under some motive like sympathy, kindness, love, etc. are not regarded as labor in the true economic sense.[4] In the context of this study, 'labor' would not be applied in the unalloyed, purely economic sense because the sociological and aesthetic implications of the same would be under consideration.

It is no secret that black workers are disadvantaged in the labor market relative to white workers, and that women are

> disadvantaged relative to men. The disadvantaged groups hold a disproportionate number of the poorer jobs in the economy, and earn less per hour, per year.[5]

Being both black and female would therefore point to a two-fold discrimination. It is to be kept in mind that being a wage earner would not be enough for a woman, less so for a black woman. This would seemingly imply indispensability of the roles of black women and as such lead to possibilities of a matriarchal set-up of the black families which has ever been a dominating tendency with them having it's roots in the African tribal culture. The American society, of which the Black-Americans are a part, is however dominantly patriarchal.

> One of the most efficient branches of patriarchal government lies in the agency of it's economic hold over it's female subjects.... In modern reformed patriarchal societies, women have certain economic rights, yet the "woman's work" in which some two-thirds of the female population in most developed countries are engaged is work that is not paid for.[6]

The complex nature of the relationships of black women to their families and to the society at large can, perhaps, be better appreciated if studied with a fresh perspective in mind. The contribution of these women to the family coffer as well as their catering to the traditional roles expected of them would undoubtedly determine their intra-family relationships and their interaction with the American society (both Black and white).

Margaret L. Anderson pointed out how multicultural studies fail to capture the underlying social structures that produce oppression—oppression that is more than cultural differences or transient cultural images because they lack the sociological perspective in their analysis. She writes: "oppression is embodied in social structures; however one conceptualizes it, social structure shapes and directs people's lives and their very ability to survive."[7] The present study has incorporated the sociological perspective to be able to explore the literary and aesthetic representation of African-American women in their work roles against the backdrop of authentic data.

The grim sociological facts that have shaped the Negro consciousness of the Negro experience in America grew from a sense of alienation and isolation as a race from the larger white American society. Richard Wright says in his moving history *Twelve Million Black Voices* that the Negroes were isolated from the dominant, white culture and forced to live in a "psychological island"[8] that cut them off from the mainstream culture as an inferior race. The high walls of racist prejudice were erected to buttress the biased convictions of the so-called superior race who appeased their moral burdens by laying the blame of victimization squarely on the shoulders of the suffering victims themselves. Any literary endeavour therefore on the part of the Negroes would be consciously or unconsciously conditioned by the socio-economic and cultural realities that have colored their existence and shaped their imagination. The interpretation or literary representation of these facts may vary from artist to artist, some may not directly deal with the physical realities of their or their ancestors' dilemma in America, some may like true artists transcend social issues or transmute them into finely honed concepts of aesthetic concern—but working at the back of every artistic representation by an African-American is the collective experience of a traumatic past that has structured their perceptions of life and art overtly or covertly.

The Black Women's Literary Movement: In *Reading Black Reading Feminist*, Henry Louis Gates Jr. quotes Anna Julia Cooper who had argued "convincingly and eloquently" for the recognition of the black women's literary tradition:

> One muffled strain in the silent South, a jarring chord and a vague uncomprehended cadenza has been and still is the Negro. And of that muffled chord, the one mute and voiceless note has been the sadly expectant Black woman.... The "other side" has not been represented by one who "lives there" and not many can more sensibly realize and more accurately tell the weight and fret of the "long dull pain" than the open-eyed but hitherto voiceless Black Woman of America...[just] as our Caucasian barristers are not to blame as they cannot quite put themselves in the dark man's place, neither should

> the dark man be wholly expected fully and adequately to reproduce the exact voice of the Black Woman.[9]

Gates writes that the challenge thrown by Julia Cooper to the authority of the Black male voice that presumed and claimed to speak of the "Negro experience" in its totality while ignoring the complex and problem-ridden questions of an exclusive Black women's experience has, after 75 years, expressed/manifested itself in the emergence of an African- American women's literary tradition of their own. Unlike most of the black male authors of the older generation who disowned any African-American influence on their writing, claiming to speak of a monolothic human experience or own only a "white paternity", black women writers drew their strength from other black women literary ancestors like Zora Neale Hurston and Anne Petry. The writers of the African-American women's literary movement write from within a tradition, inspired by a strong sense of bonding with other black women writers—sharing a literary "sisterhood"[10] as created and encouraged by writers/publishers like Toni Morrison and owning a maternal ancestry. These women are drawn together by the strong bonds of a shared and collective experience and with the intention of breaking the "conspiracy of silence" that had oppressed the selfhood of black women. In their literary representation of the African-American women characters, these writers have rejected the stereotypical images of black women not only by the white American writers but also the black male writers who have projected black women sentimentally as a reaction to the negative white racist stereotypes as the Black Goddess, Black Queen, Super Woman, Mother Goddess, etc. In defying the misrepresentations in the body of American literature of African-American women, they have exploded the myths, false notions and expected paradigms about black women's situation/experience/identity in America.

Henry Louis Gates Jr. in *Reading Black, Reading Feminist*, says that reading the text of the African-American women writers allows one to

> overhear a black woman *testifying* about (what) the twin scourges of sexism and racism, merged into one oppressive entity, actually *do* to a human being, how the combination

> confines the imagination, perplexes the will and delimits free choice. What unites these texts, what makes them cohere into that imaginary meta text we call a tradition, is their shared structures and common themes.[11]

He quotes Mary Helen Washington who places the black women writers within the tradition they created for themselves:

> Their literature is about black women; it takes the trouble to record the thoughts, words, feelings, and deeds of black women, experiences that make the realities of being black in America look very different from what men have written.... Women talk to other women in this tradition.[12]

History—traditionally the domain of men, had erased women—especially black women from its pages. Taking shape out of her "invisibility" emerged the black woman—determined to speak "herstory."

Black women writers therefore, as most black women in real life, pitted against unsurmountable odds, fall back on the nurturing support of a sisterhood and shared understanding and empathy. The black women characters they represent in their novels also rely on such a nurturing system though each woman, in her own way, is in search of an identity and selfhood—a quest amid their daily toil. The group experience and the group efforts of black women writers to express their perceptions about their own situations in a racist, classist, patriarchal White American society that has operated in terms of the worst possible exploitation for them have been instrumental in the shaping of a black feminist literary theory and criticism that has emerged as a new genre in the history of "traditional" literary criticisms. Feminist critics and writers like Anne Julia Cooper, Mary Helen Washington, Mari Evans, Gloria Wayde Gayles, bell hooks, Barbara Christian, Barbara Smith, Patricia Hill Collins, Gloria T. Hull, Valerie Smith, Jacqueline de Weever, Hortense Spillers, Gayl Jones, Claudia Tate, Melissa Walker, Michael Awkward, Houston A. Baker, Henry Louis Gates Jr., Elliot Butler Evans and many others have placed writings by black women writers in the perspective of "black feminism" that in its essence, is a search for "identification" and "expression" of a long-neglected segment of American society constituted by a thrice marginalised group, namely African-American women. Veering away from Euro-American critical practices like structuralism that have believed in the separation of the literary text from its author (to achieve objective distancing), black feminist criticism and black literary criticism as a body as such have resisted this separation. Linden Peach writes that black literary criticism has been wary about accepting Euro-American critical trends,

> ...partly because reclaiming an identity and (narrative) voice to counter centuries of denial and misrepresentation is central to much post-colonial writings. However, a major reason for this reluctance to divorce text completely from its social and political context is that literature would lose its social functions. For African and African-American writers the novel has been an important vechile to represent the social context, to expose inequality, racism and social injustice.[13]

The debate of aesthetic objectivity versus subjective authenticity may continue in the critical context, but for the black feminist writer and critic, the richness, diversity and complexity of their experience as black women in America is the inexhaustible wellspring from which they draw their inspiration and in the expression of which their imagination plays freely and untrammaled in uninhibited joy. So for Alice Walker, Black women are the most fascinating and beautiful creations in the world, who have retained their beauty despite all that they have gone through.[14] This mystery of an inner reservoir of spiritual beauty that they seem to possess has lured Walker and other black women writers again and again into their lives and compelled them to portray their lives and labors in their fiction. Black feminism therefore has emerged as a parallel movement as distinct from White feminism. Critics like bell hooks and Barbara Christian assert that black feminism, though not separatist in intentions, has wished to underscore the difference between the situations of black and white women in America and the world. No monolithic feminist literary theory could therefore hope to do justice to the peculiar problems (especially racist and also classist) faced by women of color (black and other ethnic minority races). According to Barbara Smith,

> thematically, stylistically, aesthetically, and conceptually, Black women writers manifest common approaches to the act of creating literature as a direct result of the specific political, social, and economic experience they have been obliged to share.[15]

Alice Walker, a self-proclaimed feminist, vouchsafed this standpoint when she coined the new term 'womanist' to describe black feminism. She defined "womanist" as the "feminist of color—a woman who loves other women sexually or non-sexually...and...is committed to survival and wholeness of entire people male and female."[16] Poetically, Walker relates womanism to feminism as purple to lavender thus conveying the spirituality (purple being a color that stands for spirituality), vibrancy and strength of the black women's unique experience. Being abased and abused physically, emotionally and psychically everyday, they have yet been able to rise from the morass of daily duress like Phoenixes.

Lorraine Bethel in *Some of Us are Brave* writes that at the core of Black feminism lies "Black women-identification" and that

> Black feminist literary criticism...is most simply the idea of Black women seeking their own identity and defining themselves through bonding on various levels—psychic, intellectual as well as physical—with other Black women.... Black women-identification is black women not accepting male—including Black male—definitions of femaleness or Black womanhood....[17]

Toni Morrison as an editor in Random House has played a key role in providing a "generous stewardship" to a number of black women writers including Toni Cade Bambara, Gayl Jones and Angela Davis. She has inspired by her own example a younger generation of writers, especially Gloria Naylor and created a "literary sisterhood" that promised every new talent a chance to tell her own story in her own words (voice) and encouraged good writing by publishing them.[18] Within the contours of this tradition and bonding the present study places the three authors/novelists, Toni Morrison, Alice Walker and Gloria Naylor whose novels are to be analysed in due course from the perspective already stressed earlier as the focus of the study.

Toni Morrison, Gloria Naylor and Alice Walker are contemporary writers who have registered/conveyed their awareness and concern about the socio-economic and cultural realities of the African-Americans that have established common bonds between them. Black womanhood in all its variations has formed the essence of their writings. The multifaceted dimensions and kaleidoscopic variety of black women's roles have been represented in their novels. Their standpoints are often if not always, consciously articulated through their works of art. If fiction is the artistic vision of human dilemma in real life, then at its core, it is the product of human imagination in all its richness and diversity, fashioned out of and conditioned by the awareness of socio-cultural realities and enriched by the variegated rhythms and pulses of human life. Fiction may sometimes be faithfully realistic (reflecting the patterns of society or history), sometimes escapist, sometimes creating a world of its own (magical reality) and sometimes fantastic but in its finely honed texture it contains the artistic vision of life—represents life as art and therefore is as spontaneous as it is contrived. As writers of African-American fiction, these three novelists are superbly sensitive about the special dilemma of black women who have toiled hard and received little, laboured untiringly and heroically to win the uphill struggle for existence and recognition, and regardless of success or failure have continued with their ceaseless efforts to dream and strive for a better future. The common bond of African-American womanhood has brought these imaginatve writers together, generating a sisterhood sustained by their shared concern, compassion, admiration for, pride of and above all the sense of ownness that they feel with black women in America. Their treatment and fictional representation of African-American women characters may be different, each unique in her own way—but the foundation is that of a strong empathy and identification with the suffering (physical and emotional) of black women in America. Their representation of African-American women in their roles as labor may be consciously or unconsciously, subtly or overtly made to interweave the fabric of their novels but a clear evidence of this concern can be traced in their novels. This has lent their art the power and purpose and the authenticity, the social relevance, the willingness to grasp and not evade the challenge of contemporary and problematic issues, the courage to debunk myths and explode received concepts—the motive force and dynamic power that serious fiction entails. The objective here is to examine the novels of Toni Morrison, Alice Walker and Gloria Naylor individually and in comparison to one another as also to see how this adds a new significance to their admittedly, much discussed novels. The critical discourse surrounding their work is daunting but as the review of preceding literature will reveal, very little has so far been written about the representation of the roles of African-American women as labor in their novels. In this context, the importance of the study, which would undoubtedly attempt to lend greater insight into some fundamental feminist questions cannot be overstated.

II

To begin a study on the literary representation of the roles of African-American women as labor in the novels by selected African-American women writers, one cannot negate issues that are bound to come up in the process—issues that have sociological, economic and cultural ramifications. It would therefore be essential to review the socio-economic and cultural realities of a people who had been imported to the United States from Africa to start a legalised institution of systematic exploitation, inhuman torture and moral degradation called slavery that extended over a period of three hundred years. These African peoples irrespective of their various tribes and languages were collectively categorized as "Negroes"—of the negroid origin, whose dark skin and pug features became a standard symbol for a host of negative qualities.[19] Based on the anthropological differences, the white skinned (of Caucasian origin) majority of America invented the theory of the inferiority of the Negro for legitimising their continued victimisation. In the present context, the Negro's situation as labor can be traced to the very beginning of slavery, which was begun and perpetuated to provide cheap labor to the White plantation owners of the Southern states of America.

Before the slave trade to the Americas was abolished in the late nineteenth century, at least ten million human beings had been brought to North and South America against their will, to be subjected to the most inhuman systems of social and economic oppression the world had ever seen. The first Africans were brought to work as labourers. Initially, the black people brought to Virginia Colony were not considered as slaves. They were classed as indentured servants. But by 1700, the growing plantation economy of Virginia demanded a workforce that was cheaper than free labor and more easily controlled. By establishing the institution of chattel slavery, in which a black person became not just a temporary servant but a life-time property of his or her white master (the cotton, tobacco, and rice planters of British North America) began a process of systematic denudation/ divestment of every vestige of the native African culture brought by the slaves.[20] The Negro was henceforth decivilized and primitivised for the convenience of the white slave owners.

As African men, women and children were herded, chased and forced on to the holds of slave ships indiscriminately under the lash of the whip, it is easily understood that the primary intention of the slave owners was to exploit their labor as commodity. Along with their men, the African women were denuded of all vestige of self-respect as they were put up on auction blocks to be scrutinised and handled like animals before the highest bidder claimed ownership over them. Slavery denied these men and women identity and selfhood, rendered them as "social nonperson(s)" (a term coined by historian Orlando Patterson) who, "by legal definition could have no family, no personal honour, no community, no past and no future" because the slaves "could not even possess themselves".[21] The Negro slave was therefore completely dependent on his/her master's will for survival. Given the situation, one could well imagine the Negro slave's plight/predicament whereby he was not even the owner or beneficiary of his own labor.

During slavery there were hardly any distinctions made for or privilege bestowed upon the female slave. If possible, the plight of the black woman was even worser than that of her counterpart in that she was left open to be exploited as a commodity to satisfy the white master's sexual desires. Besides her labor, her sexuality was used and reused repeatedly by the white master, first as an object of lust and then to serve as a vessel for the production of free labor (in the capacity of a breeder) as her reproductive abilities were exploited and her illegitimate children became slaves to their father-master. The three-fold commodification of black women continued and the children followed their mother's condition according to the tenets of slavery. Gradually, a distinction arose between the lighter complexioned mulatto children born as a result of miscegenation and the "nocturnal escapades of countless male aristocrats". It led to the creation of

> a privileged group of mulatto house servants who were relieved of the more arduous duties of the darker field hands. A division of labor resulted, roughly corresponding to complexion and soon hardened along class lines. The house servants living in greater proximity to their white masters, enjoyed freer access to the dominant culture.[22]

These "house servants" also called "house niggers" were trained to perform more skilled services while their more unfortunate brethren toiled from dawn to dusk at the plantations and lived in rough, wooden shacks built at the edges of the plantations. Richard Wright, the African-American writer of great renown, wrote about the socio-economic deprivation of the slaves in his *Twelve Million Black Voices*—a history of the Negros in the United States. With a number of black male authors, he shared the envy of their womenfolk, for the black man generally felt that more injustice was done to him than his woman. Richard Wright writes:

> Our women fared easier than we men during the early days of freedom.... During slave days they did not always belong to us, for the Lords of the land often took them for their pleasure. When a gang of us was sold from one plantation to another, our wives would sometimes be kept by the Lords of the Land.... They enjoyed a status denied us men, being called 'Mammy' and through the years they became symbols of motherhood...reigning as arbiters in our domestic affairs....[23]

This view did not take into account the terrible predicament of the Negro woman who was rarely if ever glad of the dubious "privilege" bestowed upon her. It also precluded the will of the slave women whose sexuality and productivity were exploited along with her labor from the tedium of which she was given no respite. Small wonder therefore that black women developed a denigrating view about themselves under circumstances that had reduced them to a sub-human level. Calvin Hernton writes about the usual practice of exhibiting black women on auction blocks during slavery thus:

> When any group of women has to submit to...atrocities, when they are denied the smallest privacy of body, when they have to stand in public before men and women naked on an auction block and be fingered in the most intimate places, it is absurd to ask them to esteem themselves.... It was in this way, then, that the Negro woman during slavery began to develop a depreciatory concept of herself not only as a female but as a human being as well. She did not have much of an alternative.[24]

Historical accounts and fugitive slave narratives bear testimony to the gruelling realities of the multiple burdens under which the Negro women labored. The responsibility of the family and children fell on her because her father, husband, brother, son or lover were rarely allowed to stay with her and contrary to the romanticized picture drawn in most of the media representations of the happy, faithful, religious and obedient "Mammy" the black slave woman seethed inwardly with a repressed sense of injustice and humiliation that often even her male counterpart did not or could not appreciate. Historical records have chronicled the degrading situation of the Negro labor prior to Emancipation.

After Emancipation (on January 1, 1863 the formal and definite proclamation was issued by which all slaves in those Southern states at War with the Union were declared free), thousands of Negroes became landless wanderers. Denied access to education, religion, skilled work of any kind and totally untrained and unprepared to face life as such, they suddenly found themselves homeless and jobless (the only labor they were acquainted with being work at the white master's house or field labor). Faced suddenly with the prospects of fending for themselves they were at a loss in the competitive world that would show no mercy for people who could not snatch a living out of it. Hordes of Negroes roamed the plantations of the South in search of willing white plantation owners who would give them jobs. Millions became drifters and millions travelled to the Northern states in search of job opportunities and economic freedom. A few of them remained with their previous masters as servants and field hands. The North beckoned the Negro with the promise of a new future and they migrated in great numbers to the North in search of a new life. However, the economic scenario far from improved in the years after Emancipation and the Negro was almost always given the most menial and difficult jobs (physically) to handle. They found employment only as unskilled laborers and occupied the lowest rung of the labor market ladder. Economically, they were the most backward ethnic race and in society they occupied the lowest strata. The urban ghettoes which developed in the North offered the Negroes living conditions that were little better than the plantation slavery and the vicious cycle of economic exploitation continued.

During the period of Reconstruction after the Civil War, some reconstruction programmes were implemented only to be destroyed by white conservatives who soon regained control of the state legislatures. Jonathan H. Turner writes that,

> (b)y 1900 blacks had been forced off their land (given to them during Reconstruction) and onto tenant farms owned by whites, or they had become part of the cheap labor pool that provided the muscle and the menial services for white enterprises. With the onset of World War I and the increased opportunities in northern industrial cities, blacks began to leave the South in search of new economic opportunities. They encountered the same white violence and economic discrimination that they had left in the South. Except during the height of war time production, blacks were excluded from skilled jobs in industry and relegated, once again, to cheap and menial labor force.[25]

Those Negroes who had not migrated to the Northern states as freedmen fell back upon the mercy of their erstwhile masters (and now Lords of the Land) and there began a new system of cruel exploitation that renewed their bondage—tenant farming or sharecropping whereby they were leased land for growing crops of which a fixed portion of the produce would have to be paid as annual rent.

As tenant farmers of the South labored under the burdens of sharecropping on land that was not their own and was mostly much poorer and less well equipped compared to the average Southern farms, they sank gradually more in the mire of poverty and backwardness with every passing year. Gunnar Myrdal writes,

> Negro farmers are concentrated in the lowest occupation in agriculture as sharecroppers or wage laborers. Non-agricultural Negro workers are for the most part either in low paid service occupations or have unskilled tasks in industry. Few are skilled workers.... The majority of manufacturing industry gave jobs to Negroes only during World War II, when they had to because of manpower shortage and the Presidential order that war contracts could be had only if there was no discrimination. Neither in the South nor in the North are Negroes in professional, business or administrative positions except in rare instances and except when serving exclusively the Negro public—and even in this they are far from having a monopoly. Only recently have Negroes been allowed into white-collar jobs and the total number of them in these jobs is not high. And, most important the unemployment risk of Negroes is very great.[26]

The grim picture that emerges of the Negro labor situation in this famous sociological work goes a long way in exposing the prejudices that have been harboured against the negroes as a race traditionally by the whites. The stranglehold of economic deprivation and backwardness tightened as "poverty itself (bred) the conditions that cause(d) poverty to continue". Myrdal points out the harsh facts that made the situation of the Negro labor more depressing in a perceptive analysis triggered off by a series of questions that he himself poses—questions that themselves illuminate the helpless economic entrapment of the Negro over the ages. He writes:

> One may ask: Why are Negroes in the poorest section of the country, the backward industries, the lowest paid jobs?

Why are they not skilled workers? Why do they not hold a fair proportion of well-paid middle-class positions? Why is their employment situation so precarious?

Part of the answer lies in the several factors of economic change. In most cases changes in the economic progress seem to work against the Negroes. When modern techniques transform old handicrafts into machine production, Negroes lose jobs in the former but usually do not get into the new factories, at least not at the machines. Mechanization seems generally to displace Negro labor. When mechanized commercial laundries replace home laundries, Negro workers lose jobs. The same process occurs in tobacco manufacture, in the lumber industry, and in the turpentine industry. When tractors and motors trucks are introduced, new "white men's jobs" are created out of old "Negro jobs" on the farm and in transportation. Progress itself seems to work against the Negroes. When work becomes less heavy, less dirty, or less risky, Negroes are displaced. Old-fashioned, low-paying, inefficient enterprises, continually being driven out of competition, are often the only ones that employ much Negro labor.

It seems that business cycles show something of the same tendency to work against Negroes as do technical changes. The Negro agricultural laborer is more likely to be forced out of depression than is the white farmer and farm workers. In fact, in almost every given occupation Negroes tend to be "first fired" when depression comes. Even in the service and maintenance occupations, where Negroes are concentrated, Negroes are fired to give jobs to white workers. When prosperity returns, unless there is an extreme manpower shortage, the lost ground is never quite made up. The general level of unemployment, depression or no depression, is always higher for Negroes than whites.[27]

Likewise the organisation of the labor market by trade unions has usually increased the difficulties for the Negroes in getting and holding jobs. Even social legislation is not an undivided blessing to Negro workers. When the employer finds that he has to take measures to protect his workers'

> health and security and pay them higher wages, he often substitutes White workers for Negroes. Sometimes sweatshop industries, existing only because of low paid Negro labor, are driven out of business by legislation as union pressure, and the Negro is again the victim instead of the beneficiary of economic and social progress. Negroes have been willing—if it were allowed them—to take the jobs at the bottom. But until the war forced a demand for them their unemployment was growing relative to that of the whites.[28]

Post Reconstruction Negro Labor Scenario: The post reconstruction period saw a continuation of the same trend in the labor market.

> European emigrants provided much of the labor for northern factories. In both the North and the South, they were given priority over African-Americans in skilled trades and personal services. Soon the carpenters, blacksmiths, coopers, ship builders, and of course, factory workers had formed all-white unions. Nannies replaced mammies and black butlers became corner boot blacks. Waiters were demoted to dish washers, and cooks were replaced by European chefs. Barbers could not use their scissors on the hair of blacks if they wished to keep a white clientele, and even boot blacks could not use the same rag on shoes worn by African-Americans and those that shod the feet of Anglo-Americans.[29]

From 1890 to 1920, while the business and professional class was fighting for the right to rise, the base of the Negro social pyramid was shifting from a peasantry to an urban proletariat. In these decades more than 2,000,000 Negroes left the farm for the factory.[30] As growing numbers of Negro sharecroppers were pushed off the land by erosion and drought, by an exhausted soil, and by the mechanical cotton-picker, they were drawn to the cities by the demands of American industry for cheap labor. The war created a labor market for thousands of black workers and under these circumstances, the urbanisation of the American Negro took place at an unprecedented rate. This phenomenon was termed in history as The Great Migration that saw the mass exodus of Negro sharecroppers from the rural southern states of America to the urban ghettoes of the northern states.[31]

The Great Depression of 1930s saw a new low in gross national produce and with the collapse of the American economic system, farm and factories closed down and unemployment soared.[32] Negroes, who at the best of times were hard put to find jobs, found themselves thrown out of the lowliest of jobs with no sources of income to support themselves. Giving a more recent (postwar) trend in the Negro job scenario and labor market representation, Jonathan H. Turner writes:

> Although the economic plight of blacks improved in the postwar period and in the early 1950s, the last decade has seen only slight change in their economic situation. Blacks are still overrepresented in menial, farm, and service occupations; they are under represented in professional and managerial positions: black unemployment has remained at twice that of white unemployment; blacks tend to be unemployed longer than whites in equivalent job categories; they earn less in the same job as whites; college-educated blacks earn about the same amount of money as high-school-educated whites; and Black income as a percentage of white income, has actually dropped from 61 per cent in 1969 to 58 per cent in 1973.[33]

Joseph F. Healey writes in "African Americans: from Segregation to Modern Institutional Discrimination and Racism" that unemployment rates have been at least twice as high for Blacks as for whites since the 1940s. These rates vary by sex and age, and black males frequently have higher unemployment rates than black females, whereas among white Americans, females always have a higher unemployment rate. Black teenagers are especially vulnerable to unemployment. In 1986, the official unemployment rate for black teenagers aged 16-19 was almost 40 per cent. In that same year, the rate for white teenagers in the same group was about 15 per cent.[34] In 1992, the unemployment rate for black female teenagers came to 37 per cent. The rates for white teenagers were 18 per cent for males and 16 per cent for females.[35]

Most social scientists like Healey, Myrdal and Turner to name a few are of the opinion that at the core of Negro poverty, disadvantage and unemployment lay discrimination, both at the individual and institutional levels which arose from long harboured and nurtured prejudice against them and racism (open or subterranean).

The "culture of poverty" theory was enunciated by certain economists who argued that "poverty is perpetuated by the particular characteristics of the poor"[36] and lay the blame of backwardness and impoverishment of the Negro community at their door. Sociologist Daniel P. Moynihan in his Moynihan Report located the cause of poverty and unemployment in the characteristics of the black family structure which is mostly female-headed. The black woman was projected as the "emasculating matriarch" who was responsible for the disruption of values (read White middle-class) and disintegration of the family which generated a host of evils including poverty and unemployment.[37] Countering this obviously prejudiced line of analysis, Healey sees the matriarchal structure of the black family as the result, not the cause, of urban poverty, and as a reflection of racial discrimination and the scarcity of jobs for urban black males. In impoverished black urban neighbourhoods, the supply of men able to support a family is reduced by high rates of unemployment, incarceration, and violence, conditions created by the concentration of urban poverty and the growth of the underclass. Thus, the burden of child-raising tends to fall on females, and female-headed households are more common than in more advantaged neighbourhoods. Female-headed African-American families tend to be poor not because of any structural weakness but because of the lower wages accorded to women in general and to minority women in particular. The poverty reflects the interaction of sexism and racism rather than a weak or pathological family structure.[38] To support his theory, Healey quotes sociologist John Farley who writes as a conclusion to his analysis that

> Black...female-householder families experience a double disadvantage in income—the low wages and high unemployment rates associated with minority group status *and* the low wages of women. Significantly, neither of these has anything to do with the effects of one-parent, female-headed families per se.[39]

Finally, the above view traced the cause of black urban poverty to the complex forces of past and present institutional and individual discrimination, racism, sexism, prejudice and the *precarious position of black women in the labor force*—a direct result of both race and gender discrimination. Concurrent with this sociological standpoint is the long and painful history of black women as labor in America for whom, more often than not, life and work have operated as synonyms to each other.

Black Women at Work: The Labor Market Scenario—Hard Facts: Angela Davis writes in *Women, Race and Class* (1981) that from the days of slavery, Black women were "workers first, women second and always black, and the three positions locked them into positions of vulnerablity. After the abolition of slavery they continued to be exploited as blacks and as women in the labor market and in the home."[40] Black women have always seen involved in the labor market, which, for them, was not a new experience. From the beginning, they had been to their men helpmates, co-bread winners and sharers of the economic burdens of the family. Compared to white women, at any point of time in history (including war time—World War I that brought in an unprecendented number of white women into the labor market), black women were "twice as likely to be employed...but their economic horizons were severely limited. Over seventy percent worked as domestics in white private homes, and another twenty percent toiled in the fields, picking crops and hoeing gardens on small farms."[41]

In spite of the fact that during war, more than 400,00 black women left their jobs as domestics to work alongside white women in defence plants, the nature of the jobs they held were of the lowest kind. While white women held clerical and sales jobs, black women got the traditional ones of janitor or scrub women even in the defence plants.[42] John Hope Franklin documents that discrimination in wage paying continued on racial and gender basis and black women were at the hard bottom of the labor heirarchy.[43]

Even during the war therefore black women were discriminated against in the matter of positions offered and salaries paid and the so-called "Economic liberation" lasted only till the war was continued. At the end of the war "black women were the first to be fired...and through economic need were forced back into domestic and other service jobs."[44] The late forties and fifties saw a continuation of the same pattern. By the sixties, the urban ghettoes that had been set up in the wake of mass emigration of black men and women to the North in lure of war time jobs had become "a permanent part of the reality of urban black people"[45] where the black women "carried more than their share of burdens."[46] In 1964, 32.5 per cent of black female workers were employed in private households as domestics, compared to 4.9 per cent of white women; and 23.4 per cent were employed in service work (hotels and restaurants) compared to 14.5 per cent of white women. Whereas 34.1 per cent of white women were employed in clerical jobs, only 11.3 per cent of black women were in this line of work.[47] Eight years of vigorous civil rights protests had not altered the position of black women in the labor market. In spite of what the prevailing fallacies about black women workers suggested in the 60s, they were the most frequently unemployed and had the highest rate of unemployment regardless of occupational category.[48]

In the year that the Civil Rights Movement began, the statistical profile of the black women was that

> she has a harder time finding a mate, remains single more often, bears more children, is in the labor market longer, has less education, earns less, is widowed earlier, and carries a heavier economic burden as a family head than her white sister.[49]

As late as 1973, "25.5 percent of (black women in the labor market) worked in the service occupation, and among this group 17.9 percent worked exclusively in private households—in other words as domestics. Of a total of 1.5 million domestics in the nation, 69 per cent were black women."[50] In "Going Nowhere Immediate: Black Women of Hopelessness", Wade Gayles traces the pattern of jobs traditionally and generally available to a large majority of black women since the time of slavery. She writes how the

> (p)oor and unskilled black women have historically been ghettoized in the labor market of white America. They are

> domestics in white homes, service workers in white owned hospitals and hotels, field hands on white owned farms, and operatives in white owned factories. In large urban areas they are often number runners, prostitutes and procurers. Of all these categories, that of domestic is the job slot most often associated in the national thinking with black women, and for obvious reasons: black women are disproportionately represented in the labor market in this category.[51]

Jeanne Noble has analysed this labor picture within the historical context and she writes that black women have been systematically programmed for the last hundred and twenty years to do that which was essentially their job to do during slavery—serve as nannies and maids for the white Americans—

> The long shadow of slavery may be fading for some, but over one fourth of all black sisters are still marketing the skills of our ancestors who washed, scrubbed and hoed in the mansion yards and cotton fields of Southern plantations, and whose daughters entered the census page of the twentieth century with little choice except to do the same.[52]

Domestic work falls into the unskilled category of labor and the black woman domestic worker shares with the nation the view that it is degrading. Jean Noble writes that black women domestics believe that they have been forced to do a work that no one else, given the option would choose to do. Since their work required little or no skill, it was work that "(n)o body would do...if they could do anything else."[53] Wayde Gayles therefore says that domestic work is "emotionally charged" for black women due to several reasons. First they have been denied a sense of self-worth or realization of their own merit or beauty because of the nature of the job that is considered worthless and degrading. Second, their work/job is a constant reminder of the "magnitude of injustice"[54] that they suffer on account of being poor, black and female:

> They leave apartments of poverty to spend the day working in homes of comfort and luxury and they return to those apartments with meagre earnings and injured pride. They see the stark constrast between the world of the have-nots

and the world of the haves they labor in to alleviate their families' suffering.[55]

Moreover, such work reinforces and confirms for these black women their cultural status or image of ugly/unappealing women of great strength who are capable of and expected to handle tasks that dainty and fragile white women (epitome of feminine beauty) are incapable of handling—tasks that are dirty, difficult and demeaning such as washing windows, scrubbing, and mopping and waxing/polishing floors and carrying heavy bags of groceries, preparing baths, washing clothes, cleaning up after meals, scouring utensils and even brushing the mistress' hair (female employer's).[56] Domestic work entails an unending list of responsibilities for the job is never simply a house cleaning job, it includes almost all the tasks identified by American culture as "woman's work". The black domestics have not only contributed their labor in return of a meagre pay to make the lives of white men and women easier, they have also raised countless white children, nursed and tended them as wet nurses and mammies and taken care of them in a way their own mothers had not done because motherhood and its unattractive realities (breast-feeding, changing diapers, cleaning up after the children) did not compliment the image of distant and frail beauty cultivated by white American women. As Gayles says, "the point being made here is that black domestics throughout history have not been just maids; they have been the great earth mother of this nation".[57] And in return for all this they get very little. The job of the black domestic is not only a job, says Gayles, it is an "institution" that has been nurtured over the ages at the cost of not only physical and material but also psychological exploitation of poor, black women. The sense of "injured pride" and violated self-worth is generated by all or most of the menial jobs that are available to black women wherein they are overworked, underpaid, used, abused and humiliated and this was the painful reality that a majority of black women faced even in the seventies. Since the 1970s though the Labor Force Participation of both black and white women rose, for the former, the reason for sustained labor force participation remained more due to economic necessity than any other factor.[58]

Poverty and discrimination in employment have led many black women into prostitution. Studies indicate that the majority of prostitutes in American cities are black.[59] Yet it is also well known that "because open prostitution is only allowed in Black neighborhoods, white men are frequently found in these areas seeking to buy some passion...[and]...making the streets at night unsafe for 'respectable' Black women."[60] Black fiction suggests that for both the "respectable" women and the prostitutes, forced to view themselves as sexual objects, there seems little possibility of growth and freedom. The image of the 'bad' black woman in black American fiction is the image of a woman anxious and afraid, seldom able to shake off her persecutors, black and white.[61]

Since the eighties (1980s), however, a considerable improvement has occurred for black women in the labor market scenario. Joseph Healey writes that in 1990, the percentage of African-American women engaged in the agriculture or domestic service dropped from 90 per cent in the thirties to less than 30 per cent and a large number of African-American women are now in the highest ranked occupational categories. Differences in the representation in various job categories in the labor market between black and white females are less dramatic now. In 1990, 19 per cent of women in the labor force engaged in managerial and professional services were black and 27 per cent white and 39 per cent in the technical and administrative category were black while 45 per cent were white. In the services category, 27 per cent were black women and 16 per cent white, in the skilled labor sector the participation rates were equal (2 per cent each) whereas in the semi-skilled labor category, 12 per cent were black women and 8 percent white.[62]

These statistical data provide sociological evidence of the changing job scenario that has placed the black women at a relatively better position than before. It cannot be overlooked however that the present picture has emerged out of a long and tangled history of discrimination, prejudice and the resultant protests, struggles, and untiring efforts of a people long subjugated unjustly.

In the light of the history traced, it becomes logically imperative that the African-American woman be inevitably associated with her work by the dominant white, racist, capitalist, sexist society that has determined her worth or evaluated her only in the capacity of a workhorse. Ironically, sometimes the black woman gauges her own self with the measuring tape of the work she does. Her existence, her essence, and even at times her expression of grief, mirth, confidence or otherwise have been bound up with her work (domestic and wage earning) to the extent of even assessing her capabilities through her work. The sociological realities operating behind this are stated graphically by Karen Dugger when she says,

> the continued exploitation of Black Labor into the twentieth century has meant the continued coercion of Black women into the paid labor force. Racial discrimination has produced high rates of unemployment among Black men and segregated them into low paying jobs, and thus the Black family needs the labor of more than one wage earner. While Black women do not work only out of economic necessity (Gump, 1980) the reality of racism continues to shape the context within which they develop and construct their definitions of womanhood.... In consequence Black women's conceptions of womanhood emphasize resourcefulness, autonomy and the responsibility of providing for the material as well as emotional needs of the family members (Ladner, 1971). Black women do not see labor force participation and being a wife and mother as being mutually exclusive; rather within the black culture, employment is an integral, normative and traditional component of the roles of wife and mother (Gump, 1980; Malson, 1983).[63]

With this understanding of the historical and social forces that have sculpted the tradition working behind the shaping of black women's roles both in society and their images in fiction, one must analyze their representation in the roles of labor in the novels by the three black women writers selected for this study.

The consistent and ceaseless struggles of the African-American woman to survive in a country where she has been the victim of three-fold discrimination (viz. race, class and gender) and yet managed to keep her "self" afloat can be termed as nothing short of heroic. Countless such women have suffered and died in this battle for survival, which the mundane business of living had come to stand for them. Their problem-ridden existence was not only a physical burden but a psychological and moral one too accounting for the raw pain that one encounters in the first-hand accounts of the lives of these women. Needless to say that literary renderings inspired by so much trauma and torture, of such determined effort and hard-won triumph would be moving in intensity. The traumatic lived experience of some famous black women that have been narrated in literature bear evidence of a past full of turmoil and toil. Literary images of black women by African-American women writers repeatedly represent them in the light of their ceaseless work and images of African-American women in their work roles are the most predominant images in their fiction. The reason for this lies not only in the personal experience of almost every African-American woman writer who has taken up the pen but also the result of a collective common experience and a persistent concern they have shared with the women of their race. Try as they might, African-American women cannot relate their peculiar predicament as women of labor to the experience of the white woman or the African-American man. Sharing the same gender with the former, their cultural realities were and to an extent still are, different from theirs and sharing the same race with the latter has placed them more at a disadvantage because of the simple fact that they have no one else to shift their burden of pain, responsibility or work as do their menfolk on them in sheer frustration and masculine aggression, irresponsibility or liberty. And work they must if they must keep their children from starvation and death and the family afloat. Karen Dugger points out the essential and basic difference in the life experiences of black and white women in their past and present relationship to the labor process. She writes,

> From slavery to the present it is precisely with regard to productive and reproductive activities that racial oppression has most dramatically differentiated them. While nineteenth-century culture in the United States stereotyped white women as too frail and dainty to undertake physical labor, Black

women were viewed as beasts of burden and subjected to the same demeaning labor and hardships as Black men.[64]

As Angela Davis asserts, slavery constructed an alternative definition of womanhood for the black woman that included a tradition of "hard work, perseverance and self-reliance, a legacy of tenacity, resistance and an insistence on sexual equality".[65] Black womanhood, therefore, in its essence became an antithesis of white womanhood in that they achieved it through a combination of "grit, shit and mother wit",[66] all of which entailed a tremendous capacity to endure pressure, hardships and toil.

Here I recount the famous life story of Sojourner Truth and refer to her historical speech to emphasize the above point. Sojourner Truth (born Isabella) was an emancipated slave who had adopted the name after forty years of struggle to become free and then to carry on the mission that she felt God intended for her. She was a crusader against oppression and by the onset of the civil war had come to represent a band of female, communitarian, vernacular African-American leadership that rivaled the masculine, individualist, literary model of the black male spokesman.[67] Truth's most famous oration titled "And arn't I a woman" had these words as a rhetorical question in her speech—words that were the crux of her challenge as a black woman to racial and sexual stereotypes that few had had the foresight to address so courageously. When white ministers spoke about women as dependents who needed to be carried over ditches and helped into carriages Sojourner Truth's powerful voice, reverberated with the thunder of hitherto unasked questions:

> Nobody eber helped me into carriages or ober mud puddles, or gives me any best place,... I have plowed, and planted, and gathered into barns, and no man could head me—and ar'nt I a woman? I could work as much and eat as much as a man (when I could get it), and bear de lash as well—and ar'nt I a woman? I have borne thirteen chilern and seen 'em mos' all sold off into slavery, and when I cried out with a mother's grief none but Jesus heard—and ar'n't I a woman?[68]

In this speech of unparalleled eloquence and candour, Sojourner Truth raised issues that had hitherto been taken for granted. The sexual and racial stereotypes that had relegated the black woman to an existence where her labor was exploited and she herself considered a beast of burden and relegated to an inferior status were challenged by her in that speech delivered during the Women's Rights Convention in Akron, Ohio in 1851. The central rhetorical question underlined strongly the difference in the life experiences of black women and white women. The latter who always "had the best place" and were "carried over ditches" and were secure in the comforts of their luxurious homes could never identify with the shocking realities of a black woman's life and labor. Turning the denigrating stereotype of towering height and immense strength of the black woman to an advantage that she should be proud of as an additional boon and a weapon she could utilise to counter male oppression, Sojourner Truth showed the budding feminists a new way to shape their one dimensional struggles for freedom from patriarchy and male domination. In this context, bell hooks (the eminent black feminist) writes:

> Racist stereotypes of all the strong, superhuman black women are operative myths in the minds of many white women allowing them to ignore the extent to which black women are likely to be victimized in this society and the role white women may play in the maintenance and perpetuation of that victimization.[69]

She posits that just as Betty Friedan's *The Feminine Mystique* ignores the existence of working-class women who were already in the labor force and could only long for leisure time and money that would allow them to stay at home and be housewives and for whom freedom meant liberty from the back-breaking routine of daily labor, so did most socialist feminists, while focusing on class and gender issues dismiss, exclude, or ignore the race problem, which was a standing reality for women belonging to the minority race. As Friedan "did not tell readers whether it was more fulfilling to be a maid, a babysitter, a factory worker, a clerk, or a prostitute than to be a leisure class housewife",[70] so did "privileged feminists" fail to take within the purview of theories that they were shaping, the peculiar situation of women of the minority race and their group experience of racist discrimination in America. bell hooks brings to the fore sociological issues that have been conveniently overlooked by these feminists. Speaking from her personal experience, she says that black women "who live daily in oppressive situations, often acquire an awareness of patriarchal politics from their lived existence, just as they developed strategies of resistance...."[71] The joy of being together and the bondage of sisterhood may be new to the white, middle-class burgeoning feminists but to black women like her, "sisterhood" was nothing new for "(she) had not known a life where women had not been together, where women had not helped, protected, and loved one another deeply...."[72] Finally, saying that her intention was not to undermine or "diminish" feminist struggle but to "enrich, to share in the work of making a liberatory ideology and a liberatory movement", bell hooks points out the peculiar dilemma of black women, who, she contends, must "recognize the special vantage point (their) marginality gives (them) and make use of this perspective to criticize the dominant racist, classist, sexist hegemony as well as to envision and create a counter hegemony."[73] The interesting parallel that hell hooks draws between the black man and the white woman exposes the inherent tendency in human beings to shift the burden of work or pain to a group whose social status is lower than theirs. In a perceptive study of the situation, she writes:

> As a group, black women are in an unusual position in this society, for not only are we collectively at the bottom of the occupational ladder, but our overall social status is lower than that of any other group. Occupying such a position, we bear the brunt of sexist, racist and classist oppression. At the same time, we are the group that has not been socialized to assume the role of exploiter/oppressor in that we are allowed no institutionalized "other" that we can exploit or oppress... white women and black men have it both ways. They can act as oppressor or be oppressed. Black men may be victimized by racism, but sexism allows them to act as oppressors of

> women. White women may be victimized by sexism, but racism enables them to act as oppressors of black people.[74]

It is not surprising therefore that the lived experience of black women would shape their consciousness in a manner different from those who have a relative advantage over them or even a relative degree of privilege compared to them. Their "world view" would therefore be different because it was churned out of a first-hand encounter with discrimination, oppression and exploitation.

Taking the cue from bell hooks' perceptive analysis of the black woman's situation in America, I would like to refer to Bernice McNair Barnett's essay titled "Invisible Southern Black Women Leaders in the Civil Rights Movement: The Triple Constraints of Gender, Race and Class," where she has enlisted three "major biases" that have been encouraged and perpetuated by the dominant white society:

> (1) a negative problem-oriented image that stereotypically connects Black women with various pathologies within the family such as female-headedness, illegitimacy, teen pregnancy, poverty and welfarism (Barnett, Robinson and Bailey, 1984; Hill Collins, 1989; Higginbotham, 1982; S. Scott, 1982);
>
> (2) a middle-class orientation that excludes, ignores, or makes inconsequential the experiences of the poor and working-class women, a large percentage of whom are Black (Bookman and Morgen, 1988; Higginbotham, 1982); and
>
> (3) an apolitical-nonleadership image of black and poor women as political passivists (Barnett 1989, 1990 and 1994).[75]

Like bell hooks, Gerda Lerner has also arrived at the difference in meaning that women's liberation has meant for different women. She writes:

> Women, as all oppressed groups, perceive their status *relatively*, in comparison with their own groups, with previously known conditions, with their own expectations. White society has long decreed that while "woman's place is in the home", Black woman's place is in the white woman's kitchen. No wonder that many Black women define their

> own "liberation" as being free to take care of their own homes and their own children, supported by a man with a job.[76] (Emphasis in original)

We can therefore assert with Giddings that "Black women had a history of their own, one which reflect(ed) their distinct concerns, values and the role they have played both as African-Americans and women."[77] Barnett quotes a black woman respondent whom she had interviewed in the course of finding out the role of black women political activists which indicated a "traditional gender stratification within Black society" that led to devaluation of women's roles:

> When you are dealing with Black men and women and the fragile position of Black males, you can expect the Black women, even though they might do all the work, will not be recognized as doing the work or leading anything.... Black women especially had to work hard, but *never ever* threaten the fragile position of their Black men. They still have to do this.[78] (Emphasis in original)

Gloria Wayde Gayles writes in *No Crystal Stair* that the assumption that black and white women were "sisters in oppression" was a "problematic one" because the differences are obvious. One cannot overlook the traditional, historical fact that

> white women have participated actively and without co-ercion, in the oppression of black men and women. They have been "ladies" who lived in leisure because black women have been "mammies". They have been protected and pampered, while black women have been dehumanized, brutalized and devalued as blacks and as females.[79]

Stereotypes and counter-stereotypes: Images of African-American Women in African-American Fiction: In *Black Feminist Criticism*, Barbara Christian defines stereotype, whether positive or negative as a "by product of racism,...one of the vehicles through which racism tries to reduce the human being to a nonhuman level" because "stereotype is the very opposite of humaneness."[80] African-American women could not therefore have avoided being projected as stereotypes either in society/real life or in literature (especially fiction where there is scope for the fullest development of characters). The "invisibility" of the African-American woman in white American literature is not difficult to understand. As Elizabeth Schultz writes:

> On national wage scales she has always been the lowest paid; in national political life she has only recently been seen; in national statistics she is categorized as the unwed mother, the welfare recipient, the maid; in national myth she is designated by multiple names all of which conceal her identity—Aunt Jemima, Mammy, Matriarch, Sometimes Sister, Black Bitch, Girl.[81]

These images are churned out by a dominant white culture and imposed upon black women as a mark of their inferior social status. It has been traditionally accepted that unlike her white counterpart, the black woman has known within the confines of her own community a freedom from sexist categories but it was easy to overlook the fact that this "freedom" was so riddled with problems and so overridden with the burdens of feeding, clothing and holding the family together that more often than not, it was a freedom that they did not desire. As W.E.B. Dubois commented, it was a dubious freedom "thrust contemptuously upon them" for which the price they have paid is very dear.[82] In an essay on the dominant images of Black American women in African-American literature, Barbara Christian traces the stereotypical images that had been constructed regarding the black women in both white American literature (Anglo American) and African-American literature. The novels of slavery and reconstruction periods including white American (esp. Southern White Literature) fashioned an image of the black woman with the ulterior motive of perpetuating the conflicts between black men and women and most importantly, to create "a dumping ground for those female functions a basically puritan society could not confront."[83] The politics of oppression that operated behind the projection of such images was condoned overtly as the audio-visual media readily accepted and encouraged without hesitation the broadcast of these negative images.

Frances Beale writes about the misconstrued images of black women thus:

> Her physical image has been maliciously maligned; she has been sexually molested and abused by the white coloniser; she has suffered the worst kind of economic exploitation, has been forced to serve as the white woman's maid and wet nurse for white offspring while her own children were more often than not starving and neglected.[84]

Of the most prominent images of black women was the mammy figure, the ever "enduring" (Faulkner's Dilsey in *The Sound and Fury*) Aunt Jemima of Southern white literature who stood as a faithful and dark foil to the white, fragile, dainty womanhood cultivated as an ideal of womanhood by the white patriarchal culture. Mammy was typically black in color, stout or obese, "nurturing, religious, kind, above all strong" and capable.

> She is related to the world as an all embracing figure, and she herself needs or demands little...she must be plump and have big breasts and arms—she is the mammy in the unconscious of the South, desired and needed since ideal white women would have to debase themselves in order to be a mother.[85]

In stark contrast to the "shimmering" and "frail", white mistress who could not be "ornamental" or "fussy" if she nursed and brought up children, mammy was physically unattractive but bountiful and all her functions were "magnificently physical"—a harmless and servile embodiment of the "gross" aspects of being female that was not compatible with southern white ladyhood. The all-pervading myth was, as Wayde Gayles aptly puts it, just as "all black people can dance, so can all black women become superhuman mothers, not only for their own people but for white people as well."[86] Shorn of every sense of dignity and self-worth, it is assumed that for the black woman, motherhood is supposedly the "chief justification" in life because it is the only "honorable, creative role in which (she) can reasonably hope to participate."[87] But according to Wayde Gayles, "the exigencies of black life in white America" have forced black women to "function heroically in the role, and their heoric functioning is often perceived as fulfillment."[88]

In *Tommorrow's Tommorrow,* Joyce Ladner writes that black women were legendary mother figures in the American thought, "stronger than other women and certainly stronger than black men".[89] The mammy figure was cultivated for the convenience of a dominant race whose set of cultural beliefs and systems of socio-economic exploitation could be maintained at the cost of a "halo" (more a crown of thorns) bestowed upon black women whose service and loyalty were needed for the purpose. In the fiction/novels written by black men, "mammy" became idealized as the creative, god-like, towering, dominating figure of the earth-mother who took upon herself responsibilities of nurturing her children and heroically performing superhuman tasks. There was also the destructive, death dealing mother figure in the novels of black (African-American) male writers who, Daryl Dance writes, is repressive only as an expression of her maternal devotion and love. The black mother became here either an Eve (death-dealing) or a Madonna (life giving) whose role however pivoted on the axis of subservience, self-sacrifice, self-denial and fierce mother-love.[90]

The concubine/prostitute is another predominant image of the black woman both in society and literature whose sexual prowess, insatiable sexual hunger, libido and absence of morality bracketed her as the Black Bitch. She was ever available to satisfy the sexual lust of the white master and supposedly enjoyed the experience of ill-disguised rape. She could be used, abused and forced into acqueisance while the blame of the action could be placed on her shoulders as she was supposed to play the role of the temptress and seductress whose "black charms" had entangled the "unsuspecting" rapist. Just as the African-American man was endowed with a legendary phallus, the Black Bitch became the symbol of the unconscious, sinful lust that haunted the psyche of puritan white America and was transferred on to the victim. Black women in this image became the embodiment of passion that was the antithesis of virtuous virginity enshrined in the beauty of white womanhood. The labels of "Jezebel" and "Black Bitch" have thus cast black women in the shadow of moral degradation had depravity.

The image of the Conjure woman is no less prejudiced and fraught with the fears of an unknown world of spirits and evil magic over which these powerful and fearsome women have supposed control. The image of the Conjure woman, in contrast to all the other images of black women is based on the role of the black woman as a professional—a witch doctor with a traditional knowledge of voodoo charms, black magic and supernatural powers who brewed magical herbs and potions for healing or killing, who could cast spells and foretell the future (fortune teller) and were thus store houses and keepers of ancient tribal culture and medicine. The white American standpoint however projected these women as harmful witches who were revengeful and wicked. It is interesting to note that the Conjure women were the only black women who could exercise any degree of freedom and power in the context of both black and white American society. The great voodoo mambo, Marie Laveau, is a historical and legendary figure of renown who, in New Orleans (a Catholic centre in the Southern states of U.S.A.), "emerged as one of its most powerful citizens for half a century."[91] It is the figure of the Conjure woman in which most contemporary black women novelists invest in their search for a selfhood and indigenous identity of black women in America.

Elizabeth Schultz, in her perceptive analysis of the reality of the "freedom" thrust upon black women refers to the harsh sociological conditions that were operative in making the image of working black women dominant in society and literature. Conformist or rebel, black women had hardly been dissociated from their work in the psyche of the white as well as black Americans. She herself has hardly ever remembered existing without the never-ending routine of work simply because she has never seemed to stop working at any point of time in her life. The society has demanded that she work and she has engaged in labor regardless of choice for she has been given none. Schultz writes:

> (d)uring the days of slavery the black woman was forced to labor in the fields and kitchens of the white masters. After slavery she continued to be pressed into farm and domestic work, with factory work only opening to her in the forties with any regularity, and clerical and professional positions only in the last decade. Slavery and poverty have kept the

majority of black American women working whereas the majority of white American women, either through lack of economic necessity or lack of motivation, have not worked outside their homes. Consequently the white woman has submitted to the cultural stereotypes of passivity and femininity, while her black counterpart has become burdened with the stereotype of masculine aggressiveness.[92]

Though the 90s trends (Healey, 1997; Labor Statistics) show an increased labor force participation by white American women in two decades, the basic argument of Schultz's theory still stands true—black women are still more likely to participate in the labor force not only as an expression of self- worth but out of economic necessity. Sociologist Karen Dugger writes much in the same vein that "Black women have had to reconcile being strong, independent economic providers with simultaneously investing a substantial part of their identity in being wives and mothers and feminine women" while tolerating the constant cultural assaults on their identities.[93] A black woman has assessed the situation in words that powerfully convey her disillusionment at the fact that regardless of their looks, skills or class they can never become "ladies": "There are two kinds of females in this country—colored women are maids, cooks, taxi drivers, crossing guards, school teachers, welfare recipients, bar maids and the only time they become ladies is when they are cleaning ladies."[94] Sociologists E. Franklin Frazier and Daniel P. Moynihan have categorized black American women as dominating matriarchs who were the decision makers in the family, who controlled the affairs of the family and community, who repressed the spirit of black men by emasculating them (undermining their masculinity by aggression instead of offering the complementary support of a submissive and feminine partner) and were responsible for the disruption of black families and black marriages.[95] This theory was countered by Robert Staples and Joyce Ladner whose books are thoroughly documented studies of the position of black women in America. They oppose the matriarchal classification forwarded by Frazier and Moyinhan by examining historically the role of the black woman as the economic provider. Moreover, they point out the folly of judging the "extended kingship family" that is more evident as a pattern of black families by the standards of nuclear white families or the black woman by the standard of white femininity.[96] In spite of this, however,

> a predicament nevertheless still faces the black woman. She must and does continue to work in order to help support her family; however, because she can qualify for the lowest-paying jobs, she is often able to find work when the black man cannot, thereby leaving herself open to the accusation of being an emasculator.[97]

It is inevitable therefore that the image of the working woman would be the most prevalent one in black American fiction. Margaret Walker's *Jubilee* (1966), Ernest Gaines' *The Autobiography of Miss Jane Pittman* (1971), Ann Petry's *The Street* (1946), Louise Meriwether's *Daddy was a Number Runner* (1970), Paule Marshall's *Browngirl, Brownstones* (1959) all had protagonists who were all working women—cook, house-keeper, gardener, weaver, midwife, domestic (maid)—physically and emotionally exhausting jobs that involved endless labor, tedium and brutality that must be endured for the sake of keeping their families and communities afloat. These novels by black women writers were written in protest against the standard assumptions adopted by the larger society. Writes Schultz:

> Poverty, precipitated by racism, sets up a relentless chain of events in the life of the black woman; it puts the man out of work, forcing his wife to become a domestic.... The black working woman is left physically exhausted by her labor, with little energy to tend to her own children and her own home, she is also left emotionally exhausted, for throughout the day she has had to contend with the degrading comments of her white employers. She is met with condescension or indifference....[98]

Gwendolyn Brook's *Maud Martha* (1953) and Alice Childress' *Like One of the Family* (1956) portray their working heroines as domestics whose self-respect and sharp tongue prevent their degradation by their employers. They not only retort but also assert their rights as Mildred in *Like One of the Family*. The working mothers of these novels by black women writers are struggling alone to keep their homes together. These women may fail, make mistakes, be angry or bitter, transform their frustrations into rage against their children or spurn or scorn their men in pent up fury or strike out at the injustice that life has meted out to them, but they are not superhuman matriarchs or calculating emasculators —they are human beings struggling against social conditions that are not under their control or fighting an inner conflict that their torn personalities give rise to. The demoralization of these women continue as their poverty does but they continue against such odds to provide the material necessities for their children and to be examples of spiritual strength. In the novels of black women writers, these working mothers/wives/ daughter/sisters are not idealized, these are complex and struggling women who have had to buy their freedom (from racist, sexist, capitalist control through sheer hard work[99]—through "grit, shit and mother wit".

Another dominant black female image was that of the tragic mulatta that abounded in African-American literature. The peculiar dilemma of these men and women, especially the women were presented again and again in literature written by black men and women. This image was a fascinating one for a people who had been subjugated physically and psychologically by a "superior" race whose physical characteristics, behaviour and value systems they held as ideals because they had no choice in the matter. Having been uprooted from their own culture and country they had been systematically debased, dehumanised and decivilized to an extent that they considered themselves as having no identity and striving for a white-like identity was the closest they could get to the "superior" race. Hence, in novels by African-American writers the tragic mulatta emerged as a lasting image for decades to come.[100] As Barbara Christian points out, the mulatta,

> (i)n her very being called up the illicit crossing between cultures. She is American in that she emerges out of the sexual relationship between a black slave mother and a white slave master, a sexual relationship denying the most basic philosophical concept of slavery—that blacks were not human beings.[101]

Though the white masters denied the humaneness of the hundreds of black women they mated with for socio-economic reasons, they must have known it themselves, but refused to admit it. Since the first novels written by black authors were aimed at a white audience, the popularity of the mulatta heroine among the white readers ensured the perpetuation of this image. The mulatta combined the physical characteristics of both races and the white race could take moral satisfaction and cover their guilt by supposing that they were lightening up the dark African race. The dilemma of the mulatta herself was that she often had a physical beauty/attractiveness that surpassed that of her mistress whom she served as a house slave and whose envy and hatred she had to encounter and endure everyday. Living in the Big House (the master's mansion) she came into daily contact with and saw the luxury, leisure and freedom in their lives—a freedom she could never get, a leisure or luxury that was not obtainable to a slave because she may be light complexioned but she was not white. The mistress hated her because she was a constant reminder of her husband's infidelity and promiscuity. The mulatta's lot therefore was alienation, isolation and mistrust from both communities. She would be different in color from her siblings and thus the object of envy and hatred. For her slave mother, she was a painful reminder of her sexual exploitation as well as an object of natural affection as her own child, who was however taken from her to serve at the Big House as a privileged slave. For her mother's black husband, she was the concrete proof of his powerlessness and helplessness as he was unable to prevent the union (mostly forced) between the slave master and his wife (the black woman). The birth of the mulatta "heightened the emotional pain of being a slave".[102] For the black field slaves, the mulatta shared physical traits of his oppressor and hence could not be trusted. She had the privilege of living in conditions better than theirs and "on the practical level, the black field slave must have wondered about the loyalty of the mulatta. Is she loyal to her father or to her mother?"[103] The mulatta therefore was a divided person torn between two loyalties, two cultures and two ways of life. She had to choose between the two and either of her choice could not be made without emotional turmoil or pain. More than the mulatto slave man (who could pose a serious danger to or threaten to damage the white master's image of power and authority in that he embodied all his qualities and so could not be shown as such even in fiction) the favourite image was the tragic mulatta woman stereotype. Such stereotypical images were found in William Wells Brown's *Clotell* (1850), Francis Harper's *Iola Leroy* (1892) and later as protagonists in Jean Toomer's *Cane* (1923), Nella Larsen's *Quicksand* and *Passing* (1928) and (1929), Jessie Fauset's *The Chinaberry Tree* (1931)—in most of which mulattas were genteel ladies whose conflicts about color and class were more hypothetical than real.[104]

The image of the black woman as "Sapphire" was one that could underscore the strength of black women as a negative quality for sapphires were shrews with acerbic tongues and violent tempers. Sapphire was the wife of the "King fish" in *Amos and Andy*, a popular early radio and television show. The black woman in the Sapphire image was loud-mouthed, strong-willed and practical, who made a fool of her shiftless, simpleminded, irresponsible husband—the henpecked husband is the one who draws sympathy and his behaviour is understandable because he has a dominating wife who undermines his masculinity and wears the pants in the house.[105] Barbara Christian writes:

> Sapphire's most salient quality is her ability to make black men look like fools, partly because she is unfeminine, that is, strong and independent, and partly because she is, by nature emasculating. Although similar to the mammy, Sapphire is not so much maternal toward white folks as she is unfeminine in relation to black men. To them, she is, cold, hard and evil.[106]

bell hooks writes that "Sapphire's shrewish personality was used primarily to create sympathy in viewers for black male lot" and today it "is projected onto any black woman who overtly expresses bitterness, anger and rage against her lot." This dominant image has caused many black women, "to repress these feelings for fear of being regarded as shrewish sapphires."[107]

Another dominant image of the black woman was spawned by the generations-old myth of the "bad" black woman. Gerda

Lerner shows how racist prejudice operated in indicting black women:

> Every black woman was, by definition, a slut according to the racist mythology; therefore to assault her and exploit her sexually was not reprehensible and carried with it none of the normal communal sanctions against such behaviour. A wide range of practices reinforced this myth: the laws against intermarriage; the denial of the title "Miss" or "Mrs" to any black woman; the taboos against respectable social mixing of the races; the refusal to let black women customers try on clothing in stores before making a purchase; the assigning of single toilet facilities to both sexes of blacks; the different legal sanctions against rape, abuse of minors and other sex crimes when committed against white or black women.[108]

Historical records indicate that the sexual degradation of black women by both black and white men could be possible because the conditions of poverty in the black community exposed black women to the many dimensions of sex at an early age which freed her from repression and enabled her to accept sexual relations without inhibition.[109] This relative sexual freedom however has also been "contemptuously thrust upon her". Only when one takes into account the conditions of poverty and work tedium of the black women can one appreciate the sexual freedom that she has been able to exercise. Ann Petry says in *The Street*,

> ...people were so damn poor they didn't have time to do anything but work, and their bodies were the only source of relief from the pressure under which they lived; and where the crowding together made the young girls wise beyond their years.[110]

The "bad" black woman was therefore defined as promiscuous, immoral and easily available as well as menial and ugly, by white America, which gave the license to use her as free game, a beast of burden (a work horse) and a whipping block.

Against the stereotypical images of black women created by received notions based on racist, sexist assumptions, one must now place the images of black women fashioned by the oral folk tale tradition and the slave narratives, which were indigenous, wonderfully original and witty. The image of the mammy is found here too, but with a difference. Here "mammy" is still a housekeeper, cook, seamstress, nursemaid, operating as the nurturer and caring mother-substitute but she is not obedient, long-suffering or meek. Here she is "cunning, prone to poisoning her master, and not at all content with her lot.... Mammies kicked, fought, connived, plotted, most often covertly, to throw off the chains of bondage."[111] Mammy saw herself as a mother, but to her that role embodied a certain dignity and responsibility rather than a physical debasement, doubtless a carry-over from the African view that every mother is a symbol of the marvellous creativity of the earth.[112]

The tragic mulatta image also appears in the slave narratives but here her tragedy is not romanticized. The account that the mulattas give of their lives speak of abuse, humiliation, alienation, hatred and frustration. Christian quotes Lerner,

> (t)here are tales of mulattas who as mistresses were abused and sold, their children scattered to the ends of the land, mad mulattas...sullen, cynical mulattas reared to be sold as high class courtesans. The narratives abound with tales of woman—be she field nigger or house nigger, mulatta or darky—as breeder, nurser, nursemaid, concubine, whipping block, put on the rack of everlasting work and debasing servitude.[113]

The worksongs on the other hand give a view apart from the master-slave relationship on which the narratives mostly focus. Here, the freedom of music that is intensely personal and not dependent on any external media to be spread, gave the scope for exploring relationships between black men and women. Here were to be found courting, love making, success and disappointment in love. Writes Christian,

> Almost always the substances of the worksongs about or by women are sifted through the cry of hard times and how that affects relationships: The men who caught trains and left for whatever reasons, the lack of money, the pervasive sense of danger, the need for a woman to be independent

> of men, an independence imposed rather than deserved, all shape the songs...slave narratives and worksongs alike project black women as caught in the vise of hard times, their spirits occasionally rising to the heights of heroism but more often tempered by the nibbling need to always be practical.[114]

Most of the early fictions by black women writers concentrated on the experiences of black women in the rural South where these women served as drudges everywhere. A gradual shift in focus began with Ann Petry's *The Street* that represented for the first time, black women as labourers in the concrete tangles of the North—the black city woman and her ghettoization and the registering and recording of a new trend of victimization. Anne Petry's *The Street* marks a change in the setting and tone in the literature of the black women. It brings the literature into the twentieth century, for the concrete plantation became the dwelling place of more and more blacks in this century. After the publication of this novel, the black city women could not be forgotten. The particular brand of slavery under which she existed meant that new changes in literature would have to occur. Christian writes:

> The novel (*The Street*) also portrays the fragmentation of the black community which was more prevalent in the concrete plantations of the North than in the rural southern town. Here, husbands leave their wives not because they are sold or had to leave town, but because they are unable to be a man in their own eyes (i.e. find a job, protect their women and children). The apparel may be different, but the substance remains the same. Here, the spiritualists are not conjure women revered by both the master and the slave, but commercial salesmen selling powders and herbs to the highest bidder. In the North, one's child would not be sold into slavery, but might be taken away to jail or reform school. The lack of money becomes the jailer; hidden and overt racism becomes the lock. And the alienation of people, one from the other, separated by concrete and the ache to survive, strangles friendship and family ties. Everyone suspects each other as slaves were expected to. The apparel changes but the substance remains the same, except for one

important factor. One was told one was free, and therefore part of the mind believed this, incorporating the attitudes of a free person into one's value systems. Frustration and confusion about who one really was further intensified an already harrowed situation.[115]

Moving away from the negative and positive stereotypes of the black women, one must now approach the work of contemporary black women fiction writers/novelists, who have attempted to portray not only the complex struggles of black women's existence but the diversity and richness of their existence, from their own perspective. Here we encounter black women who have come forward to shed light on their situations, to discover their selfhoods and identities, to register and understand their growth, to examine "(their) relationship to men, children, society, history and philosophy as she had experienced it".[116] She is no longer ready to accept the set images that society and others have imposed upon her—she has at last broken out of her mould to boldly envision new realities, new truths and new images for herself. There is no single monolothic image of the African-American women in the contemporary African-American women's fiction. According to Schultz, the celebration of the fact of survival and the search for freedom are two dominating aspects of African-American literature[117] and against this backdrop must one view the work of contemporary African-American women writers whose subjects are mainly the complex reality of their black women characters and their struggles for achieving freedom and dignity. Claudia Tate writes that a dominant theme in black women's fiction "is the quest theme—a character's personal search for a meaningful identity and for self-sustaining dignity in a world of growing isolation, meaninglessness and moral decay." She continues:

> Black women writers project their vision of the world, society, community, family, their lovers, even themselves, most often through the eyes of black female characters and poetic personae. Their angle of vision allows them to see what white people, especially males seldom see. With one penetrating glance they cut through layers of institutionalized racism and sexism to uncover a core of social contradictions

> and intimate dilemmas which plague all of us, regardless of race or gender. Through their art they share their vision of possible resolution with those who cannot see.[118]

The emergence of these black women writers has created a tradition in itself. Since the nineteen thirties, African-American women novelists and poets have made a mark on the consciousness of not only black women but the whole world. Gwendolyn Brooks, Ann Petry, Dorothy West, Carolyn Rodgers, Paule Marshall, Maya Angelou, Toni Morrison, Mari Evans, Alice Walker, Gloria Naylor, Ntozake Shange, Gayl Jones, to name a few are writers of a new tradition who have laid paths and travelled new roads by themselves. They have broken the conspiracy of silence, given voice to the muted black women and allowed their fullest development as characters in their novels. The richness of their own experience as black women in America have shaped their literary imagination and interoven the fabric of their novels. It is therefore with the hope of enriching one's own experience that one attempts to discover new possibilities and new approaches to their complex works of art and anticipates to unearth new dimensions that are yet to be probed.

For the purpose of the present study, three contemporary black women novelists have been chosen whose works, it is felt, can be related to each other in the context of the study. Admittedly, the presentation of race, class, and gender conflicts in the novels of Toni Morrison, Alice Walker and Gloria Naylor have been discussed by numerous critics and extensive studies have focussed on one or other aspect or all of them. However, though separate approaches to class, race and gender have been made or all the three aspects studied in relation to each other, no study has focussed so far on the aspect of African-American women as labor as represented in the novels of the aforesaid authors. Though there have been analyses/studies touching upon the class consciousness of these authors, they have usually found second place to race and gender questions. Also, they have only tentatively touched upon the aspect of African-American women as labor, which historically had been the primary and pivotal role of the black woman from the times of slavery upon which the whole weight of their experience pivots. The purpose of this study is to focus on the hitherto unemphasized aspect of the representation of the role of women as labor within and outside the family in the novels of Toni Morrison, Alice Walker and Gloria Naylor. Fourteen novels, six by Toni Morrison and four each by Alice walker and Gloria Naylor have been selected for analysis. These are enlisted as follows:

Toni Morrison: *The Bluest Eye* (1970); *Sula* (1974); *Song of Solomon* (1978); *Tar Baby* (1981); *Beloved* (1987); *Jazz* (1991).

Alice Walker: *The Third Life of Grange Copeland* (1970); *Meridian* (1976); *The Color Purple* (1982); *The Temple of My Familiar* (1989).

Gloria Naylor: *The Women of Brewster Place* (1982); *Linden Hills* (1985); *Mama Day* (1988); *Bailey's Cafe* (1992).

The importance of studying the role of African-American women as labor as represented in the different novels of these three authors lies in the possibility of a multidimensional approach. In studying the role of African-American women as labor, one has to keep in mind the socio-economic, cultural and historical realities that have framed their existence and their living conditions. Their roles as labor are inclusive of and affect their roles as mothers, wives, daughters, sisters, mistresses. The three-fold ramification of the term encompasses all the three concepts of race, class and gender because as laborers, theirs is an exclusive and peculiar predicament for they are black, poor and female and in their roles as labor they have faced the maximum degree of victimization and discrimination on the basis of all these three aspects. Work being central to their survival, their work roles enfold their function as the saviours of their families—and also define their identities. Often work is the only medium available to them for the expression of anger, frustration or creativity through which they may hope to transcend their circumstances. As laborers by choice or out of compulsion, as work horses of the lowest category or skilled white-collar workers, as paid laborers or unpaid drudges at home, as housewives or career-women, they function in labor roles that are entangled with their consciousness as women. The objective of this study is to probe into the fictional representations of these women in their work roles and try to find answers to questions like—whether the work roles of these women heighten their awareness/consciousness of victimization? Does the work they do liberate, confine or console? Is their work a medium of self-expression or a form of oppression to them? Have they been able to achieve any degree of freedom through their work or are they simply workhorses who have been compelled to work due to unavoidable responsibilities? Has their work lightened or enhanced their burdens? Has labor been rewarding or punishing to them? Most important, have they been able to emerge as individual women and discover their selfhood through their roles as labor? Have they been able to gain confidence, make a statement, discover their identities or compelled to submerge the same in their roles as labor? And finally have Toni Morrison, Alice Walker and Gloria Naylor been able to do away with rigidly sociological, cultural and literary stereotypes in their representations of these African-American women characters in their roles as labor to create "fluid" and nuanced characters by avoiding the traps of misrepresentation or rigidity?

In attempting to find answers to these questions, a close reading and analysis of the primary data, i.e. the selected novels of the three authors would be necessary as it would be to place them in the sociological context while viewing them as works of art transmuted as such by the literary imagination of these artists. The study also aims to find out similarities and/or differences in the approach of these three authors to the question of African-American women as labor and the handling of their fictional representations and the distinctive quality that such representations have given to their work. It is felt that a brief introduction to the life and background of each of the authors would illuminate how their personal experience could have lent a distinct flavour to their appreciation and of the roles of African-American women as labor and their fictional representation as such.

Toni Morrison (born 1931): Toni Morrison was born Chloe Anthony Wofford to Ramah Willis and George Wofford, in Lorain, Ohio. Her parents were migrants from the South, and the southern heritage influences her work. Growing up, she experienced a vibrant African-American migrant culture. Her grandfather played the violin and her mother sang and played the numbers to decode them from a dream book. At school she read the great European writers and she was also informally educated in her own culture. She studied college at Howard University, did her masters at Cornell University and then taught for two years (1955-57) at Texas Southern University and then returned to Howard to teach English. After her divorce with Harold Morrison (a Jamaican architect) by whom she had two sons, she became a senior editor at Random House, a major publishing company. Morrison's first novel *The Bluest Eye* (1970) signaled a shift in the shape and emphasis of contemporary American literature. Women, especially black women and the diversity of their experience would now occupy centrality as subjects in novels and relationships between blacks would be extensively explored henceforth. Morrison's overriding concern is to engage in major contemporary social issues. She has explored the interlocking problems of race, class and gender exploitation bringing to her novels an understanding of the African-American dilemma, the enriching experience of African-American folk culture and the conviction that the history and literature of the United States and the present world were meaningless and "incoherent" without a comprehension of the African-American presence. In 1993, she was awarded the Nobel prize for literature, the first time an African-American writer had been so honored for she championed and continues to champion the importance and uniqueness of African-American literature.

Though not a self-proclaimed feminist, Morrison's major themes have pivoted round the psychological and existential problems of African-American women. She has studied perceptively problems of the African-American history and sociology of African-Americans in America and with a writer's intuition has touched upon and illuminated the African-American woman's situation against that backdrop. Through her work, she has proved again and again her feminist concerns, though she refers only to the politics that is inherent in every human situation. She has, like a true artist, brought to bear upon her work, the consciousness of a past that has shaped the present and the anticipation of a future to be hoped for. Her narratives are powerfully authentic, interlaced with finely honed realism that often borders on the realm of the magical or the fantastic. Her fictional world of magical reality is however interrupted with persistent intrusions from a world of tough facts and uncompromising truths. Her representation of African-American women characters should be viewed with this aspect in mind. More often than not, her work is a statement in itself of her interpretation of life in all it's dimensions—she does not neglect the one to champion the other. In exploring her novels from our perspective, one hopes to acquire a deeper appreciation/understanding of her novels as works of art that help to enrich our experience.

Though it is dangerous to recount biographical details while gauging the works of individual authors, the shaping influence of a writer's personal experience on her perceptions on life cannot be denied, especially if the writer happens to be both black and female. Morrison's early life in Lorain had a profound influence on her understanding of the African-American situation. When Morrison lived there, Lorrain was a steel mill town to which workers were drawn in the 1920s. Black workers who were share croppers in the South were attracted by the brighter prospects of employment in the North. Lorain was a town that provided black migrants with jobs and where class mattered more than race. Dorothy Mbalia (1991) therefore traced Morrison's interest in class to her upbringing in Lorrain.[119] However, Morrison had her first experience of racism in her home town. Her work focuses not only on the black experience of classist exploitation but also on the black experience of white racism in America. As she acknowledged in an interview with Claudia Tate (1995), she writes from a black center, and white people constitute the fringes of the world she describes. Her interest in them is marginal. She says:

> When I view the world, perceive and write about it, its the world of black people. Its not that I won't write about white people. I just know that when I am trying to develop the

> various themes I write about, the people who best manifest those themes for me are the black people whom I invent....[120]

While writing her first novel, Morrison was a working mother who was bringing up her two children alone and the influence of her position as a black woman in the given situation is discernible in the novel. Despite being contradictory on the subject of her feminist concerns, there is clear evidence in her work that she writes as a black woman with the experiences of black women in mind. On radio in 1983, she affirmed that she was "valuable" as a writer because she was a woman,

> Because women, its seems to me, have some special knowledge about certain things.[121]

In another interview with Sandi Russel in 1986, she said:

> I write for black women. We are not addressing the men, as some white female writers do. We are not attacking each other, as both black and white men do. Black women writers look at things in an unforgiving/loving way. They are writing to repossess, re-name, re-own.[122]

The experiences of reclaiming and repossessing are crucial for black women writers who are writing from an especially difficult position.[123] And Morrison has corroborated her concern with black women's issues again and again through her novels.*

Alice Walker (born 1944): She was born to sharecroppers Minnie Lou Grant and Willie Lee Walker and grew up in the small southern town of Eatonville, Georgia. Her mother who worked as a domestic, made everything Alice and her seven siblings used herself and was known for the incredible gardens she grew. Alice Walker commemorated those gardens in her classic essay "In Search of Our Mothers' Gardens: The Legacy of Southern Black Women" (1974). From her mother's artistry, Walker learned that African-American women's experience and art are based on spirituality, especially as it relates to nature. She was aware therefore of the ways in which southern black women were artists, though they were not named or recognised as such. These women, though not admitted to libraries or schools, illiterate and burdened with hundred responsibilities of survival, lacking even the privacy of aloneness in a room of one's own (which again they did not have), nevertheless found ways and means to express their creativity. They invested their creativity in their roles as labor and expressed themselves in the only media allowed or available to them—their work: cooking, gardening, quilting and through story-telling and worksongs.

At age eight, Walker lost an eye after being shot "accidentally" by one of her brothers with a gun he had received as a Christmas gift. The loss of her eye made her feel like an outcast and she experienced early the trauma of isolation and a depreciation of self. Her heightened consciousness made her notice and observe relationships closely, impressions that she jotted down in a notebook she kept. Her experience of being different from others may have been responsible for her pursuing of "forbidden" subjects in her writing as a departure from the usual and the ordinary.

In 1961, Walker left Eatonville to go to college. She first attended Spelman, a black women's college in Atlanta and then at Sarah Lawrence, in the suburbs of the New York city. Both educational experiences had a lasting effect on her. The rise of the Civil Rights Movement coincided with her stay at Spelman, and became the subject of many of her stories, essays and her second novel *Meridian* (1976). At Sarah Lawrence, she became pregnant at a time when abortion was illegal and contemplated suicide because of the disgrace it would bring to her family's name and her own helplessness in relation to her own body. Out of this psychological turmoil began her career as a poet/writer. She began writing to channelise her dejection into the art form of poetry and soon published her first book, *Once: Poems* (1968). Written at the age of twenty-three, the book was a statement/declaration of her commitment as an African-American woman writer to explore the lives of black women. In an interview with critic Mary Helen Washington in 1973, Walker spoke of the three types of black women characters that she felt were missing from much of American Literature. The first were those who were physically and emotionally exploited, whose lives were narrow and confining and who were driven to madness like Margaret and Mem Copeland in her first novel *The*

Third Life of Grange Copeland (1970). The second were those who were victims not so much of physical as psychic violence, women who were alienated from their own culture. The third type, represented most effectively by Celie and Shug in *The Color Purple* (1982, Walker's Pulitzer Prize winning novel) were those African-American women who, despite the oppressions they suffered, achieved some wholeness and created spaces for other oppressed communities.[124]

Walker's focus on southern African-American women's voices helped to galvanize an explosion of African-American women's critical and creative expressions. In her poems, essays and novels, Walker challenged the African-American cultural nationalist position, which seldom acknowledged the oppression of African-American women and continued to articulate their resistance against injustice. She was actively involved in the Civil Rights movement.

In voicing the sexual politics of black life in *The Color Purple* Walker raised a storm of controversy and was criticised for her negative portrayal of black men. However, Walker's exploration of the lives of black women has continued through 1980s and 1990s to this day. In 1983 she coined a new word "womanist" to replace the European sounding "feminist" derived from the black folk expression "womanish" to denote black feminism and to refute any narrow definition of the word "feminist". In her famous essay "In Search of Our Mother's Gardens: Womanist Prose" (1983), Walker writes about African-American women who were unconscious artists or saints benumbed by the brutalities inflicted upon them but drawing the richness of life from the wellspring of spirituality that is embedded in them due to their close ties with nature. She writes:

> Black women are called, in the folklore that so aptly identifies one's status in society, "the *mule* of the world," because we have been handed the burdens that everyone else—*everyone* else—refused to carry. We have also been called "Matriarchs", "Superwomen", and "Mean and Evil Bitches", not to mention "Castraters" and "Sapphire's Mama". When we have pleaded for understanding, our character has been distorted; when we have asked for simple caring, we have

> been handed empty inspirational appellations, then stuck in the farthest corner. When we have asked for love we have been given children. In short, even our plainer gifts, our labors of fidelity and love, have been knocked down our throats. To be an artist and a black woman, even today, lowers our status in many respects, rather than raises it: and yet, artists we will be.[125]

Identifying herself and her maternal ancestors with these women, Walker also writes about the hard life that her mother had led as a domestic and as a sharecropper with her husband Willie Lee. Her graphic account of her mother's role as labor and the creativity she expressed through the medium of her work suggests her interest in the theme and the fictional representation of such African-American women characters in her novels. Minnie, Walker's mother, was particularly outstanding as a role model for her children. Physically strong and strong-willed, she was a hard worker who managed to create beauty out of her limited surroundings by growing flowers, and telling stories at which she was reputed to have excelled. She worked all day in the fields with Alice's father, did her traditional female tasks in the evening, then exercised her enormous and widely recognized talents as a flower gardener and decorator with flowers. Minnie made creativity an important part of everyday life and demonstrated that no form or material or setting was too humble or contemptible for its exhibition. Poor black women of an earlier day chose these unspectacular outlets for their artistic urges rather than submit to having them stifled altogether by constant and soul-numbing labor.[126]

According to Janet Gray, Alice Walker's mother was strong and hardworking and "did not regard gender as barrier to any kind of labor".[127] Walker may have been inspired by the prospect of exploring African-American women in their work roles and new and liberating possibilities unfolding for them in those roles. She writes:

> In the late 1920s my mother ran away from home to marry my father. ...by the time she was twenty, she had two children and was pregnant with a third. Five children later, I was born. And this is how I came to know my mother: She seemed a

> large, soft, loving-eyed woman who was rarely impatient in our home....
>
> She made all the clothes we wore, even my bothers' overalls. She made all the towels and sheets we used. She spent the summer canning vegetables and fruits. She spent the winter evenings making quilts enough to cover all our beds.
>
> During the 'working' day, she labored beside—not behind—my father in the fields. Her day began before sunup, and did not end until late at night. There was never a moment for her to sit down, undisturbed to unravel her own private thoughts; never a time free from interruption—by work or the noisy inquiries of her many children. And yet, it is to my mother—and all our mothers who were not famous—that I went in search of the secret of what has fed that muzzled and often mutilated, but vibrant, creative spirit that the black woman has inherited, and that pops out in wild and unlikely places to this day.
>
> But when, you will ask, did my overworked mother have time to know or care about feeding the creative spirit?
>
> The answer is so simple that many of us have spent years discovering it. We have constantly looked high, when we should have looked high—and low.[128]

Walker writes:

> She has handed down respect for the possibilities—and the will to grasp them. For her, so hindered and intruded upon in so many ways, being an artist has been a daily part of her life. This ability to hold on, even in very simple ways, is work black women have done for a very long time.[129]

Commemorating and paying a tribute to the efforts of African-American women of her "mother's generation," Walker writes movingly of their ability to "(cover) the holes in our walls with sunflowers" in the following poem:

> They were women then
> My mama's generation
> Husky of voice—Stout of
> Step

With fists as well as
Hands
How they battered down
Doors
And ironed
Starched white
Shirts
How they led
Armies
Headragged Generals
Across mined
Fields
Booby-trapped
Kitchens
To discover books
Desks
A place for us
How they knew what we
Must know
Without knowing a page
Of it
Themselves.[130]

A creative writer and a courageous thinker, Alice Walker has established herself as one of the major feminist/womanist writers of the 20th and 21st centuries. She has created women characters whose counterparts in real life have emerged through a long and tangled process of great hardships. Yet Walker, like a true artist looks forward to a brighter future for African-American women, who indeed truly deserve it.*

Gloria Naylor (born 1950): Gloria Naylor was born on January 25, 1950 in New York to Alberta (McAlpin) Naylor and Roosevelt Naylor. A dedicated reader herself, Gloria Naylor's mother passed on to her daughter the respect for the written word. She herself had been reared in a state (Mississippi) that did not allow blacks to enter libraries. Gloria Naylor is one of the first African-American women writers who has studied both her African ancestors and the European tradition. She had, as a sophomore in Brooklyn College in 1978, read Toni Morrison's *The Bluest Eye* that left a profound impression on her. She felt that she had been given the authority into a terrain that she had thought was the exclusive privilege/domain of only gifted writers. She was inspired and encouraged to tell her own story and was convinced that it was worth telling. Her first novel *The Women of Brewster Place* (1982) was immensely successful though, like Alice Walker's *The Color Purple*, it was criticised for a consciously negative presentation of black men. Along with *The Women of Brewster Place*, three other novels, *Linden Hills* (1985), *Mama Day* (1988) and *Bailey's Cafe* (1992) form a quartet with certain characters appearing in more than one book. The geographical location of the novels are important because Naylor has a Faulknerian sense of the importance of place. From the slums of Brewster Place, she moves to the middle-class black suburbs in the *Linden Hills* and then away to an island off the southeastern coast of the United States owned by a dynasty of blacks, who claim that they are not real Americans in *Mama Day* and her *Bailey's Cafe* is set in a 1948 Brooklyn neighbourhood, though it is a place supposed to be everywhere.

Gloria Naylor's novels are in themselves an emphatic statement of her concern with the diversity, richness and indiosyncracies of the African-American experience. Her African-American women characters are again a departure from set stereotypes—stereotypes that this artist has refuted consciously. Like Morrison and Walker, she has probed deep into the realities of everyday existence of black women in real life and in her representation of these realities she has unearthed the core of resilience and optimism that lies embedded in the hearts of these frustrated, abused and deprived women. Amid the mundane trials of a black woman's daily life she has discovered the glory of human endurance and courage—it has endowed her characters with that rare humanity, which lies unconscious under the trials of daily life and the tedium of toting burdens. In her work again, we find that deep concern for the problems—racist, sexist, class-based—faced by black women in the United States. She has presented in four novels different images of black women as labor—her representations attempt to find an alternative and meaningful existence for African-American women, coming from various strata of the society and belonging to different classes, but circumscribed by their roles as laborers. The bond of sisterhood that is found in Morrison's and Walker's novels is the mainstay of her novels where black women, under all circumstances, must be able to create a community of love and understanding, support and strength in order to forge ahead in collective determination.*

Some definitions related to the study and referred to in the course of analysis are discussed here.

The Gender Role Theory: The Role Theory has been broadly defined as "an approach to social structure which locates its basic constraints in stereotyped interpersonal expectations."[131] The basic idea of the gender role concept is that being a man or woman means enacting a general role definitive of one's sex—the 'sex role'. There are accordingly, always two sex roles in a given context, the "male role" and the "female role"; less commonly but equivalently called man's role or woman's role, the masculine or feminine role. The logical core of the role theory runs as follows: an analytic distinction between the person and the social position she occupies and the set of action or role behaviour assigned to the position. Role expectations or norms define which actions are appropriate to a given position; they are held by people occupying counter-positions (role senders, reference groups) and who enforce them by means of sanctions—rewards, punishments, positive and negative reinforcements.[132]

The Role of Women in the Production System: The Economic Reductionism of Engels excluded from the production system, women's production of life. Women's role in production (in reproducing new life) was seen as the sole factor in women's subordination. The role of domestic labor of women in capital production was not considered. Women's exploitation as a seperate category has its own dynamics. Gayl Omvedt in "Patriarchy" writes that "Radical feminists accepted most of the social science thinking of their time which saw male power as going back to the dawn of society. The illusions that things had been otherwise, the exaltation of the women's role in the home, the hailing of motherhood or the existence of mother goddesses, were criticised as only ways of sub-ordinating the woman by 'putting her on a pedestal'. Male power was thus seen as fundamental and a historical, and its basic aspect seen in sexual terms."[133]

The Domestic Labor Debate—Feminist Perspectives: Another new area focussing on domestic work, childbearing, child rearing—and the nurture of both male workers and children, was opened up for theorising at the end of the 1960s. Women in the movement had always been concerned about "the politics of house work" and the question of why only they, and not men, should be responsible for it. But with articles from Margeret Benson (1969) and Peggie Morton (1971), it began to become clear that house work was not simply a troublesome, tedious, never ending but trivial task, it was actually of central economic importance: it was the work of reproduction, of the production of labor power itself, the most important commodity in capitalist economy. An article by an Italian feminist Mariarosa Dalla Costa, thrust this thesis into the very center of the movement/ debate and Marxist discussion in 1972-73. She challenged the classical Marxist position that housework is 'non-productive' pointing out that what the house-wife produces in the family are not simply use-values and states that the productivity of the house-wife is the pre-condition for the productivity of the wage laborers (male). The house-wife and her labor are not outside the process of production, but constitutes the very foundation on which the process can get started. Her labor of love contributes to the process of capital accumulation as much as the bread winner's wage work.

Socialist feminists, on the one hand, confront traditional Marxist focus on economic class struggle and on the other, the insights of the radical feminists and incorporate the domestic labor debate which include sexual-psychological-cultural issues and a new version of the economics. They look at male and female role as conditioned by a set of dichotomies—

Male Role	**Female Role**
Wage Labor	Domestic Labor
Public	Private
Productive	Reproductive[134]

So Zilla Eisenstein writes:

> Power is dealt with in a dichotomous way by socialist women and radical feminists: it is seen as deriving from either one's economic class position or one's sex. The critique of power rooted in the male/female distinction focuses on patriarchy. The critique of power rooted in the bourgeois/proletariat distinction focuses on capitalism. One either sees the social relations of production *or* the social relations of reproduction; domestic *or* wage labor, the public *or* private realms, the family *or* the economy, ideology *or* the material conditions, the sexual division of labor *or* capitalist class relations as oppressive.[135]

In her discussion of capitalist patriarchy, she underscores the triple jeopardy confronted by black women in white America as, "what they share as sexual oppression is differentiated along class and racial lines." Moreover, she stresses "the need to see the process and relations of power" and avoid seeing only "sex or class, or race as class, or sex or race."[136]

The General Definition of Patriarchy: Patriarchy implies a system of male control over women's sexuality, fertility (reproduction) and labor (production and reproduction). It is a system that is seperate from but interacts with relations of production that are "class relations" in the traditional Marxist sense. Socialist feminists target the system of patriarchy as the source of women's exploitation but feel that, though men as a group are accomplices in this system of exploitation through overt participation or covert acceptance, yet because such oppression is interlocked with class system as well, men of the exploited class should also have an interest in overthrowing capitalist patriarchy. This system of male power is embodied in kinship and in the family which are the sites of reproduction and are the main areas of women's subordination. It is through the family and the kinship system that women are related to the system of production, and when they enter into 'social production' outside the family they do so in a special and subordinate way due to their bondage within their family. Taking the cue from this, the socialist feminists arrive at the gender role construct. Patriarchy as a system is embodied in or represented in particular psychological/ideological structures that function at the unconscious level and are socialised into children from their infancy, turning them into 'men' and 'women', creating gender out of what is simply biological sex.[137]

Patriarchy and Women's Labor The Production of Life: Women's labor has been defined by theorists as a special kind of labor and patriarchy as a system that works in terms of male control of that labor. In this context, Hartmann defines patriarchy as a "set of social relations among men, which have a material base and which, though heirarchical, establish or create interests to dominate women. The material base upon which patriarchy rests lies most fundamentally in men's control over women's labour power."[138] This approach adds "reproduction" to the concept of production and often makes it the ultimate foundation of the whole system of production and exploitation.

According to Delphy, the patriarchal exploitation of women by men is located in the family. In marriage women exchange their labor power, that is they provide unpaid services in return for their upkeep. The value of their upkeep, however, is less than the value of the goods and services which the woman-wife provides. At the same time, because the marriage contract gives the man-husband control over the woman-wife's labor power, the goods and services she produces are use values rather than exchange values—they cannot be sold on the market but belong to the man-husband. Thus, the marriage contract is a labor contract by which men appropriate women's labor power, and marital male-female relations characterised by the husband's ownership and control of his wife's labor power, constitute the relations of domestic production and hence structure the domestic mode of production.[139]

Sherry Ortner, in her essay "Is Female to Male as Nature is to Culture", argued in the following way:

(i) Women's physiology and her specialized reproductive functions make her appear closer to nature. Men, unlike women, have to seek cultural means of creation—technology, symbols—while women's creativity is naturally fulfilled through the process of giving birth. Men, therefore, are associated more directly with culture and the creative power of culture as opposed to nature. "Woman creates naturally from within her own being, whereas man is free to, or forced to, create artificially, that is through cultural means, and in such a way as to sustain culture".

(ii) Women's social roles are seen closer to nature because their involvement in reproduction has tended to limit them to certain social functions which are also seen as closer to nature. Here, Ortner is referring to women's confinement within the domestic domain. In the context of the domestic family, women are primarily associated with the rearing of children, and thus with the pre-social or not yet culturally created person. Ortner points out that an implicit association between children and nature is a feature of a number of societies. The 'natural' association of women with children and the family provides an additional level of categorisation. Since women are confined to the domestic context, their main sphere of activity becomes intra and inter-familial relations, as opposed to men, who operate in the political and public domain of social life. Men thus become identified with society and the 'public interest', while women remain associated with the family and therefore with particularistic or socially fragmenting concerns.[140]

The spread of feminism to non-white women and Third World countries required the incorporation of historical materialism in feminist theories for such women cannot afford one-sided views that lead to an overstress on sexuality, a tendency to over-generalize women's exclusion from the "public sphere" of labor, an inability to see the ways in which capitalism (or any other mode of production) is not only shaped by patriarchy but also by factors such as race and caste.[141]

The African-American Woman and the Gender Role Perspective: Gender is more a cultural than a biological construct and "gender roles" have been assigned in recognition to those cultural constructs. Thus, in the sexual division of labor, it became traditional to argue that the male/man of the superior strength would take up heavier, more strenuous, difficult tasks and take up innovative, creative leadership roles while women would be given lighter tasks of house keeping, child bearing and child rearing—expressive, supportive work that was designated "woman's work". It would not be possible to apply such a concept to the roles of African-American women as labor who have always toiled in the fields and handled the most strenuous jobs along side their men, exibiting exemplary courage, determination, iron will and leadership qualities. They have been decision makers at home. However, ironically, though they have done "man's work" and more than man's work, their work has not been associated with or accorded the prestige that such labor usually finds—their work and they as workers have been devalued and relegated to the inferior status of the menial. Thus, as working women they have undertaken double shifts and often multiple shifts of work within and outside their homes but have not been paid in equivalent terms in money, social standing or even appreciation. It is to be noted that Negro men as such may be hoped to have sympathies with overthrowing the patriarchal structure as they have seen the worst kind of class exploitation from a dominant white capitalist patriarchy that has reduced them through a process of sexual reductionism to "boys", shorn them of their "manhood/masculinity" and dignity thus linking the racial bias with the gender role construct. On the other hand, African-American women of the privileged class have been confronted with the same gender-role assignations and assumptions that have created problems for white women. Again, even working-class African-American women in spite of full participation in the labor force, have faced role discrimination based on gender constructs.

The Beauty and the Beast: The concept of ideal womanhood posed peculiar problems for black women. African-American women were supposed to be embodiments of the very qualities which were thought to be degrading and offensive in women. The idea of softness, vulnerability, feminine delicacy went with a corresponding delicacy of constitution. Great strength, extraordinary appetite or ability to bear excessive fatigue required physical attributes akin to masculinity and hence violated the accepted image of feminine fragility that the white women were expected to cultivate. For the African-American woman however, it was essential to be endowed with the very qualities which were distasteful in her white counterpart. These were features to be emphasised in the promotion and selling of the black female field hand at a slave auction. Hazel V. Carby writes: "...a delicate constitution was an indicator of class as well as racial position; woman as ornament was a social sign of achieved wealth while physical strength was necessary for survival of women in the cotton fields in the factories or on the frontiers" and also that, "(t)o qualify as a 'true woman', position of virtue was an imperative."[142] In terms of literary conventions, the qualities of piety and purity were manifest in external physical traits such as skin color, hair color or the the color of the eyes. In literature, these qualities could be represented in a physical aura that surrounded the heroine and were displayed through strict codes of action and behaviour. The dark physical presence of the black woman who lacked these essetial qualities were constructed in opposition to the heroine. The idea of modesty and virtue in a black woman may only be ridiculed and overt sexuality emerged in the images of black women that were projected in literature and the media.

The Myth of Matriarchy: The dominating tendency of the Afro-American families has been matrifocal where the mother is at the center of the family. The Afro-centric families have been said to derive their matrilineal and matrifocal tendencies from their roots in African tribal culture. These female-headed households have been assumed to be matriarchal in the same way as white American households are said to be patriarchal, which means that the term 'matriarchy' evokes the same impression of power that is associated with patriarchy. However, the vision of matriarchal power that is conjured up is often superficial. Despite the fact that black women shoulder multiple responsibilities, including the earning of a livelihood and the onus of household chores, she is often powerless and oppressed. The African-American woman is the matriarch mostly out of compulsion and not by choice. They are the centres of their family in the sense of serving as pillars of strength and support, as cohesive factors endeavouring heroically to hold the dispersing family together and to maintain a foothold on life and not as dominating power figures. Arguing that "survival...was the prerequisite of all higher levels of struggle," Angela Davis points out that black women's survival oriented activities were and are a form of resistance.[143] With the powerful demands of poverty always pressing upon her and with the desire to have her husband proud in his own eyes and the eyes of others, she does not fulfill the criteria for being a matriarch; a figure of strength, she is not a figure of power.[144]

The various terms/names used to refer to/designate Negroes in the United States of America and their connotations have been discussed in the Appendix ["Terms and Concepts", *cf.* Appendix, pp. i-iii]. The terms Negro, black, Afro-American and African-American have been used interchangeably and at random in referring to members of the said race.

The Hypothesis of the Study

Women as 'labor', in the sense used here, encompasses all her roles (domestic and breadwinning) and therefore middle-class women who need not 'labor' outside their homes in the labor market also come within the purview of this study. It is therefore not a study based only on classiest, or racist or sexist exploitation but all the interlocking/interlinking facets forming a chain of imprisonment and exploitation. As workers outside and inside the home African-American women meet with discrimination—racist from the white society, classiest from the capitalist society dominated by white and middle-class blacks and sexist from men both black and white. In their roles as labor, they would not have faced racist discrimination had they not been black, would not have faced sexist exploitation had they not been women and would not have faced classiest exploitation had they not been poor, which was again a direct consequence of racist discrimination. Therefore, in their roles as labor, black women, irrespective of class and because of class have had to face problems of different nature. The study posits the following hypothetical model as an analytical tool:

I. The Slave Women: The first category of women as laborers in America were black women imported as slaves from Africa along with their men and children. They were beasts of burden, "mules of the world", social non-persons, work horses, whipping blocks—the most despised, denigrated and oppressed group of people in America before emancipation— after which they were theoretically free but captives of poverty and degradation.

II. Poor Black Women: In their roles as labor have no alternative but to work outside and inside their homes but free from middle-class taboos and class codes of superficial decorum, they sometimes may create spaces for their "self"s in unexpected places—through the tedium of work or through their work roles at home and express their art and creativity through the medium available to them. These are both domestics and housewives, tackling multiple roles and working double and multiple shifts to cope with the business of living.

III. Middle-class Black Women (Urban and Rural): Though not facing the physical abuses and harsh conditions that poverty engenders, they are still locked in a prison of disillusionment and alienation. As belonging to a different class that automatically imposes restrictions modelled on those tenets of white society that they imitate, these are women locked in a psychological prison, where their labor is considered useless and where the tedium of housekeeping makes them listless and apathetic. Having no compulsion to work, their potential of creative labor is translated into meaningless, decorous activities. Nor are their responsibilities as mothers, daughters or wives as pressing as those of poor black women. They are relegated therefore to a status very like that of white ladyhood, which however does not extend beyond the sanctuary of their homes or their communities. In the larger arena of white American society, their racial reality looms large where class does not gain them any extra privilege or protect them from racist assumptions and discriminations. They are afraid to mingle with poor negro masses for fear of being associated with them or becoming like them—carefully avoiding their funk and passion and sterilising their own feelings and emotions. These are women who labor for decorum, neatness, order and stability—assimilating the white society's standards and alienating themselves from their cultural roots.

Rural middle-class black women live lives of imprisonment under sexist domination as unpaid laborers (domestics) at home. However, as house laborers their contribution towards the family coffer goes unrecognized. Their 'respectable' and self-righteous husbands expect them to "stay in their place(s)" at home, obey their dictates, and act as objects of their lust and labor without demur.

IV. Rich Housewives: Few and far between in real life and rarely found represented in fiction, who are again alienated from the realities of most black women in America. Surrounded by luxury and wealth, they have compromised their souls. They need not labor outside or inside their homes (because they can afford to employ domestics), need not earn money and lead a pampered and ornamental existence, however, most often than not having bartered their peace of mind for material comfort.

V. (a) Career Women, Successful Models, Executives: These are black women who have achieved success, fame and wealth through their determination, drive and labor—that is hard work. Yet, at the top after achieving or in the process of achieving the pinnacle of success, they have been alienated from the realities of the large majority of negro masses laboring under the burdens of poverty and degradation. They are, in their incessant upward strivings, cut off from their cultural roots and rich folk tradition that has been kept alive largely amid poor black folk. It seemed that these women could not fall back on any support structure generated by community ties and sisterhood. Existing in self-created cocoons—isolated, extraordinary and alone, these women languish in their niches, unable to reach out, communicate, love and be loved. They seem to suggest a loneliness of the soul that is frightening in its absolute hopelessness. It seems also that the success and fame attained by these women, their jobs that should have given them fulfilment, fills them with a sense of emptiness as if they were floating in a vaccum where their 'self's had no anchor.

(b) **School teachers,** shop owners, academicians, nurses, clerks—black women with blue or white collar jobs—living a middle-class existence and circumscribed by middle-class confinement or decorum.

(c) **Prostitutes,** pimps, sex-workers, brothel-owners, night-club dancers and owners, call girls and street walkers—black women who confirmed the stereotype of the oversexed, bad black woman, but achieved, in their own way material independence, liberty and amoral pleasure.

VI. Political/Social activists like Meridian Hill of *Meridian* or Kiswana Browne of *The Women of Brewster Place* who had no particular compulsion to leave their homes to work for the upliftment and betterment of negroes or labor in their own way to change the situation, to ask for legitimate rights or to share with the large majority of African-Americans their poverty, trials and frustrations while trying to drag them out of the mire of apathetic acceptance and stagnation. These are workers who have shunned upper middle-class or middle-class affluence and security in order to experience firsthand the underside of American life, the seamy side/dark underbelly of African-American mass experience. Moving away from the 'elite' or the 'respectable' these are laborers for freedom and in search of new horizons for African-American womanhood.

VII. Black Women who Defy Categories: Those like Sula or Pilate in Morrison's *Sula* and *Song of Solomon* respectively, Miss Lissie or Fannie Nzingha in Walker's *The Temple of My Familiar* and Cocoa or Ruth in Naylor's *Mama Day* and *Linden Hills* respectively who defy categorizations and are untrammelled in their roles as *women*, defying relationships, social expectations, delimiting circumstances or gender constructs—the freest and fullest expression of self their sole quest/aim.

VIII. The Conjure Women: The wise magicians and healers who functioned as doctors, midwives, fortune-tellers and were able to achieve a relative degree of freedom from constraints burdening other black women and who were respected and feared by men—both black and white. These were women whose roles extended beyond the arena of their homes to encompass social roles—they often made a living out of their medicinal skills and wisdom—they were also the repository/reservoirs and keepers/ guardians of black African folk tradition, culture, heritage and knowledge, the ancient and pagan wisdom of African tribes. Regarded as evil and feared as such by the white society, they were held at a distance when not hounded as witches. In a way, these were the practising professionals among black women, though a shroud of mystery cloaked their methods of practice and brewing of medicine. In the black society, they were held in high esteem.

The hypothetical framework has been applied to analyse the fictional representation of African-American women as labor in the selected novels of Toni Morrison, Alice Walker and Gloria Naylor. Their correspondence with real-life counterparts may be deliberate, overt or covert. The hypothetical framework has been used to identify and systematise the diffuse pattern of role-assignations in the fictional representation of African-American women in their various role-categories. The flexibility of this kind of categorization allows for/accomodates the multiplicity of roles in which they operate and their movement from one category to the other or allows their simultaneous operation in one or more role categories.

The present study is divided into five chapters. Chapter 1 titled "Introduction" makes a brief survey of the history of the Negro as labor in America with special emphasis on African-American women as labor. Exploring the socio-historical background, it then examines the socio-cultural and literary traditions by focussing on the social and literary stereotypes of African-American men and women generated by years of misconception and prejudices nurtured against the Negroes as a race. The literary images of African-American women in particular as represented by white American, black American and black women writers in their novels has been discussed. The role played by Black Feminist Criticism and the new insights lent by feminist critics in analysing the fictional representation of African-American women has also been stressed. The study is then placed within the tradition of African-American literature and the three writers whose particular novels have been selected for the study are introduced biographically and aesthetically. The justification of the choice is also stated. In the light of the existing literature on the novels of Toni Morrison, Alice Walker and Gloria Naylor, the importance of the study is stressed. A definition of the term labor both traditional and as used in the study along with some terms and concepts that have emerged in the course of analysis are incorporated here. The Introduction also includes a review of existing literature on the novels of these three authors.

Chapter 2 titled "Changing Roles: African-American Women as Labor in the Novels of Toni Morrison" is devoted to a detailed analytical narrative of the roles of African-American women based on the hypotheses. In attempting to bring the kaleidoscopic range of complex African-American women characters created by Morrison within the framework of the said hypotheses, the chapter has attempted to make a systematic and ordered analysis also allowing for the flexibility of the roles and the fluidity of the characters. The chapter underscores Morrison's concern with African-American women's issues, though she is not a self-proclaimed feminist to bring out her artistic standpoint through her representations.

Chapter 3 titled "From Despair to Fulfilment African-American Women as Labor in the Novels of Alice Walker" is devoted likewise to a similar analysis of the roles of African-American women as represented by Walker in her novels selected for analysis. Walker's novels are mostly centered on black women fron the rural South or small towns of the South, though she does represent some urban women characters in their roles as labor.

Chapter 4 titled "Towards New Horizons: African American Women as Labor in the Novels of Gloria Naylor" deals with her representation of African-American women in their roles as labor, her stated standpoint regarding the black women's experience in America *vis-à-vis* the standpoint that emerges in the novels as they are analysed from the study's stated perspective.

Chapter 5 titled "A Comparative Analysis of the Representation of African-American Women as Labor in the

Novels of Toni Morrison, Alice Walker and Gloria Naylor" puts forward a brief comparative analysis of the novels of the three authors from the perspective of the study. Discussing the similarities and differences in their approach, treatment and representation of black women as labor, their distinctive qualities as individual writers are brought out. The "common bonds" (socio-cultural realities) that shape their imagination are traced while the aesthetic beauty of their "different voices" are highlighted. Writing from within the same tradition, these writers are still capable of transcending, as true artists, the topical and the particular.

Chapter 6 titled "Conclusion" gives the summary of conclusions arrived at after the attempted analysis on the basis of the hypothetical framework provided in the "Introduction".

NOTES AND REFERENCES

1. "Sister in Black" refers to African-American slave women in the folktale. In the context of the study, the term connotes/denotes all African-American Women.
2. From Zora Neale Hurston's *Mules and Men,* 1935, Reprinted in *The Norton Anthology of African-American Literature.* Eds. Henry Louis Gates Jr. and Nellie Y. McKay. W.W. Norton & Co.: New York, 1997, p. 111.
3. An expression borrowed from Zora Neale Hurston's *Their Eyes were Watching God.* New York: Fawcett Publishers, 1965, p. 16.
4. P.N. Chopra, "Factors of Production", *Principles of Economics.* New Delhi: Kalyani Publishers, 1996, pp. 28-29.
5. G. Lloyd Reynolds, "Labor Market Policy: Discrimination," *Labor Economics and Labor Relations.* New Haven, London: Yale University Press, 1978, p. 158.
6. Kate Millett, "Theory of Sexual Politics," *Sexual Politics.* London: Sphere Books Ltd., 1972, pp. 39-40.
7. Margaret L. Anderson, "Foreword", *Race, Class and Gender: Common Bonds, Different Voices.* Eds. Esther Ngangling Chow et al. Thousands Oaks, London: Sage Publications, 1996, p. xii.
8. Richard Wright, *Twelve Million Black Voices.* New York: Thunder's Mouth Press, 1988, p. 30.
9. Anne Julia Cooper, quoted by Gates, Henry Louis Jr. Ed. *Reading Black, Reading Feminist: A Critical Anthology.* New York: A Meridian Book, Penguin Group, 1990, p. 1.
10. *Ibid.*, p. 4.

11. *Ibid.*, p. 7.
12. *Ibid.*
13. Linden Peach, *Toni Morrison.* New York: St. Martin's Press, 1995, p. 2.
14. Alice Walker, "An Interview With John O'Brien", *Alice Walker: Critical Perspectives Past and Present.* Eds. Henry Louis Gates Jr. et al. Amistad Press, 1993, p. 331.
15. Barbara Smith, "Toward a Black Feminist Criticism", *Conditions: Two.*1977, p. 32.
16. Alice Walker, quoted in "Profile: Black Beauties" by Suchanda Gupta, *Sunday Statesmen,* 17 June 2001.
17. Lorraine Bethel, *But Some of Us are Brave.* Eds. Gloria T. Hull, Patricia Bell Scott, and Barbara Smith. Old Westbury, New York: The Feminist Press, 1982, p. 184.
18. Henry Louis Gates Jr., *Reading Black, Reading Feminist,* p. 4.
19. Elizabeth Schultz, "Free in Fact and at Last: The Image of Black Women in Black American Fiction", "*What Manner of Woman, Essays on English and American Life and Literature.* Ed. Marlene Springer. New York University, 1977. Oxford: Basil Blackwell, 1978, p. 323.
20. Henry Louis Gates Jr and Nellie Y. Mckay Eds. *The Norton Anthology of African-American Literature.* New York: W.W. Norton and Company Inc., 1997, p. 130.
21. *Ibid.*, pp. 130-31.
22. Robert Bone, *Down Home: The Negro Novel in America.* New Haven and London: Yale University Press, 1958, p. 12.
23. Richard Wright, *Twelve Million Black Voices,* pp. 36-37.
24. Calvin Hernton, *Sex and Racism in America,* New York: Grove Press, 1965, p. 125.
25. Jonathan H. Turner, *American Society: Problems of Structure.* 2nd edition. University of California. New York: Harper and Row, 1976, p. 190.
26. Gunnar Myrdal, *An American Dilemma.* New York: Harper, 1944, pp. 68-70.
27. *Ibid.*
28. *Ibid.*
29. *The Norton Anthology,* pp. 464-65.
30. Myrdal, *An American Dilemma,* pp. 191-96.
31. Robert Bone, *Down Home,* pp. 53-54.
32. *Ibid.*, p. 111.
33. Jonathan H. Turner, *American Society: Problems of Structure,* p. 191.

34. U.S. Bureau of Census, 1988, p. 368. Quoted in Joseph F. Healey, *Race, Ethnicity and Gender in the United States, Inequality, Group Conflict and Power.* Thousand Oaks, California: Pine Forge Press, 1997, pp. 137-38.
35. U.S. Bureau of Census, 1993, p. 40. Quoted in Joseph F. Healey, *Race, Ethnicity and Gender in the United States,* pp. 137-38.
36. Joseph F. Healey, *Race, Ethnicity and Gender in the United States,* p. 132.
37. Daniel P. Moynihan, *The Negro Family in America: The Case for National Action.* Washington, D.C.: Government Printing Office, 1967.
38. Joseph F. Healey, *Race, Ethnicity and Gender,* p. 132.
39. John Farley, 1995, p. 80; quoted in Healey, p. 132.
40. Angela Davis, *Women, Race and Class* (1981) quoted from Gloria Wade Gayles. *No Crystal Stair.* New York: The Pilgrim Press, © 1984, p. 6.
41. William H. Chafe, *The American Woman: Her Changing Social Economic and Political Roles, 1920-1970.* New York: Oxford University Press, 1972, p. 136.
42. Gloria Wayde Gayles, *No Crystal Stair,* p. 24.
43. John Hope Franklin, *From Slavery to Freedom.* New York: Random House, 1969.
44. Gerda Lerner, *Black Women in White America: A Documentary History.* New York: Random House, 1972, p. 239.
45. Wayde Gayles, *No Crystal Stair*, p. 33.
46. Horace Layton and St. Clairs Drake, *Black Metropolis.* Vols. 1 and 2 New York: Harcourt, Brace and World, 1945.
47. U.S. Department of Labor, *Handbook of Labor Statistics,* 1978; Bulletin 3000. Washington D.C.: Government Printing Office, 1979, pp. 75-79.
48. Allen Walter, "Family Roles, Occupational Statuses and Achievement Orientation among Black Women in the United States," Signs 4 (Summer 1979): p. 679.
49. Pauli Murray, "Jim Crow and Jane Crow", *Black Women in White America.* Ed. Gerda Lerner. New York: Random House, 1972, p. 597.
50. Jeanne Noble, *Beautiful, Also, Are the Souls of My Black Sisters.* Englewood, New Jersey: Prentice-Hall, 1978, p. 75.
51. Wayde Gayles, Gloria *No Crystal Stair,* p. 114.
52. Noble. *Beautiful Also*, pp. 75-76.
53. *Ibid.*, p. 75.
54. *Ibid.*

55. Wayde Gayles, *No Crystal Stair,* p. 115.
56. *Ibid.,* pp. 115-16.
57. *Ibid.,* p. 116.
58. *Journal of Marriage and The Family,* 55 (May 1993): p. 317.
59. Robert Staples, "Bodies for Sale: Black Prostitutes in White America," *Black Women in America: Sex, Marriage and the Family.* Chicago: Nelson Hall Publishers, 1973, pp. 73-94.
60. *Ibid.,* p. 90.
61. Elizabeth Schultz, *What Manner of Woman,* p. 330.
62. Joseph F. Healey, *Race, Ethnicity and Gender in the United States.* 1997, pp. 137-38.
63. Karen. Dugger, "Social Location and Gender-Role Attitudes: A Comparison of Black and White Women," *Race, Class and Gender. Common Bonds, Different Voices.* 1996, pp. 34-35.
64. *Ibid.,* p. 34.
65. Angela. Davis, *Women, Race and Class.* New York: Random House, 1981, p. 29.
66. Angela Davis, "Reflections on the Black Woman's Role in the Community of Slaves", *The Black Scholar,* 3 (December 1971), p. 7.
67. *The Norton Anthology,* pp. 196-97.
68. *Ibid.,* p. 200.
69. bell hooks, "Black Women: Shaping Feminist Theory," *Feminist Theory: From Margin to Center.* Boston: South end Press, 1994, p. 13.
70. *Ibid.,* p. 2.
71. *Ibid.,* p. 10.
72. *Ibid.,* p. 11.
73. *Ibid.,* p. 15.
74. *Ibid.*
75. Quoted in *Race, Class and Gender: Common Bonds, Different Voices,* p. 268.
76. Gerda Lerner, (1979, pp. 81-82)—Quoted by Barnett in *Race, Class and Gender,* p. 267.
77. Paula Giddings, (1984, pp. 5-6)—Quoted in *Race, Class and Gender,* p. 268.
78. Barnett—Quoted in *Race, Class and Gender,* p. 279.
79. Wayde Gayles, *No Crystal Stair,* p. 9.
80. Barbara Christian, *Black Feminist Criticism: Perspectives on Black Women Writers.* New York: Pergammon Press, 1985, p. 16.
81. Schultz, *What Manner of Woman,* p. 316.

82. W.E.B. Du Bois, *Darkwater*. Reprinted in *To Be a Black Woman*. Eds. Mel Watkins and Jay David. New York: Morrow, 1970, pp. 234-35.
83. Barbara Christian, *Black Feminist Criticism,* p. 3.
84. Beale Frances, "Double Jeopardy: To Be Black and Female," *The Black Women*. Ed. Toni Cade Bambara. New York: New American Library, 1970, p. 92.
85. Christian, *Black Feminist Criticism,* p. 2.
86. Wayde Gayles, *No Crystal Stair,* p. 59.
87. Daniel Thompson, *Sociology of the Black Experience*. Westport, Conn.: Greenwood Press, 1974, p. 81.
88. Wayde Gayles, *No Crystal Stair,* p. 59.
89. Joyce Ladner, *Tommorow's Tommorow.* New York: Doubleday, 1972, p. 63.
90. Daryl Dance, "Black Eve or Madonna? A Study of the Analytical Views of the Mother in Black American Literature," *Sturdy Black Brides*. Eds. Roseann Bell et. al. New York: Doubleday, 1979, pp. 123-32.
91. Barbara Christian, *Black Feminist Criticism*, p. 3.
92. Schultz, *What Manner of Woman,* p. 318.
93. Karen Dugger, *Race, Class and Gender*, p. 36.
94. Louis D. Stone, "What It's Like to be a Colored Woman," Washington Post. November 13, 1966. Quoted in *Black Women in White America*. Ed. Gerda Lerner. New York: Random House, 1972, p. 217.
95. This is the general thesis of E. Franklin Frazier's *The Negro Family in America,* Chicago: University of Chicago Press, 1939, a thesis which became the basis for governmental policy upon the publication of Daniel P. Moynihan's *The Negro Family: The Case for National Action*. Washington D.C.: Government Printing Office, 1967.
96. Ladner's *Tommorrow's Tommorow: The Black Woman*. Garden City, New York: Doubleday, 1971 and Staple's *The Black Woman in America: Sex, Marriage and the Family.* Chicago: Nelson Hall Publishers, 1973.
97. Schultz, *What Manner of Woman,* p. 318.
98. *Ibid.*, p. 319.
99. *Ibid.*, pp. 320-22.
100. Sterling. Brown, *The Negro in American Fiction*. 1937: Reprint, New York: Atheneum, 1969, pp. 1-89.
101. Christian, *Black Feminist Criticism*, p. 3.
102. *Ibid.*
103. *Ibid.*

104. *Ibid.*, p. 8.
105. Gayles. *No Crystal Stair,* p. 29.
106. Barbara Christian, *Black Women Novelists: The Development of Tradition, 1892-1976.* Westport, Conn.: Greenwood Press, 1981, p. 90.
107. bell hooks, *Ain't I a Woman? Black Women and Feminism.* Boston: Southend Press, 1981, p. 86.
108. Lerner, *Black Women in America,* pp. 163-64.
109. Schultz, *What Manner of Woman,* p. 328.
110. Ann Petry, *The Street.* Boston: Houghon Mifflin, 1964, p. 206.
111. Christian, *Black Feminist Criticism,* p. 5.
112. John Mbite, *African Religions and Philosophy.* New York: Doubleday Anchor, 1970.
113. Lerner, *Black Women in America,* pp. 71-72 quoted by Christian. *Black Feminist Criticism,* p. 5.
114. Christian, *Black Feminist Criticism,* p. 7.
115. *Ibid.,* pp. 11-12.
116. *Ibid.*, p. 16.
117. Schultz, p. 342.
118. Claudia Tate, Ed. "Introduction", *Black Women Writers at Work.* New York: Continuum, 1983, p. xx.
119. Doreatha Drummond Mbalia, *Toni Morrison's Developing Class Consciousness.* Selinsgrove: Susequehanna, University Press, 1991.
120. Toni Morrison, "Conversation with Toni Morrison". Interview with Claudia Tate. *Black Women Writers at Work.* Ed. Claudia Tate. New York: Continuum, 1983, p. 118.
121. 1983 Radio Interview quoted in Peach. *Toni Morrison.* 1995, p. 14.
122. Nellie Y. Mackay, Ed. *Critical Essays on Toni Morrison.* Boston: G.K. Hall and Company, 1988, pp. 46, 54.
123. Linden Peach, *Toni Morrison,* 1995, p. 14.
124. 1973 Interview, with critic Mary Helen Washington. *The Norton Anthology of African American Literature.* Eds. Henry Louis Gates Jr. and Nellie Y. McKay. New York: W.W. Norton and Company Inc., 1997, p. 2375.
125. Quoted in *The Norton Anthology,* p. 2384.
126. Wilfred L. Guerin, et al. *A Handbook of Critical Approaches to Literature.* 4th Edition. New York: Oxford University Press, 1992, pp. 62-63.
127. Janet Gray, "Alice Walker", *American Writers: A Collection of Literary Biographies.* Supp. III, Pt. 2 Ed. Lea Beachler and A. Walton Litz. New York: Scribner's, 1991, p. 521.

128. Quoted in *The Norton Anthology*, pp. 2384-85.
129. *Ibid.*, pp. 2386-87.
130. *Ibid.*, p. 2387.
131. R.W. Connel, *Gender Power: Society, the Person and Sexual Politics.* Cambridge: Polity Press, 1987, pp. 47-48.
132. *Ibid.*
133. Gail Omvedt, "Patriarchy and Matriarchy," *Feminist Concepts.* Part I: Contribution to Women Studies. Series 7. Research Centre for Women's Studies. SNDT Women's University, Vithaldas Vidyavihar, Santacruz West Bombay, p. 8.
134. *Ibid.*, p. 11.
135. Zillah R. Eisentein, "Some Notes on the Relations of Capitalist Patriarchy", *Capitalist Patriarchy and the Case for Socialist Feminism.* New York: Monthly Review Press, 1979, p. 47.
136. *Ibid.*
137. Gail Omvedt, pp. 12-13.
138. Heidi Hartmann, "The Unhppy Marriage of Marxism and Feminism: Towards a More Progressive Union," *Capital and Class.* 8 (Summer 1979): p. 11, quoted by Omvedt in *Feminist Concepts,* p. 16.
139. Annette Kuhn, "Structures of Patriarchy and Capital in the Family," *Feminism and Materialism: Women and Modes of Production.* Eds. Annette Kuhn and AnnMaria Wolpe. London: Routledge and Kegan Paul, 1978, pp. 99-100.
140. (i) Ortner, Sherry. "Is female to male as nature is to culture?", *Women, Culture and Society.* Ed. M. Rosaldo and L. Lamphere. Standford, California: Standford University Press, 1974, p. 77.
(ii) *Ibid.*, p. 78.
141. Omvedt, p. 27.
142. Hazel V. Carby, "Slave and Mistress", *Reconstructing Womanhood.* New York: Oxford University Press, 1987, p. 25.
143. Angela Davis, "Reflections on the Black Woman's Role in the Community of Slaves," *The Black Scholar* (Dec. 1971), p. 7.
144. Joyce Ladner, *Tommorrow's Tommorrow,* pp. 34-35.

* *Note*: The biographies of the three authors have been based on information gathered from various sources as already acknowledged in the notes. The framework and general information of the biographies have been taken from *The Norton Anthology of African-American Literature*, pp. 2094-98, 2375-77, 2542-43.

Changing Roles: African-American Women as Labor in the Novels of Toni Morrison

2

Toni Morrison was awarded the Nobel Prize for literature in 1993. It was the first time that an African-American writer had been so honored and since then Morrison came into national and global consciousness. Nancy J. Peterson writes: "it is not only in the field of literature that Morrison has become the touchstone...she has become the symbol of African America, of human struggle against various kinds of oppressions, of a global longing for liberation".[1] Significant debates of American literature, culture and ideology have amassed around her name including those about the relation of slavery to freedom, the possibility of creating literature that is aesthetically beautiful and politically engaged, the interlocking relation of racism, sexism and classism and the possibility of laying claim to our 'self's', our lives and our imagination from within a society that is postmodern, patriarchal and capitalist.[2]

Morrison's role as spokesperson for the black community came to the fore in her 1989 interview with Bonnie Angelo for *Time*.[3] Since then she has been regarded not only as a talented and visionary author but also as a leader of the black community. Represented as such by newspapers, journals and magazines, she has been evoked and credited in the words of intellectuals like bell hooks, Patricia Hill Collins and Cornel West for providing new paradigms, using her voice to raise essential issues that affect black women, and as a "political intellectual" who can work effectively both in the academy and on the streets.[4] However, Morrison's emergence as a writer of international repute has not been easy. Her story of success has been punctuated by disappointment and difficulties along with triumph.

Toni Morrison's concern with the African-American woman and her work is undoubtedly one of the major forces which lend the power of authenticity to her novels and weave the strength of tough realism in the fabric of her finely chiselled narratives. Morrison has the unique experience of being both black and female, which means obvious and immediate relegation to the lowest strata of a highly stratified White American society variously distinguishable into rich and poor, white and black, male and female. This society has operated in terms of the worst possible exploitation of the African-Americans in general. The structure of the dominant patriarchy of the same society has made the black woman it's victim in a different way. Put together, this has been instrumental in making the black woman sufferer of a three-fold oppression resulting from class, race and gender distinction: "The black American woman's struggle of survival and liberation has been won against dual traditions of racism and sexism in America".[5] Added to this, is a history of starvation, poverty and economic deprivation. Under the circumstances, the role of black women as labor in context of the white society and the black family as projected by Morrison in her novels, acquire an added significance.

Although it is dangerous to recount autobiographical details while gauging the works of individual authors, the shaping influence of a writer's personal experience on her perceptions of life cannot be denied. Morrison's early life in Lorraine, Ohio had a profound influence on her understanding of the African-American situation. She has admitted that she writes from a black center (interview with Claudia Tate)[6] and also that she writes for black women (interview with Sandi Russel)[7], her major themes having pivoted round the psychological and existential problems of African-American women. Having studied the history and sociology of the Negro woman's experience in America, she has explored and illuminated the African-American woman's present situation against that backdrop. The 'politics' inherent in every human situation permeates her novels and she has proved her feminist concerns again and again through her work.

In the 1960s, Toni Morrison was a divorcee, a working mother and a single parent bringing up her two sons alone in Syracuse, New York. Her days were spent in working as an editor for a subsidiary of Random House. She has mentioned in various interviews the isolation, loneliness and the difficulties she had faced as a black woman in the given situation. At night, when her sons had gone to sleep, she burnt the midnight oil to write her first novel *The Bluest Eye* that was published in 1970. The influence of her personal experience as a struggling African-American woman trying to perform in the multiple roles of mother (nurturer), breadwinner and creative writer is discernible in the novel. Tracing this as a major concern in her other novels is not difficult and this chapter attempts to explore Morrison's narratives in her six selected novels as mentioned in the "Introduction" to examine her representation of African-American women characters in their roles as labor. The complexity and diversity of the black women characters represented by her range from Category I of the hypotheses to Category VIII and include their roles as slave women to conjure women. Geographically, the location of her novels change from small town Lorraine, Ohio (Northern state of USA) in *The Bluest Eye;* small town Medallion City, Ohio in *Sula*; small town in the Northern City of Michigan, USA in *Song of Solomon*; small semi-rural township, Ohio in *Beloved*; a Carribean Island named Isles des Chevaliers inhabited by local blacks in *Tar Baby* and Harlem, New York in *Jazz*. She concentrates as such more on semi-rural and urban characters, representing them in their roles as labor and projecting the trajectory of African-American women's experience in America and their changing roles, against the backdrop of historical, sociological and cultural realities.

In *Beloved*, Morrison presents the story of a fugitive slave Sethe Suggs based on the true story of Margaret Garner, a fugitive slave from Kentucky who attempted to kill her children rather than have them suffer the atrocities of slavery at Ohio in 1850. As a writer, Morrison, ever concerned with the untold stories and blank spaces/gaps left in historical narratives attempts in *Beloved* to lend a voice to the unspoken saga of an oppressed people rendered mute by years of violence, oppression, torture and racial discrimination. Since in all of this, the worst possible deal was meted out to black women, their "extremely painful and unattractive"[8] history bears testimony to their roles as mothers and laborers and the work they have been required to do at the fields alongside their men and in the house of the white master—roles that have demanded both physical toughness and the ability to endure immense hardships and pain. Using the technique or device of re-memory, Morrison, defying chronological or sequential presentation, has pieced together bits and pieces of information about the past, little details that are missed out or ignored and the day-to-day accounts of the unbroken routine of endless work that these black slave women had to do. Because slavery was an institution that meant the owning of a personal labor force, it is obvious that slave experience would be tied up inseparably with the gruelling and strenuous physical labor/work that was forced upon the slaves. They had no identities but as beasts of burden who were "moved around like checkers". They were "hanged, (they) got rented out, loaned out, bought up, bought back, stored up, mortgaged, won, stolen on seized" (*Beloved*, 29) like commodities. As Alice walker says in *Meridian*, there was no concept of a "sick" slave, just a "malingering" (*Meridian*, 144) one and there was no respite or rest for the slave except in death.

In *Beloved* therefore Morrison has represented the protagonist Sethe Suggs, her mother (anonymous), her mother-in-law Baby Suggs, Nan, her wet nurse, the thirty-mile-woman, Ella and a host of other unnamed women as slave women, belonging to Category I of the hypotheses, whose collective and individual experiences weave the rich tapestry of the novel.

The experience of Baby Suggs' slave life was no different than that of countless black women of that era. She was bought and sold several times as a field laborer, lost every one of her eight children she had by six different husbands except Halle and had never known stability in her life. The gruelling physical labor that she had to perform and the physical abuse and atrocities that she had endured as an inseparable part of slave life had broken her physically and mentally till, due to a fall in her price on account of her broken hip, she was bought by

Mr. Garner of Sweet Home plantation who ran a "special kind of slavery" (*B*, 173) by treating his slaves as paid laborers. Here she was spared from the harshness of field labor as also the humiliation of having to "couple" with boys half her age at the master's order and the lash of the whip. When Halle bought her freedom with his own labor, initially freedom meant nothing but separation from the only child she had left with her as she had already lost everything she had loved or cherished. The only thing that freedom could give her was a chance to "sit down for a change" (*B*, 13), Baby Suggs had, like Sethe, and countless other slave women, waded through rivers of blood to arrive at a safe shore where they could at least be mistresses of their own bodies and minds. In the light of what she had actually lived through, Baby Suggs' statement that slave life had "busted her legs, back, head, eyes, kidneys, womb and tongue" (*B*, 106) was an understatement.

During her ten years at Sweet Home, minus the burden of back breaking field labor, the exhausted numbness of her mind loaded and hazy with grief for all that she had lost, lessened as she gradually came to herself. The freedom that had been bought at so dear a price however filled her with an intense exhilaration as she absorbed the fact that at last she was the mistress of her own body, emotions and thoughts and was free to sell her labor to earn money and lead an independent life. For an ex-slave woman, it was unbelievable at first that the worth of her labor would be gauged in money and paid in cash. Her transition from a slave woman to a free one and then a self-styled preacher and social worker wrought changes in her personality, allowing her "great heart" and great kindness to embrace men and women of her race at Cincinnati where she emerged as a messiah for needy Negroes. As a fine cobbler and seamstress, she could pay the rent of her doubled-storied house to the Bodwins—a white brother-sister duo who hated slavery—as also get regular orders to support herself and her daughter-in-law and grandchildren. Supplementing her income by taking in washing and planting her own crops allowed for an abundance in her house that enabled her to extend a warm welcome and hospitality to any hungry stranger who appeared at her door that was always open for any one in need. "Giving advice; passing messages; healing the sick, hiding fugitives, cooking, preaching, singing, dancing and loving everybody like it was her job and hers alone" (*B*, 168), Baby Suggs' mission was to teach her people how to love their abused bodies and tortured flesh. So she, an "unchurched preacher," (106) led them to a clearing in the woods where, blessed with the "word" by God, "called" (218) to the great spirit of nature and nature responded.

In Alice Walker's *The Temple of My Familiar*, Fanny Nzingha discusses with Robin, her psychiatrist, the strong community ties engendered by black women—the heritage of bonding that enabled them to pool their strengths to combat hostile forces that threatened to tear them apart. In that tradition, many renegade black women became preachers who founded their own church which they called a 'band'—a prayer band or a spiritual band comprising a group of people who shared a common bond or purpose and whose idea of spirituality was radically different from prevailing or mainstream ones (*TMF*, 299). The call and response tradition was solidly grounded on community ties and deep faith. Baby Suggs was lovingly called "holy" (*B* 24) by the grateful black people of her community whom she "loved, cautioned, fed, chastised and soothed" (106). Ironically, her bountifulness and generosity became the cause for envy to the people whom she had given so much, as there seemed to be no poverty in her house. She had built a new world for herself after gaining freedom only to be betrayed by her own community as the abundance in her house became a sore point for them and motivated by jealousy at her extraordinary capabilities they deliberately abstained from warning her that slave catchers had followed Sethe's trail and were approaching her house.

Baby Suggs' role as social worker cost her dearly and with all her love and "great big heart" (107) she could not prevent the terrible tragedy in her shed where Sethe killed her daughter Beloved rather than yield her to her white master. Losing faith in herself and everything she had preached, she lapsed into a silence and withdrew from the community.

Baby Suggs' heroic struggle ended in futility but this black slave woman with her inherent sense of dignity and self-worth would wrest a grudging respect from anyone. After spending a lifetime as a slave and laborer, she tried to search for a self that could have been a mother, a sister, a daughter or a daughter-in-law. She had attempted to rediscover herself in her role as a loving and protective mother-in-law and grandmother. She had found in herself a God given power to "call" to nature and rejuvenate the flagging spirits of her kin—her beloved community of Negroes. In her role as a preacher and social worker always ready for community service, she had found fulfilment. But after the "bloodspill in her backyard" (217) she was totally disillusioned and the great faith in love that had been her anchor was shattered. Her tenacious grip on life loosened and in the last years of her life she retreated into an apathetic and indifferent silence. Her days now consisted of mechanical routine work, which was necessary to earn a living and in silence she delivered the mended shoes and washing to the white homes, carefully avoiding company. Her estranged friend Stamp Paid (a Negro who had saved numerous fugitive slaves) realised after eighteen years the enormity of the grief that she had contained within herself and the magnitude of tiredness that had broken her marrow after all these years of fight and hope, determination and survival and the tremendous efforts of this lone black woman who had struggled to keep afloat despite the mire of terrible memories sucking at her feet to bog her down. Stamp had regarded Baby as superhuman, the "mountain to his sky" (209) and had expected too much of her. In subverting Baby Suggs' image of stereotypical and extraordinary strength, Morrison brings out poignantly in her abandonment of the "word" and "call" as useless, the vulnerability that lay beneath that laudable toughness. Forces beyond her control in a racist society brought her to her knees and when she said: "I'm looking for what I was put here to look for: the back door" (220), she put in a nutshell the sum total of a black woman's existence. No matter what she did or how she labored, she could not get out of the circumscribing circle hemming her in.

There were other slave women like Sethe's mother whom she could recall only vaguely and whom, as a child she attempted to identify/distinguish from the long line of similar looking backs stooped over the watery fields of rice, indigo or cotton, engaged in field labor, her mother's figure. In that era, thousands of slaves in the United States who existed in a state of dazed numbness emotionally, exhausted physically, their minds a blank void and already at work long before sun up and at it long after sun down. The mothers hardly met their children, the fathers did not know them. The slave children were brought up collectively by slave women like Nan who could not tackle the harsh labor on account of being handicapped. Their job was to nurture the future labor force. Sethe's mother—a black slave woman who had lived and died as a laborer (she was hung—a fate common to all slaves who attempted rebellion or escape) and whose life had been a long saga of endless suffering and mindless labor—had nevertheless tried to point out to her daughter her individual identity as her mother. Sethe had then been too young to realise the implication of that brand burnt into her mother's skin or begin to apprehend the horror of such anonymity that erased their individuality and made them represent a faceless, nameless mass of people like herds of animals to be bullied, tortured, pushed, beaten and forced to work at the numerous cotton, indigo or tobacco plantations spread all over the Southern States of USA. The mark represented the brand of ownership over a unit of labor that, if it happened to be female, had the potential of reproducing more units of labor. The spark of rebellion in her had made her refuse to mother babies forced on her by rape and even in that enslaved state, she had wanted to protect Sethe from the same fate. Nan, on the other hand, had functioned in the role of Sethe's mother and confidante, trying to shield her from further pain.

Similarly, Ella, who had been "beaten every way but down" (318), whose broken bottom teeth and scarred waist bore testimony to a traumatic past, was not one to allow the past to take an upper hand, had fought tooth and nail to survive and had learnt to live the hard way in a society that had shown no mercy to them. As a free black woman, she then became instrumental in saving the lives of many fugitive slaves with Stamp Paid—a woman of the community in her social role as saviour—action-oriented and tough though, as a benefactress, she did not have Baby Suggs' "great heart" or "great love" to embrace unconditionally.

Again, even amid their endless toil and existence as laborers, there emerged slave women like Sixo's thirty-mile-woman who created a mark by defining new possibilities of relationships between black men and women (their relations had always been strained due to socio-historical reasons. As a "friend of his mind" (335), she and Sixo had shared an unusual comradeship, a woman who could be both ship and harbour to a man.

Morrison also represents the women of the black community collectively, women who had once loved and adored Baby Suggs and who come forward on Ella's request to drive away the spirit of Beloved. These are all working women as indeed almost all black women represented in fiction by Morrison, Walker, Naylor and most black women writers are—black women whose lives are invariably bound up with their work roles. Many of these women have been slaves and now as free blacks belonging to the semi-rural black township near Cincinnati they can be grouped under Category II of the hypotheses. They handle the multiple roles of bread winners, mothers, wives and also community women participating actively in community rites and rituals. Religious, self-righteous and hard-working, they have wrestled with life's hardships and performed simultaneously in multiple roles. On regular work days they did the laundry at the orphanage or asylum and worked at the slaughter house (the jobs available for them in town were menial, unskilled and usually brutal, offensive, dirty or demoralising—yet, the pay in cash meant a lot to them). They cleaned fish, shucked corn, rinsed offal, cradled white babies, swept stores, scraped hog skin, pressed lard, case-packed sausages or hid in taverns while cooking food so that white people's appetites were not put off to see their "black hands" handle the food because they associated blackness with dirtiness (317). Ironically, black women like them were expected to render the most intimate and personal services for them without seeming to notice what they were doing. So they wore detached expressions on their faces, masking their revulsion, appearing unconcerned because they had no choice but to earn their livelihood. The tribulations of daily life was sufficient to sap their strength in a world of racist prejudices. The sexist domination is not pronounced in this community of blacks, suspended as they are in a time setting when black men and women stuck together in a racist solidarity that made nothing of sexual bias. Morrison however subtly interjects comments and presents situations to foreground the black woman's dilemma as more acute than that of the black man's as they had to combat sexual commodification along with being exploited as laborers. These are black women who have, like the rural Georgia women in Morrison's *The Bluest Eye*, and black women in real life, have lived, loved and "lasted" amidst overwhelming odds.

In *Beloved*, the protagonist Sethe's role is the anthithesis of that of her mother-in-law Baby Suggs. While the latter had emerged from slavery with a "great heart" that readily embraced her community and made her reach out to them with a message of love, peace and surrender of hatred, Sethe murdered her own daughter in a violent rejection of the same fate of bondage for her children—a "staggering crime" (250) in the eyes of the community that shunned her—leaving her to face intense loneliness, isolation and alienation for eighteen years. Sethe has deliberately repressed the memory of her unbearable past and as the novel unfolds, her memory yields up from its layers/folds, incidents of shocking cruelty, exploitation and torture as she re-memories her past trauma. Sethe's superhuman struggle to survive for the sake of her children, to keep the child in her womb alive, her desperate bid for freedom that led the act of murdering her daughter and her effort to put the past behind her can be appreciated and justified in the light of the soul-shaking experiences she had been through. Her resignation has been interpreted as arrogance and the stigma of being in jail has hounded her name and poisoned her daughter Denver's childhood and adolescence. Traditionally, black women, torn from their roots, anchorless as their men, laboring under burdens hoisted on them by an alien people in an alien land, carrying the savage imprint that slavery has left on them and living on the edge of a precipice, have learnt to form strong bonds of trust and affection—community ties that have sustained and protected them. Yet, from amidst them have emerged women like Sethe,

Sula (*Sula*) or Pilate (*Song of Solomon*) who have been shunned by their communities, for violating its systems of values and beliefs. These are black women who have thought differently, acted according to their independent wishes, never bothered to justify their actions—good or bad, broken away from typified roles and finally transcended their situations to gain an insight into life that was rare and precious. Sethe has been therefore hated for her arrogance, Sula branded as a ' pariah' and Pilate feared for her supernatural powers. Sethe had attempted to protect her children from a fate worse than death as her "mother love" (162) propelled her into committing the "staggering" crime that condemned her for life in the eyes of the black community that could forgive murder of all kinds but not that of one's own child. However, unlike Sula who is unrepentant in death and Pilate who is triumphant in death, Sethe, at the close of the novel, comes back full circle to be poised on the threshold of a new beginning with Paul D—her husband Halle's friend. Though Morrison has championed the toughness, aggression and innate strength of black women in representing Sethe as the slave girl with "iron eyes and a backbone to match" (10), the vulnerability, femininity and the need for love that reaches out from these women is also underlined through Sethe's trusting acceptance of Paul D's affections.

Bought as a young teenager by Mr. Garner as a replacement of Baby Suggs, she had been pretty and strong (combining paradoxically femininity and strength in herself)—her steely reserve making the six black men at Sweet Home keep a respectable distance from her. When she chose Halle as her life partner, there was no ceremony (religious or otherwise) to mark her changed status as his "wife" as in her youthful naivette, she had not realised that for slaves, who were non-persons socially, no social or religious sanction was thought necessary to "marry" them—their owner's permission was sanction enough. Their animal-like status was re-inforced by the fact that their choice of mate was indicated by their co-habiting and the pregnancy of the female slave. Sethe was fortunate to have her choice approved by the stamp of her mistress' authority and staying together was privilege enough. She was also fortunate to be able to have a husband for six years and that all her children were fathered by him, though they could never meet at daytime because Halle was out working in the fields all day and Sethe was working at the homestead late into the evening. Sethe was admired then for her shy reserve, obedience, devotion to Halle and capacity for hard work. Nothing seemed to tire her, not the children she bore each year, nor the labor at the homestead—she seemed to handle all her roles with equal determination and efficiency.

In trying to impart some personal and lively touches to break the tedium of routine chores, she did at the kitchen by bringing in wild flowers, decorating the door knob or the handle of the flat iron, she had always been different, an individual wanting to assert her distinctive self even as a slave—a woman whose innate sense of self-worth distinguished her from others. Mr. Garner's death brought to the fore the fact that years of devotion and loyal service from her black slaves was not enough to erase Mrs. Garner's prejudiced fear lurking in every white person's heart for Negroes. The sense of betrayal that filled Sethe and the six black men was immense as they understood that their status as paid laborers had been illusory. Subjected to physical abuse in a heavily pregnant state, Sethe's soul was lacerated more by the violation of her dignity and the ultimate insult inflicted upon her motherhood by the "stealing" (84) of her milk by the white boys than the physical hurt of the vicious whipping she had received that cleaved her back. Powerless to prevent Sethe's humiliation at the hands of the white boys, Halle lost his sanity but Sethe had to endure in grim silence, having already sent her children on their way to Cincinnati on a wagon with other slave women and determined as she was to escape to freedom. For Sethe, there was no sweet relief of insanity because she was a mother who could not afford to forget the responsibility of her children.

Repeated references to Sethe's pride in the text underscore her independence—a pride that broke her but did not allow her to bend. She never justified her actions to the Negro community befriended by Baby Suggs—she held herself aloof in stony silence to endure lifelong alienation. So it was natural that Sethe as a mother would not allow the white people to sully her children, as she knew from personal experience that any white person could take away the 'self' from a black woman/person and work, kill, maim and more frighteningly, "dirty" (308) her irrevocably. She was ready to work at the slaughter house yard, but as a mother could not allow that degradation of her daughter. Convinced of her right to take back the life she had given to save it from a worser fate, Sethe has been portrayed as the slave mother whose protective love could turn violent when threatened.

Interspersed throughout the narrative are references to Sethe's extraordinary strength of will, physical hardiness (she was as good as any man in chopping wood, hoisting heavy burdens), inflexible determination, the capacity to bear unflinchingly extreme physical pain and mental pressure—the 'iron' that was in her. If it gives the impression of towering strength and invincibility, the impression is reverted when Sethe begins to break down in mind and body eighteen years after committing the "staggering crime". Unlike Eva, the matriarch in *Sula* who had, godlike, dealt death to her son because she thought he was unfit to live, Sethe was caught up in a paradox of life that was as complex as the "mother love" that motivated her. Neither she nor Baby Suggs had been matriarchs, though theirs had also been an all-woman household. They had simply absorbed the truth of black women's existence that they could never afford to rely on anyone in the world except themselves because forces beyond their control would take away their men—as Halle was, by insanity, as Paul D who failed to understand Sethe, by Howard and Buglar—Sethe's teenage sons who had left them one by one never to come back again. So Sethe had left Sweet Home without a backward glance, her resolve undeterred by the horrifying sight of the headless, feetless torso hanging from the tree. The same indomitable will to survive had driven her to cover large distances on foot and the circumstances in which she had given birth to Denver in the middle of a jungle and arrived at Baby Suggs' doorstep with the newborn baby strapped to her chest would strike terror in the hardiest of hearts. Sethe's presence of mind and ability of endurance had been phenomenal once. Yet, beneath all the toughness and contained aloofness there lay such vulnerability and trusting simplicity that it made her turn to Paul D with a deeply buried longing for understanding. Sethe's quiet strength had never been and was not castrating. As Paul D said, she was woman enough to "give him back his manhood" (335) even when he was powerless to comfort her.

After Sethe's return from jail, Baby Suggs took to bed, leaving upon her the responsibility of running the household and feeding her three children, Baby and herself. From Sethe's scattered reminiscences it becomes clear that as a social outcast in her community it had not been easy for her to find a job. She had worked at the stone mason's shop—work that was most certainly strenuous. However, she was saved from working at the slaughter house (a filthy, bloody, brutal work) by the interference of Mr. and Miss Bodwin who recommended her to Mr. Sawyer—the owner of a restaurant in town. He had been kind enough to hire an ex-convict and for Sethe, the job as a help to the main cook that brought her 3.40 dollars a week plus daily dinner was manna from heaven. She was quiet, punctual and efficient and for eighteen years she had no problelms either with her work or with her boss. Sethe shuddered when she recalled her mother's lips stretched in a permanent smile—a smile that had been etched there by the prolonged holding of a bit in her mouth. This grotesque smile—the symbol of the white man's dehumanization of slaves—had been superimposed on her own genuine smile that Sethe could not recall. The same zombie-like smile was on the face of the "Saturday girls" (250) who worked at the slaughter house—a work that drained them in body, mind and soul so that, come pay day, they drank themselves into oblivion or stumbled in exhaustion to the local store to buy the week's ration for their families or buy things that their children needed. Sethe had been spared this gruelling routine and she was grateful for her work at the restaurant.

Sethe, for whom no sacrifice was too great for her children, who had allowed sexual favours to the gravedigger to pay for her dead child's tombstone, could also, without a second thought, give up her job for them. As willing as she was to work herself to the bone to feed her children, she would just as soon forget practical considerations to be with them. So when her long dead daughter Beloved appeared to reclaim her love, she grew obsessed with her. The 'ghost' that haunted Sethe's house may well be her traumatic past and sense of guilt haunting her psyche—the guilt, self-blame and pain that she had repressed for years and never allowed to surface. Taking in the strange young girl who appeared at her doorstep unquestioningly was not unnatural as it was usual in those days to ecounter such black women seeking shelter or running for safety from the lust of roving groups of white men and the certainity of rape, torture and murder in a territory infested by whites. Gradually, like Denver, she was convinced that this girl was her dead daughter Beloved who had taken flesh to return to her. Morrison's richly layered narrative interweaves the supernatural with rational reality leaving the text open to different interpretations. Sethe immersed herself in her role as a mother who had long neglected a beloved child, atoning for her past actions by giving back the "mother love" that she had once withdrawn from her and neglecting the stable job that had given her her livelihood. Sethe's transition from an efficient, unproblematic employee to a moody, temperamental one was not taken kindly by her employer. After several instances of uncharacteristically late arrivals, leave without prior notice and being answered back, he dismissed her. Driven by a primitive, instinctive love that lay so deep-rooted within a her womb, Sethe did not pause to think of the consequences of losing her job. Her preoccupation with motherhood and its pleasures had come into conflict with her work and for an ex-slave woman, always denied her claim over her own children, practical considerations would have to take a backseat. For the psychologically traumatised woman, it was a way of absolving her guilt and reclaiming a lost child.

As a slave woman Sethe had felt unable to love her children to the fullest extent due to her awareness that they didnot belong to her. A slave woman was separated from her family and her children by the white master in order to better utilize her labor as well as exploit her motherhood. She was deliberately delinked from her family—physically and emotionally—so that she wasted no time or invested little emotion in her roles as wife or mother. In trying to wrest her own and her children's freedom, Sethe had tried to reclaim her right to love them totally. Ironically, the ultimate expression of her "too thick" (250) mother-love found violent expression in her slitting of her beloved child's throat in order to protect her from a fate she considered worse than death. Morrison plumbs the depths of the undefinable and infinite sea of instinctive primeval love that has bonded mother and children in an inexplicable and complex womb-tie. The helplessness and defiance of a slave-woman who has been denied this right is poignantly foregrounded here.

Finally, it was Denver who took matters into her hand when Sethe began to starve herself to feed Beloved as she had lost her job and there was no other source of income. So Denver approached the neighbors to ask for help, take up a job and reverse roles to become a mother to Sethe. Sethe emerged from the grip of past grief cleansed and free and was at last at peace with herself. Paul D, who had left Sethe, aghast at the revelation of her crime by Stamp Paid, had failed to understand the depth of her emotions as a mother. When he had moved in with Sethe he had, for a time taken over the role of the man of the house. He expected Sethe to do the little, womanly chores like sewing buttons to his shirt and cook his food while he handled the "man's job" of splitting firewood or mending furniture, forgetting that this was a woman who had survived suffering that could drive a man insane, take without squinting the lash of the whipping wind on her face, take final goodbyes in her stride after having lost so many loved ones and calmly accept betrayal. Paul D had given a conditioned response to Sethe's love, feeling betrayed by her closeness to Beloved and believing that being a man meant possessing a woman—being able to "choose" a wife or a horse, being able to "buy" a mother form her boss. Yet by withholding blame, she had given him back his "manhood".

In the end, Paul D reclaimed Sethe in his understanding and acceptance of her actions and the possibility of a future with him brightens her horizon. Sethe's final yielding leaves the reader with the image of a vulnerable, trusting woman, who still has enough faith left in her to trust a man, to take again the risk of betrayal, the courage to reach out for a meaningful relationship and the promise of a new life. In the broken remnants of iron-eyed Sethe's former self, one finds the emergence of a young girl who has truly "(laid down) her sword and shield" (105) to become Paul D's "friend of his mind". She has indeed "lasted" (247) while others have failed.

True Belle, a twenty-seven year old black slave woman in *Jazz*, was compelled to leave her husband and family to accompany her master's daughter who was banished from her home for her liaison with a Negro man and consequent pregnancy. Working as her personal maid for years, True Belle, an "unputdownable" woman, took her job as an opportunity to see Baltimore—the great city of her dreams. Hard as it must have been for her to leave her daughters behind, she was accustomed to take things in her stride as she was an irrepressible optimist. So this young woman, choiceless as she was, left her family behind, suppressed the pain of separation and served Vera Louise for twenty-two years, giving her "whole well life" (*J*, 164) in her service to experience, as she said, a more sophisticated way of living. Her "cushiony" (122) job had demanded a life time of service, yet she had no regrets when, in 1888 she returned as a free woman with her wages (ten dollars for eight years) after she had convinced her mistress that she was dying of an incurable disease. After the civil war was over and the Emancipation Proclamation liberated all Negro slaves, Vera Louis had begun to pay wages for True Belle's services, though she held the money in trust just in case her servant ran away. Ironically, years of unconditional and faithful service on True Belle's part had not generated enough trust in her employer for her servant not to resort to such a measure to ensure her services. Like Sethe in *Beloved* who had tended to a sick Mrs. Garner with as much solicitious care as she would have accorded her own mother but was bitterly disillusioned to realise that the status of a slave never changed, True Belle got from her employer the same callous disregard for her feelings and a lack of faith that hurt. Unlike Sethe however, True Belle accepted it as a part of her role as laborer. For white people, Negroes were like animals who could be occasionally indulged but always kept under a tight leash of control. In the end however the money she had earned enabled her to return to Rome (Vesper County) in answer to her daughter Rose Dear's desperate pleas to take up the reins of her shattered household. Like the ingenuous and cunning slave women of folktales, True Belle had managed to wrest her freedom and her wages from her mistress. The inexhaustible energy of this old slave woman filled her granddaughters with love and admiration for her. She was always there for them, "chuckling, competent, stitching by firelight, gardening and harvesting by day" (126) tending to her granddaughters' bruises, inspiring them to work hard, keeping them working at their tasks by telling them spell binding and fascinating tales of Baltimore. Like Louvinie of Walker's *Meridian*, True Belle had a flair for story-telling and as she worked to hold together her daughter's family, not only feeding them but also generating confidence, she also imparted in them her own toughness, appreciation of beauty, joy of living and tremendous will for survival. Her creativity was expressed through her daily work, her "classy" ironing, the wonderful quilts she made, the dresses she sewed and the tales she spun with her rich imagination. She was a woman, unfazed even by her daughter's suicide, saying, "Thank God for life...and thank life for death" (125)—suggesting even in calm acceptance the true story of a black woman's life where death was a release from a hell-like existence. When Violet and her sisters grew up, True Belle encouraged them to leave for Palestine, giving them an opportunity to break out from the poverty and confinement of country life as also the exposure and the taste of adventure that only financial independence could give them. True Belle had seen enough in life to understand Violet's decision when she did not return and not resent it. This particular characteristic of black women—their courage to let go and the unconditional love that expected nothing in return let them have the last laugh in life. Like True Belle, a black slave woman bringing up her employer's mulatto son, seeing him showered with every luxury that money could buy by his white mother, laughing aloud and delightedly at the poetic justice of the situation, they could live in their multiple roles, handling all the toil with panache—not embittered but wise.

Toni Morrision's interest in the historical dimension of the female Negro experience can be traced clearly in her representation of the roles of black women in her novels. Besides her representation of individual characters, there are lengthy descriptions in her narratives of the situation of black women in America and how, in every age, they have learned to counter racial discrimination, sexist domination and classiest in exploitation. She has written in each novel about communities of black women from varied backgrounds—rural, semi-rural, small Southern town, Northern ghettoes and even an exotic Carribean island which has a black community of its own speaking a French dialect. The collective experience of these women may vary according to the geographical location/setting but essentially, in every age and everywhere, Negro women bear testimony to lives full of trauma and toil. Their "broken eyes", "sore feet", arched backs, bent arms, toughened soles of feet and palms are only physical evidences of their lives as laborers. The psychological agony and the laceration of their souls at being denied human dignity is a weight they have carried in their minds. It is perhaps this consciousness of the commodification of black women's labor as the most exploitable commodity (sexuality and fertility being incidental and secondary, an interest on the principal amount, over and above) that has made Morrison present the experience of black women as the sociological backdrop against which her novels unfold and her characters develop. As, historically, the black woman's role has been primarily that of a laborer, they were always workers first and women last where their sexuality and fertility could be taken for granted because they were available as possessions. The African-American women she represents are conscious of the disadvantage they suffer. Seventeen black women spanning the six novels of Morrison selected here come under Category II of the hypothesis. Mrs. Macteer and Pauline Breedlove from *The Bluest Eye,* Eva Peace and Nel Wright in *Sula*, Circe and Mrs. Baines in *Song of Solomon*, Ondine and Thérèse, Rosa, Francine and Cheyenne in *Tar Baby*, Denver and Janey in *Beloved*, Violet, Rose Dear and Malvonne in *Jazz* and a host of women—the Georgia women in *The Bluest Eye*, the community of black women in *Sula*, the women of Alabama and the domestics and maids in *Song of Solomon*, the poor women of the island and the poor women of black ghettoes in *Tar Baby*, the Saturday girls and other black women of Cincinnati in *Beloved* and the cotton pickers, share croppers, city women of the ghettoes of Harlem, New York in *Jazz*, fall in this category. These are poor black women who have had to operate in multiple roles who, as laborers, are in the non-skilled and manual category and as housewives are houseworkers or drudges. In rural communities, these women come together to form strong ties of affection and mutual understanding wherein they share their sorrow and joy with each other. In small towns or semi-rural areas, they come together as church groups or otherwise, communicating with each other and working in an unspoken understanding of each others' problems. In urban ghettoes, they are more alienated and alone—yet, even amidst the mundance routine of work and more work they reach out to break through individual and private shells of defence to forge ties with other black women.

In *The Bluest Eye*, Morrison uses the geographical backdrop of a small steel mill town of Lorrain, Ohio. Black families from the rural South migrated to this small town in search of job opportunities and employment, though low on wage scales, were available for the men. While men worked at the factories, women found jobs as maids, cleaning women, cooks and washerwomen with the prosperous white families. Poverty was accepted as a permanent threat and those black women who did not have to work as domestics or engage in manual labor outside their homes were considered more fortunate than the others, though they too were engaged in a compulsive, ceaseless and almost frenzied effort of saving money through their labor at home because the "real terror of life" (*TBE*, 11)—that of being put "outdoors" (11) loomed large in the horizon. The threat of being dispossessed that haunted them drove them to their roles as labor and in their ceaseless struggles to make ends meet, the existence of these African-American women were intertwined inseparably with their work. The narrator of the novel is a young, black girl named Claudia whose parents are grimly engaged in a struggle for survival, a situation that she summarises thus:

> Being a minority in both caste and class, we moved about anyway on the hem of life, struggling to consolidate our weaknesses and hang on, or to creep singly up into the major folds of the garment. (*TBE*, 11)

So black women, not able to enhance their income, tried with their labor to control expenditure, saved money, supplemented the family income by their own contribution towards the family coffer and dreamt of owning their own house one day. These women seemed to be incomplete without a job at hand and in a world which tried its best to dislodge them from their precarious hold on stability and security, they tried to find their identity through the equation of work.

Mrs. Macteer was the narrator Claudia's mother. Though she had her own house and a husband who worked, which placed her in a relatively securer position than many other black women, Claudia's description of the house as both old and cold where icy blasts of wind through the cracked windowpanes made them shiver in winter and a single kerosene lamp lit one room while the others were in darkness indicate that they had not yet been able to "creep...up" into the "major folds of the garment". Their peripheral existence as a minority group could not be helped and therefore Mrs. Macteer, like other poor housewives tried her level best to prevent being put "outdoors". So Mrs. Macteer was never found whiling time away in idle chatter. She did not ever stop working, was always engaged in an endless stream of household chores—a grim and determined woman who was a model of industry and thriftiness. Besides the sequence of routine housework like cleaning, washing, making meals and rearing her children, there was also canning, pickling, baking, preserving and stocking. The tedium of constant work bore down upon her—work that required day long involvement with hardly any leisure to call her own—roles that she must perform as a mother and housewife with growing children and growing needs, a limited income source, sickness, and the haunting fear of being dispossessed from their shelter and livelihood. Her role as laborer was necessary for the survival of her family as it was necessary to supplement her husband's income. She therefore took in a tenant, charging him five dollars every two weeks and took extra responsibility and extra burden of labor upon herself in catering to his needs in addition to those of her own family. Spending the major chunk of her time and life in the kitchen, she had very little leisure to call her own. No wonder therefore that she was irritable and snappy most of the time, resenting even the sickness of her children that added to her already harrowing burden of work. So often she was brisk and dominating with them, issuing orders and giving instructions rather than wasting time to explain things gently to them. This hard working, tough and practical woman found time amid her work for love, for gossip, for charities (she took in Pecola, a poor black girl of the community) and for singing in a voice that evoked her daughters' dreams.

As a mother, Mrs. Macteer was rarely tender and never demonstrative, not even when her daughters fell ill. Her rough and down-to-earth efficiency did not allow room for sentimentality. She maintained strict discipline in the house and took a stick to her children as punishment for misdemeanours. Yet when Pecola attained puberty, she gave her the maternal care and attention that Pecola's own mother had failed to give her. Claudia remembered, amid a haze of fever that her mother's hand, while replacing the quilt on her, had rested awhile on her forehead—a hand that belonged to a mother who wanted her to live, who cared. This black woman, so occupied in the business of living as she was, was still capable of weaving dreams transluscent and pure, as they were churned out of pain and hard labor, sweat and blood.

Pauline Breedlove belonged to a family of eleven children in Alabama where, as a handicapped child she was restricted within the confines of her house. At Kentucky where her parents had migrated due to the availability of jobs, she was left to manage the household. Her enjoyment of the house work she did and the neatness and order that gave her pleasure became the sole focus of her life later on. Her marriage to Cholly Breedlove brought her to Lorraine where the isolation and alienation she experienced on account of being left alone drove her to work. Also, a wish to measure up to the standards of the town women by buying stylish clothes that Cholly could not afford motivated her. However, her self-sufficiency irritated Cholly and beginning with initial bouts of quarrel, their relationship deteriorated steadily.

Pauline's reminiscences about the steady, live-in job she had taken up with a white family of modest means reveal the predicament of black women working as maids in such houses as domestics and the kind of personal and often degrading work they had to do for their mistresses. Like Mrs. Hill in *Meridian*, Pauline's contempt of her mistress was cutting when she recounted her slovenly ways and dirty habits. However, she endured because of the money till Cholly forced her to leave precipitately in a show of husbandly possession. The white mistress was ready to re-employ her on the condition that she left her husband but a traditional notion of the wife's 'place' and racial solidarity held Pauline back: "...it didn't seem none too bright for a black woman to leave a black man for a white woman" (93). In the end, she was deprived from her rightful claim on her accumulated wages of eleven dollars. For Pauline, her employer's insistence that she leave Cholly was unreasonable as was her insistence that she owed the lady money for a broken bed and an uniform she had allowed her maid to use. The concrete reality stood thus for Pauline: that the gas supply had been cut off because the bills had not been paid and she could not cook, that she needed the money desperately, even if it was extended on loan and that expecting Cholly to do his husbandly "duty" as the man of the house by paying the bills was as ridiculous as the idea of asking him for alimony to maintain herself. As a black woman her reality was one that a middle-class white woman could not even begin to comprehend in her protected existence and conditioned as she was to expect men and women to behave according to traditional role expectations. For black families, there was no division of the "breadwinner male" and the "homemaking female" roles as black women functioned in both roles simultaneously—paying the gas bills and also cooking the food.

After giving birth to two children, Pauline took up in right earnest the role of a strictly religious, church-going, long-suffering, self-righteous wife and mother who convinced herself that it was her monumental self-sacrifice that kept the family from disintegrating. So she took up a job (she considered herself fortunate in getting it) as the Fisher family's cook-cum-housekeeper-cum-washerwoman-cum-maid. For Pauline Breedlove, "all the meaningfulness of her life was in her work"[9] and in her role as a breadwinning mother, she "bore her children like a cross" (98). Morrison here probes the complex psychological depths of a black woman faced with the unenviable task of bringing up single-handedly her two children and assuming the role of both a father and a mother. Pauline does not have so much of the inner reserve of strength which Pilate in *Song of Solomon* has. Nor is she rooted as firmly in her roots, folk tradition and culture as Pilate is. Witnessing the gradual crumbling of her home, disruption of all forms of order in her household and sensing that her relationship with her husband and family were falling to pieces, she turns to the only solace she can think of, the comfort of work. She thinks that finding a permanent job in an affluent white family as the only (ultimate) blessing in her life—a role she can assume with confidence and firmness—a role devoid of emotional complications, soothing because mechanical and predictable. The disorder in her life which she is incapable of organising can be sorted out here, in the precincts of her white master's kitchen. The coherence which her life lacks can be found in the stability that her job offers her.

Morrison has represented Pauline Breedlove in her role as an embittered wife and mother who took pride in her own upright character, her capacity for hard labor and the fact that she was the breadwinner of the family. All the spontaneity and love that was lacking in her life was made up many times over by her role as surrogate mother to the doll-like white baby girl and as an "ideal servant" (99) to the Fisher family. The creativity she was capable of as a good cook and housekeeper could find expression only amid the abundance of the white master's kitchen. Here she could forget the scorching humiliation at the indifference of white doctors towards her as a black woman who according to them, could give birth painlessly "like horses" (97) while white women needed solicitous care and tender deference during their labor pain. Here, hearing praise for her work, she felt the justification of her labor, recognition of her efforts and a peace that she could never find at home. So, Pauline Breedlove deadened her love for color, "june bugs" (101) and her children, to excel in her role as labor, channelising all her energy in her work that became a medium of self-expression for her as she conceived it. It was beyond her to feel insulted at the fact that even the baby girl she cared for called her by name—"Polly" (99) (Claudia and Frieda had felt angered and insulted on her behalf on hearing her being addressed so by the little girl). Ironically, her own children and even Cholly addressed her as Mrs. Breedlove, the formality of the address removing every vestige of closeness or affection in their relationships. The snappy, ill-tempered, sharp-tongued Pauline underwent a transformation when she was in the Fisher family's kitchen. Here a different personality emerged—confident, efficient, smug and even affectionate—a 'Polly' who would readily abuse her own child to 'protect' her 'darling'—the dainty and frail white baby or 'her' clean kitchen or 'her' pie. So Pauline Breedlove had created a dream world of her workplace where she spent as much time as possible, experiencing borrowed/second-hand power and luxury in handling her employers' money, the inexhaustible stocks of food, her employers' baby, her rich clothes—none of which belonged to her.

Morrison's *Sula* is dominated by the towering mother-figure Eva Peace. She is Sula's grandmother and the proud, domineering matriarch of that all-woman household consisting of Eva, Hannah and Sula herself. She has been portrayed as the sovereign, a queen in command who holds court as people mill around her, who rules the house from her wheelchair upstairs and whose command is law in that house and area that no one dares defy. This imposing character then may seem to be the typified image of the black matriarch capable of great love and great hatred, mighty and undisputed in her rule over her domain. However, the multidimensional aspect of Eva's character, which offers scope for further analysis, resists simple and straightforward interpretations that project her as the head of the household, in-charge of all affairs, the economic provider and controller of purse strings or the suffering, self-sacrificing black woman. When Eva had first arrived at Medallion city, Ohio as a young bride with her husband Boy Boy (who was a carpenter) to live in the one-room cabin built by him, she had been in love. Her husband had persuaded her to leave her family in Virginia to come with him to Medallion. He was given to womanizing, drinking and abusing her and after five years of marriage fraught with quarrels, he left Eva for good. The stark reality of African-American women's existence is brought out forcefully in the helpless situation in which Eva found herself where the absence of a husband meant death for the family while his presence had given her nothing but trouble. The African-American man had the alternative of moving off to greener pastures, which they did whenever they were fed up with their responsibilities and did without compunction, leaving behind their wives to fend for themselves and the children who were, as always, their sole responsibility. In Morrison, as also in Walker and Naylor, one can find the familiar motif of absconding or errant fathers and husbands who have the choice to "fly away" leaving their commitments behind while the African-American women carry on with their business of survival, alone and independent. Like Eva they nurture a hatred for their betraying menfolk, like her their independence is forced upon them by their circumstances, like her, hatred is often the mainstay of their independence and like her they long for the stability of marriage and the love of their men, which is expressed through their insatiable "man-love" (*Sula*, 41) or man-hunger (a steady stream of men friends are entertained by both Eva and her daughter Hannah). Perhaps because of this and their suppressed yearning for a man's steady presence and stable family structure, their love is as fierce as their hatred and as destructive. They have, in their fight for survival, learned instinctively to defend themselves and their children with ferocity.

On examining Eva's role as labor in the novel, she can be placed in Category II of the hypothesis as she was, before and after Boy Boy's desertion, first a poor black woman and abused housewife and then a struggling single mother trying to provide for and keep alive three children and herself amid the avalanche of surmounting problems that were caving in to crush out her existence. Eva's transition from a poor, black woman to a fairly moneyed one took place after she came back from eighteen months of unexplained absence with money enough to set herself up comfortably with her children. She exuded a confidence and strength that created an impression of towering personality so that even as she sat in her wheelchair as a handicapped woman with one leg, people looking down at her had the illusion that they were actually looking up at her. One could not or was not allowed to glimpse the underlying vulnerability, regrets, the indescribable pain caused by well-meaning but soul-wrenching decisions she had to take or the toll they had taken on her. The complexity and intensity of emotions that Eva displayed closely associates her with the mammy of the oral folktales (see "Introduction") who was cunning, conniving and unscrupulous—in stark contrast with the image of the kind, religious and asexual mammy promoted by the media and the white society (for its own convenience), Eva is not only practical and scheming she is also "arrogant, domineering and mean-spirited."[10]

The ironical humour with which Eva's supposed sale of a leg is described underplays the shocking and horrifying reality—that a 'nigger' girl, driven to the end of her tether, with no money and three children in hand, abandoned by a husband, had perhaps no other alternative but to cut-off cold-bloodedly a part of her body in order to claim insurance payment to support herself and her children. No plausible explanation is offered for Eva's eighteen-month-long absence at the end of which she appears with ten thousand dollars, minus a leg. The very mystery which shrouds that period activates conjectures about the means by which Eva earned the money. The enormity of the pain she brought upon herself is lost in the glitter of the money she brings back, which makes her powerful enough to rule her roost with an iron-hand for the next fifty years. The role that Eva Peace assumes is that of a stern father, a masculine briskness is evident in her running of the affairs of the house. She becomes, in the words of Bryce Bjork, "the embodiment of a black feminist self-determinism that defied the odds against abandoned black women in 1921."[11]

When Eva's husband Boy Boy abandoned her, she was young and dependant. Her situation is described with graphic realism by Morrison when she is said to have $1.65 in hand, five eggs, three beets and no idea as to how to support her three children (32). The only way to earn money was by taking up domestic work which required her to leave her children and go to the white village in the valley where work was sometimes (not always) available. The white Americans living in the vicinity were not rich and they did not require maids. Whatever job there was, the work was in the nature of "hard-labor help" (33) which required her to work from early in the morning until after dusk. Her neighbours had been helping her all through summer and Eva knew that come winter, their generosity would be strained as they themselves were not very well-off either. Other than begging or scrounging, her only alternative was to return to her people in Virginia but her pride kept her from going home. Her other vague plan was to somehow tide over the bitterly cold winter and when her baby boy was old enough to be left behind, she would hire herself out to farms in the valley to weed, sow or feed stock, may be plant some crops herself till steadier jobs came along at harvest time when job opportunities were better by far even though due to the nature of the work (outdoor, fields), men were preferred to women. Meanwhile, "the children needed her; she needed money, and needed to get on with her life.... She was confused and desperately hungry" (32). The poignancy of her situation was that she had been left with no time to grieve over or indulge in any emotional outlet to her frustration as she was totally pre-occupied with the business of staying alive and keeping her children alive. The luxury of anger and hatred would come later, practical considerations had to have their priority.

Eva gave up her role as the nurturer, suppressed her maternal instincts to assume the role of breadwinner. She has had no time for play—none to cuddle her children or express affection for them. Shouldering the monumental responsibility of keeping her family afloat single-handedly had rendered her hard-headed and sharp tounged. Her children must have missed this natural quality (playfulness and warmth) of mother-love subconsciously, but they never dared to question it. When Eva said that there had been no time for her to play with her children in a passionate repudiation of Hanna's question, one can visualise the young mother's valiant struggles to maintain a precarious foothold on life and keep afloat her children. Her sharp words hide a plea for her child to understand and appreciate the situation that conditioned her relationships with her children and shaped her, toughening her inner core into a rock-hard resolve shorn of gentleness.

In 1917, black men were recruited to fight during the First World War. The violence and discrimination that Negro men faced in the army had the devastating effect of demoralising them and driving some of them to insanity as is Shadrack in *Sula*. Eva's son Plum is also a victim of war atrocities and when the laughing, energetic boy returns from war, he is a shadow of his former self. With the men away at war, the African-American women had to fend for themselves and their children. The story of the days of slavery was re-enacted as families were estranged from fathers, brothers and sons and African-American women were once again left alone to cater to their families' needs. When the war was over, thousands of African-American men returned wounded, shell-shocked, disoriented and insane. They had now become burdens whom their mothers, sisters, wives or daughters had to bear.

Sethe in *Beloved* had murdered her child rather than see her brought up in slavery. Eva kills her only son, the son whom she had fought with her life to protect, to free him from the chains of a vegetable-like existence. She offers no explanation or excuse except for saying through blinding tears that she had held her son close to her bosom before giving him up forever. The mother here assumes the frightening role of a destroyer who kills, out of compassion, her only son, to spare him the trauma of a degrading existence. According to Bjork, Eva, in doing so, "underscores her own lack of a loving, sensitive center. It is a center that long ago was diffused in desperation by her need to assume a position of pragmatic matriarch, possessive and domineering."[12] This view does not take into account the frustrations of a fiercely loving mother who assumes the god-like role out of an instinctive arrogance with which mothers try to arrange/shape the lives of their children by claiming to have given them life. So Eva, who had burnt her son to death, risked her life in trying to protect her daughter Hannah with her own body when her dress caught fire. The instinctive urge to protect her child makes Eva fling herself out of the window, regardless of her own incapacity or safety. She is still the fiercely protective mother trying to shield her child from danger with her own body. The contradictory roles of protector and destroyer combine in

Eva as she is both the father who provides and controls and the mother who protects.

Though Eva has been portrayed as the matriarch of the Peace family, her innumerable lovers (her men friends) constantly surrounding her as she held court like a queen, yet in her heart, she still valued a family structure where the man and the woman functioned according to traditional role expectations. So she chided newly wed brides (her tenants) when they neglected their cooking or housekeeping. When Sula came back after a ten-year absence, Eva confronted her with accusations about her ingratitude and selfishness telling her that she needed the stability of marriage and children to "settle" her. When Sula reminded her that both she and Hannah had lived their independent lives unburdened/unhampered by the complications of marriage or husband, Eva pointed out that they had had no choice. Like most black women in real life, Eva had not assumed the role of a matriarch by choice—life had given her no other option and though at heart she craved for the traditional household set-up, circumstances had compelled her to be independent in order to survive. Eva's association with the oral folk tale's mammy figure was further confirmed by the African-American ambience of her household (that fascinated Nel, Sula's friend) where people came and went as they wished, there was no father-figure looming as a threat to restrict freedom of action, movement or speech, no discipline or strict rules, a constant stream of relatives and friends and a grandmother who distributed "goobers" (84) to young children, read dreams and told stories. With Sula's return Eva's regime came to an end as the former put her grandmother in an old home—a decision that horrified the black community for whom it was unthinkable to put their elderly out of their houses. The strong bonds of loyalty generated by kin-ship African-American families did not allow such breach of faith. A lifetime of being admired, envied and looked-up-to culminated in a journey to the town's old home strapped to a stretcher and helpless to prevent being put out of her own home by her own grandchild. The futility of her role as labor is underscored by the irony of Sula's nonchalant placing of her own name in the official papers of the old home as the 'guardian' of Eva Mae Peace.

In Morrison's *Song of Solomon*, Mrs. Baines (Guitar's grandmother) and Circe are African-American women who can be grouped under Category II. Circe, a professional mid-wife had also worked as a maid for a rich white family. She was bitterly resentful at the denigration and abhorrence of her work by her white mistress. She was also courageous enough to give shelter to Pilate and Macon Junior at the risk of her job. A typically frail southern lady, Circe's mistress had preferred to die rather than take upon herself the jobs hitherto performed by the African-American servants—an insult that had released a violent destructive anger in Circe. She had systematically destroyed all the beautiful furnishings in the castle-like house by allowing them to fall to pieces due to lack of maintenance. It was in a way her statement of rebellion against a white patriarchy which had fashioned it's code of the 'genteel lady' who was white, vulnerable and feminine and the black woman servant of the house who was a workhorse capable of the toughest and coarsest works.

The black woman's labor had always been necessary to maintain the beauty and cleanliness of the houses of white people and cherished items—yet, their labor was devalued so that they lost their own self-worth and self-respect. Circe had spent a lifetime working for her employers, tending to their needs, delivering their children, nursing them. Her white mistress had been forced to give up all her staff for financial constraints and kept only her—not out of affection but because she was dependent on her for housekeeping and even her personal needs. Circe's justified anger at having lost the dignity of her labor made her abandon her role as laborer deliberately and in calculated vengeance—to prove to herself and the world the true value of her labor. She spent the rest of her life in her master's house letting it fall to ruins and tending only to the dogs, her last wish being that when she died, she be found by someone and given a burial before the dogs ate her body. An unusual woman, Circe was (as milkman found her) a combination of grace, apparent frailty and fierce self-pride.

Guitar Baines' grandmother struggled to hold her family together after the death of her son and his wife's elopement who left behind a string of unfed children. Black women, who have been fighting for mere survival are for ever faced with the danger of being rendered homeless. Guitar Baines' grandmother is grim eyed and resigned as she tries to think of ways and means to avoid being turned out on the streets with her grandchildren. For women like Mrs. Baines life has been a series of problems, a daily fight to overcome them and even in old age, they have not been spared from shouldering responsibilities that circumstances (a dead son, an absconding daughter-in-law) have placed on them.

Pilate's daughter Reba and her daughter Hagar both did not have legitimate fathers. The three lived together in a house that had no electricity, gas or any other modern amenities. Poor as they were, these black women lived in contentment, singing as they worked and working as and when they wished. Pilate was the head of the household but not the matriarch in the way Eva Peace had been. These were women whose labor was spontaneous, whimsical and need-based. Whatever profit they made from wine-selling was gone in a few days as they never could save money and had no material ambitions. Reba spent her money on her boyfriends and Hagar was pampered by both Pilate and Reba. As Pilate made a steady living making wine and cooking whiskey, the skill allowed her more freedom than any other work a poor, black woman had the choice of doing besides trading her sex. So, her bootlegging offered her an independence and leisure that was extended to both Reba and Hagar who also were not compelled to work either as domestics or prostitutes. Their alienation and isolation from society made their home different from that of Eva's household which had always been the centre of social activity and filled with the hubbub of visitors. Pilate, Reba and Hagar made an all-woman household where only love reigned. Yet, in spite of the spontaneity and richness of love that prevailed here, Hagar's wilfulness grew, leading finally to her disastrous love affair and subsequent death. If Morrison had deliberately pointed out the problems that resulted from a too indulgent and lenient rearing of the child Hagar, she does not seek to do so by projecting the patriarchal family set up (Milkman's family) as the ideal one. As Guitar puts it after witnessing Hagar's disintegrating 'self' at Milkman's betrayal, she needed the guidance and constant, vigilant watch that Pilate, in her own independence and Reba in her simplicity had not realised or thought to provide.

Reba, Pilate's daughter, like Hannah, Sula's mother in *Sula* was fascinated by every man she came into contact with. Like Helen, she was generous and giving, because of which her never-ending series of men friends exploited her. She did not work outside of her house because her mother's wine-making business fetched them what little money they needed for their upkeep. Both she and her daughter helped in the plucking and picking of berries from which they fermented and distilled wine. They had enough to do at home, though there were no routine household chores. They ate when they were hungry and not necessarily cooked food. Money was not a problem because they had no electricity, no pump to run water and the basic ingredients necessary for living (soap, medicine, etc.) was made at home by Pilate and they grew vegetables and collected fruits. Reba was as uncomplicated and foolish as a young child and Pilate protected her as fiercely as a tigress did her cubs. There was an unspoken bond between mother, daughter and granddaughter—the three generations of women because Pilate, unlike Eva did not seek to dominate as a matriarch. They existed as an independent family unit, least concerned with the ways of the world, as insulated and isolated from the townspeople as if they were living on an island. As they did not work as menials, they hardly came into contact with the white society. The strong ties of love that had held the three women together had not been snapped under any circumstances. With Hagar's death, all prospects of developing the familial chain was dashed.

In *Tar Baby*, Morrison represents Ondine and Thérèse as the cook and housekeeper and the washerwoman respectively of a large mansion owned by a rich white man called Valerian Street of Philadelphia, USA, on the tropical island (Carribean) named Isles Des Chevaliers. Though both these women can be grouped under Category II of the hypotheses, their situations are different in that Ondine reigns over the kitchen as the undisputed authority and Thérèse is the paid help employed temporarily as she is the resident of the island—Ondine has worked with the Street family since her marriage to Sidney (the main butler) thirty years ago while Thérèse has come to work for them only since they have shifted to the island. Also, Ondine is addressed as 'Ma'am' by the temporary helps, indicating the difference in their positions. Morrison's richly layered narrative makes the differences only the surface reality. Ondine's advantage at being the cook-cum-housekeeper whose dictates have to be obeyed by Thérèse or Alma Estée collectively called (the Marys) or Gideon (the yardman who did odd jobs) is only apparent. In reality, there was no difference between them as both were employed by the white man and both their jobs subject to his whim. The traditionally overplayed distinction between the "field niggers" and "house niggers" (see "Introduction") is seen here where the former identified the latter as in league with the master in their oppression and as the privileged and snobbish Negroes who tried to emulate white culture and capitalist values, and the latter saw in the former's way of life a threat to all that they had built through hard labor, a negation of everything they had accepted as important and a confirmation of such 'negative' racial traits as they consciously denied and deliberately distanced themselves from. Ondine's husband Sydney proudly professed to be a descendant of the industrious Philadelphia Negroes who had risen from poverty and subjugation by dint of hard work and uprightness. The 'house niggers' of the days of slavery had later emerged as the Negro middle class, denigratingly termed as 'bourgeoisie' by both white Americans and the Negro proletariat or the masses of poor black folk. Ondine and Sydney had spent a lifetime working for Valerian Street and had been well set-off by their 'considerate' employer but they cannot be considered as middle class or 'bourgeoisie' by economic standards because their work still falls in the manual labor category in spite of their superficially glorified status as the dignified butler and the reigning queen of the kitchen. Despite the euphemisms, they were servants subject to the employer's vagaries of temper. The myth of the distinguished status of house-servants in comparison with the outdoor workers is exploded forcefully in the loaded scene of the novel where Valerian Street and his wife Margaret (the rich white master and mistress of the mansion) sit down with their "loyal" servants to have a Christmas dinner together.

The under-currents of tension that had hitherto never surfaced because there had been no formal occasion of meeting as such, come to the fore that night. Ondine's repeated cries of "(y)es my kitchen. Yes my kitchen. I am the woman in this house. None other..." (*TB*, 210) reinforce the poignancy of an old servant's claim for recognition of her years of dedicated service that had entailed not only physical labor but also compromise, tactful silence and suppression of bitter resentment. The confrontation and subsequent revelations made by Ondine about Margeret's perverted pleasure in physically torturing her son when he was a child underscore the enormity of her compromise. It was less out of loyalty than her own need to keep her job that had kept her silent. Ironically, her 'privileged' position as a house servant had made her more dependent on her employer than Thérèse or the other Marys because her insecurity was greater than theirs. Ondine refers to her past when as a strong young girl she had worked at a butcher shop with her mother and grandmother, doing work that was bloody and brutal. She had slogged for long hours standing on her feet—a job that she had given up and a life that she had left behind after marrying Sydney at only seventeen years of age. After that it had been another lifetime of standing on her feet, working away at her white master's kitchen, cooking food for his family and guests, trying to meet his wife's constantly changing demands and catering to his own fastidious choice of meals and drink through the day for thirty years. It was not surprising therefore that Ondine constantly complained of aching and tired feet—the recurring motif in Walker's portrayal of poor, black women. Yet her present job had given her financial security, comfortable quarters to live in and at least more consideration than most white employers would accord their Negro servants with. For Ondine and Sydney, it would be doubly difficult to think of taking up positions in some other place with another employer because they could not contemplate facing the humiliating contempt with which Negro servants were treated by their employers. Apart from this, they were beholden to Valerian for having put their adored niece Jadine through college who had graduated from Sorbonne as an art historian and also established herself as a model. For

Ondine and her husband, it was unthinkable to revert back to the ignominious lifestyle of domestics and their allegedly 'burgeoisie' mentality is a natural if not admirable outcome of a single-minded effort to keep their jobs and deny links with the 'common' Negroes who were illiterate, poor and inferior in both material and social status. On no account can Ondine think of reverting to that life of degrading and harsh labor and after thirty years, as an old woman herself who has hardly found time to rest her feet, she is not even capable of it. Her predicament makes her compromise understandable. As Sydney says, they have known no other home besides their workplace, which has been a home to them for years. It has taken a lot of adjustments and compromises but at her age Ondine could not work like one of the Marys employed at the mansion "shucking crayfish on a porch" (101)—work that was more manual and strenuous than the one she was doing at Valerian Street's kitchen, which gave her at least a relative degree of freedom and basic comforts they had grown used to. The apartment in which Ondine and Sydney lived was above the downstairs kitchen and by no means as well-furnished as the other rooms of the mansion. Their separate quarters indicated their status as employed servants. Yet they had made a home there and had found comfort, solace and privacy—all of which depended upon their job and their staying employed at Valerian's home. Ondine has not been represented as the stereotypical 'mammy' figure who fawns over her employer and condones their faults in trying to hold her job. She has always nourished a deep resentment against Margaret and her surliness has been directed quite pointedly at her mistress. She has however not divulged the secret of Margaret's abuse of her son because, her practical foresight has intervened to stop her from speaking up. The diplomatic silence she has maintained at the cost of the young boy's psychological and physical torture makes her a party to it indirectly. One cannot however overlook her efforts in trying to provide her employer's son with as much protection, love and stability as she would her own son to make up for the compromise. Her relationship with her employer's son defies Son's (the fugitive convict and Jadine's lover) accusation that like the traditional white man's 'mammy', she had brought up obediently her master's son—an accusation black men have always made against black women. Ondine's submissiveness or obedience has not prompted her genuine affection for Michael nor has she denied her own child in order to bestow its share of affection upon Michael. Ondine's character resists conventional interpretation and simplified assumptions in that her motives have been selfish but her affection genuine. She is therefore neither the docile mammy whose primary role has been to nurture her employer's child nor is she so headstrong or assertive as to endanger her own security and stable job to reveal Margaret's sadism.

Sydney and Ondine had no house of their own, no place to go and no savings. They had been promised by their employer that their interests would be taken care of in his will. With Ondine venting her long-suppressed ire and slapping her mistress, the future has become very bleak and insecure for them. Ondine has had no children of her own but as she says later with controlled grief, she had taken both Michael and Jadine to her breast, loving them like her own children, to be paid back with disrespect and unconcern. Jadine was Sydney's brother's daughter and when her parents died, Ondine cared for her like her own mother. Both Sydney and Ondine had been ready to sacrifice their own comforts and work to put Jadine through college. Valerian had volunteered to finance Jadine's education in return of their services and over the years, having worked to secure their only niece's future, they had begun to expect a reciprocation of their concern. When, towards the close of the novel, Jadine announces her intention of going back to Paris and makes a token offer to them of accompanying her, Ondine, sensing her withdrawal voices for the first time her natural expectations from her niece. Reminding Jadine of her casual indifference to their fate or unconcern about what they would do if they were dismissed from their job or if they wanted to leave it, Ondine tells her:

> Jadine, a girl has got to be a daughter first. She have to learn that. And if she never learns how to be a daughter, she can't never learn to be a woman. I mean a real woman: a woman good enough for a child; good enough for a man—good enough even for the respect of other women. (283)

Jadine's retort that she did not want to be "that kind of woman" (284) cuts her to the quick and resigns her to accept the inevitable. For Ondine, a woman's role as a mother, daughter and wife contained the meaningfulness of her existence and proved her worth as a "real woman". Black women had functioned in those roles unflinchingly and courageously, thinking no sacrifice as too great than their commitment and responsibility to elders, to their husbands and their children. So, Ondine had "take(n) another one in (her) heart" (285) but her earlier claim that she had no regrets whatsoever at having overworked herself for Jadine's sake is sadly reverted by her disillusionment. This childless African-American woman had spent the best years of her life slaving in a white man's kitchen for her beloved niece. So her weary feet "talk back" (162) as they have endured so much stress. The payment asked by her in return of love was concern and care—a "parenting" (283) Jadine was not ready to or capable of giving her then. Ondine had no choice but to work along with her husband till death because they had only themselves and their own capacity for labor to rely upon—a labor that would at least guarantee them comfortable coffins if not ensure the emotional support or commitment from a niece to "bury (them)" (286). If Ondine regrets her failure in her role as a mother to 'guide' Jadine towards an appreciation of the roles of her maternal ancestors, she herself has been circumscribed in her role as a "real woman". As Walker insists in *Meridian*, black women have often had to perform in the roles of heroic martyrs for their children because they have had no other choice. Ondine had no such compulsion but her ingrained sense of responsibility towards a child in her care and her genuine affection for her niece whom she had grown to love as a daughter motivated her labor. For herself she had the only wish to die in peace and in familiar surroundings—in her workplace that had grown to be Sydney and her home, which was possible only if they continued to work—there was no other option left.

Thérèse and Alma Estée were the Marys whom Gideon brought with him everyday from the mainland to work at the island mansion of Valenian Street. These were native black women of Dominique—poor, but sullenly proud of their race and local culture. Their attitude towards American Negroes, especially Ondine, Sydney and Jadine was resentful and distrustful and try as she might, Ondine could not make them enter the precincts of her kitchen because they insisted upon doing all the work out on the porch. Their pointed aloofness was an indication of their rejection of any suggestion of proximity with the uppity American Negroes. Their identities had merged in the eyes of the Americans (both blacks and whites) because they had never been noticed as individuals. They were addressed as Mary irrespective of their age and appearance simply because they were recognized only in their capacity as laborers—the paid 'helps' whose anonymity suggested an erasure of distinctive personalities in the eyes of their employers. However, Thérèse was an old woman now whose "broken eyes" (150) were as much an evidence of a tough life as Ondine's tired feet. Appointed as a washerwoman at Le Arbe de La Croix, she was now incapable of handling the entire load of laundry and relieved at Ondine's decision to send most of the washing to the laundry at the mainland. Thérèse had been a wet nurse in her younger days and had made her living by nursing white babies until formula milk flooded the market and she was forced out of job. Initially (during slavery), black women had nursed white babies out of compulsion, which later became a source of livelihood for them. This commodification of motherhood, where the natural flow of a mother's life-giving/nourishing milk is bought in exchange of money has continued through the ages and has been instrumental in promoting the image of the black woman as the all- embracing and universal mother. Thérèse is proud of her nurturing role and her "magic breasts" (291) that are symbolic of that traditional and noble role. Both Ondine and Therésè therefore despite their apparent dissimilarities, believe in the cultural role of the "real" black woman as primarily maternal and life-giving. So Thérèse is affronted by the news that American women think nothing of undergoing abortions—a henious crime in her eyes. Thérèse as a poor, black woman who has had to labor all her life and was still working as a sixty-year old woman, was a counterpart of countless such women in America. In New York city and other metropolitan areas, such black women were no longer found on the streets—they had been driven underground with children, their identities had been submerged in the facelessness of poverty and degradation so that they were no longer visible as individuals. Confined to the poor ghettoes, some of them still labored to work their way up the socio-economic ladder like Ondine while others languished in the anonymity of a life of frustrations and toil.

The black women of north Florida (Son's home town Eloe) have been described as tough and capable. Son's own mother had roped horses when she was a girl—she later died of overwork. Francine was athletic, Cheyenne a great huntress and could drive a truck at the age of nine, Son's aunt Rosa and grandmother had built a cowshed by themselves and Rosa had built her additional room single-handedly. These were the African-American women whom Son admired and Jadine compared herself to subconsciously and who haunted her dreams with Ondine and her own mother and the magnificently beautiful black woman she had seen at the store at Paris. These women seemed to remind her of her own lack and inadequacy as they themselves had accomplished all that rendered her own achievements as meaningless. These were women who had existed for others, had lived in their roles as the bearers of an African heritage that had demanded a negation of their own needs and comforts. Morrison has raised here the question of choice raised by Walker in *Meridian*. The poor black women of Eloe, driven to death or insanity or rigidly moral women with definite ideas about the duties of a woman had had no choice in their lives but to be what they were. Their roles had been those of nurturers and builders, they had had to combine aggression and sacrifice and had accepted their labor as the sum total of their existence. Betrayal of commitment towards one's family or husband could perpetrate death. So when Cheyenne, Son's wife (who is very appealing sexually) is caught by him with her lover he kills her by running her down with his car which he drives into the shack where they lived. So these women lived and died within their close-knit community in Eloe, confined within its codes of conduct and systems of values that were as chauvinistic and patriarchal as the white American society, the only difference being that here, the women were expected to function in multiple roles while they themselves took pride in their strength and ability to handle tough labor.

In *Beloved*, Denver and Janey come under Category II of the hypotheses. Denver was Sethe's youngest child—the only one who remained with her till the last. Her traumatised childhood had left her withdrawn and reluctant to speak and she came to be known as slow-witted and strange. A natural talent for quick learning had made her a topper in her class during the one year she had attended school, after which she was psychologically devastated by her classmate's reference to Sethe's crime. Building a case against Sethe in her mind, she built a defensive cocoon around herself to exist in her isolated dream world of fantasy. With the appearance of Beloved, she came into her own. Sethe's growing obsession with Beloved and vice-versa excluded Denver from their attentions—a fate that had seemed to haunt her from the very beginning. This time, however, Denver had attained enough maturity to take an independent decision to save all three of them from starving to death.

Sethe had been dismissed from her job and the precious savings accumulated over the years were spent recklessly in buying expensive dresses and exotic food for Beloved. Denver served both Sethe and Beloved, washed, cooked, cajoled Sethe to eat a little and provided sweet things for Beloved. She was now convinced that it was Sethe who needed protection from Beloved. Finally, the sight of her weak and starving mother drove her to step out of the isolated world at 124 and approach the community of neighbouring Negroes for help. It was a bold step on Denver's part to take up the challenge of meeting new faces and braving stares to knock on Lady Jones' door for help and work. The colored people of Cincinnati were not so well- off that they could hire help and, bred under the influence of Sethe's inherent self-respect, she recoiled from the thought of accepting charity. However, her positive gesture of timid plea for help was accepted gladly by the Negroes of her neighbourhood who could now pity Sethe and appreciate Denver's sensibility and caring responsibility towards her mother whom providence had brought to her knees. Denver's predicament had been that of a strange childhood and an isolated youth. Her growth and maturity is registered by her positive step towards the forging of a new kinship with an estranged community.

Denver hired herself out for odd jobs in between household chores and caring for Beloved and Sethe and she managed to bring home some food and also squeeze a little time out every week to learn Bible verses from Lady Jones. Denver discovered a self in the middle of this crisis. She realised that unless she found work none of them would survive. The idea of preserving herself was as new to her as was the sense of responsibility and protectiveness towards her mother. To save her mother from total destruction Denver was forced to approach the Bodwins and was called for an interview at their place for a night job that would require her to stay there for the night—a position that was convenient for her because she could then look after Sethe in the day and work at night after putting her to bed. She secured the job and her confidence in herself grew. At Cincinnati, Denver came across the realities of black people's existence when she realised that for Negroes, only the back doors of the houses of white people were permissible for entry and that too only in the capacity of laborers. The equation of black and white relationships began to dawn on her and she learned the ways of the racist white society and its discrimantory policies. However, there was a quiet courage in Denver that refused to let her be daunted by her newly acquired understanding.

In the end, Denver emerges not only as the survivor but also the saviour of her own mother. Having taken upon herself the responsibility of caring for Sethe, she could now greet Paul D without bitterness and she has been represented in the role of a caring, loving, considerate daughter who had now assumed the protective mother's role, strengthening the mother-daughter bonding and ready to labor to provide her once invincible mother with the support that she now needed. With the acquiring of her job, her self-esteem grew as she also discovered what she was capable of as a person. The worthiness of her self was confirmed and re-affirmed through her work, in her role as laborer, daughter and breadwinner. At eighteen years, Denver had evolved into a mature, hardworking and sincere woman—so like Hal in her readiness to labor tirelessly for her loved ones and as protective of Sethe as he had been of Baby Suggs. When Paul D met her, she was on her way from her night shift of a maid's job at the Bodwins to the shirt factory in town where she had heard about an afternoon job that would help her to supplement her present income and enable her to save a little money after providing for her mother and herself. Her steady friendship with Nelson Lord was blossoming into love, thus opening up a vista of possibilities for her. Miss Bodwin had taken up her education in her hands and with the requisite qualification she hoped to find a better job in future. She had saved Mr. Bodwin's life when Sethe attacked him in madness after the black women of the community drove Beloved away thus winning the trust and friendship of her employers. With her job, her education and the possible fruition of a love relationship, she was now poised on the verge of a new life that beckoned her with the hope of a fresh start. When Paul D wonderingly told her, "you grown" (327)—his words summed up Denver's evolution from a poor, black girl to a confident young woman determined to fulfil her commitments towards her mother and fashion a life of her own with the limited options available to young black women in that day and age.

Janey had been the Bodwins' resident servant for years now, at their beck and call for twenty-four hours. Middle-aged and still working, financially she could not afford to leave working altogether and would have to retain her day job for livelihood. However, the night work was too much of a strain, especially because she was needed at home. She voices the sentiments of poor, black maids (whose work always extended beyond the appointed time because housework is unlimited and there are no fixed hours for arrival or departure) when she says: "I don't want to quit these people, but they can't have all my days and nights too" (313). Like the other black women of the community Janey was one to stand by one of its members in times of trouble. In a way, it was Janey who initiated the process of reforging ties with Baby Suggs' kin by seeking help on their behalf because Baby Suggs was a woman whom she greatly admired. The transition from slavery to freedom in that age meant for black women and men a shift from a status of unpaid labor to paid labor but the category of work available was invariably menial and poverty dogged them even if as free persons they were at least owners of their own bodies and their labor. Like most black women of her community Janey was independent, forthright, down to earth, capable, managing both housework and her job as maid while finding time to help people of the community—trying to create as much space as possible for her 'self' within the confines of social, historical and cultural situation.

In *Jazz*, Morrison represents Violet, Rose Dear and Malvonne as poor black women from rural and urban backgrounds. Violet, who had migrated to Harlem in New York from the South had had her experience of labor in both settings while Rose Dear (Violet's mother) was from the rural South and Malvonne from the urban North (Harlem, New York). Morrison has presented in her novels comparative pictures of African-American women at work both in the rural South and the urban North. While women like True Belle, Violet and her sisters grew tough from their exposure to a hard life and to the elements, there were also women like Rose Dear who were broken by the hardships, poverty, degradation and betrayal of their menfolk. Again, while there were urban black women like Malvonne who had survived the hard life of ghettoes, there were others who were driven to depravity, insanity or death.

Morrison's representation of Rose Dear defies stereotypical images of black women of iron will and immense capacity of endurance. Rose Dear's very name is symbolic of her vulnerability and fragility. Traditional expectations are thwarted as Morrison underscores the point that there is a limit to one's endurance—even a black woman's—and also that not every black woman is heroic or extraordinary. There are certain traumas in life that one can never get used to—so Rose Dear, who should have become accustomed to her husband's long absences and sudden reappearances over the years, buckled and keeled over after his latest disappearance. She lived in an abandoned shack in Southern county with five children in 1888, after being dispossessed of her house and land, surviving on neighbours' charity. Apart from a few borrowed pallets, there was nothing else and whatever food they ate was brought by neighbours. By the time True Belle came back to take up the reins of her daughter's shattered household,

Rose Dear had managed to live for four years even after her last disillusionment. A piece of paper bearing her absconding husband's signature entitled unknown men to take away their household articles and even the chair she was sitting on by tipping her over to the edge of the floor, where she sat bewildered and silent. The crushing poverty of the family had left them helpless with no father to provide for them and a mother who had sunk into an abyss of grief and was not capable of doing so. With the arrival of Rose Dear's mother, the family regained stability but just when every thing had settled back to normalcy, Rose Dear committed suicide. Violet could never fathom why her mother killed herself when their situation was changing for the better. Perhaps, she told herself, because Rose Dear at last knew that her children were in safe hands that she let go of her grip on life—a life that had been too much of a burden for her, filled with too many disillusionments and too much pain—that asked and expected too much from a black woman. Like her husband, life itself had "misjudged and misunderstood her particular backbone.... This here particular spine" (122). So Violet, haunted for years in her sleep by the nightmare of her mother's suicide made a resolution never to have children because "(w)hatever happened, no small dark foot would rest on another while a hungry mouth said, Mama?" (126).

Malvonne lived alone in an apartment in the same building where Joe and Violet lived. She worked in the evenings and late into the nights cleaning and polishing office buildings, 'sparkling' them up for the day when work would start. Malvonne was a poor black woman of the urban ghetto belonging to the great underclass of the city constituted by black men and women who had migrated to the cities of the Northern states of America in search of new horizons and occupied the lowest rung of the labor market. The limited sky that was available to them here was the metaphor of their lives. The reality of African-American female experience was that they were laborers first and then reproducers and sexual objects. The heads of the female-headed households (both rural and urban) were both breadwinners and nurturers. In fact, due to the pressing economic needs, they were breadwinners first and then nurturers. Small wonder therefore that their charges turned out to be bad as Malvonne's robber nephew and Alice Manfred's unruly neice Dorcas.

Violet, the central character of *Jazz* had been born in the South in a poor black family, her childhood fraught with insecurities as she watched the gradual disintegration of her psychologically broken mother and the absence of her perpetually absconding father. Amidst the pangs of hunger and fear was the bewildered confusion of an innocent child unable to comprehend the import of events taking place around them. So Violet and her sisters breathed a sigh of relief when their grandmother True Belle came back from Baltimore to take up the responsibility of caring for them. After her mother's suicide, Violet could not forget the sight of her crumpled body in the narrow well. It was True Belle who wove dreams of a different life for her grandchildren through her stories of Baltimore. At seventeen, Violet was sent to Palestine with her sisters to work as a cotton-picker at the plantation where there was a high demand for labor that season. As a migrant laborer in the South, Violet had experienced the same discrimination as she does as an unskilled worker in the city. In the plantations, for the female pickers, the wage rate had been ten cents while for male pickers it was a quarter. In her reminiscences of the past, Violet recalls the humiliation she had felt at being relegated for second-picking with the children as she was not nimble enough to keep pace with laborers of her age in picking cotton. Her chagrin turned to determination once she met Joe Trace, a young black boy who worked at the ginning factory. Unbearably hurt by Joe's betrayal of her (he took a young girl named Dorcas as his lover late in life), Violet relives past memories, thinking of the time when as a young girl she was so much in love with Joe that she had been desperate to do any and every kind of work just to be with him. It was her love that motivated her to become "the powerfully strong young woman who could handle mules, bale hay and chop wood as good as any man. It was there where the palms of her hands and the soles of her feet grew shields no gloves nor shoes could match" (131). To be near him, she could work herself gladly to death. This love-starved young black woman from a broken family had at last found an anchor for all the emotions and love she was capable of. So she did not return to Rome and instead moved in with a family of six in Tyrell as a domestic-cum-field hand working desperately to keep her job—a job that could keep her in Joe's vicinity.

As Schultz points out, when black women are able to work in harmony along side their loved ones or for them, the work, no matter how laborious, may be liberating.[13] From her separate musings, the work conditions of the rural South for migrant laborers in the late nineteenth century becomes amply clear. The overseers of the plantations who supervised cotton-picking lined up the laborers at dawn and many a time, Violet was whipped for being late in the line-up because she had spent her night in Joe's arms. She would chop twice the wood that was needed to avoid being summoned when she had a rendezvous scheduled with Joe Trace. For Violet who had found emotional security and a safe haven in Joe Trace, the "hollering" of the "crackers" or the "welts" from the "two-tone peckerwood" (119) were irritating or painful inconveniences—much like inclement weather or hostile natural forces that needed to be avoided or accepted because one had no control over them. Functioning for the white people solely and purely in the role of laborers had become habitual for African-American women like Violet and the tough and time-taking work they had to do was as inevitable as the job hazards they faced—odds that had to be overcome before they could get back to their families or lovers. As cotton-pickers, field hands and domestics they functioned with their bodies while their thoughts were concentrated on their loved ones.

After marrying Joe Trace, Violet and he worked as sharecroppers for two years. The worst plots of soil were usually leased out to Negroes in those days and Recks' place was no exception. The soil was soon exhausted and yielded no crops and Violet and Joe had to survive on the game Joe hunted. When the land was sold to another white landlord named Clayton Bede, their debt to the original landlord accrued interest and rose manifold (from 180 dollars to 800 dollars). To work off the debt, Joe hired himself out, working in sawmills and lumber factories while Violet had to tend single-handedly not only their own leased land but was also required to plow Clayton Bede's personal land. The tremendous physical labor that she was forced to do in order to stay afloat made her tough and capable. For five years they worked to pay the debt and Violet then was not only the co-breadwinner but also the housewife, functioning in both roles simultaneously. When Joe got a railroad job after having paid off their share cropping debt, they risked buying a piece of land but were driven from it and dispossessed by white people who usually snatched property from Negroes. Like Dorcas' father who was burned out of his poolroom business in the city of New York, Joe and Violet were run out of their land in the rural South. The instability and financial insecurity of their lives continued. It was an age of transition and change and hordes of African-Americans roved the countryside in search of jobs as migrant laborers and families were scattered and dispersed as fathers, brothers and husbands left, never to return. The economy of the South had collapsed after the abolition of slavery, making it extremely difficult for African-American people to find work for their livelihood. It was then that masses of black people migrated to the cities of the North in search of work. Violet moved with Joe to Tenderloin where she took up service (as a domestic obviously) in three houses a day, and Joe took up all kinds of work that was available—both day and night work till he got a waiter's job. They moved then to Lenox in an uptown apartment and Violet began her hairdressing work at home while Joe went out to work. In spite of the improvement in their standard of living and financial security, the alienation that they encountered in a big city began to weigh them down.

As a hairdresser who was a house worker, Violet was liked by her customers as with her deft hands and friendly gossip, she made a name for herself among them. She managed the dual roles of housewife and hairdresser without a hitch, combining the two smoothly at the kitchen sink or the chair by the window where her customer's hair was shampooed and she was seated comfortably while Violet styled her hair as she cooked or planned her next housekeeping chore. When the reader meets Violet, she is so accustomed to work that rest for even an afternoon seems to become a burden for her. Her inner craving for a child has reached a point where the acuteness of that longing has occasionally disoriented her, to take a toll on her external behaviour. Relationship with her once-loved husband has reached an all-time low as communication between them has collapsed. Violet's sanity and marriage are now held by the single thread of her work and routine chores which lend stability and restore a modicum of meaning and sense into an otherwise meaningless, empty shell her life has turned into. For women like Violet,

> ...it is impossible to have nothing to do, no sequence of errands, lists of tasks...she thinks she longs for rest.... This notion of rest, it's attractive to her, but I don't think she would like it. They are all like that, these women.... They are busy and thinking of ways to be busier because such a space of nothing pressing to do would knock them down. (26-27)

Here, the role of an African-American woman as labor has acquired a different dimension as it is interwoven with the psychological complexities of the character and work becomes the steady and inevitable factor in a topsy-turvy world where no one can be trusted, not even a beloved husband. Violet's struggles to hold on to her self-esteem through her profession and housework throbs with poignancy and intense frustration as her customers refuse to come to her out of fear after her attempt to cut open the face of her husband's dead mistress and her housekeeping efforts and elaborate meals are no longer appreciated by Joe. Notably, it is not only Violet who suffers from such disorientation and suppressed sorrow. There are others like her who are outwardly normal and poised enough not to show the chasm within—women who would rather prefer thoughtless periods of sleep than the joys of leisure which saves them from feeling restless and uneasy. Pauline Breedlove in *The Bluest Eye* derives pleasure from her work as she is able to experience second-hand all she has been denied in life. Violet's character has the nuance of a more profound psychological turmoil which goes beyond any stereotype or repetition in the poignancy of it's delineation. Violet functions automatically and out of habit while her mind is preoccupied with a sense of overwhelming loss—the loss of a child—earlier never regretted. Violet's 'other self' has detached itself from her and seems to be in control while she looks on, a wondering spectator. The merging of these two selves will take place gradually as Violet's raw emotional wounds heal.

In the South, the reader encounters a young, vibrant and determined Violet who, along with her husband and a trainful of hopeful black people travel from the South towards Harlem, a place of dreams. Violet is determined to work her way up the economic ladder. Violet's sheer willpower and persuading capacity has stood her in good stead:

> She liked, and had to get her way.... She had butted her way to a spacious uptown apartment promised to another family by sitting out the landlord, haunting his doorway. She collected customers by going up to them and describing her services ("I can do your hair better and cheaper, and do it when and where you want"). She argued butchers and wagon vendors into prime and extra ("Put that little end piece in. You weighing the stalks; I'm buying the leaf"). (35-36)

Later in life, we find this bubbling, confident young Violet being replaced by the old brooding one whose dissociation with work goes on parallelly with her dissociation with herself. She loses sleep as the "fist of fatigue" (39) due to physical hard work is no longer there to knock her to sleep. Both Joe and Violet come from such backgrounds that prompted their voluntary refusal to have children, though it is only Violet who has to suffer the psychological consequences of maternal deprivation, which has been the lot of her race-women since slavery times, of her grandmother True Belle, of Joe's mother Wild (who refuses to nurture her child) or Beloved's mother and Baby Suggs (*Beloved*) Violet's divided personality is the result of the alienation, violence, isolation, and the harsh realities of African-American experience in the urban ghettoes of cities that had lured them into their midst.

The trajectory of Negro history (1888-1927) is projected in *Jazz* in the transition from plantation slavery to share cropper/ migrant labor to urban proletariat—crude slavery to disguised slavery. Joe and Violet are not true proletariats with stable jobs in the organised sector. Joe is a waiter and small salesman. Violet is a self-employed hairdresser. She has no degree or licence so she is doubly exploited—paid 50 cents whereas legal hairdressers charge 2 dollars. Nor is her work stable—it fluctuates according to the whim of her customers. She and Joe have to go into homes and wait on doorsteps with their bag of tools, their jobs have provided them no social security. This insecurity governs their actions (Violet's "madness" and unpredictability, her silence, Joe's longing for company and comfort). The theme of alienation of labor through proletarianisation and urbanisation is explored in *Jazz* by Morrison. Joe and Violet are penniless after they are literally burned out of their farms and settlements down south and are forced to migrate. The city has offered them opportunities but at the cost of isolation and alienation, making them slaves of its relentless and mechanical system.

For the working class and especially for black women, the theme of Jazz music is especially relevant. Its relation to the women workers of the city, its underlying violence, the promise of dark desires, of escape, has its effect on women like Alice, Dorcas and Violet. The theme of "feminization of labor" is a continuation of old sexual division of labor—male work and female work. It is noteworthy that though of the same age and background, Violet is shown as much more intelligent than Joe "who stopped somewhere around sixteen" (145). However, Joe has always had better paid work than Violet. When she is a cotton-picker, he is a "ginner", i.e. working the ginning machine, hence better paid. In the city too, his jobs which entail going out to public places—hotels, restaurants, slaughter yards, railroad cars, the streets and shops as seller, are much higher paid than those available to Violet which are confined to domestic and feminine areas as house cleaner or hairdresser in homes or exclusively female beauty parlours, which are less well paid. It is assumed that he pays the bills, Violet's work is only a side business for the extras and that she supplements his income. It is only when he misses work after his traumatic experience that Violet has to bustle about to keep the pot boiling. The myth of the male breadwinner and female homemaker is as strong and pervasive in African-American society whereas the reality is totally the opposite (*cf.* Alice, Malvonne, True Belle, Rose Dear due to the absent father, unwed mother Wild, politically victimised father—Rose Dear's husband, a slave sent for his master's work—True Belle's husband, a railroad porter on long journeys—Felice's father). When Violet and Joe are sharecroppers, she does the hard work of managing the farm and keep them going while he goes out and does the paying jobs that will repay their debt. The African-American woman is therefore left with a raw deal either way—in the town and in the city.

Jazz music operates here as the metaphor for African-American life and experiences and also as the structural principle of the novel. Jazz music emerged in the first decades of the twentieth century and developed primarily as a city phenomenon, attempting to capture in music the cadences, voices, and even the rising skylines of new, urban America. The knowledge that permeates Morrison's *Jazz* as also jazz music is that though life dismembers African-Americans every day, they still rise somehow to face another day—the sum total of their experience in America.[14]

Giving an account of the Georgia women of *The Bluest Eye* where Cholly Breedlove was born and brought up, Morrison catalogues the work they did in minute detail, creating the deliberate impression of identities, personalities and experience merging with the taste of sweat on their brows—the remembrance of pain, back-breaking labor and toil. These women have grown old together and as one of them (Cholly's aunt Jimmy) is dying they sit around her remembering "all of the bruises they had collected from moving about the earth—harvesting, cleaning, hoisting, pitching, stooping, kneeling, picking—always with young ones underfoot" (*TBE*, 107). For them, the process of growing up has been painful, being adults has been torture:

> Everybody in the world was in a position to give them orders. White women said "Do this", white children said "Give me that". White men said , "Come here". Black men said, "Lay down". The only people they did not take orders from were black children and each other. But they took all of that and re-created it in their own images. They ran the houses of white people, and knew it. When white men beat their men, they cleaned up the blood and went home to receive abuse from the victim. They beat their children with one hand and

stole for them with the other. The hands that felled trees also cut umbilical cords; the hands that wrung the necks of chickens and butchered hogs also nudged African violets into bloom; the arms that loaded sheaves, bales and sacks rocked babies to sleep. They patted biscuits into flaky ovals of innocence and shrouded the dead. They plowed all day and came home to nestle like plums under the limbs of their men. The legs that straddled a mule's back were the same ones that straddled theirs men's hips. And the difference was all the difference there was". (108)

When they grew old and "were through with lust and lactation, beyond tears and terror, were they in fact and at last free". (108)

In this passage of unparalleled eloquence, Morrison has crystallised the essence of poor black women's role as laborers and jolted the reader into an awareness of the trials of their existence.

In *Sula*, the women of the black community of Medallion have, like the African-American women of Cincinnati, Ohio in *Beloved* lived hard lives amidst the insecurities and poverty that have dogged African-American people in America. Spanning 1917 to 1965, before and after World Wars I and II, the novel depicts changing times that were difficult for these families and they had to work hard to find a toehold on life. The winters were especially tough and both jobs and food were scarce. The menfolk were grim and silent, the women harsh and bitter from trying to cater to their families' needs. Struggling against the odds of life, these African-American women had developed their own systems of beliefs and values—their own ideas of virtue and worthiness. By the time they were thirty they had lost teeth, put on weight and suffered bruises that had destroyed their beauty and appeal. The circumscribed lives had "dusted their bronze with ash, the eyes that had once opened wide to the moon bent into grimy sickles of concern. The narrower their lives, the wider their hips" (*S*, 121). The "starched coffins" (122) that their married lives had become were burying them alive. Women who were not attached to men became like "sour-tipped needles" (122)—hardened and empty-eyed, those who had their men "had the sweetness sucked from their breath by ovens and steam bottles" (122). These African-American women made their children the sum total and the centre of their existence and it was their young innocence that made them stop short of murder or suicide. Frustrated and broken, these were women who battled racism, segregation, natural calamities, sickness and evil with stony-eyed silence and stoic endurance, knowing how to behave in the role of helpless victims. Self-righteous but limited, they were, writes Morrison, "afraid of losing their jobs" (119) that is, their job as wives of husbands who may discover their sameness and reject them. Afraid as they were to break their own society's accepted norms and codes of behaviour, for fear of being branded as deviant and become a pariah or outcaste, they clung to the webs they had spun around themselves, unable to break free, and terrified of the "free fall" (120). They tried to find meaning in their roles as wives, mothers, daughters or mistresses and clustered together in their sameness to support each other and morally desparate in their effort to condone or condemn others' behaviour within their limited understanding. Combating the harsh realities of life had drained them as persons and their 'self's had been long submerged in their role identities.

In *Song of Solomon* in Shalimar, a small town in the backwoods of Virginia in the South, the protagonist Milkman is struck by the appearance of the women. None of them carried anything in their hands when they walked on the streets unlike the black women he had seen in his hometown who invariably carried purses or pocket books. The difference in their lifestyles is underscored by the apparent dissimilarity of appearance. These were African-American women who, like Pilate, were accustomed to labor in a different manner than the town women. These were women who hoed, plowed, chopped, planted, washed, cooked, raised children, raised vegetable gardens, bred poultry and in fact, their men relied on them and their children (who looked after the chickens and pigs) for food. The men did not own any land and they found employment only when white men came to pick them up when they needed laborers. So they spent their days chatting and drinking at Solomon's General Store while the women managed the business of living by themselves. To Milkman, these were upretentious, unselfconscious, true daughters of the soil and the salt of the earth who, like Pilate, were free from the urban society's artificialities and pretentions. He could not appreciate however in his newly acquired enthusiasm for country life, the confinement of their lives and the roles that had been imposed upon them and in which they were compelled to restrain themselves, not by choice. Poor black women both in rural and urban areas, in the North and in the South, were tied to their work roles—their commitments anchoring them to their families in a bondage greater than slavery. Yet they survived, though some like Ryna—left behind with the responsibility to fend for herself and her twenty-seven children by her husband Solomon who "flew" away (the absent father/male/protector—recurring motif in African-American women writer's fiction)—went insane in her inability to tolerate the emotional barrenness and crucifying burdens of her life. Ryna's story brings out with poignancy the African-American women's dilemma who are invariably the ones to be left behind to drag on and stumble forward with the staggering burdens, unable to bring themselves to "fly away", leaving their bodies behind. Like the soldier ants of Isles des Chevaliers in *Tar Baby,* they march in singleminded determination toward the nests they have built, "(b)earing, hunting, eating, fighting, burying" (*TB*, 294). The lives of the soldier ants are a metaphor for the lives of African-American women who have "no time for dreaming" (294) their lives comprising of unrelieved labor—a life that "requires organization so tight and sacrifice so complete there is little need for males" (293) except for the act of procreation and a brief period of sexual gratification. They have so much work to do, "so many to be born and fed, then found and buried" that their work is "literally endless" (293). So Morrison writes in *The Bluest Eye* that they wait for old age with resigned anticipation, knowing that only then, after being through with "lust and lactation" can they claim a private world of their own.

In contrast, Morrison's citified black women are aggressive and confident as in *Jazz* or *Tar Baby*. In *Song of Solomon*, the black maids of the Northern towns are, for Milkman's sister Corinthians, "grown-up women" (196) who do not hide their reality or deny the demeaning labor they have to do in order to survive. They are proud of their commitments and their ability to shoulder responsibilities—practical women who carry shopping bags of uniform and aprons to their workplace unashamedly and wear flat shoes because they know their feet could not stand working on high heels the whole day. In *Jazz* as Alice and Violet share confidences and recount incidents from the past—tit bits of information related to their past occupations, experiences as well as changes that were taking place in the society then are thrown up. Citified black women handled jobs and men with a confidence born out of a primitive instinct—self-preservation. Armed with lethal weapons, they protected themselves while others came to terms with the brutalities they faced everyday from every quarter. Those that went about unarmed were either resigned or insane. Still others tried to hoard money for protection or attached themselves to armed men. Desperate black women found ways to support themselves, supplement family income and survive (98-99).

Category III of the hypotheses includes rural and urban middle-class women who are privileged in the sense that they do not have to work outside their homes as financially their positions are securer than that of poor, black women. In emulating white middle-class values, they distance themselves from the common "niggers" who represent all that they have tried to eliminate from their lives. Very few middle-class women come together in community sisterhood, though they attend churches regularly and meet at discreet ladies' clubs or charity organisations as symbols of their improved status. The illusion of their superiority remains intact within the confines of their homes or in the community, beyond which however their reality remains the same as that of all African-American women irrespective of their class or qualification. The superficiality of their existence is underlined by the meaningless chores in which they involve themselves, the decorum, neatness and order that they labor for with fanatic precision and their confinement in their roles as housewives and mothers where their imagination is "driven underground" (*S*, 18) and their 'self's repressed.

In *The Bluest Eye*, Morrison has represented Geraldine as a middle-class housewife and mother who has realised her dream with her single-minded effort. She has conformed with the norms of the white society, accepted and adopted their standards of behaviour as ideal and moulded herself to fit the niche of those privileged African-American women promoted to the category of 'coloured' as distinctly different from common blacks. Like hundreds of aspiring young African-American women, she has succeeded in wiping away the stigma of poverty from her existence. In the process, she has sterilized her passions and emotions and circumscribed herself within a strict pattern of dos and don'ts. In eliminating the funkiness[15] (a legacy of her race) of passion from her behaviour she has achieved respectability and economic stability. Her neat precision, obsession with cleanliness and moral propriety belies the fiercely curbed desires. She has worked painstakingly and laboriously to remove every trace of the unpredictability and irresponsibility of her race from her behaviour, speech and action. She is grounded solidly in the middle-class comfort of her immaculately maintained house, polished furniture, carefully groomed flower plants, spotless laundry and well-stocked kitchen. Her well-fed and neatly dressed husband and son have no cause to complain because she is the ideal housewife and dutiful mother. She goes to church regularly, reads morally uplifting passages from magazines, represses her sexual longings, allows her husband only a partial privilege over her body, responds mechanically to his lovemaking, and bears one or two children without a fuss. She has cultivated the image of a prim and proper lady and has worked hard to maintain this image.

Women like Geraldine have had college education and have settled down in quiet colored neighbourhoods. The respectability that has been consistently denied to black women by the white patriarchal society has been thus achieved by these women and they have clung tenaciously to it. Having gone to land grant colleges and having been trained in House Economics, they are fit for skilled work and better paying jobs. But, due to the limited choices available to an African-American woman for work, she can either opt for manual labour (unskilled work) or trade in sex. The only other option is marriage (which stands for security and dignity) which the middle-class African-American man offers her in exchange of looking after his house, bearing his children and being the exemplary housekeeper-cum-wife. They are industrious and self-righteous and have spared no effort to keep a distance from the demoralizing poverty of the African-American ghettoes. They have, as Geraldine had, cooked, cleaned, starched, pressed, trimmed, polished, decorated, ordered and re-ordered their houses to perfection. Through diligent work, they have built a fortress of material security around themselves and have at last succeeded in achieving the African-American woman's ultimate dream—to possess a house of her own. To barricade themselves against possbile invasions of despicably poor and dirty negroes, they have forbidden their children to mix with them for they are unwelcome reminders of a past they have left behind. Geraldine's terror of the black street urchins with their unblinking, questioning eyes speaks of an ingrained insecurity which sees in their deprived childhood a threat to her own neat, ordered secure world.

Geraldine is one of those "sugar-brown" girls who are "as sweet and plain as buttercake" (64). In her representation of Nel's mother Helen in *Sula* and rich housewife Ruth in *Song of Solomon*, Morrison has used food metaphors like "custard" (*S*, 22) for Helen and "moist and crumbly like unbleached sugar" (*SOS*, 16) for Ruth and the young "high-yellow" girl at Claudia's school named Maureen Peal was nicknamed "Meringue Pie" (*TBE*, 57) by her envious classmates. Most of Morrison's middle-class and rich women are high-yellow or light brown in complexion—Ruth is lemon yellow, Helen a creamy brown and Geraldine is sugar brown, Corinthians and Magdelene in *Song of Solomon* are both light complexioned and Jadine of *Tar Baby* has honey-toned skin (*cf.* Appendix, pp. iv-vi). The color and the food metaphor mingle to reinforce the theme of "edible", "buyable", and commodified, carefully maintained beauty of these middle-class and rich women who have bought respectability in exchange of the services (however mechanical) they render to their husbands and families in their roles as wives, mothers and daughters. The image is also strongly suggestive of appeal that these women have in the eyes of men—both black and white and the beauty that they sometimes flaunt as a commodity to take advantage of the sexual appetites of men—buying a better and securer ways of life from themselves. There are those like Ruth, however who suffer psychologically at the barrenness of their existence and the uselessness of their labor—women (like Corinthians and Magdelene) who are daughters of rich men in *Song of Solomon* who face patriarchal domination and sexist discrimination within their homes.

In *Sula,* Morrison represents Helene Wright as a middle-class housewife and mother. Helene Wright was the daughter of a Creole prostitute and had inherited her great beauty along with a disgust of her profession and lifestyle instilled into her by her grandmother, under whose strict vigilance she had been brought up. Being married by Wiley Wright was in a way a dream come true for her. He was a cook on one of the boats travelling extensively over the Great Lakes. He was well off and had a beautiful house which Helene loved to keep in order. In fact, the house became the center of her existence and the symbol of their marriage because Wiley was away at sea for long periods and was a distant if comforting presence at best. Helene did not have to worry about money or material stability but her labor was one of single-minded determination to make herself and her house (representative of her class and social status) as different from the yellow house of her childhood as possible. The yellow house she was born in was, to her, the embodiment of evil, degradation and moral depravity, a past which she needed to erase in order to bolster her self-esteem. Hence, her ceaseless and untiring effort to maintain herself as a model of perfection—religious, self-righteous and industrious. Even the role of motherhood was assumed by her as an exemplary role to project herself in. Her professed pride in being the ideal mother and ideal housewife and her aspirations to move upward in the social scale did not leave much room for warmth and easy friendliness with her daughter. She was always well-dressed, authoritative and impressive and Nel had always been in awe of her. She carefully emulated the whites and her dealings with the people of her neighbourhood had in it the same aloofness and distance which the whites cultivated towards the African-Americans. Nel was convinced about her mother's self-pride until that fateful day on the train where she flashed a dazzling, fawning smile to placate the abusive white conductor. That glimpse of uncharacteristic bonelessness and absence of steel in her disturbs Nel so much that she decides to be on guard always lest she lose her backbone too. Nel's "me-ness" (29) develops only after witnessing Helene's humiliating experience of being black in a larger white society. Through this experience of Helene, the complex nature and inherent tensions of the black-white relationship comes to the fore as Nel feels the acrid disgust of the other blacks in the compartment rising in her against the "Uncle-Tommish"[16] quality of her mother's smile. Helene who had 'risen' in life, refuses to acknowledge her mother of whom she is bitterly ashamed. Counterpointed here is the natural poise and grace of Helene's mother which impresses little Nel as against the cultivated hauteur of Helene Wright which belies the "custard" lurking beneath. For Helene Wright, the respectability acquired in the role of wife and mother justify her sacrifices of freedom in the bondage of marriage. She has gained material advantage in that she is esconced in a comfortable house and has no financial worries but she has achieved it at the cost of her self-respect. Despising her mother for prostitution, she has "sold" herself in marriage and has been a prostitute—if only to her husband. Both the alternatives available for black women—labor and prostitution—entail the sale of themselves, their hands or their bodies—and the illusion of dependence on men is broken when they fail to deliver the commodities—the wifely acquiescence and yielding of body, the surrender of freedom and the services of a housekeeper. Helene has sacrificed her mother's "freedom" for her "unfreedom". The "inner" core of dissatisfaction and unhappiness of having an economically supportive husband who is nevertheless absent and probably whoring with other women (*cf.* Grange and Brownfield in *The Third Life of Grange Copeland*) Helene learns to hide by only living for the "outer" shell of perfection and show of satisfaction in a clean house, church going and public service—activities that demonstrate her efficiency, taste and quality of leadership. She believes that a fine dress will insulate her from the reality of

African-American existence in the world outside her community where she is much admired for her cultivated virtues (hence the rich dress she makes to wear in her journey to the South) but the facade crumbles in her encounter with the white train-conductor. The smile she gives him compromises her self-respect and Nel is horrified to glimpse the "custard" beneath her mother's proud carriage. Like Geraldine, Helene tries to erase all memories of a past stigma (of her mother's prostitution) because the "red shutters" (*S*, 17) of Sundown House had haunted her with the threat of a fate she thought was worse than death (red-suggestive of the scarlet woman—the slut). Motherhood therefore was for Helen a noble role to which she "rose grandly" (18) and inculcated in her daughter Nel her own values which she had imbibed from her grandmother Cecile who had rescued her from whoredom. It was under Helene and her combined persuasion ("pressure"—coercion) that Cecile's grand nephew married Helene to take her away to Medallion—a town far away from Sundown House and all reminders of it. Faced with the limited options that life offered black women, these women opted for compromise and respectability rather than the "degradation" of prostitution that ironically gave more freedom than marriage.

Helene's daughter Nel was Sula's best friend. These two are drawn together in a friendship where each complimented and completed the other. A similarity of apparently different situations had drawn them together. Coming from a house which lacked order, Sula preferred the calm neatness of Nel's house while Nel, accustomed to the rigid order of her house, preferred the warm diffuseness of Sula's household. Each of them, in their own way had felt the necessity of a friend. Early in their lives the two girls had come to realise the disadvantage of being African-American and female. They also knew that they would have to create a space for themselves. The marginalisation of the African-American female is sensed by the young teenage girls.

Nel's wedding was a "real" one—complete with a church service and reception afterwards which was unusual for the people of the Bottom—the acme of middle-class respectability. Deep-rooted in the African-American man was the eternal urge to be a man, the head of a household, the bread-winner and decision-maker—an urge to be the master, not at the beck and call of white superiors. The only way it was possible was through marriage to a black woman. The past history of slavery and continuing racial discrimination had not allowed the African-American man to recognize and revel in his manhood. Shorn of every claim to a human existence, disallowed the natural claims to wife, children and family, bought and sold like animals, they had been reduced to the status of permanent boyhood devoid of maturity and masculinity. Regaining and reclaiming it was possible only through marriage to a docile wife who could be subjugated, his wishes made her command and a family which would give him a purpose for taking up jobs beneath his dignity. The middle-class African-American woman's role within the family therefore becomes primarily that of a wife and mother. She is expected to manage the household chores, bring up her children and provide the much-needed psychological mooring to her bitter and complaining husband whose hurt ego constantly needs the balm of her soothing care. If the husband loses his job, indulges in fights or simply leaves, out of boredom and tedium, the black woman has then to assume the double role of breadwinner and nurturer. Nel assumes this caring, nurturing role with a placid contentment which reminds the reader that Jude had wanted Nel to submerge her identity in his and give him a wholeness which he lacked. This he has indeed achieved and Nel gives herself up so completely that "Krumholz (1993) observes: 'In *Sula*, Morrison both cherishes and criticizes the character Nel, who (ambiguously) embodies the myth of the black woman as a nurturing, self-sacrificing, infinitely strong burden bearer'"[17] when Sula takes her husband away, the betrayal leaves her desolate, and no amount of work can even distract from the throbbing pain or the yawning emptiness within her. Jude is another African-American male who needs the African-American female's dependence on him to boost his self-esteem and erase his sense of unworthiness or inadequacy.

For Sula, Nel's wedding had been a betrayal of all that they had shared. Like the ash-skinned, narrow-eyed and bitter Medallion women, enmeshed in their own web and avoiding at all costs the "free fall" into the unknown territory of unleashed passions, unconventional behaviour or rebellion, Nel had settled into her marriage with Jude, esconced herself in middle-class expectations, surrounded by domesticity and stagnating in her role as wife and mother. The "me-ness" that Nel had discovered in herself as a girl is submerged in her role as Jude's wife, and she did not realise till the last (till after Sula's death) why Sula had forced upon her the bitter pain and disillusionment of Jude's betrayal. As Ajax said about African-American women like Nel, the tight shield of sorrow which they had built around themselves in defence against more pain was a necessity that had turned into a shackling habit. Middle-class housewives like Nel knew only to function in their expected and accepted roles because they repressed the awareness of exploitation and burdensome relationships and resisted the free expression of their 'self's. Conditioned to behave 'nobly', 'honorably', with 'responsibility' and 'commitment', they did not have the courage to exercise the freedom of choice, to act according to their own will and not the will of others as they had done as slaves and laborers. The recognition of one's desire and the courage to claim it was something girls like Nel had forgotten in their circumscribed roles.

So, in 1940, when Sula is dying, Nel is a woman of thirty, staid, matronly and past her yearning desires for emotional and physical companionship from men that has been replaced by a "monstrous" and "thick" love for her children and the smug knowledge of her "goodness" in having labored to be the ideal mother. She has assumed full responsibility of her household as there is no longer any possibility of Jude's return or his earnings to support her. She had taken up a cleaning job and recently had got a better job—that of a chamber maid in the same hotel Jude had worked in. She does not earn as much as Jude did but because of the timing she can both maintain her job and look after her children, for which she is thankful. As usual, African-American women got the worst deal when it came to jobs and even in 1940, a large majority of them were engaged in the unskilled labor sector doing work that they had been doing all their lives—at home and outside. As Nel stresses the limitations of being a woman and insists the women are incomplete without men as she is, a "maple struck down" (139), Sula points out that she has lived for others and even her loneliness is a "secondhand lonely" (143), given to her by someone. Nel has borne her life as a sentence, inflicted upon her by Jude but she does not realise in her justified and self-righteous anger the cruel kindness of Sula's action. Years later (in 1965) at the close of the novel, Nel identifies the true yearning of her 'soul' as a mourning over the loss of a cherished friendship. All these years she had moved in a rigid anger that had obscured the true cause of her grief. In a final acknowledgement of that relationship and recognition of Sula as her soulmate, Nel's cry of profound sorrow reverberates with the agony of missed years of friendship and self-knowledge.

The relationship between Hannah and her daughter Sula is unusual. Hannah had never assumed total responsibility of her child, which was shared with Eva who took major decisions. The disorderliness of Eva's household did not make way for traditional bonding between mother and daughter or the sharing of confidence. Hannah's role as mother was confined to occasional concern. Her role as labor was limited to her running the house and cooking for the boarders which she did with whimsical pleasure and no orderliness but in a way earned her keep. Since her husband's death, she had come back to live with her mother, never therefore having to worry about money. They had rented their outhouse and had always a steady stream of boarders, which was another source of income for them. She was a compulsive man-lover and had a steady stream of boyfriends. She gave her body generously, gracefully and unashamedly and was so undemanding in return to their caresses that men were enchanted with her. The family in which Sula grew therefore was an all-woman household, with no cohesive or binding factor of stable relationships and no presence of a father-figure. The women in the household were pre-occupied with their own problems and pleasures, where a young girl was not paid much attention to. These circumstances probably led to a strange indifference between mother and daughter, so much so, that Sula watched her mother's body twitch and dance in a flaming fire in an agony of death with detatched interest. Eva carried with her forever the bone-chilling memory of Sula's indifference to her dying mother.

Hannah is like Reba in *Song of Solomon* though she is not poor, but middle-class. However, she is totally free from middle-class taboos or codes of decorum. Her "sootiness" (122) is much discussed in the locality and despised by the prudish and primly proper Helene Wright. The absence of inhibitions in Hannah and her enjoyment of sex with every available male is a formative influence on *Sula*. Hannah exasperated all women, including the prostitutes. So all erect and proper middle-class women disapproved of her as did the prostitutes who were as such hard put to find customers among black men who could not afford to or would not pay for sex and Hannah's generosity affected their trade badly.

Susan Byrd and Grace of *SOS* are both middle-class women. The former has inculcated all the lady-like virtues of the white American female and her snobbery has isolated her from the neighboring village where all the inhabitants are black. She does not need to work for a living as she has a small legacy left for her by her parents. Unconsciously, Susan Byrd tries to uphold the Southern image of a delicate and decorous white lady, holding herself aloof from the vulgar negroes. The latter is garrulous and effusive, her unattached state no boon, as she is really insecure about her future which stretches bleakly before her with no immediate prospect of a change towards the better.

Morrison has represented Ruth, First Corinthians and Magdelene in *Song of Solomon* as a rich housewife and daughters of a rich man respectively. Ruth herself was also the daughter of a rich African-American doctor. The emotional barrenness one encounters in the lives of these three women brings to mind the question whether material advantage does not suit the African-American women and whether personal success (as of Jadine in *TB* or Laurel in Naylor's *LH*) always leaves them with a feeling of betraying the community or an emptiness of soul that is staggering and frightening. For women like Ruth, Corinthians or Magdelene or the Needed wives in Naylor's Linden Hills, existence is nothing short of slavery—the only difference being that they are slaves in their own homes.

Ruth Foster was the daughter of the first colored doctor in town. Widely respected, he was actually selfish and class-conscious, with a pronounced color bias. Between her father whom she literally worshipped and her husband whom she hated in her fear of him, Ruth's personality was stunted to an extent where she seemed like a pale wraithe to her son, as insubstantial and ineffective. Ruth was brought up according to the rigid tenets of white upper-class values which her father had embraced and emulated. She learnt how to keep house, to arrange flowers and all the other little tasks which befitted a doctor's daughter. When her father was alive and she unmarried, she had found pleasure in her household chores and she walked long distances to gather driftwood and flowers for subtle effect in arrangement. Her father had appreciated her efforts though he was stifled by and more than a little uneasy with the singular devotion which his daughter bestowed upon him. With the death of Ruth's father, Macon became the head of the household but Ruth had never been and never became the mistress of the house. She exchanged the role of an obedient daughter with that of a submissive wife, whose opinion was never sought and whose existence was circumscribed by a series of meaningless rituals and mundane duties. From the patriarchal protection of an indulgent if dominating father she passed on to the dubious protection of a fiercely jealous husband. Ruth was an indifferent cook at best and Macon's sharp criticism of the food she prepared had the effect of making her more nervous and jittery. All her careful attempts at baking and cooking ended up in a mess of inedible food and provoked Macon's violent ire or disgust.

In spite of Macon's evident wealth, there was no servant employed for housework. Ruth was expected to cater to Macon's physical needs (not sexual ones as he had stopped sleeping with her since her father's death) and maintain the house with the help of her two daughters. The trembling nervousness that the three women felt in the presence of Macon was reflected in their clumsiness and inefficiency. Ruth's situation is a replica of any patriarchal, white American household where the male is the head automatically by virtue of his gender. Clearly, it is expected and accepted that he would be obeyed without demur and that his temper and tyranny were to be borne as Ruth and her daughter bore Macon. It is ironical that Ruth was relegated to the status of a glorified housekeeper-cum-hostess in her father's house which was her own only in name. Starved of physical contact or any expression of love from Macon, Ruth sought emotional satisfaction through breast-feeding her son Milkman till he was quite old and visiting her father's grave once every month. Ruth's question to her son: "What harm did I do you on my knees?" (124) echoes with the helplessness of a mother who had fought to keep her son alive in her womb but had no control over his present or future. She is denied the choice of making decisions because she is a woman. Condemned by Macon for her necrophyllic love for her father and her unhealthy possiveness for her son, Ruth's natural adoration for her only son is deliberately distorted as a Freudian complex.

The story of Ruth's life is put in a nutshell when she, confronted by her son, explains her behaviour for the first time: "...because the fact is that I'm a small woman...I'm small because I was pressed small. I lived in a great big house that pressed me into a small package" (124). The isolation which Ruth had experienced from her childhood, the envy of classmates, the loneliness and insecurity become poignantly clear as she continues with her low voiced revelations. The story of Ruth's life was confinement—both physical and psychological. Her delicate taste, her finer sensibilities, her lady like grace had been encouraged and cultivated by her father so that she could become the ideal hostess in his house after his wife's death. She dutifully catered to his every need and the intense joy she felt in serving him shone in her eyes. In return he cared for her well-being like any father would for his child. He was the economic provider and physical protector and he had passed on the mantle to his son-in-law. She was also unaware that she had been exploited and circumscribed, albeit in the name of fatherly love. She had made her father the purpose and sole focus of her existence due to which, with his death, she lost interest in her own life. She had never had the opportunity to come into contact with people outside her narrow social circle. Even within that exclusive coterie, she felt alienated and lost. Her relationship with her husband deteriorated with every passing day. Normally, under such circumstances, she should have drawn closer to her daughters because they, like her, feared Macon. Traditionally, African-American women had always clubbed together in sorrow and joy to combat the odds of life, including the indifference, hatred and abandonment of their men-folk. Ruth and her daughters however had no such traditional group heritage to support them with the strength of collective wisdom. They could fall back only on their upbringing which was a replica of a Southern white lady's. As Barbara Christian puts it, Ruth represented the underside of white Southern ladyhood. Perhaps because of Ruth's own passivity and lack of initiative, her daughters remained enclosed in their own world, though they did have sympathy for their mother.

A desperate Ruth turned to Pilate who helped her by giving her moral support, engineered the conception of her son (using potent herbs to excite Macon's sexuality temporarily) and also taught her methods to protect the baby in her womb in the face of Macon's furious attempts to get her to abort the baby. With the birth of her son all her attentions focussed on him who gave her joy, a purpose for living and even physical pleasure as she suckled him. Being, supposedly, the privileged daughter of a rich doctor and wife of a richer real estate man had brought little happiness in her life. There had never been any pressing necessity for her to work outside her home that would suggest that she had a much better deal in her life than most African-American women. But the freedom from a breadwinner's responsibility had not given her any degree of independence or self-confidence. Over the years her identity had become submerged in the roles she was performing as daughter, wife and mother. Milkman's dream regarding his mother acquires an ominous significance as, in it, Ruth is being slowly and surely strangled by the giant tulips with evil yellow pistils. In her fight against hatred (her husband), Ruth has been dominated, over powered, smothered and taken for granted in her love for her father and passion for her son. Ironically, none of the men in her life whom she has loved have ever thought of her as an individual apart from her role identity. She had become an increasing embarassment to her father towards the latter part of his life and to her son she was too "shadowy" and "insubstantial" (75) to evoke his love. He also knows that his sudden urge to protect his mother from his father's physical violence stemmed from a latent masculine aggression born out of his own newly acquired self-confidence. In a way, he has now taken charge and demonstrated through his actions who the new dominator or head of the household would be.

Ruth had in effect passed, in the last phase of her life, into the hands of a new protector—her son. However, Ruth's submission and passivity vanished when her protective instincts were aroused and she rediscovered her inner strength and a new purpose of motherhood as she took up her last fight to save her son's life from Hagar. The same grim resolution also made her force a reluctant Macon to yield a substantial amount of money for Hagar's funeral—a gesture of loyalty and solidarity towards Pilate—her true sister in spirit.

Megdalene, Macon Dead's eldest daughter, is now an old maid with no chances of ever getting married. She stays at home, helps her mother with her household chores and her one pastime is making red velvet rose petals, which she sells at the store. The colourful and soft scraps of velvet provide a welcome distraction to her otherwise monotonous and meaningless existence. Lena acknowledges that she had taken to that stupid hobby of making artificial rose petals because it kept her hands and mind occupied. She compares herself to the residents of an asylum who are made to weave baskets and rag rugs to keep them quiet. Otherwise, like her, "they might find out what's really wrong and...do something. Something terrible" (154)(*cf.* Fanny Nzingha of *TMF*). She had not been able to go to college because of her fear that her father would harm her mother. Her father had provided expensive dresses for Corinthians and her and paraded them as a measure of his wealth and power. She had even as a child felt humiliated and on display. He had however been quick to curb them if they showed any signs of friendliness or inclination towards poor Negroes, his class consciousness becoming a jail for the young girls who gradually lost their spirit and finally zest for life. In a confrontation with Milkman, she challenged his chauvinistic right to interfere in Corinthians' life. For Lena, after years of subjugation by her father and the natural fear towards the patriarch of the family, it was intolerable that a younger brother whose dribble she had wiped, food she had cooked, clothes she had cleaned and bed she had made should assume the mantle of the male "protector" only to start domination and torture in another form.

Megdalene had never been thrilled with the idea of richness or luxury. The claustrophobic life she had been confined to on account of being the daughter of a wealthy Negro emulating white materialism and values had driven her to the brink of insanity as she herself realises. The natural sexual urges of a young girl and her spirits had been smothered by this isolation and cloistering. She had hated it but not dared to voice her thoughts. After all these years, after losing every opportunity of finding a life partner for herself, she was happy that Corinthians had had the courage to find work and also someone who gave her a sense of purpose in life. She therefore rose to defend her sister's happiness, as ferocious as a tigress protecting her cub. She was no longer prepared to suffer domination lying down and with all the intensity of a slow-smouldering coal fire, her indignation and anger at the sense of injustice done to herself and her loved ones burst into a conflagration at the final provocation—Milkman's interference that shattered Corinthians' new found happiness.

As a rich man's daughter, First Corinthians faced an unusual dilemma—she was rejected by eligible bachelors because of her father's wealth, her ladyhood, elegance and privileged status. After completing her education, she had to settle down to a vacant life of endless waiting—for a suitable boy (according to her father's definition) to come along and propose marriage to her. She waited in vain because though she was admired, she was never approached—men preferred to keep formidable Macon Dead's daughter at an arm's length. As in her childhood, when she, along with her mother and sister were dressed up fashionably to be paraded and flaunted as status symbols, so in her youth she became a symbol of class privilege. The barrier which was created by her father's status-consciousness and money power was too high for her to break down and come into contact with real emotion or affection. She had witnessed early in life, the passive apathy of her mother's existence. The three women in the house cowered for fear of abuse and harsh words. The day Milkman knocked his father down for hitting Ruth, she and Lena understood that he had now assumed power. Frustrated with the fruitlessness of her education and life, she decided to step out of her house to find a job for herself.

Unlike most African-American women who have had to work for a living, in First Corinthians' case, it is not bread-winning compulsion that forced her to break out of her respectable middle-class mould. To keep up the facade of respectability, she told her family that she worked as the "amanuensis" of the famous white woman writer Michael Mary Graham. In reality, she worked in the writer's house as a maid—hard work that entailed physical labor. She had to go down on her knees literally as well as metaphorically and she never let any one know the pain and humiliation of being taken as an illiterate person when in reality she was college educated and held a degree which should have guaranteed her a better job. This was again a reminder of the grim fact that beyond the precincts of home and family any African-American woman was always a maid, a manual worker or a prostitute—either strong and sturdy enough for hard physical labor or with enough sexual prowess and libido to satisfy their customers. Even as late as 1961, the African-American woman hardly had any identity beyond this for the white American society.

Corinthians' search for a job had resulted in a frustrating failure as she discovered with dismay that in the white dominated American work world, colored girls were wanted only for a certain kind of work. Her education gave her no advantage therefore as it left her unequipped to deal with strenuous physical labor as also the nature of a maid's work that was debasing and humiliating. Unfortunately, her expensive education and finishing school training did not prepare her for a working woman's life. It was taken for granted that she would eventually marry a wealthy man—work of any practical useful kind was not taught as earning a living was out of question. There was this complacent thought at the back of such ambition that if marriage did not materialise after all, there were always "alternative roles:

teacher, librarian, or...well, something intelligent and public spirited" (188). The practical problems faced by Corinthians when she stepped into the world of working-class women made her come to terms with the bitter truth that her education at Bryn Maur had "unfit her for eighty percent of the useful work of the world" by "training her for leisure time, enrichments and domestic mindlessness" and by implying that she was "too good for such work" (189). In the long years that had lapsed between her acquiring a degree and her search for work, she had lost all contact with the fast paced world of education and had become outdated in every sense. That is why she was left with no other option but to forget about her college degree and take up the only work available to a colored girl, irrespective of her background. First Corinthians had to grit her teeth sometimes to swallow the indirect insults and embrassment she had to face as an educated maid. For a sensitive woman, it was especially difficult to accept the prejudice against her race. On the other hand, she refused to stagnate in the prison of decorous dependence that had been imposed upon her as a rich man's daughter. The need to reach out, break barriers and communicate with others like her became overwhelming. She was stifled by the absence of feeling and emotions in the intra-family relationships in her house where she had every material comfort but no self-respect. Shunning Porter initially because of his obviously inferior class and social status, she however could not prevent reciprocating his continued interest in her that fuelled her emotions and gradually, a new world of emotions opened up before her eyes, a vista of earlier never known feelings and sensation rocked her to the core of her being. Corinthains' rebellion and her work was responsible for this new found happiness in her life. The angularity of a bitter spinsterhood gradually disappeared as she acquired a radiant glow of inner satisfaction. The quiet but obvious change drew Milkman's attention and upon discovering Corinthians' liaison with Porter, in a typically male gesture, he reported the affair to his father who immediately forbade Corinthians to go out for work.

Corinthians was extra careful in maintaining the secrecy about the nature of her work and the elegant book she carried gave no clue as to her occupation. Despite the humiliation of working as a maid, her job gave her the satisfaction of earning her own money as well as a sense of purpose and responsibility which had hitherto been lacking in her life. Delighted at her ability to read, write and appreciate good books, her employer suggested that she take typing lessons to enable her to take dictations. Moreover, her salary was quite substantial and she was on her way to being promoted to the post of a real "amanuensis". She had also learnt enough tact not to reveal her college education or knowledge of French before her mistress.

The rich and so-called enlightened white lady's attitude towards her maid is presented by Morrison in an ironically humorous way. Morrison's impish satire is at play here as she says that Michael Mary's "mild liberalism" was a "residue of her bohemian youth" (190) which allowed for taking pleasure in her maid's ability to appreciate books by Walden instead of the run-of-the-mill money hungry maid. It suited her house and her image perfectly to have a maid who was different and whose lady-like elegance amused and delighted her. It added to the exotic touch which she had carefully affected in her house. Miss Graham's "(p)osture of sensivitve lady poet" (190) is just that—a posture affected for the benifit of her image—cultivating a generosity and charity which caused no great inconvenience to herself nor any objectionable change in the present set-up of social affairs. The envelope of money which was expected by her previous maids at Christmas filled her with boredom which was laced with contempt for their ignorance and inferiority. With all her "sensitivity" she had never realised that for her maids, money meant survival because these African-American women came from a class which was and always had been deprived of the superior comforts of life including education and cultivated appreciation of fine arts. For these women life has been an endless series of struggle and hardship comprising work at home and hard labor at the workplace, long uncomfortable, sweaty rides in buses to and from work, humiliation and insults. To them, the gift of money meant making ends meet, food, clothes and shelter—the basic necessities for survival. The poet laureate had interestingly never stopped to think why her extraordinary maid preferred receiving a book for a gift and seemed to be able to appreciate great works of literature. That Corinthians did not really need to work for survival set her on a different plane from the usual working class women but Micheal Mary Grahams was too self-centered (as befitted a poet) to notice much difference except for the refreshing "uppity manners" (190) of Corinthians which amused her because it suited her image. Interestingly, Corinthians too felt that she was a cut above the rest because she came from a wealthy family—a different class background altogether. She knew for certain that she was superior to these women who worked for a living, who were "common" enough to be contemptuous of and to look down upon. Yet, when Porter accused her of not being a real woman but a doll, she knew that she lacked the earthy contact with life, the real taste of life's joys and sorrows, which had left her emotionally immature. She was incapable of dealing with the unpalatable truths of life—one of which was that if she refused Porter's offer of a sexual culmination of their affair, she would have to revert back to the scraps of red velvet petals—symbolic of a barrenness and emptiness which frightened her out of her senses. It was only after acknowledging her physical and emotional needs urged by a deep inner conviction, that she achieved womanhood for the first time in her life. Having discovered her self-worth through her job, she also found her love—both of which gave her confidence and she blossomed, having gained a new taste of a hitherto unknown aspect of life that added a new dimension to her one-dimensional and colorless existence.

Category V(a) of the hypothesis includes African-American women who have established themselves as successful career women—black women who have achieved fame and wealth through their determination, drive and labor. In their incessant strivings upward, they have left their struggling sisters behind somewhere along the line. The alienation that they feel at some point in their lives from the people of their own race cannot somehow be justified by the individual and singular success they have attained. Black women writers have tended to express their faith in experience and achievement that is both collective and communitarian. Morrison's strong community ties as an artist has already been established by writers like Bryce Bjork. Walker and Naylor also seem to articulate through their representations of women characters the same necessity to fall back on a sustaining sisterhood that could provide emotional support and fullness of experience where individual quests for success may leave one drained and isolated. On the other hand, there is the possibility of restricting values imposed upon these extraordinarily talented or beautiful women, fettering their flight and leaving them frustrated and cloistered as Jadine is in Tar Baby. An interesting and complex metaphor for these ambitious and modern black women who revel in their roles of power flexing, money handling, order-barking, decision-making, top-ranking career women, has been used by Morrison in the symbol of *Tar Baby* (from a famous African-American folktale[18] or the Tar Baby figure in the novel by that name. The aloof, disdainful Tar Baby acts as the lure or the trap for the cunning rabbit (the black man) who embraces it only to get stuck, to the glee of the farmer (the white man). However, Morrison's use of the metaphor is layered in that the above interpretation stands true from the point of view of the black man Son (Jadine's lover in *Tar Baby*) who sees her as the Tar baby and Valerian (the rich white man) as the white farmer—and Eloe (his hometown) as his briar patch or natural habitat.

Inverting the metaphor and viewing it from Jadine's point of view yields a different meaning. Jadine regards the "night women" (*TB*, 265) who haunt her dreams as the tar babies who beckon her to the briar patch of life, flaunting a way of existence that negates all that she has striven to achieve. Their "superior" and haughty disdain of Jadine's efforts has rendered meaningless her womanhood and her role as the emerging, modern and successful black woman who has made her presence felt in the upper echelons of a classist, racist, sexist society. The choice that confronts Jadine is difficult, in fact, it is not even a choice that could be rationally made as it demands great sacrifice—and an erasure of one's self in one's role as mother—the measure of a "real" woman in the eyes of African-American women themselves.

Jadine in *Tar Baby* is a professional model, somewhere near the top rung of the occupational ladder, well-paid and famous. She is also a Sorbonne graduate (from Paris) in Arts history and has therefore the additional choice of opting for a career in academics when her modelling days are over. Jadine's priveleged upbringing and education are both courtesy Valerian who has paid for it in exchange of the service of Ondine and Sydney, Jadine's aunt and uncle who have been his faithful servants for many years now. The novel's early references to her phenomenal success comes through her aunt's proud observation that not every girl had the talent or beauty to be selected for the cover pages of the most prestigious magazines of Paris—a feat more extraordinary for an African-American woman because she has to battle not only ordinary competition but also racism. Apart from her modelling assignments, Jadine has done a small role in a film that has given a substantial boost to her bank account so that she has now begun to contemplate the establishment of her own business—a boutique or a gallery—according to the capital available. She has other avenues open too for consideration like the prospect of marriage to a rich and handsome white European named Rak. Jadine's education allows her the freedom of choice and she can capitalize on her cultivated assets. In the world of modelling, one had to survive cut-throat competition and the amount of ruthlessness required to stay in the business could drain the glamour of the job. Yet, this career stood for the acme of accomplishment and material achievement that she could not deny. The other option of intellectual fulfilment could be acquired through her Art history degree that guaranteed her a lucrative academic job. Toying with these possibilities and at the peak of self-satisfaction and well-deserved happiness, Jadine is suddenly swamped with a feeling of guilt and uneasiness at her social and financial success. Her unease has begun with her encounter with an African woman of majestic beauty whose contempt of Jadine has shattered her peace of mind and driven her from the glitter and lure of her social circle in Paris to Isles des Chevaliers to spend some time with her aunt and uncle while working temporarily for Margaret, the wife of her patron and mentor Valerian Street—both pretexts for the real reason buried in her subconscious mind.

Jadine is projected in the narrative as a self-centred, practical and hard-headed woman who aims to continue her upward climb towards status and recognition by belonging to the coterie of successful negroes who are ambitious and modernized enough to be accepted by the white Americans in their midst—exclusive and privileged and totally devoid of all traces of negritude—in behaviour, attire or accent. So Jadine feels totally out of place in Eloe (a small town in the South) where the black women seem to her to be mindless and circumscribed—women with whom she cannot relate and roles in which she can never imagine accomodating herself. In aligning herself with the white tenets of fashion and beauty, Jadine has negated her authenticity and denied her African roots while, Sula-like, she has shunned traditional African-American womanhood by refusing to cast herself into the roles of a responsible and caring daughter, wife or mother. She has tried, in her own way (and in the way she has been trained in) to transcend the limitations imposed by these roles by avoiding them altogether. In doing so she has existed for herself alone, shrugging commitments aside and apoligising or justifying herself to no one—not even her old aunt and uncle who had been responsible for her upbringing in the first place. Unlike Sula, Jadine's quest is not that of the freest and fullest expression of her self and soul—her quest is that of individual gain and material advancement. So she would like to forget her blackness, get out of her skin or the limitations of skin-color, to be not white, but a human being. However, in denying her commitments, in refusing to "parent" her old uncle and aunt who are in need of her emotional support and company, she fails to combine the strengths of African-American womanhood (nurturers, all-embracing mothers, sacrificing daughters, bearers of cultural heritage, both ships and harbours, protectors, fighters) with the intellectual and material freedom that she craves. Ondine has not been able to generate in Jadine the natural bond of care and concern that a daughter has for her mother and Jadine feels even now her motherlessness acutely. She feels betrayed when her mother appears with the "night women" to silently condemn her for having failed to measure up to their standards of womanhood.

Jadine's class-consciousness and ambition may have culminated in the ultimate step in the process of shedding her racial identity with her marriage to the rich Parisian (Rak) who has gifted her with a sealskin coat that operates as a symbol of ruthless materialism. Significantly, when Jadine leaves the island with the anticipation of growing love (to join Son) she leaves behind the expensive coat. When she returns after having broken her relationship with him, she takes the coat with her in her flight to Paris. The gleaming, black fur of the seals is a stark reminder of the system of oppression that lies at the base of Euro-American capitalist economy that churns out such highly priced luxury items—a system of which Jadine is a part. Ironically, however, in her turn, Jadine herself is a commodity in that her beauty and talent are marketable products. So Jadine too is in the process of assuming the role of object and commodity, which makes her feel "lonely and inauthentic".[19] Jadine is aware of a sense of lack which is aggravated by the "vision" of a "tar-like" African woman described in the narrative as a "transcendent beauty...that woman's woman—that mother/sister/she; ...unphotographable beauty" (43) who leaves Jadine transfixed. Symbolically, she is the black Superwoman, black Madonna, black goddess, black motherhood personified, the keeper of ancestral heritage, the proud bearer of African tribal culture and tradition and fertility (the three eggs she holds aloft in her hand) and she leaves Jadine with a feeling of inadequacy, falseness and an undefinable incompleteness. Bjork observes that Jadine's "desire to resist any identification with the woman's maternal difference"[20] stems from wish to negate the possibility of such a role for herself. She later tells her aunt, "there are other ways to be a woman Nanadine" (284). She is consciously impervious to the possibility of a maternal role and to her African-American identity by denying the limitations and inhibitions imposed upon her by skin color. She is stifled in her relationship with Son when she realises that he is trying to fashion her into a role model of his dreams connected to his past—a role which demanded her to "settle for wifely competence when she could be almighty, to settle for fertility rather than originality, nurturing instead of building" (271). In an interview with Claudia Tate, Morrison has observed that "Black women seem to be able to combine the nest and the adventure."[21] Jadine's inability to combine the two roles and her dissociation from and denial of her ancestral roots leaves her in the end with an emotional numbness. In her final resolve, she trades the complexity, responsibility and possibilities of such a dual role for the ambitious, surface-deep, glamorized and momentary life she leads as a modern career woman as she feels in control and secure in such a role. She is ready to forego the emotional challenge of parenting an old couple or the uncontrolled passion and violence of sexual love for the mechanical challenge of job hazards and mundane decisions.

Jadine's love relationship with the fugitive African-American man named Son makes her abandon, temporarily, her ambition and her hauteur. In her dealings with the white and black men and women of her social circle, Jadine has tactfully avoided emotional involvement. She knows how to handle confidently white people's attention or admiration in that she allows them to be patronising and condescending, convincing them of their superiority and her inferiority that kept their relationship perfect. The black people she knows have aspirations similar to her own and therefore are easy to deal with. With Son however, she is like a fish out of water as he unleashes in her a primitivity she has never known to exist in her and is able to draw out her wild desires and stir up emotions that she is afraid to acknowledge. All her life she had fought tooth and nail against being reduced to a helpless state due to sexual urges that she has kept under tight control. For the first time in her life Jadine relaxes her guard to allow herself the full taste of a sexual, emotional relationship with a man.

During the days of developing commitment and growing love between Jadine and Son, she was the one who earned more money and supported themselves. As an educated woman, she earns more than an illiterate man (Son) who can only qualify for menial jobs. So he earns only $150 a week and leftover champagne at the hotel he works while Jadine makes $2500 catwalking in shows and posing for picture spreads. Jadine knows that she has only a few more years in the profession where only fresh and girlish, teenage looks are in demand. So she has to maintain herself, fight a battle against time and make the best of the years left to her before the tell-tale signs of maturity creep into her face. Competitive fields like modelling did not give one many chances and the work was nowhere as interesting as supposed. It was only the wealth and fame that held people in its world of artificial glitter. In any case, it is Jadine who attempts to chalk out their future plans, fills up forms for Son, tries to persuade him to enroll for courses, none of which efforts are appreciated by him. According to Son, Jadine is the tar baby who is trying to lure him into her way of life (educated, cultured, refined, wealthy) and he resists her efforts fiercely. Jadine is however doing only what she thinks is the only rational way of trying to make a life together. She fights the memories of the "night women"—her tar babies who beckon her to their briar patch and Son who wants her to become like them. Son is another black man for whom a woman exists only as a sexual object—he commodifies women in that sense no less than the white man. Jadine is angered when Son denies her the right to think for herself and for telling her "what a black woman is, or ought to be" (121) and Son is incensed because she has refused to accept the traditional role of a black woman (defined by him, a black man, and not as defined by the world or the black woman herself) and nastily suggests that she has got her success by granting sexual favours —an age-old accusation levelled by frustrated and powerless black men against up and coming black women. Jadine is an African-American woman who has known from experience the limited choices available for her in America. With her education and upbringing, she could hope to have three choices—marriage to a rich man, pursue modelling as a career or teach art—options that she thought would not give her fulfilment or allow her creativity to flower. So she had come to Europe where racism was sub-terranean and she thought there was a "fourth choice" (226) for educated and "refined" black women like her. Ironically, it is in Paris that her authenticity and identity are jeopardised and her achievements insulted.

Having agreed to accompany Son to his hometown Eloe, Jadine is taken aback by the conservatism and censure she meets there and feels as if she has moved back in time. Son's friends gaze at her with pride and at him in adoration as if she were a prize car he had managed to possess (won, stolen or bought—the means did not matter). She cannot envisage a future here with Son who refuses to acknowledge that a narrow, codified traditionalism is all that is left in Eloe and that it is no longer the symbol of warmth, charm and security as he had sentimentally come to believe. It is here that Jadine is confronted with the "night women" who crowd her dreams. In the cramped windowless room in Rosa's house Jadine spends her nights in the hold of a suffocating fear. In her nightmare all the women of Eloe (dead and living), all the other black women she knew except her city friends, Ondine, Thérèse and even her own dead mother jostle each other to come near her, pushing their sagging breasts out at her. Ironically, their sagging breasts suggest that they have been drained by motherhood while their faces, smug and haughty in the knowledge of their superior virtues and the greatness of their sacrifice proudly project their lives and their roles as the ideal ones. Jadine's protests that she too had the power of procreation and the capability of nourishment goes unheard. The roles that Jadine had chosen to forgo inevitably seeped the vitality of these women whose folded stomachs and shrunken breasts bore the marks of exploitation—sexual, material and physical and a deprived womanhood. Given the choice most modern black women like Jadine would rather forgo the dubious glory of a life time of sacrifice to take the easier and rational way out. Analysing her haunting nightmare, Jadine comes to the conclusion that "they seemed somehow in agreement with each other about her, and were all out to get her, tie her, bind her. Grab the person she had worked hard to become and choke it off with their soft loose tits" (264). Jadine cannot resolve the disparity between the African woman's role recollected by her cultural memory and the role she has chosen willingly. Her predicament is that ironically what she takes as freedom and power of choice is in reality an undermining of her own potential strength which would have flowered had she acknowledged or tried to establish her connections with her past heritage. On the other hand, it is also true that an imposed African traditionalism cannot define the African-American identity and at one level restricts the opportunity for growth and intellectual development for black women.[22] So in New York, the "black woman's town" (223) they were allowed the freedom to express themselves, could earn their livelihood independently, could give commands, be incharge and were heard and obeyed. So educated girls could work their way up to the top ignoring the harsh reality of starving prostitutes, disillusioned children and helpless old black men and women huddled and clustered in poor ghettoes of New York. One could only hope to escape by distancing oneself from the "crying black girls" (217) of New York city or denying that most black women were masking their pain in gestures of defiance and arrogance. Jadine therefore fiercely resists Son's efforts to teach her the black woman's "ideal" role—a role that suits his convenience and restricts her. In the face of his accusations that she is also the white man's whore, Jadine forces Son to acknowledge the reality that his original dime (the symbol of male fraternity and bonding) comes originally from a black woman consorting with a white man. Son's expectations of Jadine are too chauvinistic for her to accept, their conflicts are irresoluble, his verbal and physical abuses too much to endure. In a final decision, Jadine breaks her relationship with him, flies back to Isles des Chevaliers, reclaims her mink coat and resolves to return to the lifestyle she is familiar with, a way of life that operates predictably, that has no emotional pitfalls and does not demand more from her than hard work, a life she can cope with and is manageable as it poses no questions that can unnerve her or shatter her self-esteem. After the emotional and psychological upheaval of her affair with Son, she is unprepared to face the complications of another responsibility—towards her aunt and uncle and hardens herself in the face of Ondine's expectations to tell her, "I don't want to learn how to be the kind of woman you're talking about because I don't want to be that kind of woman" (284). She hurts her aunt immeasurably by negating her lifetime's sacrifice and rejecting her concept of a "real" woman. Jadine has left behind the legacy of misery and exploitation (as sexual animals and workhorses) to insulate herself in her self-created world of luxury and comfort, secure at last if lonely, unperturbed and majestic in a self-defined role that is intellectually and materially rewarding if barren emotionally.

Few women in Morrison's novels come under Category V(b). Lilly and Marcelline of *Song of Solomon*, Lady Jones of *Beloved* and Alice Manfred of *Jazz* could be categorized as blue collar workers. However, Violet of *Jazz* is a hairdresser now and her transition from Category II to V(b) has brought improvement in her financial status and standard of living. She is not a licensed hairdresser and because her rates are lower than professional hairdressers, they complain that she takes away their business. Unlike them, she is a houseworker and has often braved chilly winds, freezing temperatures and many a time in her hurry to keep an appointment has slid on ice to reach a customer's house. In hard times, she has done hair for prostitutes whom others viewed with contempt but she could testify to their generosity. Because Violet has come to this category later in life and by dint of her labor having been originally a poor, black woman so she has been included in the latter category.

In *Song of Solomon*, Lilly and Marcelline were both hairdressers who jointly ran a hairdressing saloon and catered to the local African-American women, most of whom were their regular customers—judging by the fact that their business was doing fine. Both women were engaged throughout the day and often they hardly had time for a hurried bite between attending demanding customers. The reasonably "respectable" status of hairdressing seems to suggest that here was one job for African-American women which could not be denigrated as unskilled labor. Some basic professional training was necessary to maintain this kind of a job which required skilled hands. Still, it was "woman's work" and the white women hardly ever attended saloons run by black women. Their clientele was limited within the confines of African-American society.

Lady Jones in *Beloved* was addressed so with a respect that she deserved. She had received education because it had been her privilege to be chosen for a colored girls' normal school in

Pennsylvamia on account of her light complexion and yellow hair—assets in particular circumstances and a curse in others. Her complexion indicated her mixed blood and being a mulatto placed her at an advantage in comparison to her darker siblings. So she was sneeringly referred to as the "white nigger" (*B*, 304) by her own siblings and other people of the community. After her husband's death, she lived alone in her house, teaching black children till they became old enough for chores or jobs. Her invariable politeness and her 'superiority' by virtue of her education and complexion made her a lady in others' eyes. To make up for the advantage of education she had acquired, she taught those children who were not chosen. The Negroes of Cincinnati had no school or hospital to serve their needs. So, she decided to run a school and started her coaching classes at home, in her parlour—a private institution where she taught the neglected children of the local black community, charging a minimum fee of a nickel a month. She loved the innocent, young faces of her students, their clear eyes and unpolluted smiles. She derived a satisfaction from her job that was rare and precious. It was her dignified way of answering back her own community that had hated her fair skin and mixed lineage. In Denver she had recognized an intelligent student with a will to learn and when she stopped coming to school, she approached Baby Suggs to offer free coaching for the child. It was her attachment to her students and the personal care she took with them that encouraged Denver to approach her after twelve years.

Lady Jones' mission in life has been to impart education to black children so that they could have better options in life and their chances of moving out and acquiring better jobs would improve. It was important for her because she believed that they had been deprived sadly. So she labored to better the lot of the children of her community—a job that was more a mission than a livelihood and that added meaning to her life. In her role as a schoolteacher, she achieved dignity and respect. Lady Jones' generous and loving heart could, even today, motivate her to find the energy and willingness to help Denver and old and tired as she now was, she took up another mission late in life—arranging help for her through the Church committee, encouraging her to meet people, giving her gifts of food and teaching her in her free time. She initiated Denver into a new world of confidence and self-dependence, thus "inaugurat(ing) her life in the world as a woman" (305).

Beneath Lady Jones' lady-like grace, polished manners and self-contained aloofness, lay a vulnerable woman who had been hurt and humiliated by inverted racist snobbery and the pain of being misunderstood by her own community. She had spent her life making amends for a fault that was not hers but without rancour or bitterness. Having the courage to face censure, she did not alienate herself in trying to prove her superiority which she well could have done. Instead of attempting to move up in the color scale, she reclaimed her race by marrying the darkest man available. Though not condoning or supporting the superstitious beliefs of the ignorant women of her community, she still believed in community ties and the strength of bonding in sisterhood. Lady Jones' role as labor was a rare one in that era where black women were mostly illiterate and is laudable in that she had labored for community development instead of individual advancement and in so doing not only proved a point but gained a depth of understanding, humane concern and set an example in her own small way.

In *Jazz*, Alice Manfred is the aunt of the girl who was killed by Joe Trace for betraying his love. Surprisingly, a strange bond develops between Violet and Alice. Alice is a reputed seamstress who is known in the ladies' circles for her impeccable taste, expertise as a seamstress and her housekeeping prowess. She cannot tolerate slovenliness and her obsession with neatness is admired by less efficient women. The restraint, femininity, decorum and maidenly virtues which make up her exterior are some of the essential features of white womanhood which middle-class black women emulated. Alice Manfred is like the "genteel", usually light colored or pale-skinned Negroes who work in semi-skilled occupations (fine stitching). Family appearances are all important for them, though reality is otherwise and the fear of unwed pregnancy (the norm in lower class Negroes) makes them repress their natural urges. She keeps under careful control the dark thoughts and wild desires that rage inside. Inside, she is that wild, black woman who crushes to a pulp the body of her husband's mistress by riding over her again and yet again. It is this private dream that makes her identify with Violet who had tried to violate her dead niece. The two African-American women have in common their husbands' betrayal, though each deals differently with her turbulent emotions.

Alice is almost always working when Violet pays her visits as they converse, she continues to work at ironing her laundry or stitching or cooking. The discipline under which Alice was brought up, the middle-class values which were imposed on her, were responsible for her becoming the way she was, claiming to be a perfectionist, very proud of her work. Alice Manfred lived in her Clifton apartment home where she brought up her younger sister's only child under strict vigilance. Alice had been afraid all her life—her insecurities having taken root in childhood where a conventional, middle-class upbringing had taught her to remain on guard against any possibilities of "wild" or "immoral" behaviour. Obsessed as she was by the haunting fear of danger that lay just beyond the boundaries of her home, she "gathered her rope" (75) to leash her life and her charges within the safe boundary of her neat and well-kept apartment. When her job required her to work away from home for two months, she left Dorcas in the charge of the Miller sisters who looked after four other children of the building while their parents were out working. She prided herself at her calmness, controlled dignity and self-respect that did not allow her to plead with her two-timing husband or fight his lover. Like the Millers who trained their charges to ignore temptations and the call of the heart because it could lead one to dangerous paths, so Alice warned Dorcas about the white men who beckoned black girls with folded dollar bills between their fingers and the "low-down" (73) music that promised primitive pleasures. She shepherded her niece into the sanctuary of her home, did not allow her to wear stylish dresses, tied her luxuriant hair in braids but could not prevent her from thinking "wild" thoughts. The "rope" that she had "gathered" could not hold back the natural sexual urges that she had tried to repress. Like Sister Carrie in Naylor's *Bailey's Cafe* and Helene wright in Morrison's *Sula*, she tried to confine and control her niece but failed. The prim and unfailingly polite woman, much admired for her impeccable taste in clothes, excellence in her profession, perfection of her housekeeping, the flawless presentation and laying out of her dinner table, first-class ironing and virtuous, sex-less, unexciting single life, found herself conversing with the woman whose husband had killed her niece. After having failed to protect the one person in life for whom she had been responsible, Alice began to see things with more clarity and sharpness. So when Violet came to visit her each day, she let her in and shared personal information of a kind she had never thought to share with anyone before. The alienation that Alice Manfred and Violet both feel bring them close, though they belong to different social classes and Violet is the kind of woman whom Alice had always consciously avoided—women who could not control their passions or their violence, black women who picked up the knife to take revenge. In essence, Alice's friendship with Violet is the bridging of a chasm between the middle-class, profession-proud, lady-like seamstress and the psychologically unstable, struggling, black woman who had, through sheer determination and grit, worked her way up to an uptown apartment. So when Alice makes clear her prejudiced contempt against the prostitutes, Violet points out that the profession they had chosen was often a compulsion, not a choice. Alone, working, secure in her apartment house and totally without responsibilities after Dorcas' death, Alice Manfred is at last confronted with all that she had held at an arm's length in Violet—a woman whom she first abhorred, then pitied and finally shared a friendship with. The breaking of barriers forges ties that could give new meaning to both their lives—women from disparate backgrounds—one a woman who had been afraid of the streets, the other entirely comfortable walking them. Their roles are inverted when Violet, with all her strangeness, brings a measure of self-understanding in Alice and Alice lends to her the calm composure that she lacks. The satisfaction of work well-done had once been enough for Alice but after her niece's death there arose in her an acute need for soul searching, which she could do only in Violet's unpretentious presence.

Category V(c) consisting of prostitutes, pub-owners, brothel-owners, street-walkers, call-girls include women of a tough profession associated with the stigma and the raunchiness of sex. Besides menial work, trading of one's body was the other option available to most black women both in rural and urban areas. The rate of prostitution in Negro localities was exceptionally high (see Introduction, pp. 24-25, 44) due to which white men haunted black neighborhoods for the easy availability of sexual gratification. Morrison's representation of prostitutes is varied and complex. In *The Bluest Eye*, she presents three prostitutes who have taken up the profession not out of pressing and unavoidable circumstances but because they saw it as the easier alternative than being a domestic—a lifestyle that may have branded them as fallen women but gave them a security and comfort they could not have afforded otherwise. Of course, the early exposure of young black girls to the seedy side of life and the easy pleasure of sex have contributed towards their dissipation and Morrison's awareness and concern about the sociological factors and attitudes that have worked behind the making of such women has emerged in her narratives through the weaving of little details in the fabric of the backdrop of her novels.

To Pecola of *TBE*, the three prositutes who lived in an apartment above the Breedloves' house were fascinating. The interchanges between Pecola and Mari, interspersed with spicy comments from China and silent laughter from Poland, their easy banter and dirty talk, project them as hard-headed and calculating sex-workers whose pride in their sexual prowess is evident in the obvious relish and carelessness with which they describe their sexual exploits. In describing them as "three merry gargoyles. Three merry harridans" who "did not belong to those generations of prostitutes created in novels, with great and generous hearts...taking money incidentally and humbly..." (*TBE*, 42) for their services, Morrison, clearly, does not want to romanticize their reason for turning to prostitution. "They looked back on their own youth as a period of ignorance and regretted that they had not made more of it.... They were whores in whores' clothing, whores who had never been young and had no word for innocence" (43). Upon learning that their bodies and sex were commodities they could sell, they had never looked back again. Their hatred for all men and respect for "good Christian colored women" (43) are pointers to their identification of the former as the ultimate enemy as perpetrators of sexist exploitation of all women and sympathy with the latter for their being victims of a system of male domination which they bear so heroically and the duties and labor that they undertake in tending their families as also a craving for respectability that they refuse to admit. However, underneath their cock-sureness and brimming-over audacity, they are insecure and worried about a future that promises nothing but failing youth, dwindling business and emotional barrenness.

Rochelle, Helene Wright's mother in *Sula* was a Creole prostitute (of mixed European and African blood) who worked in an exotic brothel frequented by well-to-do men. She led a life of freedom and luxury, able to afford a lifestyle impossible for black women of that age. Helene, reared under the vigilant eye of her grandmother, was trained to fear and abhor this life of moral degradation. Ironically, her mother's profession had freed her from inhibitions while Helene had traded her freedom for the dissatisfaction of the confined life of a middle-class housewife.

As the owner of the local pubhouse and brothel, Mary of *SOS* may have enjoyed the independence of a businesswoman but the insecurities that are inherent in a business of this nature, the stigma attached to it and the dangers with which it is fraught cannot be overlooked. One is bound to view this situation vis-à-vis the white American scenario where this kind of work is naturally accepted as "man's work" requiring enough mettle and toughness not expected from women, especially white women. Black women, except those who had achieved ladyhood by virtue of belonging to the moneyed class, on the contrary were supposed to be stronger and tough enough to handle such situations.

Sweet of *SOS* was unique in her own way, not one of the stereotypically bitter and foul mouthed prostitutes one finds in *The Bluest Eye*. Sweet is an African-American woman who takes pleasure in her 'work'—the question of morality does not cloud the clarity of purpose—she is willing to provide every comfort to her tenants from whom she earns her keep. Her lack of inhibitions points more to an amorality than immorality. Morrison, in representing Sweet, seems to hold hypocrisy at an arm's length and we find a woman neither at odds nor dissatisfied with her socially degrading 'work'. Again in *Tar Baby*, the teenaged Nommo is a streetwalker, beneath whose foul mouth and burning eyes is the hurt, bravado and loneliness of a young girl exposed at such a young age to the harsh realities of life—realities that had toughened her but had not erased the vulnerability in the shape of her head or the bewilderment in her eyes.

Under Category VII comes Morrison's Sula in *Sula*, the brilliantly delineated, utterly unconventional, thoroughly unpredictable central character who defies every attempt of defining, limiting or casting into a mould her role or behaviour. Sula was an only child in a matriarchal household headed by her grandmother Eva. Growing up in a household where there was the constant hubbub of voices, people coming and going as they pleased (boarders, Hannah and Eva's menfriends, children adopted by Eva and guests), noise and disorder, Sula retreated into her girlish daydreams in the uninvaded privacy of the attic. The women of the household were preoccupied with their own problems and pleasures, where a young girl was not paid much attention to. Unlike Pilate and Reba in *Song of Solomon* who showered all their love and attentions upon Hagar, Eva was dominating and Hannah indifferent. There was no cohesive factor of stable relationships for a young and growing girl to anchor upon in that crowded house. Sula therefore preferred the calm neatness of her friend Nel's house where Nel's mother's attentions seemed to be focussed always on Nel. In reality, Helene's attentions were more upon Nel's external behaviour, appearance and manners than on her as a person. So both Sula and Nel were "(d)aughters of distant mothers and incomprehensible fathers" (*S*, 52) due to which they were drawn to each other in a friendship where each complimented and completed the other, an emotional bonding that they could not forge with their mothers and the absence of a father figure that both felt in their houses. During their formative years, both were acutely conscious of the disadvantage they suffered as African-American females and they "use(d) each other to grow on" (52). Apparently (during those years), Nel was stronger and more consistent of the two—Sula being whimsical and unpredictable. However, Sula's fierce independence and protectiveness towards Nel made her slash off her own fingertip once, to frighten a group of white boys who had blocked their way to bully them. As Morrison says later, Sula was "like any artist with no art form" (121) whose unexpressed but great creative potential found no outlet and therefore became dangerous, making her restless and pre-occupied. Sula felt no compulsion to be consistent with herself, and the life she lived was experimental. She experimented with situations in her life to taste to the full every aspect that life had to offer—fear, hatred, violence, love—pleasing only herself in whatever she did and pleasing others only when their pleasure pleased her. Sula could not confine herself within the codified norms of accepted and expected behaviour. Knowing well her limitations as an African-American woman, and that "all freedom and triumph was forbidden" (52) to her, she began a quest of finding her true "self" and transcend limitations instead of existing in self-imposed or society-imposed roles. For Sula, Nel's friendship had been the central relationship in her life for they were two persons but one soul, their thoughts and deeds matched in perfect harmony. Nel's marriage to Jude was for her a betrayal that made her leave Medallion to go North on Nel's wedding day. The singling out of Nel by Jude and her acceptance of him established his priority over Sula in her eyes and "selected her away" (84) from Sula's friendship. Sula left Medallion without a backward glance, severing her ties with her hometown as swiftly as one would the birth-chord choking the newborn child. She returned to Medallion after a gap of ten years, accompanied by a plague of robins, to die, like them, in her nest.

Sula mentioned after coming back that she had been in college, ostensibly wanting to complete her education after graduating from high school in Medallion. However, she had not come back even after college was over and from the scattered references and rumours that rose surrounding her mysterious occupation and whereabouts indicate that she may have taken up prostitution to keep herself, as she insisted that she was not one to "work" for a living. African-American women, even educated ones, were hard put to find jobs, other than menial in the 1930s, even in the urban areas. It was only after 1950 that the job scenario began to change gradually. For a woman like Sula, who was not ready to labor with her hands the only other option was to sell her body. From her reminiscences it can be assumed that she had men friends who supported her during those years in the city. Her lovers gave her money and gifts and for Sula, who had always as a child seen her mother and grandmother consort with a constant stream of boyfriends, especially Hannah who had always looked refreshed after the act of sex, it was the easiest thing to have chosen as an enjoyable means of livelihood. When Sula returned to Medallion, she was dressed like a "movie star" (90) and had just arrived from Cincinnati in style. All this is a clear indication of the lifestyle she had followed or her past occupation as a high level prostitute or hired escort, which had given her enough financial independence to pursue her pleasures. However, as Sula admits to Nel, the big cities she had been to (Detroit, New Orleans, New York, Philadelphia, Macon and San Diego) after leaving Nasheville (where she had lived initially) were like big Medallions. Sula's quest for novel experiences, new joys and new relationships had culminated in her turning inward upon herself where she found her true mate. So external circumstances ceased to matter for her as the more she travelled, the more restless she grew. Only when she turned her mind's eye upon herself did she discover the true joy she was looking for. Sula was possessive about no one, as she had not attached herself to any relationship, unlike other women including Nel and having grown up in a household where all men were thought available, she saw no reason not to have an affair with Jude. The hurt that Nel felt at her best friend's betrayal was incomprehensible to Sula for she had never experienced the intimacy of marriage. Sula's return to Medallion changed not only Nel's life, but the men and women of Medallion's black community because Morrison says, Sula's presence helped others to define themselves. For Nel, the return of her best friend was like "getting the use of an eye back, having a cataract removed" (95), who brought back the humor into her life and the mundaneness of routine chores acquired new significance in her presence. Even the customary love for Jude that had become a habit of her conjugal life acquired a new dimension. It was Nel's predictable and conventional reaction at the betrayal that shattered their friendship in the end because Nel, like the other women of Medallion, chose to suffer in her role as the victimised and wronged wife, choosing self-righteous anger and bitterness instead of the freedom that Sula had forced upon both her and Jude. When Sula left Jude for other men, he chose to leave for Detroit—a choice he could make because of the freedom thrust upon him.

With the same disregard towards responsibilities, Sula sent Eva to an old people's home soon after her return. She did not see eye to eye with her grandmother who wanted her to get married and settled, pointing out that she and Hannah had lived as they had lived because circumstances had compelled them to do so. Sula was living as she did, by choice, for no decisions could be forced upon her. Totally free of ego, ambition and greed for money, status, property, attention and compliments, she had no need to justify herself to others, or even to herself, due to which she often acted wilfully, without guilt or afterthought.

She set her own paradigms of behaviour and soon the community of blacks in Medallion had convinced themselves of Sula's evil nature and branded her as pariah. The most damning rumour against her was her supposed liaison with white men with whom she was known to have lain willingly (not raped)—a crime that merited no mercy in those days in the eyes of black people. So the women of Medallion, smug in the knowledge of their own righteousness, envious of Sula's slim and youthful looks and life free of burdens and bondage, angered at her casual rejection of their men after one or few sexual encounters, hurt at her disinterested sampling of their elaborate dishes prepared for Church dinners or suppers, and in effect her shunning of all gestures of communication and participation in community activities, turned their hatred upon her with a vengeance. Sula had violated all conceivable norms of social behaviour and her sins were unpardonable according to the tenets of the African-American community of Medallion. Hated as she was as indifferent, even cruel in her roles as daughter, granddaughter and lover, her negative qualities ironically inspired the Medallion women to assert their goodness and display their positive traits. As they could, unlike Sula, claim identity as persons only in their imposed roles, in her presence they became solicitious wives, caring daughters-in-law and conscientious mothers. Sula's presence acted as a moral catalyst, because her amorality had been labelled as immorality. In essence, it was Sula's freedom of choice and her ability to live life as she wanted that these women could never achieve and therefore condemned. The "free fall" and danger of living only for oneself, to test the pain and taste the pleasures of life, was beyond them. So they hung in their meaningless existence, suspended from the web of their own making, out of their own spittle clinging desperately to the secure but shackling bondage lest they "fall". So Sula's isolated victory can never be theirs because Sula lives and dies by choice.

In her role as a lover, the most intimate of all relationships physically and emotionally, Sula disliked the position of surrender beneath her sexual partner because in that instant of coital exhilaration she exulted in the knowledge of her own limitless power. With Ajax, her fulfilment was complete in that he was not like any other man she had met. Where her earlier lovers spoke "the same language of love" and "taught her nothing but love tricks, shared nothing but worry, gave nothing but money" that had made her realise that a lover could never be a true comrade for a woman, Ajax spoke a new language of love which was free from commitment but full of passion. He surprised her with unusual and imaginative gifts and seeing in him a version of herself, she longed to "reach out and touch with an ungloved hand" (205) his inner self. She had touched her own inner self thus, and was intimate with it and she had wanted but not been able to do the same with others. For the first time in her life, she discovered a possessiveness in herself about Ajax and sensing Sula's newly developed emotional dependence upon him and the expectation of commitment in their relationship, Ajax withdrew precipitately, abandoning her with a finality that left her face to face with her own introspections and loneliness again. Earlier, admiring in Sula her independence, toughness and wisdom, he had refused to baby or protect her. He thought her as a woman who was living her own life, taking her own decisions, dealing efficiently with life and disinterested in "nailing him" (127). During their lovemaking, Sula had always been positioned above him, flushed, ecstatic and free. On the day Ajax left her, for the first time in their lovemaking, he dragged Sula beneath him—her gesture of surrender driving him away from her forever.

In 1940, as Sula lay dying in her house, Nel came to look after her friend, to meet Sula who was, she thought, as arrogant as before. Sula's forthright honesty had always disconcerted people who had taken it as pride. She had refused always to make her role as labor or work the pivot of her existence and even in penury, as she lay in pain and with no money to buy food or medicine, she refused to do so. Nel's words put in a nutshell the community women's prejudice against Sula who had transcended the limitations that held them captive in an invisible slavery:

> You can't do it all. You a woman and a colored woman at that. You can't act like a man. You can't be walking around all independent-like, doing whatever you like, taking what you want, leaving what you don't. (142)

Nel had designated independence, irresponsibility and freedom, to be the prerogative of men, and women, especially African-American women, could not hope to have that freedom, tied as they were to their burdens and responsibilities—especially their children. In Sula's reply, we hear the triumph of a black woman claiming her freedom of choice and her innate strength in defining herself:

> You say I'm a woman and colored. Ain't that the same as being a man? (142)

The individualised existence that Sula champions shatters the notion of the collective and the communitarian bonds that have traditionally sustained black women and that she has despised. Unlike Sethe in *Beloved* whose isolation was forced upon her, Sula chooses to live alone and die alone—an African-American woman who has subverted the role of the female, living only for herself, rejoicing in her loneliness, shunning others even when she is in need of help. Earlier, she had refused to offer sympathy to Jude when he whined a tale of injustice done to him. The biting sarcasm of her words, though relieved by the witty humor, however did not deter from the African-American woman's consciousness of the difference between the African-American male and female situation.

As Nel turned to leave Sula after a futile exchange that left her more convinced of Sula's pride and "bad" ness, Sula asked her a question that startled as well as shook her—a question that overturned the paradigm of goodness and badness as society defined or interpreted it, and by the double standards it applied for men and women. So Sula asked Nel how she could claim that it was she who was "good" because she chose to behave in the way people expected a mother and a wronged wife to behave and Sula was "bad" because she had chosen not to live in a misery inflicted upon her by others. In 1965 (at the close of the novel), Nel visits Sula's grave—an African-American woman whose funeral had not been attended by her community (that gathered on the death of even prostitutes—their "fallen sisters") unpardoned even in death, an outcaste still—only to be hit by the sudden realisation that in all those years of dry-eyed mourning and contained grief—she had been missing Sula, not Jude. Unlike Pilate in *Song of Solomon* who, in spite of her alienation had not shunned people, Sula lived in a glorious loneliness and even in death, rejecting communitarian values, content in the knowledge of her 'self', defying mediocrity and role definitions.

Pilate in *SOS* stands out in the novel as a solitary figure of nobility, self-pride and immense willpower. She is an African-American woman who has transcended the troubles in her life to acquire an imperturbably calm attitude towards life, as if its trials and tribulations could be taken into stride as casually as she chewed bits of strings, twigs or rubber bands. The absence of her navel was to all a sign that she had no link with the past. However, it is Pilate who has always borne responsibility for past action, who has never denied facing the consequences of her own actions and who has taught Milkman the meaning of taking on life's responsibilities.

The male protagonist Milkman's life is tied to Pilate even before he is born. She saves him from being killed by his own father (her brother) while in his mother's womb. Pilate has always been helpful, generous and broad-minded, ready to offer warm hospitality to every person who stepped inside her threshold. She would harm no one unless they hurt her daughter or granddaughter about whom she was fiercely protective. Unlike Ruth, Pilate has had no formal education but she has travelled widely. Her one geography book, the only book she has ever read, has been her guide and comfort. Pilate is that widely travelled, vastly experienced, totally self-sufficient African-American woman who has never needed the aid of any man to conduct her life. When her brother and she parted ways, she had to fend for herself. She had never looked back and never shed a single tear since the time they had spent in hiding to escape the white men who were on their trail. The confinement had driven her wild as she was used to open spaces, freedom and direct contact with nature, revelling at the feel of vibrant earth beneath her unshodden feet. Pilate was grounded solidly in the roots of her African-American identity and culture and had forever carried the memory of the race within her. Ironically, she had always been denied stability, roots and security. In a way she had defied them always, had been as free as the wind and as impulsive. It was Pilate therefore, and only Pilate who could act as guide to Milkman, lead him towards his roots and help him to rediscover his racial and cultural identity.

Pilate's experiences of work had been varied and colourful. For her, labor has been spontaneous and need based. As a young girl, she had seen her father shot at and blown off the fence he was sitting on, guarding his property. Since then she had always been on the run, at first with her brother at her side to protect her and later, after their separation, alone, journeying through the woods and hills, from town to town and state to state. Her own account of the amount of travelling she had done and the numerous jobs she had undertaken to stay alive, clothe and feed herself and provide for her family is an understatement in itself. She has always, very casually, side-stepped the painful details of her own hardships but one only has to be sensitive enough to realise what unsurmountable trials a young, pretty and defenceless African-American girl must have faced and overcome to achieve the contained confidence she had today. Her still eyes and animated mouth spoke volumes and told untold stories.

In the course of her travels, Pilate had sustained herself by taking up any job that came her way. The first job that she got was with a preacher's family as a resident maid in exchange of bed and board from where she was dismissed by her mistress on account of her husband's sexual misdemeanour (an innocent victim, she had to suffer the consequences and was the one to be blamed—a job hazard for young and unattached girls always). Having accumulated no wages, she was penniless when she was turned out, nor could she find another job in that area where the preacher was well known. The only advantage she had gained in this job was that she had been sent to school where she acquired her precious geography book. She then joined a group of migrant laborers (cotton pickers) with whom she travelled for three years moving from state to state. She made friends easily but was abandoned precipitately as soon as the absence of her navel was discovered. Regarded with fear and pity as one born unnaturally, she was alienated again and again wherever she went. Knowing how to team harvest, she looked for job opportunities with such regent groups but was prepared, from experience, to rely on herself and only herself to fight it out with fate and great odds. The steady pattern in her life since then became travelling, new jobs, new bonds and abandonment/betrayal. She was also engaged in seasonal work such as brick making, working in shipyards or in iron factories but the hostility of the women on account of her prettiness and innocent appeal did not allow for settlement. On one occasion, after being left behind by yet another group she had joined, she took up work at the local laundry, having rejected the option of trading sex in the whorehouse—the only other option available to black women for earning money. She worked, ate and slept at the laundry itself, saving boarding charges and was given staunch support by her fellow workers when the blood running from her split knuckles spoilt the white sheets—a pointer to the group loyalty and solidarity of black women who usually covered for each other. From washing clothes at a hotel next, she joined a colony of economically self-sufficient island Negroes where her hard work (she hoed, fished, planted, helped out at the stills) and resilience generated a goodwill that stood her in good stead. It was there that she became an unwed mother as she refused to marry the father of her child (her island lover), after which she continued with her travelling to finally settle in her brother's town as a bootlegger. Pilate's belief that one should atone for one's past actions by taking responsibility for the same is a pointer to the remarkable sense of morality that is inherent in her. Her posthumous connection with her father suggests that she had inherited from him the rich legacy of independence, commitment, courage, and strong ties with the earth—a legacy that her brother had forfeited in his avarice.

In Pilate's life, there had been only a few stable relationships with men. Her father whom she loved and adored was shot before her eyes. Her brother, who had been very caring and close to her, had changed into a cold-hearted, hard-headed man, for whom real estate and money were the be-all and end-all of human life. Her island lover was the only man who had given her love and was ready for lifelong commitment. Hers was an all-woman household where men came and went (Reba's countless lovers) but never were allowed to call the cards. Pilate chose bootlegging as a means of earning money because at that time, with the price of foreign liquor shooting up, people looked for local stuff which was cheaper and readily available. The market was ripe for wine trade and she knew how to brew it. Though unlicensed, she was hardly ever troubled by the police because she never allowed her customers to drink within her premises and there were no drunken brawls in her compound. She has managed to procure the basic necessities of life for her family naturally and it seemed effortlessly. Pilate was and is that side of African-American womanhood which is the most natural, unhampered and unafraid. Pilate's fight was against hatred. In her roles as mother, granddaughter, aunt and sister-in-law, she had shown deep compassion. Pilate's grief at Hagar's death is a dark, tangible mass of pain which only a woman who had sheltered, protected and cherished her only child's only child could feel. Her untiring labor of love had not achieved fruition. There was no solace, and no way to reconcile oneself to this untimely and needless death. Especially for a woman who had such a positive outlook towards life, who had taught others to live, it was difficult to accept the defeat which her granddaughter's death meant for her. It was doubly painful because the man who had been responsible for Hagar's death was her nephew whose life she had saved even before he was born. Her astounding capacity of forgiveness is tested when Milkman meets her after this tragedy. One cannot help admiring the ability of this woman to rationalise in a situation where anyone would be prejudiced. Powerful emotion as that she has felt has never clouded her thought. She has taught Milkman and Guitar how to appreciate the colors of nature, the flavour of good wine, the taste of a perfectly boiled egg. Her finer sensibilities have defined the animated vital persona that she exudes and Pilate is a fictionalised representation of African-American womanhood that is so appealing because so warmly humane.

Pilate stands out as an extraordinary figure of African-American womanhood—competent and confident, passionate yet level headed, independent and generous—a marvellous combination of will, funk, humour and eccentricities—kind hearted and compassionate. She has the capacity to handle her roles with pluck and aplomb—she has never neglected her past nor ever denied her present. She has learnt from her mistakes, never to repeat them. She has the strength of a matriarch and the vulnerability of an affectionate woman—in all her roles and responsibilities she has never let herself down. She has, above all, never been self-righteous, which puts her on a separate plane from Eva in *Sula* who had been proud of her self-sacrifice. In Pilate, there is a wonderful balance of the past heritage, present need and future thought—an openness and receptivity which places her as a sensitive and complex character at the centre of the novel. More than Milkman, she is the protagonist in *Song of Solomon*, her story providing the very fabric of that process of self-discovery, which she initiated in Milkman.

Category VIII includes conjure women—the only women of the race who have an indigenious profession—the only occupation involving skill and knowledge (traditional) and that gives them power, respect and freedom. These are healers, doctors, root-workers, functioning with the wealth of traditional tribal knowledge of medicinal herbs, roots, magic, lore and myth—thus acting as bridges between the past and present. Morrison's *The Bluest Eye* and *Sula* have two conjure women—M'Dear in the former and Ajax's mother in the latter novel are represented in their roles as such.

Ajax's mother was an evil conjure woman by profession, respected and feared widely, whose neglect of her children amounting to absolute freedom given them made her an object of worship in their eyes. She was the only woman whom Ajax had admired and found interesting in all his life before meeting Sula because of her toughness and independence. The weight of her "hoary knowledge" (*Sula*, 126) drew adoration from her seven children and esteem from others. The freedom she allowed them was in effect the freedom she had exercised for herself by refusing to labor in conventional roles or exist only as a mother or a woman. She had not conformed to the role of an ideal mother and had stubbornly continued in her pursuit of the occult and had remained pre-occupied with her exciting occupation that allowed the free play of inventiveness and imagination, wisdom and practice of medicine. Because she had lived her own life independently and efficiently, expecting nothing from her children and having no possessive love for them, she aroused her son's admiration, generosity and thoughtfulness. The nature of her job made her elusive, and also indifferent to conventional modes of behaviour, inspiring her children's awe and unfailing faithfulness and love. This African-American woman did not bind herself even to her children in love and they in turn did not feel hemmed in by a possessive mother-love. In making space for herself, she allowed space for her children. However, parhaps because of the absence of strong family ties, her son Ajax was afraid of emotional commitment for whom expectations spelt the end of a relationship and personal freedom was more valuable than any relationship. He was unequipped psychologically to deal with emotional bonding and the thought of loving anyone other than his mother was unthinkable. His mother made a modest income out of her skills and needed no one to support her. Yet her children plied her with gifts out of adoration, reflecting the

African-American society's attitude towards these wise conjure women in whom they had unshakeable faith and whom they approached for the remedy of all maladies and ailments—physical, emotional, psychological and supernatural.

M'Dear lived alone in a shack near the woods and was a competent woman reputed as a midwife and diagnostician. Unlike most conjure women who summon up a vision of old age, strange appearance and a stooped and wrinkled frame, M'Dear was a woman of towering height and youthful looks, who used her cane not for support, but for communication. M'Dear like Miranda Day in Naylor's *Mama Day* functioned more like a doctor than a magician and the people of the community had great faith in her diagnosis and cure. The fact that she lived alone and that the preacher took the trouble to provide transport for her indicate her independence and the special reverence and respect that was accorded to her by everyone.

The emerging pattern in the course of the analysis based on the hypothetical categorisation of African-American women as labor indicates the changing labor roles of these women from slavery to the present times. In tracing the "labor of sorrow" and the "labor of love" (terms borrowed from Jacqueline Jones) of African-American women, one can identify progression and improvement in their situation that is heartening, as also peculiar problems that have been inherent in their new labor roles.

The changing roles of African-American women as labor from slavery to the present can be traced clearly in Morrison's novels and one is left with the possibility of more meaningful roles opening up for them in future. Their evolution from the status of laborers in menial jobs where work was a necessity to the status of educated, conscious women for whom work is a matter of choice, however limited, marks a change in their situation—though the process of change has been, slow, long and full of strife.

NOTES AND REFERENCES

1. Nancy J. Peterson, "Introduction: Canonizing Toni Morrison," *Modern Fiction Studies, Toni Morrison Double Issue.* Vol. 39, Nos. 3&4, Fall/Winter, 1993. Purdue Research Foundation, p. 464.

2. *Ibid.*, p. 465.
3. Toni Morrison, "The Pain of Being Black: An Interview with Toni Morrison." With Bonnie Angelo. Taylor-Gurthrie, pp. 255-61.
4. Peterson, *op. cit.*, p. 466.
5. Elizabeth, Schultz, "Free in Fact and at Last: The Image of the Black Woman in Black American Fiction." *What Manner of Woman.* New York: Basil Blackwell, 1977, p. 317.
6. Toni Morrison, "Conversation with Toni Morrison". *Black Women Writers at Work.* New York: Continuum, 1983, p. 118.
7. *Ibid.*, "An Interview with Sandi Russel," *Critical Essays on Toni Morrison.* Ed. Nellie Y. McKay. Boston: G.K. Hall, 1988, pp. 46, 54.
8. Rosemarie K. Lester, "An Interview with Toni Morrison," Hessian Radio Network. Frankfurt. West Germany. Quoted in Nellie Y. McKay, pp. 48-49.
9. Patrick Bryce Bjork, *The Novels of Toni Morrison: The Search for Self and Place Within the Community.* New York: Peter Lang Publishers, 1992, p. 64.
10. *Ibid.*
11. *Ibid.*
12. *Ibid.*, p. 67.
13. Elizabeth Schultz, *What Manner of Woman,* p. 322.
14. Henry Louis Jr. Gates and Nellie Y. McKay. Eds., *The Norton Anthology of African-American Literature.* New York: W.W. Norton and Company Inc. 1997, pp. 55-57.
15. A term used by Susan Willis in her essay "Eruptions of Funk: Historicizing Toni Morrison". *Black American Literature Forum* 16 (Spr. 1982), pp. 34-42.
16. A Negro character popularized by Harriet Beecher Stowe's *Uncle Tom's Cabin* (1852)—projecting and reinforcing the stereotype of an obedient, submissive, self-sacrificing, slave.
17. Quoted in Linden Peach, *Toni Morrison.* New York: St. Martin's Press, 1995, p. 44.
18. The plantation adaptation of the original Tar Baby folktale which ran as follows: A white farmer (the fox) wanted to catch a rabbit who he thought was stealing his cabbages. He set up a doll made of sticky tar whose aloof hauteur angered the rabbit and instead of avoiding it, he embraced it and got stuck, to the farmer's glee. Finally, however, the rabbit outwitted the farmer by asking not to be thrown on to the briar patch. The farmer, convinced that it would be a painful punishment for the rabbit, threw him into it, only to be hoodwinked as it was

the rabbit's natural habitat, who made good his escape. [*The Norton Anthology*, pp. 120-21]

19. Patrick Bryce Bjork, *The Novels of Toni Morrison: The Search for Self and Place Within the Community*, p. 113.
20. *Ibid.*, pp. 115-16.
21. Claudia Tate, "Conversation with Toni Morrison", *Black Women Writers at Work*. New York: Continuum, 1983, pp. 117-31.
22. Linden Peach, *Toni Morrison*, p. 85.
23. Terms borrowed from *Jacqueline Jones' Labor of Love, Labor of Sorrow: Black Women, Work and the Family, From Slavery to the Present. New York: Vintage*, 1985.

[Quotations from novels have been indicated by abbreviated names of the novels followed by page numbers within parentheses initially. Thereafter, till another novel is alluded to, numbers in bracket indicate page numbers of the same novel.]

From Despair to Fulfillment: African-American Women as Labor in the Novels of Alice Walker

3

As a novelist, poet, short-story writer, womanist critic, social activist and "apologist"[1] for African-American women, Alice Walker has created her own space in the history of American literature. She has stated emphatically her chief concern as the problems of African-American women and inspired many by her example. Experiencing first hand the rigours of poverty, racial and sexual oppression and degradation (in the lives of women she knew personally, in her mother's as well as in her own life) she grew up to be extremely sensitive to the plights of Southern black women. Growing up in Eatonton, Georgia allowed her daily glimpses into the lives of black women around her, women who suffered daily the abuses of the society and frustrated black men, who labored in the dazed and benumbed state that resulted out of prolonged suffering and who, in spite of their degradation, continued to labor for their homes, their children, their families and their communities keeping alive the spirituality that was embedded in their souls. For Walker, the inexhaustible source of inspiration has been the diverse and richly complex life experience of Southern black women whose endless labor amid the daily violence they endured had rooted them in a cesspool of inexpressible pain and yet, who struggled heroically to achieve a space for themselves and their children and find fulfilment in their severely circumscribed roles. Since the identities of these women had been until recently, submerged in their role identities as laborers and since, for them, all relationships, all emotions and creativity converged on their existence in their roles as laborers, it is not surprising that Alice Walker would explore the possibilities and limitations of their situations in their roles as laborers, wives, mothers, daughters, sisters or mistresses. She represents them in her fiction as women who may or may not overcome the shocking brutalities of their lives—as women who may or may not transcend their realities, who may go mad or die or achieve freedom through their work roles. As an artist, Walker has envisioned the representation of three types of African-American women through her work—black women who were physically brutalised, tormented and driven to a point where they succumbed to death, women who were physically so violated and tortured that they were driven to insanity, and women who, in spite of the ordeals they have endured, have emerged as figures of resilience and fulfillment.[2] Within this framework, the present study attempts to place its hypothesis with its eight categories of women laborers—the slave women, the poor, struggling, working women of the lower class, the middle-class housewives who simulate Southern white ladyhood, the rich housewives, the up and coming professionals, top-ranking officers and successful business women of the emerging black elite class, the black women who defy all categorizations and cannot be confined or limited in their roles—public or private, the political activists and social thinkers who have laboured to achieve goals that are not personal or private and the conjure women—once the figures of power and keepers of African tribal heritage in their labor roles that are largely public/social. Walker's deep involvement, passionate concern and personal identification with the black women of the South has motivated her to represent the lives of these women in her fiction—both short stories and novels as also in her poems. Taking Walker's famous poem[3] dedicated to her mother and the black women of her mother's generation as the central metaphor operating behind her representation of African-American women as labor in her novels, it would be possible to probe into questions posed in this study and arrive at hitherto unearthed dimensions. Walker writes proudly in this poem of the women of her "mama's generation" whose "husky voices", "stout steps" and determined "fists" and "hands" were raised to "batter down doors" for their children. These women spent their lives laboring in the houses and fields of the slave masters and land owners, ironing shirts, scouring, cleaning, cooking, lifting burdens to make a place for their daughters to move into, to "discover" books that they knew they "(m)ust know/without knowing a page/of it/ Themselves." Walker pays tribute to their heroic efforts, which had made a better life possible for their progeny, though they themselves had to stifle their own creativity and natural talents to be drudges and laborers—or to channelise their creativity into mediums available to them—cooking, gardening, quilt making, story telling—that they transformed into art. The four novels by Walker to be examined here are *The Third Life of Grange Copeland, Meridian, The Color Purple,* and *The Temple of My Familiar.*

To begin with, one must refer to the three generational cycles[4] of African-American women that Walker has taken up as a paradigmatic periodised representation in her novels. The first generation of women represented by her belonged to her "mama's generation", the oppressed women who were the mothers, grandmothers, and great-grandmothers of contemporary African-American women. These were her "suspended" women, acknowledged and existing only in the roles of laborers by the era in which they lived, these women were defeated by the external circumstances of their lives—the racist, sexist, classist oppressions and the pain, violence, poverty and degradation of their times. These were women who were, according to Walker,[5] unconscious artists, whose "springs of creativity" could find no release, driving them to a "numb and bleeding madness" and whose spiritual richness ran to waste as their "work-worn, sexually abused bodies" couldn't endure the strain of their "unused and unwanted talent". For Walker, these women who had been rendered mute and caught in the relentless and vicious grip of crucifying circumstances, still attempted, though mostly unsuccessfully, to break free from the shackles of three-fold oppression that threatened to destroy them. These were women who belonged to the first and second category of laborers posited in the hypothesis of this study—women who were primarily laborers (as slaves) and women relegated to the lowest rung of the society (poor, black women)—women for whom life and labor were synonymous, more by compulsion than choice. Walker's personal construct of the black woman's history has operated behind the conscious expression of her instinctive concern for the experiences of black women in her novels.

In *Meridian*, Walker acquaints us with the history of Meridian's maternal ancestors. Meridian herself recalls the story as told by her mother who spoke of their sacrifice with great pride. These are women who belong to Category I of the hypothesis—slave women whose lives were those of bondage, endless labor and unspeakable pain. Mrs. Hill's great-great-grandmother had been a slave. As was usually done, her two children were sold off while they were still very young. Desperate, she followed the man who had bought them and after days of chase, she was able to steal them back. Three times she risked her life to steal back her children from the different owners to whom they had been sold. The third time, she was whipped for her offence till the flesh of her back was ripped open to expose the bone beneath. Even after the inhuman torture, she was not ready to give them up. So she was allowed to keep them on condition that she provide for every scrap of food they ate, which meant that she would have to pay for this with additional labor. They managed to survive somehow, pulling through on account of their mother's determination until they reached teenage when their mother died due to years of overwork and starvation. This slave woman had laid down her life to keep her children with her—motherhood being the only role through which she could claim human dignity in an animal-like, sub-human existence. Her labor of a lifetime bore no fruit however, as on the day of her burial, her children were sold. She had died protecting them from a fate like her own—only to be defeated in death.

Mrs. Hill's great-grandmother had also been a slave whose creativity as a painter was widely reputed. She used to paint beautiful decorations on the barns and was able to earn money for her owner who allowed her to keep some for herself. Over the years, she accumulated enough money to buy freedom not only for herself but also her husband and children. Her paintings were scattered throughout the length and breadth of the state on hundreds of barns and each of the figures she drew had her own trademark—a small contorted face at the centre of each figure. This slave woman had kept alive the artist in herself and exceptional though her case was, there were, even in the times of slavery, women like her (real life counterparts of these fictional representations) who had, through innovative means and the medium available to them, expressed their spontaneous creativity. Walker, who has been lured always by the mysterious reservoir of creativity in black women and their ability to overcome mountainous odds, has represented through this slave woman the potential she has witnessed in real life black women. Historically, slave women of the South, leading degraded lives and laboring endlessly in a benumbed state, yet found the time and the inner strength to use their medium of work as an expression of their art. The small, contorted face that this woman drew at the heart of all her paintings symbolized the excruciating pain of a crying soul craving liberty and the freedom of expression. Perforce, women like her sought joy from their work and made their work their joy.

In *The Third Life of Grange Copeland*, Walker represents Margaret Copeland (wife of Grange Copeland) and Mem (Brownfield's wife) in their roles as laborers, suffering tortures from their husbands who were in turn victims of a racist society. Margaret was a gentle woman whose delicate beauty and clean fragrance filled her son with a sense of security and comfort. However, her gradual degradation and decline as a consequence of her harsh married life, the brutalities she endured from her husband and the poverty that dogged her family in spite of her work from dawn to dusk is a pointer to the hopeless situation in which black women like Margaret were trapped in that era of sharecropping in the South. Her husband Grange was, like thousands of African-American men, a share cropper submerged in debt to the white owner and literally everything he "owned" including himself was mortgaged to the landlord. Margaret worked at the bait factory, pulling bait for long hours while her husband was out working at the fields. She could not take her baby to her workplace, and had to leave him on the front porch every morning as she rushed to work. Brownfield's earliest memories were those of his mother leaving sweet-smelling and clean to return in the evening covered with evil-smelling manure, mud and slime up to the knees from pulling bait. The "ready money" (*TLGC*, 6) that bait pulling offered was the dire necessity that kept Margaret working at this nasty, filthy job. Her husband was out in the fields all day in the sun to return home sullen, demoralised and bitter. The steady decline in their relationship is marked by Grange's growing silence, indifference and finally unconcern as his frustration grew in direct proportion to his helplessness and he channelised upon his wife his pent up anger at the injustice of it all. Walker set the tone of Margaret's future by referring repeatedly to her natural grace, cleanliness and gentle submissiveness and the mud and slime that literally coated her at the end of her long and harrowing day of labor—the spiritual waste and physical and moral degradation that would eventually come in her life.

In spite of belonging to the South (so rich in its folk tradition and culture) and living amid a community of Negroes, the Copeland family was alienated from other families as is indicated by the physical fact of living in a house that sat apart from the others, isolated and off a dirt track with a wood at its background. Margaret's life, writes Walker, had become a cycle of repeated events that followed the same pattern week after week. She was a slave to Grange's whims and the vagaries of his moods, alternately quarelling with him and trembling in terror at his murderous rages, living in an unspoken fear of his predictable dissatisfaction, irritability and leashed violence all through the week till Saturday evenings brought on his drunken bouts of rage. She could have travelled North with her sister where there were better job opportunities to attain freedom from the hopeless situation in which she was trapped. However, in one of her rare casual conversations with her husband, Margaret expressed her pity for her sister who had severed ties with her Southern roots and now flaunted bleached hair like a streetwalker. Ironically, it is this sedate and self-righteous Margaret, the submissive wife and long-suffering mother who, after five years of physical and mental abuse and unrelieved labor, would launch on a desperate path of rebellion that would eventually lead to her demoralization and death. It was whispered by Brownfield's cousins that his father was attempting to "sell" his mother to get them out of debt. Through Brownfield's innocent musings, Walker subtly presents the complex situation of the poor African-American woman, confronted by the impotent failure of her husband to provide for his family, compelled to wade through dirt and squalor to supplement his meagre income but unable to claim the sacrifice or thanks for it as her own, lest it rob him of his "manhood". Laboring hard to keep her family afloat she was always burdened by insecurities and the danger of being "sold" as a commodity to the white man who was her husband's boss, by her husband who was, in reality, her boss. In this complex tangle of male ego versus injured pride and manhood versus poverty, the black woman was the one to be victimized, commodified (by the sale of either her labor or her sex) and humiliated—it was her self-respect that was destroyed in the process of keeping her family alive and her man's "manhood" intact. Added to this was the ultimate degradation and stigma of being unable to avoid society's assumptions that a black woman, sooner or later, would have a broken marriage, a trail of affairs and a string of bastard children, all due to her promiscuity and castrating personality. The operating metaphor in Margaret's life was the wheel of oppression that spun in the same groove week after week more firmly rutted in the quagmire of mounting difficulties with every passing year.

When Margaret gave up her job to begin a life of mindless pleasures, her rebellion was as ineffective as her submission had been—it brought no positive change in her own life, nor did it in any way alleviate the already excruciating circumstances in which she existed. She forfieted the adoration and love of her son, while the liberty that she wrested for herself turned out to be nothing but sexual indulgence. In her role as wife and mother, she had been a drudge, and to Grange she had been a tiresome burden along with her son. Now she was the sober, submissive wife only on weekdays, gathering food and hunting game from the woods, cooking and keeping house, but with a hardened heart and cynicism that was not there before. With her changing role from a home-making, quiet housewife to a woman who now sought good times and had no compunction in sleeping with any willing man, in her passage from a caring, loving mother to a woman of loose morals, Margaret's is not a journey to liberty from the confines of restricting role expectations. Her actions were only a futile expression of rebellion and a means of venting long suppressed anger and emotions at the injustice that life had meted out to her. Her new dresses and store-bought perfumes may speak of her financial independence that had liberated her from the need to wait for the time when Grange would be able to afford a new dress for her, but this independence had been bought at a cost too dear. Unlike Josie who had made a profession out of her sexual prowess, Margaret had found no fulfilment in her present role. If her new role provided any consolation to her, it was to strike out at life and Grange—her way of finding an alternative source of involvement in life. Her burden had not been alleviated in reality but her weekly escapades had rendered her indifferent to the worries and cares of routine poverty and oppression.

Margaret's consciousness of victimization was not one that she could clearly identify in terms of racist or sexist oppression. As a bait factory worker, she could never be able to earn enough to alleviate their poverty. Nor could she achieve enough financial independence to leave Grange. She was pushed into catering to the white boss's sexual demands—a common enough job hazard that black men were unable to prevent and often pushed them towards it in order to get extra favours from the boss. The menial role of black women's labor was inevitably tied up with sexual exploitation. Forced to work for survival, they could not avoid contact with white men, resulting in their oppression that led to the accusation of being accomplices in their own exploitation. Margaret's labor was fruitless in that it led to no change in their situation. The tedium of labor coupled with frustration and hopelessness led to her demoralisation. No alternative way, no other avenue or scope was available to black women of her generation, the inevitable consequence being degradation and self-abasement. So she had to acqueise when Shipley compelled her to grant him sexual favours, while Grange turned a deaf ear to her pleas of help. Ignorant, confined and poor, all her efforts and labor rewarded with pain and heartache, she had found solace in a process of self-degradation and self-destruction. In the "drama" of their family life, she could not do justice to her role as mother or wife in spite of her sincere efforts.

Walker has portrayed Margaret's failure against the backdrop of the heroic struggles of laboring African-American women who have fought to keep afloat at all costs. Here is a woman who has broken down and accepted defeat. She ended her own life after poisoning her unwanted baby a week after Grange's abandonment of his family and in death she appeared as lonely as she had been in life. Walker has combined here with the finesse of a true artist the suffering—physical and psychological—of an African-American woman who, in her role as labor, is *not* superhuman, *not* exemplary, *not* courageous and a victim of debilitating circumstances, but who in her self-destruction and spiritual degeneration wrests understanding and sympathy from the reader if not from her son or her community.

The same pattern is replicated in the story of Mem, Brownfield's wife and Margaret's daughter-in-law. Like Margaret, Mem was also a demure, quiet woman with natural grace and loveliness. She was also educated, well mannered and naive. Mem was the antithesis of the "bad black woman image". She preferred to keep to herself and take lonely walks in the nearby woods rather than have a good time in the company of men at Josie's rowdy bar. Her father who had abandoned her mother appeased his conscience by sponsoring her high school education at Atlanta once her mother was dead.

Mem has been physically described by Walker in stark contrast to the mother-daughter duo Josie and Lorene to underscore her unspoiled beauty. For Brownfield, Mem was the essence of womanhood with her gentleness and beauty. She reminded him of his mother as she was in his childhood—clean, fragrant and innocent. In Mem's role as wife to Brownfield too, the life-giving mother-image persists in the self-less and nurturing love she offers Brownfield. Ironically, the same cycle of abuse and torture that Grange had accorded his wife with would be begun by Brownield once he had reduced his lovely wife to a dried-up, harsh-looking drudge. Blaming his father for his mother's downfall, Brownfield knew no better than to repeat the same process of psychic stress and physical brutalities that his father had indulged in. Mem, like her predecessor, was another Copeland woman who, entrapped and helpless, had to endure daily the violent beatings of a frustrated and ignorant husband who was up to his ears in debt to the white landlord.

Educated and trained in teaching, Mem had been, before marrying Brownfield, a grade school teacher who taught the children with a passionate and sincere intensity that indicated her pleasure in her job. She was a good teacher, dedicated and involved and she took up the task of teaching an illiterate Brownfield the letters and grammar. Before he had convinced Mem of his love, Brownfield had used the lessons as an excuse to stay near her. By the time he had impregnated her with their third child, he had begun to resent her superiority and her lady-like conduct. Where once he had considered himself "dirt" in comparison to her goodness, beauty and refinement, now his male ego found satisfaction in bringing her down to his own level. Though, unlike Margaret, Mem had had a proper education, a teaching career and an option of finding herself a better life-partner than Brownfield, she could not escape the fate of her predecessor—doomed to the same cycle of frustration and exploitation that was the lot of Southern women of that period. She was totally demoralised and broken by Brownfield's ill-treatment of her and her children despite her ceaseless labor to improve their situation. With the intuitive perception of an artist, Walker again refutes the stereotype of invincibility of black women. Mem too was dehumanized and brutalised to the point where she deliberatley burnt her precious and once-coveted books and lapsed into the slack and unrefined diction that she had so despised. Mem, in pursuing her own career had been financially independent as well as emotionally free. In her role as Brownfield's wife, she was reduced to a mechanical and slovenly drudge, who was consigned her demeaning place and forced to stay there by a brutish husband whom a racist society had forced into a situation where, try as he might, he could not extricate himself from the quicksand of mounting debt and poverty. Nor could he salvage his manhood or male pride with the consolation that he was the father figure and sole economic provider of the family who could expect his wife to "stay in her place", confined in her gender role as obedient wife and dutiful mother. Brownfield's guilt is the guilt of thousands of black men like him, who, in their inability to provide adequately for their families, transfer their rage against the white racist society and their own impotence on to available victims—the institutionalized "others"[6] that is, their wives and children (lower than them in social status). In her essay, "In Search of Our Mother's Gardens: Womanist Prose", Walker has written about the predicament of African-American women like Mem whose labors of fidelity and love have been "knocked down (their) throats" and who have been "given children" when they asked for love.[7] Mem and Brownfield's passionate love for each other and their joyous participation in sex culminated in yearly pregnancies that broke Mem in body and spirit and added to their already harrowing problems and burdens. Indebted and overworked, Brownfield gradually grew impatient with the bondage of sharecropping and the increasing needs of a growing family. Characteristically, he sought relief through heavy drinking and physically abusing Mem for becoming a burden and producing more burdens for him with an additional mouth to feed each year.

In the initial years of their marriage, Mem had been content in her role as a wife, mother and working woman. She, Walker writes, "sang while she cooked breakfast in the morning and sang when getting ready for bed at night. And sang when she nursed her babies, and sang to him when he crawled in weariness and dejection into the warm, life-giving circle of her breast" (49). Yet, it is this wonderfully happy woman of few wants and fewer complaints whom the degradation of marriage to a working-class and uneducated man eventually destroyed. The sexist oppression that Mem faced within the precincts of her own household has been graphically described by Walker, consciously and deliberately, to challenge the prevailing sentiments of racial solidarity that demanded the relegation of black women's problems to the backshelf and the subsuming of sexist oppressions under the "greater" considerations of racist prejudice and oppression. Walker's attempt to probe into the depths of the black man's psyche and the reasons that motivate him to inflict torture upon the black woman (his mother, sister, wife, daughter or mistress) is ample proof of the breadth and depth of her artistic vision and her understanding of and sympathy with the black man's moral predicament. She seems to suggest how an alternative way of life is possible for the black man and woman once the African-American man comes to terms with the racial oppression and does not allow it to demoralise or break him. He would then be ready to deal with social and political circumstances that have been instrumental in the estrangement of relationships between black men and women. In understanding the trauma of the black woman, in appreciating the multiple roles in which she has operated for his and his family's sake, in percieving the immensity of her sacrifice, in accepting her shortcomings and faults and in lending her his strength by standing shoulder to shoulder with her, the African-American man could well regain his own lost self and achieve his manhood by recognizing the potential of black womanhood. He would then be able to join hands with his woman to prevent the collapse of his family and community instead of destroying both in a mindless violence born out of frustration and thwarted hopes. Only if black men reclaim their responsibilities and transcend sexist attitudes through an enhanced perception of the problems of their women, can black women look forward to a better future.

In his own household, Brownfield was the lord and master and every insult that he faced during the day from his white boss and the white society was in a direct proportion transferred upon his wife and daughters. His daughters would step into a future that society had already shaped for them. He was now an overseer of his own children on a farm owned by a white landlord and the only future that his daughter could expect him to give her was a repetition of the pattern already set for her mother, Mem. Mem's decline is described graphically by Walker, as with every passing year, Brownfield's abuse and accusations increased as did Mem's passivity and silence. She was accused of being unfaithful to him by her husband who knew, even as he beat her for it, that she was innocent. His own guilt at not being able to provide for her was so acute that the only way of appeasing it was to imprint the story of his own failure on her face. Mem was forced by her husband to leave teaching at school because his pride was hurt by her obvious superiority. So he debased her to establish his power over her and negated her self-respect to find a measure of his own worth:

> It was his great ignorance that sent her into white homes as a domestic.... His rage could and did blame everything, *everything* on her. And she accepted all his burdens along with her own and dealt with them from her own greater heart and her greater knowledge. He did not begrudge her the greater heart, but he could not forgive her the greater knowledge. It put her closer, in power, to them, than he could ever be. (55)

In this passage of deceptive simplicity, Walker condenses an entire body of historical, social and cultural concepts that have emerged out of the complex history of the African-Americans in America. Mem's is the classic situation in which most African-American women of that era were trapped—combating on the one hand the gruelling pressures of domestic survival, the anger and frustration of their men and the accusation of having liaisons or illicit affairs with white men, and on the other, fighting off unwanted attention from white men, proving their fidelity and innocence, accepting their men's burdens (physical and psychological) along with their own and finally, forgiving their men from their "greater heart" (that was ignored) and "greater knowledge" (that was begrudged). Like Mem, their labor was endless, thankless and futile and nothing they did could, it seemed, to bring a better future for themselves, their children or families. As Mem and her daughters were moved about from shack to shack by Brownfield wherever he found work, she and they never knew the security or stability of a permanent home. As a rural domestic, Mem earned meagre wages after a hard day's work, wages that allowed her to pull through in the rough times when Brownfield spent his time at Josie's bar, reliving their past relationship, cursing Mem and drinking. Josie gave him money to pay his rent and he left his wife to cater to the domestic needs of their family with her own small income as best as she could. Earlier, when Mem was working as a school teacher, both she and Brownfield had saved money to buy a house—Mem's "big dream" (57). A house of her own would be precious for a black woman not as a material possession but as a sanctuary, a secure shelter from the innumerable storms that broke upon her in life—uncertainties that robbed her of the steady protection of a husband and family. However, like thousands of black women in real life, Mem's dream could not be realised because in drunken bouts of anger, Brownfield stole her hard-earned money to spend it whimsically. Mem was more bewildered than angry at how, whenever they moved a step ahead or upward towards owning something or achieving some improvement in condition, he found a way to check them. In tracing the "unbelievable decline" (55), that had come over their relationship in their years of married life, Walker pens a horrifying picture of ignorance and cruelty in the systematic degradation and torture that Mem faced from her husband. To his friends, he crudely hinted about his sexual domination over her and proudly professed his ability to keep her under control by his violent beatings. In his ignorant bravado, Walker has embedded the essence of patriarchal domination over women—violence (exercising the power of superior physical strength) and rape/enforced sex (exercising the superior power of the phallus). The third factor—that of material control is not applicable in the case of black women of this category as they are more than co-breadwinners—like Mem, they are often the sole supporters of their families. Yet, in a way, material control does exist in terms of controlling income and expenditure. Moreover, a perverted satisfaction in impoverishing the woman, seizing her money or property by force, disallowing her to continue with her blue collar job show how black men like Brownfield replicated patriarchal domination in all dimensions as existed in mainstream society. Their "manhood" had to be manifested and vindicated by dominating and oppressing black women, the only possible ventilation of their pent-up frustration and ire. As Mem calmly handed Brownfield some old copies of *True Confessions* for starting up a fire, she symbolically relinquished "all that she had been to all she would become now" (57). The author's sociological standpoint becomes amply clear when she refers to the "culture of poverty" theory and how black women like Mem "barely escaped it" only to "slip back into that culture" (56). Denied the stability or comfort of a good home, Mem still had her cherished dream of buying her own house one day and she kept alive that dream by maintaining her personal cleanliness and by planting flowers wherever she went. As Brownfield changed jobs, Mem was forced to change homes, each worser than the last and with each step down she was a little more broken, a little more demoralised.

Mem's journey from passive acceptance to active rebellion took place through a slow process of transformation against the backdrop of routine injustice that she suffered. Walker uses Brownfield's hand as a symbol of his patriarchal control over his wife and daughters—hands that had been sensitive, slender and beautiful once but had, over the years, become wrinkly, tough and huge—hands whose bestial control Mem hated but was terrified of. Through a telling scene, Walker represents fictionally the exact position of the black woman within her family while making it clear throughout the novel her role as conceived by the white society, as well as the black society. As Mem and her three daughters huddled together at the dining table poring excitedly over brightly colored catalogues of houses, Mem's love reached out to encompass all of them in a warm glow. She had envisioned a different future for them than hers and she seemed ready to combat singlehandedly all that came in the way of her children's happiness. Brownfield's absence had granted them a temporary respite though, in spite of the lateness of the hour, they had not dared to have dinner before his arrival. Mem's dream of an idyllic future and the temporary and illusory peace that had settled over her household were rudely shattered with the usual noisy entry of her husband who grinned in sadistic pleasure as Mem burned herself in her haste to serve him and as her daughters winced at his crude eating habits. The whole scene highlights the household drama that took place each day and was a regular feature of their lives and pivots on the silent acceptance of the control exercised by the "man of the family" on his wife and daughters who waited till he had had his fill before daring to eat their own food.

To the members of the African-American society, women like Mem who had committed the folly of marrying beneath themselves, had sealed their own fates. For the white society, Mem was only a workhorse, a work machine, a good cook, a good housekeeper or a good worker. Their present employer Captain Davis had secured their services in exchange of the tractor which he lent his brother for a season who no longer needed Mem's services, now that his wife was dead. Now, he wanted to move Brownfield and his family to his son's farm where he was sure that his wife would appreciate Mem's good cooking. Mem herself viewed her life's labor in a different light. Finding a rented house with modern facilities in town after months of tireless search and sore feet was a great accomplishment for Mem and Brownfield's outrage at her presumption at having signed the lease (he could not sign having forgotten whatever Mem had taught him before marriage) could not deter her. Mem who had taken the first step towards breaking the shackle of "unrelenting misery" (86) that had been the cost of allowing Brownfield to be the man of the house, would not relent anymore. Her new spurt of confidence that she was capable of supporting her children alone without the disrupting influence of her husband's evil ways made her declare as much in the face of his violent anger.

True to her word, she hunted for and found a job that would pay her 12 dollars a week. For Mem, the job was manna from heaven, the gateway to freedom and a new life. She spoke of it with as much excitement and hope in her voice as, writes Walker, a bird poised for first flight. The comparison throbs with the poignancy of the horrifying consequence—that the wings of this bird would be cruelly clipped and her hopes crushed, that her fragile nest would be destroyed and she with her children exposed again to the vagaries of Brownfield's whims. Not knowing then about the unbelievable low that she would eventually face, now, for the first time in nine years of married life, Mem decided to take matters into her hand. For the first time in his life, Brownfield was afraid of the wildness he had provoked in Mem as she, a tigress defending her cubs, struck terror in his heart by wielding the gun with a grim determination that held him frozen. In a grotesque reversal of the nine years of cruel masculine regime she had tolerated, Mem had now inverted the power dynamics within her family and stood controlling the gun—a physical symbol of the phallus and a death-dealing weapon, threatening Brownfield to obey her commands if he wished to move with her family to town and commanding him to address her respectfully and trembling in terror, Brownfield obeyed.

However, Mem's victory did not last long. In the city house, with Mem's good income and Brownfield's own job at the pie factory (that was much easier and pleasant than the farm work that involved back-breaking labor) there was considerable improvement in heir living standards. Yet, in spite of enjoying the comforts of a gas heater, electric lights, indoor toilet (and the cleanliness), the refrigerator, Brownfield plotted to pay his wife back for the humiliation she had brought upon him. Two consecutive pregnancies were forced upon her by Brownfield's apparently genuine and renewed attraction for her and the inevitable cycle followed. None of the pregnancies bore fruit but Mem's health was devastated and she was too weak to continue with her job. By the time she had recovered and went in search of new jobs, she had become so emaciated that prospective employers refused to employ her, thinking she was not fit to handle strenuous work. As an urban domestic she had earned more but her work obviously entailed manual labor—the only jobs available to black women in that era. Having long forgotten her books and totally out of touch with studies or learning of any kind, Mem could not hope to fall back on her former education and training as a teacher to acquire a job of such category. Jobless, she could not pay the rent for the house they occupied and Brownfield having waited long for his chance, flaunted the eviction notice in her face—he had deliberately not paid the rent, though he still had his job. This was the third reversal in Mem's life when, after a brief period of relative comfort, peace and harmony, she fell back into the same abyss of despair from which she had risen with uncharacteristic determination. Her financial independence on account of her job had bolstered her courage, losing which had become the curse that pushed her back into the same degradation.

In the last phase of her life, Mem did not make even the occasional protests she used to earlier. However, she did not relinquish her hopes of recovering her health and finding a new job that would give them the financial freedom to leave Brownfield for good. In the next few years, her abasement was total though eventually Brownfield lost his job and Mem began to work again, earning seventeen dollars a week, paying the rent for Mr. J.L.'s house and supporting herself and the family. With stoic determination she cleaned up the filthy house, repaired the floor, leaky roof and cracked walls, split logs to lay steps for their tumble-down, aslant porch, cooked food, catered to the children's needs and did everything in her power to survive and keep the family afloat. On Christmas Eve that year, Mem returned late from work and was dropped off at her gate by her kindly employer in his car. She had bought some oranges and candies for her daughters, though she had not been able to afford their wishes for other gifts. As her lurching and drunken husband appeared on the porch waving his shotgun, she called out a tired but cheerful greeting and kept walking towards him as he aimed the gun at her face and fired, killing her instantly.

Walker has recounted in an interview with Mary Helen Washington,[8] how in Eatonton, Georgia she had been horrified as a child by the sight of a friend's mother laid out on a stone slab, shot in the head by her husband and the first thing that struck Walker about her was that her frayed shoes had gaping holes in their soles from which wads of newspaper were sticking out. Mem is remembered in exactly the same way as she lay in death by her daughter Ruth. In the biting cold of mid-winter, she had been wearing tattered shoes padded with newspaper pieces. Her life ends in the same way her life had been, amid violence and bloodshed. She was the faceless martyr, one among the countless women in the South, who had laid down their lives for no other reason than their wish to rise above the quagmire of poverty and mindless labor and dared to dream for a better future for their children. Mem's failure cannot be the measure of her life's labor and though she had not been accorded with even a word of token appreciation in this world, she had been given one by the author in her death—the bright yellow oranges were scattered around her head like a halo as she lay faceless in a pool of blood. Her youngest daughter, now suddenly and sadly realised that Mem was the Santa Claus who had always bought their presents and who had broken herself in trying to bring them up and combat the harrowing pressures of daily life. In her lifetime, Mem's voice had been literally strangled and her self-expression choked cruelly. In death, she had been relegated to the faceless anonymity that was the lot of black women like her—the loss of face an insistent motif used by many black women writers—a motif that underscores the erasure of the black woman's 'self' or personality as she is forced to deny her own needs and suppress her own talents, qualities and creativity. Mem had tried to channel her love for all that was beautiful and clean in planting flower seeds and maintaining cleanliness in the house and on her person—the only avenues allowed her. Mem's callused and tired feet encased in battered shoes bear testimony to the harsh life she has lived and the magnitude of her love, labor and sacrifice.

Mem's life should have been a movement forward but she too is trapped in marriage to an uneducated, working-class man. In the end, there was no redeeming situation for her, as like her mother-in-law, she had to die. Her education and privileged status as a school teacher does not give her the anticipated liberty. Instead, she falls back into the pit of poverty and degradation. In town, she had provided the house rent and earned enough money to call the cards and maintain psychological pressure on her husband to obey her—making it clear to him that he was not indispensable. Yet, she did not leave him, giving him an option to stay. Where her work had given her strength, her generosity proved to be her undoing as it precipitated her fall. She was reduced to a menial worker as circumstances, particularly black male ego forced her down to occupy the traditional slot alloted to black woman in the labor hierarchy of a white-racist, black-male dominated society. The question arises as to why Mem had to leave her teaching job? Was it because she could not combine the double burden of work both outside and at home? But Mem had always handled multiple labor roles and taken up the entire burden of work both outside and at home till the very last. Was it because she wanted to avoid confrontation at home and could not tolerate the psychological pressure put on her? But when she achieved a temporary phase of freedom, it was through confrontation. She was caught in the relentless grip of sociological circumstances that victimised her because she was a black woman. In contrast with Brownfield who had succumbed to these circumstances and abandoned his responsibilities, Mem had, as a responsible mother, continued to work for the sake of her children. In doing so, her labor attains a dignity and nobility that makes her sacrifice worthy of respect.

In *TCP*, Walker's heroine Celie is again another African-American woman who can be categorised according to this study's hypothesis as belonging to the second category of poor, overworked black women whose labor was taken for granted by the men in their lives. In her role as daughter and housewife, Celie faced all kinds of abuse, less from the larger white society (she hardly had any contact with the outer world) than within her own family.

In this novel too we find Walker's uncharitable portrayals of black men and the horrifying brutalities they inflict on their womenfolk is noteworthy. This is so regardless of the multiple roles in which they operate and in spite of their tireless labor to share their burdens. Here, there is no redeeming excuse of cruel white landlords shackling Celie's stepfather or husband in the bondage of sharecropping or undermining their manhood so that they turn their frustrations upon their womenfolk. Both men are relatively well-off compared to Grange or Brownfield in *TLGC*. However, with changing times and a movement forward into history (Walker has placed *TCP* against the backdrop of changing times, 1900-44, though no direct mention is ever made in Celie's letters to God of the historical events or their influence on the lives of her characters in the novel. The socio-historical perspective is provided by the letters sent by Celie's sister Nettie from Africa). The lot of downtrodden African-American women like Celie did not change in any way and they seemed to be frozen—"suspended"—in history with no movement forward or no movement at all. Celie's situation was different from Margaret or Mem in several respects—poverty was not her problem because she was 'poor' in a different sense. She was a slave to her own husband in that she had to pay for her upkeep with her labor. Unlike the former two, her children did not live with her and she had only a vague idea about their whereabouts. She was married to a man who was well-off and though she had to work very hard to earn her keep, she was not lacking in food or the basic amenities of life as the former two women, the twin taboos of incest and lesbianism added complexity to her role as labor and finally, she of all the three, emerged from the absolute hopelessness of her situation and the emotional impasse into which she was locked, to claim her identity and personhood, to declare her passionate love for Shug Avery and establish a career of her own as a designer and seamstress of repute. She moved forward towards an affirmation of self with the help of bonding with other African-American women, a nurturing sisterhood that neither Margaret nor Mem had been able to achieve. The poetic justice of the moment when she tells her husband Mr.—whose first name she had never even dared to utter before—that his "dead body" was "just the welcome mat(she) nee(ed)" (*TCP*, 181) to make a fresh start in life, is worthy of cheer. Celie belongs to Walker's third cycle of women—women who have been brutalised physically and scarred psychologically but who emerge from their trauma with new determination, women who make space for themselves and inspire others, thus making space for them too.

In *TCP*, Walker uses the epistolary form to present Celie's first-hand account of her own life through her letters to "God". The first letter opens with Celie recounting her rape by her father (she later comes to know that he is her stepfather) at the age of fourteen when her mother is pregnant and too sick either to cook or to meet the sexual demands of her husband. Young as she is, even from Celie's naive point of view, her "pa" is a monster whose incestuous desire for her is shocking and cannot be disclosed before her sick and "cussing" mother. A mean and evil man, Celie's stepfather expected all kinds of service from his wife—she must be a good cook, a good housekeeper, an ever willing sexual partner to satisfy his insatiable libido and somehow, miraculously she must also know how to avoid pregnancies that created a host of complications. Meanwhile, as his wife lay indisposed in bed, he could use his eldest step daughter to cater to his domestic needs and sexual appetite while the entire blame could be put on her for getting "spoiled" before marriage. Celie is utilised and exploited in the worst ways imaginable and the horror of her situation is doubled as she does not even know that she had been raped or that she was pregnant, not understanding the changes in her body or why she took so long to finish work that she had been always habituated to finish promptly:

> I'm big. I can't move fast enough. By time I get back from the well, the water be warm. By time I git the tray ready the food be cold. By time I git all the children ready for school it be dinner time. (12)

Celie and her younger sister Nettie could understand only one thing about the entire situation—that their mother was as helpless as they were to prevent the course of events and that their father was the tyrant master of the household whose word was law and whom no one dared to disobey. Celie, in spite of her physical discomforts, had to continue with cooking, other household chores and tending to her younger brothers and sisters. Celie's mother's death perpetrates her open exploitation by her father. Prevented from acquiring education, her labor was utilised to the full while her sexual exploitation and harassment continued, to render her emotionally and literally sterile. Celie had accepted unquestioningly that she being the ugly one, must take on the entire burden of housework and be a nursemaid to her younger siblings. Her own children were taken from her without her knowledge and disposed of. She was given to understand that they had been killed in the woods and she bore the pain of this knowledge as stoically as she had all the injustices and tortures inflicted upon her. Though Celie's stepfather was actually living off her and her sister Nettie's property that had been bequeathed in their names by their mother, he played the role of overlord too well for them to understand that he was only the guardian and keeper of the estate, not the legal heir. Celie had been so terrorised and the truth that he was not their biological father so well-hidden by him that until after his death and till the estate fell to Celie, she had no notion of the fact that her childhood and teenage had been spent as a drudge and unpaid servant in a house of which, legally, she was the mistress after her mother. On one occasion Celie writes of how she is asked to "look decent" by putting on "something" and she says, "But what I'm sposed to put on/ I don't have nothing" (13). Even in her husband's house Celie does not own anything, not even a new dress of her own and when her sister-in-law insists that she choose material for her dress, she writes, "I can't remember being the first one in my own dress" while her husband looks at her "like he looking at the earth. It need something? his eyes say" (28). Walker uses the earth metaphor to underline Celie's unquestioning obedience, generosity and service and like the earth she is taken for granted, exploited, utilised and stamped upon. The transition from her father's house to her husband's brings no change in her role or her situation as a drudge whose labor is taken for granted, except for the fact that there her use as a sexual object had been illegal while here it was legalised rape under the license of marriage. Albert is desperately in need of someone to look after his four children, Nettie is not available, Celie is accompanied by a cow by way of dowry, she is a good worker and therefore he marries her on the rebound and out of sheer necessity.

More than one references are made to Celie's capacity of handling strenuous jobs. Her step father says: "...she can work like a man" (18) and Celie herself thinks nothing of hoeing in the fields with her step son Harpo, chopping cotton for hours on end, working out in the farm all day to come back and cook lunch or dinner, wash clothes and tend to all the children. She is as used to hard work, unwilling/forced sex, as beating, all of which she calmly accepts as a part of being a poor, ugly, black woman and in her role as daughter or wife she must, of necessity, endure. Her situation is reminiscent of slave women who were whipped to be kept under control. In Celie's case, as in the case of poor black women of this generation, sexist domination had been added to the burdens of racist exploitation. More acute than the pain of physical torture is Celie's feeling of humiliation and degradation at this routine abuse which is even more intolerable than his nightly ritual of sex of which she is again the wooden, passive, partner. The association of Celie with the earth, and the wood reminds one of the bountiful benevolence of nature, which is afraid of man's forcible entry and violation of its precincts. Yet, Celie does not revolt, though her sister-in-law Kate advises her to fight her own battle and not take abuse lying down. Celie thinks about her sister Nettie, who she assumes is dead because she had fought against her lot, Kate too had to leave because of her confrontation with Albert. For Celie, staying alive is more important than fighting back. Like a tree or the earth, Celie stays in her place and does whatever she is asked to in her role as a wife cum servant and laborer.

Walker develops early in her novels a sense of sisterhood and shared perception of oppression among black women who draw together despite their apparently clashing roles/relationships. For example, Celie is her own mother's rival after she is taken by her stepfather but her sympathies always lie with her and when she remarries after her death, Celie and Nettie become naturally close to their stepmother who is a fellow victim in the politics of male oppression. When Nettie leaves her father's house her only worry is about her stepmother. This theme of solidarity among black women is further developed in the central relationship between Celie and Shug Avery who is Albert's erstwhile lover and present mistress. Even before her marriage, Celie had been informed by her step-mother about Shug who was a reputed blues singer and very popular and beautiful. There was no stirring of jealousy in Celie despite Albert's obvious attraction for Shug as she felt drawn to her as soon as she saw her photograph and later in the novel the sexual attraction between the two women becomes clear. It is Shug who liberates Celie from her slave-like and dependent state, encourages her to find a career of her own through which she could achieve the fullest expression of her artistic self, i.e. her creativity as also realise to the full her own potential and claim her own identity and selfhood as she had never dared to do before. Raising Celie's self-esteem was the first positive step towards the rediscovery of her selfhood and dignity. Also, there is Celie's natural and protective love for her blood sister Nettie and vice versa. Each puts the other's welfare before herself and each is ready to protect the other even at the cost of her own life. Such instances of sisterhood and a sense of belongingness to each other permeates the novel and this shared concern, the similarities and commonalities of experience, the sexist, racist, classist oppressions they encounter bind them together and draw even a Spelman graduate (Corrine) to the almost illiterate Celie thus transcending the barriers of class and social status. The common bonds are strong enough to form a nurturing support structure, but the individual clashes must be overcome and the oppressors (not only whites, but black males) must be identified and combated. A shared sense of victimization is not enough to overthrow patriarchal domination—the confidence, awareness and affirmation of self must be first achieved that in turn is possible only through economic independence. That is exactly what Shug—a true sister to Celie—helps her do. Recounting the experience of writing of *TCP* in an essay,[9] Walker refers to it as a historical novel inspired by the story of two women—one the wife and the other the mistress of the same man sharing their "drawers". Obviously, the history, or rather, her story Walker is referring to here is the unspoken understanding between two women who have traditionally figured in the roles of rivals but who, as black women, identify more with each other's confinement in the narrow space of race and sex (to borrow Gloria Wayde Gayles' expression) and sympathise with each other's consciousness of pain, injustice and indignation. For Celie, who has come into contact with other black women who have rebelled against their lot (Nettie, Kate, Sophia, Shug) a gradual change in her formerly passive acceptance is not surprising. At the end of the novel, she comes a long way from her conviction that fighting back was no solution to the problem and staying alive was more important than resisting torture. Yet, even in passivity, the grain of determination is evident in Celie—she is not ready to die despite all that she has been through.

Despite the fact that she and her step son work together to produce the best crop in the country, which indicates Celie's pivotal role as labor in their economic solvency, her participation in labor not being confined to house work only, her work is thankless and taken for granted as wifely duty. Because she serves as free labor for her husband who owns the fields, it is her labor that is instrumental in bringing in profit. In that sense, she is the breadwinner of the family, while Albert is only the overseer of his plantation. Again, in her mother's house, Celie's stepfather hunted game with white men during the hunting season, and Celie had to dress and smoke-cure venison at home, earning a lot of money for him—as many black women did during those times—a job alternative that served Celie no purpose as she was not a beneficiary of it despite her contribution. Her labor was owned by the men in her life and she remained poor, victimised and severely limited. So she was astonished to see Corrine handling money—the first black woman in her knowledge to do so. Though most people who watched Celie stuggling with the double burden of housekeeping and field work over the years were sympathetic towards her, none could imagine an alternative existence for the unfortunate woman. For Celie, work has been a part of her life from her childhood and when Nettie before leaving her house tells her that she is worried to leave her with Albert and his children because "(i)t's like seeing (her) buried", Celie thinks: "It's worse than that.... If I was buried, I wouldn't have to work..." (26). By "work" Celie means here not only the labor in which she is involved from dawn to dusk while her husband sits smoking on the verandah, but also her work as his whipping block and licensed whore, all of which is entailed in her role as his wife.

With Celie's changing role from a passive wife to an independent, working woman, she also changes as a person, recognizing new dimensions in her own flat existence. She begins to express her opinions as, with the recognition of her self-worth, she recovers her power of speech and her own voice. Celie says: "I don't even look at mens...I look at women, tho, cause I'm not scared of them" (15) setting the tone of all her future relationships, where she would form meaningful and sympathetic bonds with several women—beginning with women who try to help her, the special woman she falls in love with and finally with women whom she helps. Her educated sister Nettie had tried to alleviate her condition earlier by teaching her to read and write, realise her self-worth, and also protest against her lot. Her love for Shug becomes a means of finding fulfilment through her work that transforms her from a drudge to a creative worker.

Celie fashions dresses for Shug and the latter inspires her to make pants for women (an idea which seems ridiculous to Celie at first but when she is reminded of the inconvenience of hoeing, chopping and ploughing in a long dress, she concedes that it would be more practical and comfortable if working women wore pants). The idea of women "wearing pants in the house" does not go down well with the men, affronted as they are by Celie and Squeak's decision to go to Memphis with Shug to explore new possibilities. Shug, Celie, Squeak and Sofia join in laughter in a shared appreciation of the joke that while the men thought that the ultimate goal for every woman was to get a man for herself, women knew better than to argue or prove them wrong. These were women capable of handling problems better than their men but they pampered their fragile egos only to withhold hurt and humiliation, which they, in their ignorance took for granted as weakness or fear. Albert tried to dissuade Celie from going by undermining her confidence saying that she had no beauty, talent or spunk. His spiteful evaluation of her worth reveals the black male's callousness towards the black woman's feelings and his role in denigrating her self-esteem:

> But what you got? You ugly. You skinny. You shape funny. You too scared to open your mouth to people. All you fit to do in Memphis is be Shug's maid. Take out her slop-jar and may be cook her food. You not that good a cook either. And the house ain't been clean since my first wife died. And nobody crazy or backward enough to want to marry you, neither. What you gon do? Hire yourself out to farm? He laugh. May be somebody let you work on they rail road. (186)

Albert tries to frighten Celie that she, untrained as she was, would find no other means of livelihood in Memphis except domestic work—the only work she was "fit" for. In saying "You black, you pore, you ugly, you woman. Goddam,...you nothing at all" (187) his definition of Celie is exactly the one which the world, including black men, accorded black women—that they were "nothing" beyond their role identities as labor—a labor over which their men now had control. Celie declares in words that state her arrival as a woman of consequence:

> I'm pore, I'm black, I may be ugly and can't cook, a voice say to everything listening. But I'm here. (187)

The "voice" that has declared her independence and the air that has rushed in to shape words in her mouth to state her arrival as a person warns everyone not to take her for granted anymore and Shug fervently says "Amen" to it. This turning point in Celie's life changes her personality and in a way it can be called a rebirth as she rises from the ashes of the past.

At Memphis Celie stays with Shug at her house as a close friend and unashamed lover, her newfound selfhood giving her courage to assert her wishes. Whatever work she does is voluntary and here she is free to spend her time as she likes. Beginning her work with Shug's inspiration, she designs her dresses. Every week, Shug gives her money to buy enough material for the making of pants, which Celie takes as a diversion to occupy her hands while she worries about finding a means of livelihood. She is unaware initially that she is being encouraged and guided by Shug towards making a successful career out of a work that she does spontaneously and beautifully—a work that she enjoys doing. Her creative potential as a dress designer has been long discovered by Shug during the times when she sewed dresses for her and quilted for hours together with Sofia to design original patterns. The first perfect pair she makes is for Shug—pants that are stylish and comfortable—in keeping with the requirements of her profession as a performing artist. After that there is no looking back for her, as every member of Shug's musical band places orders for pants and Celie is literally swamped with orders from everyone in the neighborhood and her family. Thus, she begins her career as a seamstress, working as an entrepreuner to establish her own small business and running it herself. Guided by Shug, she turns the dining room into a factory, appoints two girls to assist her, "raises the price a hefty notch" and places advertisements in the newspapers. Celie has come a long way from being an enslaved housewife-cum-maid and fieldhand. She is now her own mistress, no longer dependent on anyone financially and the proprietor of her own dress-making enterprise named "Folks Pants Unlimited". In this new role, Celie emerges as a totally transformed person—confident and outspoken. Where earlier she had detained Shug at her home to shield herself from Albert's beatings, now she travels to her hometown alone to attend Sofia's mother's funeral, passing Albert's house without turning a hair as he sits alone on the verandah gazing out but unable to recognize the well-dressed, poised woman passing by his house as his own wife. In her relationship with Shug, Celie is an equal partner now, revelling in the love she gets as well-deserved. Earning money and fame, enjoying her work and also the leisure time which she had never had before, Celie is at peace with herself at last. Added to this is the news of her sister's return from Africa with her two children who had been given away to Corrine and Samuel (the missionary couple who had taken Nettie in and offered her not only shelter but also friendship, education and advice). Also, after her stepfather's death, she has come to own the house, dry goods store and estate that had been her own father's property originally but both sisters had been deprived of their own father's property by their stepfather who had taken advantage of their ignorance. At last Celie knows the happiness of owning her own home where Shug can stay with her and she can accomodate, Nettie, her husband Samuel (they had married after Corrine's death) and Celie's two grown-up children—Olivia and Adam. Coming full circle, Celie has at last known the pleasure of a relationship that is not a burden, nor is it purely sexual. Knowing each other, commitment and a space to move and grow is entailed in this relationship that has helped her to find her own identity through her creative work. At the denouement of the novel, Walker places her heroine Celie at the centre of a complete circle of love and trust, surrounded by Shug, Nettie, her children, Samuel, her relatives and friends—in the role of a host who is now the proud owner of house, a store where she sells her pants, has employed a white storekeeper and also Sofia to attend to the colored customers, and above all has an independent business of her own. Celie has moved from Category II of the hypothesis (a poor black woman, a domestic and a drudge) towards a fulfilment of self and material well-being that is rare among poor, black women. She has indeed arrived, and arrived to stay.

In *The Temple of My Familiar*, Olivia, Celie's daughter appears again, this time as a fully developed character and through her recountings of the past we are introduced again into Celie's life, where we find her as a mature, contained woman, not given to much talk and in the role of a mother and grandmother (to Olivia's daughter Fanny Nzingha). Olivia remembers her mother's fascination with colors and how she could weave magic into the dresses she made out of fabrics of different vibrant shades. She also mentions that in addition to being the best seamstress around, Celie was now also an expert midwife who delivered her daughter's baby. Through her imaginative work Celie has created her own world, achieving wealth, recognition and liberty. Together Celie and Shug (Big Mama and Mama as they were addressed) were the two "queens" of that household where there were no male heads. Olivia also recounts how Celie always wore pants—however so subtly designed that only women noticed that they were so. This is a layered reference to Celie's evolution from a work horse and mule to a confident woman who had taken up the reins of her life in her own hands. Her new personality is reflected in the "power blue" of her dress—an electrifying and vibrant color. Walker here underscores the point that independent, hard working, self-assured and accomplished black women need not be abusive or castrating.

Walker has introduced in *Meridian*, the protagonist's grandmother (Mr. Hill's mother) who had formerly been a maid and worked as a domestic laborer in the houses of white people. Over the years she had had enough experience about the nature and behaviour of her white employers, especially white women to arrive at her own theory about white Americans in general. Her views tallied with her daughter-in-law in that both had nothing but contempt for white people in general and white women in particular. As an 'erect' former maid, this African-American woman had obviously encountered enough oppression from her white mistresses to come to the conclusion that white women above twelve years of age, having become aware of the difference in their positions with their maids began to treat them with the same disrespect and insensitivity as their men folk. As women they have always been a privileged group as compared to their African-American counterparts who have had to work hard in order to survive and save their families from starvation. In contrast with the tough, hard-working black women, they were useless and decorative, their only roles being as breeders of white children who would grow up to oppress black women in their turn. Finally, white women were habitually unclean and since they were not capable of doing any useful work and were dependent on African-American women (their maids, washer women and cleaning ladies) for even their personal cleanliness (including bathing and changing clothes), they were lost without the services of black women whom they treated with such indifference and callousness. Mrs. Hill's long years of service experience had rendered her cynical. She had now become a mid-wife, a job that was treated with more respect than that of a domestic and that did not require her to go into the houses of white people as they preferred white nurses. Having confined her arena of work within the black community, she was now free to speak about her erstwhile employers without reservation and express the suppressed discontentment and pent up hatred of all these years. Her work within her own community and her earlier reputation for erectness that obviously indicated her moral strength made the black people of the town value her opinion. Senior Mrs. Hill was one of those African-American women who were positive, righteous, efficient, capable of strenuous labor and justly proud of their attributes. Along with this, these women considered their roles as labor as an integral part of their roles as mothers, wives, and women and their concept of womanhood included toughness and resourcefulness as against the frailty and ornamental uselessness of white women.

Mrs. Hill's own mother too belongs to Category II of the hypotheses. Her life was one of tremendous hard work and toil combined with the physical and psychological abuses inflicted upon her by a husband who was not poor but refused to pay for his daughter's education. Whenever Meridian remembers her maternal history and the stories told by her mother about her mother, grandmother and great-grandmother who had been women of iron will and inflexible determination and who had laid down their lives for the sake of their children, she is filled with an intense shame and feeling of inadequacy. These women, felt Meridian, were worthy of their maternal ancestry and the sacrifice of their mothers, which she was not. In contrast with Meridian or African-American women of a latter age, Mrs. Hill's mother and her ancestors had had few or no options. Their role had been to "batter down doors" so that their progeny could walk through them into a world of freedom and liberty and it had been their role to secure for their daughters the advantage of education that they themselves had never had. Walker herself had great admiration for these sturdy, grim-faced women who had lived and died for their children and had toiled throughout their lives to make a better, brighter future possible for them.

Mrs. Hill's mother should have been able to live her life as a rural, middle-class housewife, working at home as a housewife and mother, rearing her children and dealing with housework. However, her husband's tyranny (he beat his wife and children and worked his wife like a mule) forced her to work as a washerwoman in order to fulfil Gertrude's (Mrs. Hill) dream of becoming a school teacher. Gertrude could never forget the grim resolution imprinted on her face as, pregnant with her twelfth child and already white-haired as a consequence of the immense strain and toil she had endured, she trudged off to earn the extra money (after doing her own washing and works in the fields) "with her rubboard under her arm" (122). Exhausted, she refused to voice complaint or speak of her hardship, attaining through her immense and silent sacrifice and labor a dignity and stature that made her children adore her. With her first pay as a school teacher, Gertrude bought her mother a pair of shoes (a lingering motif in Walker's representations of black women's lives and symbolic of their wasted lives, weary feet and exhausted bodies).

Walker has herself paid tribute to the labor of such African-American women in her poem "Women". In acknowledging their debt, Walker also suggests that admirable as their lives and labor had been, one must acknowledge that they had had no choice whatsoever in the matter. The difficulty of African-American women like Meridian in accepting heroically courageous black women (their grandmothers) as role models is in that the latter had lived circumscribed lives of workhorses while the former lived in an age where, though limited, they did have the opportunity to choose alternative lives for themselves and work through which they could find fulfilment. Whereas women of an earlier era had made the best use of the worst deal in life, women of Meridian's (and Walker's) generation could choose the best deal out of the options offered to them.

Mrs. Mabel Turner and Agnes of *Meridian,* Eula Mae of *TMF* and Anne Julia of *TCP* all belong to Category II of the hypothesis. Among them Eula Mae, who was initially a poor and ignorant housewife, but after stagnating for years in that state of indifferent and routine labor, began to plant her own kitchen garden. Soon, she started to sell the surplus to her neighbours and opened a little shop. From the income that she got from selling her produce, she bought a little boat on which she often went out fishing. She became, over the years, an expert fisherwoman, catching enough fish to sell and supplement her husband's income, improving herself in every way to establish herself as a small-scale, successful businesswoman. From being a mother who was considered "stupid" and "clumsy" by Lissie and an indifferent housewife—a poor, black woman wallowing in her squalid surroundings—she emerged as a woman willing to change her lot through extra effort and industry—thus raising not only the material status of her family but also changing for the better their food habits, their health and their outlook. Lissie witnessed the positive changes in her mother and the blossoming of qualities that poverty, laziness and boredom had suppressed and over the years, they became more than mother and daughter, friends to each other.

In Walker's *M*, one encounters fringe characters, who make up the fabric of the novel. The setting is a small town in the Southern state (Georgia) of U.S.A. and the economy presents a mix of rural and urban job opportunities where black American women can find work as field hands, domestics and even school teachers. Nelda, Meridian's friend, belongs to a fatherless family of several children where the mother is the breadwinner.

Nelda's mother has been described as a stout, tall, bald-headed woman who worked as a domestic outside her home while her eldest daughter handled the task of bringing up all the younger children in addition to cooking, washing, shopping and assorted household chores. On Sundays her mother took the children to church while Nelda was given a day off to wash her hair, do homework and in the evenings see a movie with Meridian, Delores and their boyfriends. At fourteen she was pregnant already by an older boy from school who was gentle with her and came by to cut grass on their front lawn and to help her on weekdays (when her mother was out working) in bathing the children, giving them supper and putting them to bed. Nelda was seen on Saturdays, struggling to the market with her five younger brothers and sisters, the youngest baby strapped to her back and the two toddlers holding on to both her arms while the twins raced ahead. The family's burden of housework had been accepted by her without demur, she went to school only about six or seven times in a month and after her first pregnancy dropped out of school. Walker hints at the general indifference of the society and the law towards black teenagers like Nelda, who, having been left to take the burdens of their's families while their parents were away at work, sought the early pleasure of sex out of ignorance and curiosity with inevitable consequences. As Petry writes in *The Street*, these young girls had very few means of entertainment or pleasure, hardly any money and usually guardians who were indifferent to these problems.[10] They came in contact with sex very early in their lives and sought sex as the only diversion from tedium. Eventually, demoralised and pregnant, like Nelda, they were forced to drop out of school and follow the same course of endless labor and child rearing as the sole purpose of their lives.

There are other young girl children like Daphne and Ornette of *TLGC* who are exposed to a different kind of degradation. When still very young (a frail, five year-old pickaninny), Daphne became a child labor in the cotton plantation of a white landlord for whom her father Brownfield worked as overseer and sharecropper. Her mother Mem worked outside as a domestic and she very early in life, began to share her burden of responsibilities as a natural consequence of her being the eldest girl-child in the family. Daphne's early exposure to harsh labor and psychological and physical abuse left indelible scars, turning her into a high-strung, nervous girl. In Mem's absence, she acted in the role of surrogate mother and also, by the time she was thirteen, handled all the work at home like an adult. She is not only Mem's daughter but also her closest friend and her labor has always been motivated by and directed towards lessening her mother's burdens. After Mem's death she was taken away to the North by her maternal grandfather where, having lost her mind, she was put into an asylum. The heart-wrenching picture that Walker presents of a love-starved young black girl, craving for the times when both her parents loved her and were in love with each other, brings to mind the fate of so many young black girls like her (Pecola of Morrison's *TBE*) who have been forced into their roles as labor from their very childhood and whom disillusionment and degradation have led to insanity or death.

Squeak, as she is nicknamed, is Harpo's girlfriend in *TCP*, who moved in to live with him after Sofia left with her children and Harpo turned their house into a juke joint. Her real name is Mary Agnes, though she is not called by that name initially—a subtle underscoring of the submerging of her personality and selfhood in her role identity as Harpo's sweet little girlfriend whose constant, clinging loyalty and possessiveness Harpo finds flattering.

Squeak's gradual evolution into Mary Agnes and her assertion of self is witnessed in the course of the novel where she emerges from Category II of the hypothesis to Category V—that is, from a poor, black woman who is exploited and taken for granted in her role as a meek bystander in the drama of Sofia and Harpo's lives, she launches into a career as a performing artist (singer) with help from Shug, Albert's former mistress. Accustomed to being ignored, she has earlier scurried round Harpo, trying to get his attention. After her experience of rape by the white jail warden (her uncle) in trying to get Sofia released from jail, she is left a changed person. In standing up to declare that her name was Mary Agnes when Harpo tries to embrace her, she has literally and symbolically stood up on her feet and at last understood the import of Celie's advice who had asked her to insist that everyone including Harpo call her by her real name. Her awareness of victimization and newly awakened sense of sexist domination gives her the courage to retaliate. Soon after, Mary Agnes discovers her own talent at singing. Her voice, though lacking Shug's deep huskiness, has a high-pitched treble and a sex appeal that gains popularity with the audience. Braving Harpo's mockery, she asks his permission to sing at his juke joint and soon, guided and encouraged by Shug begins to earn money. She manages both her budding career as a singer and the household chores at home. From being a timid, girlish person, Squeak takes upon herself the responsibilty of Sofia's six children and one of her own and struggles to handle all the extra work that it entailed. Squeak does not complain about the extra work she has to do on account of Sofia's children, the youngest of whom is not easy to manage, not because she is dependent on Harpo for her upkeep but because she truly sympathises with Sofia and admires her courage. Bringing up her lover's and his ex-wife's children is not an enviable task and no mean feat but she does "carry on". In the twelve years when Sofia is working as a maid for the Mayor's wife, it is Mary Agnes who holds the family together. Here again Walker develops the theme of friendship between two African-American women who, having shared the love of the same man are not at each other's throats as the world has always expected them to be. Instead, after the initial fight, instinctively they draw closer. It is due to Mary Agnes' sacrifice that Sofia is set free from jail and sent to work for the Mayor's wife. During those years Sofia is hardly able to visit her family but she acknowledges gratefully Mary Agnes' sacrifice and labor in bringing up her children.

On the day Sofia returns home, Mary Agnes announces her decision to leave for the North. Mary Agnes breaks out from her role as unpaid labor and surrogate mother, housewife and lover that she has hitherto shouldered uncomplainingly, becomes a singer, moves in as Grady's girlfriend, travels with him to several places to finally settle in where he owns his own plantation. However, after a few years she is disgusted by his drug-taking and flirtation and returns to live with her own mother and her children at her house while making comfortable living out of her singing. She has also finally grown into a maturer person whose independence and self-confidence has flowered with her crossing the threshold of domestic labor and stepping into the wider arena of an independent career. Mary Agnes' career is a foil to Celie's more dramatic one but like the letter, she too breaks free from the confinement of her earlier role to discover her hidden talent and develop it into a career of her choice. As a singer, she achieves an identity for herself and asserts to everyone that she is not Harpo's appendage—his little "Squeak", but a woman called Mary Agnes with her likes and dislikes, love and hatred and capability to earn her own livelihood, fend for herself and sort out her own life. In her new role as a professional singer she makes an emphatic statement of her individuality and freedom.

In *TCP*, Shug Avery's aunt is a roadhouse cook in Memphis who is reputedly "wild" (116). When Shug gets pregnant by Albert for the third time, her parents turn her out of their house and she is taken in by her aunt who, according to Shug's mother, is just like Shug: "She drink, she fight, she love men to death. She work in a roadhouse. Cook, feed fifty men, screw fifty-five" (116). Shug's aunt, an independent, single woman, led a life of her own choice. She earned her own livelihood, worked hard—her job as a cook in a roadhouse was not an easy one—it needed toughness, strength and ability to fight in self-defense—the ability to survive. Unlike her sister who had married into a rural middle-class, respectable family (not affluent but neither short of three meals a day or the basic amenities of life), she was uninhibited, headstrong and free. Having broken away from a family that had rejected her as wild, this African-American woman revelled in her freedom and unashamed enjoyment of sexual pleasure. She could fight tooth and nail for the men she loved, bare her claws in defence and if need be, provide shelter to a relative in need of help and support. Unshackled by the society's sham values or hypocritical standards of gauging a person's worth, she could generously offer help to a kin or friend as she was not bothered by the consequences or the stigma to her reputation for she had already been branded as "wild". Whatever she earned could be stretched by her to accommodate someone in need. Such African-American women in real life were often mis-represented in fiction as over-sexed, libidinous, bad black women—an image that has persistently overlooked the hard labor, the tough menial work in which these women were engaged throughout the day so that, in the evenings their only entertainment or outlet from the day's routine of untold stress was sex with their male partners. However, Walker refutes this stereotype of the bad black woman not by insisting that poor African-American women engaged throughout their lives in back breaking labor needed the respite of sex but by suggesting that it is that woman's personal choice and subverting judgmental assumptions to celebrate their amoral sexual prowess. Like Shug, her aunt enjoys sex in a totally guiltless, amoral way and the shallow moral measures of "good" or "bad" cannot gauge women like them because these are women who are capable of deep compassion and profound love. These are women who break gender role constructs by their ability to perform all kinds of labor, their ability to enjoy physical/sensual pleasures and above all by their honest acknowledgement of their faults. These "wild" women come forward to help a sister in need where their "respectable" counterparts draw back for fear of social stigma. These are women who, having shunned the traditional roles of wives or mothers, have had the courage to work alone, love alone and live alone. They work with as much gusto as they love and live life to the full.

Under Category III of the hypothesis come African-American women from the middle-class, who have not been required to work outside their homes because the pressure of poverty has been relatively less as compared to the poor, black women of the second category. As Walker mostly centres her novels in the rural South or the small towns of the Southern states of United States of America, her women, middle-class or otherwise, are also mostly (with a few exceptions) from the rural background. Examining Walker's representation of their roles as labor, one can locate a common feature in that all these women have husbands who hold middle-class jobs or in case of rural counties have their own land and house or store. In other words, they have a modest means of income and their wives are therefore found in the traditional roles of housewives and mothers. The husbands are the proud patriarchs within the household and respected in the community, often self-righteous, rigidly "moral" and religious fanatics. The women remain confined within their homes, slaving at the kitchen, washing, cleaning, cooking, keeping house and raising children—unpaid domestics and house-laborers whose labors are more often than not taken for granted and unrecognized as such. Their contributions to the family coffer are not taken into account and they are expected to work for their upkeep. They are invariably pregnant each year, because willingly or unwillingly, they have to submit to their husbands' nightly lust for sex. They have accepted that their position in society has been ensured and safeguarded by their marriages to "respectable, colored" men and the only appreciation they can expect to gain is as ideal housewives, "good" mothers or efficient workers at home. Within the precincts of the home they hold the status of glorified servants at the beck and call of their overlords who deem it their birthright, as members of the dominating sex, the absolute control over their wives' labor, bodies and minds. Subjugated as they are, they may occasionally break free from their submissive moulds and assert themselves when the question of defending a child arises, but apart from that they have rarely, if ever tried to achieve freedom or find their own identities from amid the multiple labor roles that enmesh their selfhood. The middle-class African-American woman (rural) has submerged herself in the roles she performs, stays in the "place" assigned to her and plays second fiddle to her husband not only because she is afraid of retribution and physical abuse but often because she has taken upon herself the wifely duty of pampering her husband's injured male pride and bolstering his sagging ego that very often takes a racist beating in the larger arena of the white society. Unlike their urban counterparts, these women have also to labor outside in the fields (serve as field hands when they cannot afford to employ extra labor) and shoulder both material and emotional responsibilities as the sole confidante of their growing children, especially the daughters, who are also subject to the rule of the father/patriarch. Also, unlike their urban or white counterparts, there is no concept (it is unthinkable) of employing paid help at home due to which they hardly have any leisure time in hand to pursue activities of their choice—creative or decorous. A progression from the state they were in in their Category II labor role, they are yet confined in their roles as housewives and face a different dilemma.

In the third Category come a number of women from Walker's four selected novels. Josie's mother in *TLGC*, Sofia's mother, Shug's mother, Celie's mother, May Ellen, Daisy, Odessa (Sofia's sister) can belong to the rural, middle-class background. Where some like Sofia and Josie's mother are obedient housewives who are only allowed to function in that role, laboring at the kitchen and terrified of their husbands' wrath lest they are thrown out of the house and material respectability, there are those like Shug's mother who have formulated their own strict codes of conduct and enforced them in their houses, working with grim dedication in their roles as exemplary housewives and mothers, clinging determinedly to the respectability that marriage has given them and shunning unpredictable and untraditional behaviour for fear of the moral stigma attached to it. Some like May Ellen and Celie's mother are exploited, harassed housewives—the former unable to meet her husbands criteria of a "good" wife, who should be, in his view, a skilled and strong worker, an efficient housekeeper, servant and sexually gratifying mistress all rolled into one and the latter a propertied widow (formerly a contented housewife and mother who had lacked nothing) who became an easy target for a fortune-hunting man, as she herself is unable to manage her husband's flourishing business. Failing to act in her role as labor, she has withdrawn from life, work, her children, responsibilities, clinging to the memory of her dead husband and trading all that her first husband had acquired through his labor in hiring a protector-husband who, traitor and wily cheat that he is, deprives her daughters of their legal heritage. Languishing in an emotional void, she fails to take up the reins of her own household and dies in disillusionment, demoralisation and degradation. Placed against the backdrop of courage and mettle of African-American women in tiding over hostile circumstances, she comes across as a weak and helpless Southern Belle, more in the image of a Southern white lady than an African-American woman accustomed to fight back at all costs.

A variation in this category is Odessa, who with her husband Jack is represented, perhaps deliberately, as the ideal couple along with that of Samuel and Corrine and Samuel and Nettie. Jack and Odessa have their own farm, which they work and house but no children of their own, so they embrace in love others' children and rear them with care. Odessa is not the subjugated, cowering, middle-class housewife, leading a confined existence as labor. Her efficiency, strength and capability do not undermine her husband's masculinity as they take their decisions mutually and share all work and burdens. Her forthrightness is backed by her husband's quiet reserve and in their relationship there is space for growth, free expression of her emphatic views—a relationship that gears on mutual love and respect. Here is one African-American woman who has achieved balance and harmony between the free expression of her self and the unforced and spontaneous performance in her work role as labor because she has been fortunate enough to get the fullest support and loving care of an African-American man who is neither bitter nor weak. Odessa therefore as a middle-class housewife and mother operates in her role as labor in perfect harmony and is represented as such. Walker has, through the relationship of Jack and Odessa, shown an alternative family life for African-American women and men where there is no "head" of the family but equal partners in labor (work), emotions (love) and responsibilities (problems). Placed against the stereotype of the female-headed Negro families, such a family brings forth the positive influence of the African-American kinship families where mother, father, uncle, aunt, brothers and sisters, cousins, grandparents, friends, neighbours and even ex-girlfriends, ex-boyfriends, ex-husbands and ex-wives sit together for meals, share laughter and tears, take care of each other's children, sort out problems and share burdens.

Daisy on the other hand has married Alphonso because her parents and family work on his land and having no choice but to marry a much older man, she has made the best out of it by way of material advantage. Her compromise represents the middle-class woman's sale or bartering of her sexuality instead of her labor as the easier option. She is in reality a "respectable" prostitute and her marriage nothing but legalised/licensed prostitution to one man. In return, she is "set up" handsomely and her family is helped financially by her husband.

Alice Walker has created in *M* the complex character of Mrs. Hill (the protagonist Meridian's mother)—an ex-school teacher and now, a middle-class housewife and mother. As a young, educated African-American woman in a small town, she had earned both money and respect in her job as a school teacher. She was contented with her job and knew the luxury, rare to African-American women, of getting up late from bed on weekends, of owning good clothes, her own small car and the joyous freedom of earning her own money. She was independent, carefree and unshackled with the responsibilities of anyone other than herself. She was also free to do as she liked, examine her options, measure her future possibilities, enjoy leisure and feel the calm pleasure of an undisturbed single woman's life. A few years later, however, the delights of a single existence began to wane and as many of her friends began to fall in love and settle for marriage, she sensed in herself a need for change. Earlier, the pleasure of toying with the possibility of moving out of her hometown to find a job in another town was adventure enough for her but now she had begun to feel the stagnation in her life and the unspoken pity in the eyes of married women who seemed to have a "mysterious inner life" (*M*, 40). She sensed that a greater fulfilment in life awaited her and felt that her single life, so pleasant and trouble-free, so calm and predictable and minus the unnecessary burdens of forced labor was incomplete in some way. She needed to experience life in all its fullness and depth and the mystery of marriage, family and childbearing intrigued her. So she married Meridian's father, her colleague at work who taught history and was a scholarly, gentle and quiet man.

She was contended and at peace even after leaving her job until her first pregnancy disrupted forever her hitherto untrammelled existence. Motherhood demanded a division of herself in a way she had never anticipated and she in her anger, blamed everyone for not having "warned her against children"

(40). The physical discomforts she experienced during pregnancy, the feeling of entrapment at being at the mercy of the changes in her body, the pain of labor when Meridian was born, embittered her forever towards her husband and children. She executed her duties as a mother and dragged the burden of household chores with a suppressed resentment and grudge while she held everyone responsible for having stolen her selfhood and peace of mind by failing to warn her about the tedious toil that motherhood entailed. The representation of Mrs. Hill's reluctant and resentful labor for her family shatters the image of the fiercely loving and protective African-American mother who toils bravely for the sake of her children and sacrifices everything including her own happiness for them. Mrs. Hill is harsh and strict and blames Meridian for the loss of her own identity as a woman, a person, and more than that, her freedom and independence.

The stereotype of contented or blessed motherhood (a dominating image for the African-American women) receives a jolt through Walker's representation of the unwilling labor of a mother that is often taken for granted as a mother's duty, motivated by a natural love and the sum total of her existence. Mrs Hill, unlike the enslaved African-American women of old for whom the greatest blessing was to be able to or allowed to retain their children (most of whom were sold to other masters), had endured the pain and toil of motherhood out of a moral obligation and an acceptance of the society's codes laid down for a woman. The blessing had turned into a curse for her and as she labored to feed and dress her children, the "starch of her anger" (73) enfolded them daily in the crisp perfection of their ironed dresses. She cooked, washed, mended, ironed—all with the precision of an automaton, never mellowing, never relenting—long suffering and hardened till the last. Her layered question thrown at her innocent child (who represents for her the first link in her chain of bondage) jolts the reader into an increased awareness of an unprepared woman's anger at having motherhood thrust upon her. Barbara Christian in her essay on motherhood as a theme in Walker's *M* in *Black Women's Fiction*, writes that, according to Walker, motherhood should not be a mere function that entails the sacrifice of the mother's freedom—rather it should lead to a fullness of life that is the mother's right as a woman.[11] Walker also points out the risk of imposing societal values and mores upon women who often internalize those values and force themselves and other women to function according to those standards. Walker is treading slippery ground by focusing on the tedium of child care and child rearing that is expected of a mother as her labor of love. It is especially tricky to foreground the lifelong labor of a resentful African-American mother where the traditional image of the black woman has been synonymous with bountiful motherhood. Even Mrs. Hill before her marriage had felt that the overweight, hideously dressed, harried or passive mothers of the school children she taught had an "inner life" that was not achievable as a single, independent career woman and that she was missing out on the prime experience of life. In her new role as a mother, she has to labor for her children and put their needs before her own. Also, her liberty is gone forever, she can no longer think about her own pleasures or discomforts and cannot even express her disatisfaction at her lot—or for having been "caught". When people made jokes about the corpulent and fecund women who were burdened by broods of children, she felt their pain as her own and was disgusted at such obscene merriment because "it was like laughing at a person who is being buried alive, walled away from her own life, brick by brick" (41). The sense of doom is carried forcefully by such a description where the mother's natural life is disrupted, freedom is curbed and her existence is rendered meaningless by the endless cycle of chores she has to perform and the unending demands of her growing children—she is hemmed in from all sides by the walls of expectations that have been constructed over the ages through accumulated ideals to serve the needs of the society. Often a mother's forced labor is given the euphemistic name of selfless care while her protest goes unheard to suit the society's convenience.

Once her children grew up and were no longer as tiresome burdens as before, Mrs. Hill thought of resuming her former career as a school teacher. However, the world had changed in those long years and even in that small town one had to pass new exams to enter service again. She soon lost interest in this pursuit, found that she had no patience with young children anymore and turned to filling her leisure time with the trivial hobby of making prayer pillows and paper flowers—ornamental things that were never of "everyday use"[12]—that served only to occupy her vacant time. Her creativity she had curbed forcefully because she was perpetually "at war" against the world and though she had the talent, she never allowed herself to become a good cook or braid hair prettily or make any effort towards any expression of her creativity. When Meridian wanted to give away her son because she had won a scholarship to college, Mrs. Hill highly disapproved of her daughter's "selfish" and "monstrous" act of rejecting her own child. Grimly, she reminded Meridian that she too had not enjoyed being a mother but had never failed to perform her duties as a mother of six children. Self-righteous and religious, she had accepted a mother's labor without demur, though simmering inwardly in a consuming anger. She expected the same of her daughter for whom, she believed she had set an example by her own life of sacrifice and "blind, stumbling endurance" (71). A middle-class, church-going woman, she had had no serious financial worries as her husband's modest wages and his acres of prize crops kept their table supplied with fresh vegetables and good food. Her job therefore would not have been missed had she found fulfilment in her role as housewife and mother. For her, her job had symbolised freedom and independence, a labor that was dignified, well-paid and respectable. Confinement at home as a mother and housewife angered her and in revenge, she curbed her own spontaneity, moulding herself in the image of an ideal mother and whiling away her leisure in making tiny prayer pillows and paper flowers symbolic of the emotional barrenness and the mechanical artificiality of her existence. She had not been able to achieve fullness or completion or even the fullest expression of womanhood in her role as labor at home. For Meridian, she would always remain an imposing if exemplary figure of sacrifice and discipline whose moral rigidity questioned her daughter's attitude towards her child and pointed an accusing finger at her negligence of her motherly duties. She also thought her mother worthy of the maternal history of African-American women who had always laid down the lives gladly for their children.

Mrs. Hill had made a wrong choice and she had not gained insight from her mistake—she had no compassion or sympathy for younger women, not even her own daughter, who failed to measure upto the standards that society had set for them. In her own confined and severely circumscribed existence, she had added meaning by assuming a self-righteous attitude and she could not tolerate younger girls escaping the trap that she had gullibly fallen into. This embittered African-American woman has, in submerging her own self in her role-identity, destroyed her own natural affection and tenderness. Her transition from Category V(b) to III, albeit a conscious decision, had stifled her spontaneity forever and the only outlet for her frustration was piling complaints against her idealistic, philosophical, impractical husband and her family. Unlike Celie, who had created space for herself and established an identity of her own, Mrs. Hill not only remains largely unconcerned about the larger political issues of the society, she also withdraws from anything beyond the church and her family. Meridian's friend Nelda feels the same betrayal that Meridian had been unable to voice when she blames Mrs. Hill for not having warned her about the consequences of adolescent passion, which as an older woman of the community she ought to have done. In limiting her own boundaries, she has severed connections with the wider community and remains confined within the precincts of her home, withdrawn and aloof from social and political changes. In her role as labor, she has undergone a reverse journey—from liberty to confinement because hers had not been a true freedom of self or soul even in the beginning. She had achieved material freedom and physical comforts in her job as a school teacher but had remained confined in mind and soul. Later, as a housekeeper she was contemptuous of the school teachers who taught her children because they were poor housekeepers, though qualified teachers. This estrangement from the throbbing community life was surely the brick wall that ensured the slow burial of her selfhood in the role identity she had donned permanently with long-suffering patience.

She sometimes worked as a temporary help in white homes to bring in some extra income at Christmas. Her interaction with white people filled her with contempt for them. From personal experience, she knew that white men always saw black women as objects to be used for their convenience with the assumption that their labor and sex were always at their disposal irrespective of their age or class. Where she worked, she was approached both by the master of the house and the young teenage boys come home on holidays from school. The only difference now from the days of slavery was in that she could refuse—however, politely or tactfully. For a white man, black women's bodies were gateways to a forbidden and adult world of lust and sexual enjoyment—a pleasure they could automatically demand and was their prerogative by virtue of their being whites, males and employers. Like her mother-in-law, Mrs. Hill had a very low opinion regarding their capabilities. In Meridian's eyes Mrs. Hill was a superwoman and the ultimate mother figure who had accepted and shouldered enormous responsibilities. In the work arena as manual laborers black women had no identity except as bodies—for labor and sex—so they had no respectability, were assumed to be available and there was no improvement in this situation.

A progression from the state in the Category II labor role, African-American women of this category are still not able to achieve independence or break free from the domestic bondage of labor. The conflict between work and mothering may become central in this category, their labor-role or work-role dilemma is like that of white women, while, as members of the African-American society, they are faced with another dilemma—the ego of their menfolk who resent the fact that their women are more hard working and advanced than they are. In their work arena outside their homes as menial or manual laborers, they have no identity except as bodies, whose labor and sexuality are taken for granted by the white employers, so they are faced with the same debasement. Such work erodes their self-esteem and is demoralising in that they are assumed to be available and hence there is no improvement in situation. If they are educated like Mrs. Hill and have opted for marriage by foregoing their careers, they have to accept the burdens of traditional roles and housework, which again limits their possibilities and curbs their creativity.

One or two women of that generation were able to assert their wish due to certain circumstances like Feather Mae of *M*, but in the main, their work roles remained the same. In *TMF*, Walker represents Marcia and Frudier as urban middle-class women, the former as a helpless mother and wife trapped in marriage to a psychologically devastated, war-returned husband, the latter a dominating, shrewish woman in the image of Sapphire who, in marrying into middle-class stability and respectability had been venomously jealous of her beautiful and reckless younger sister for refuting the decorum and traditionality of behaviour by refusing to remain confined within set standards of societal codes/norms. Both are therefore circumscribed in their roles, one in helpless surrender and the other on account of her limited understanding. For Frudier, her sister epitomised all that she could never be and in hating her she recognizes her own limitations—the same hatred that the Medallion women of the African-American community feel for Sula in Morrison's *Sula*. Respectable, religious, overweight, old before their age and restricted to their work at home, women like Frudier epitomize the negative aspect of the rigid moral stance that middle-class women impose upon themselves and other women as a mechanism of self-defence.

In *The Third Life of Grange Copeland*, Walker represents Rossel Pascal, a beautiful African-American girl as a rich housewife belonging to Category IV of the hypothesis. She is the wife of a rich black man old enough to be her father. Rossel carried herself with a lady-like grace that every one envied and an aloofness that made her unapproachable. Mem's daughter Ruth found in her a heroine to be worshipped with ardour and when Rossel got married to Walt Terrel (an old war veteran, the richest man in the county after whom the school was named and who was respected and fawned upon by everyone), Ruth was stricken by her choice. She was too young to understand Rossel's decision or the reasons that prompted it. Close as Rossel was to her father, she could not depend upon him for her upkeep because he had become an alcholic after his wife's death. The parallel drawn between Rossel and Southern white women extends beyond the similarity of speech. Like these "dumb" but beautiful and ornamental but useless creatures, Rossel too was confident only of the "empty perfection" (*TLGC*, 192) of her own lovely face. She told Ruth that she had no choice but to marry a rich man who could give her an alternative lifestyle from the choice of degrading run-of-the-mill "stinking jobs" (192) that black girls were offered in towns. Walt Terrel could keep her in comfort and luxury and for Rossel, her marriage was a business contract—a deal in which she would get the security, respectability and wealth that no job could give her. She had deliberately, calculatingly compromised her self and soul for a lifestyle she thought she deserved, enchantingly beautiful as she was. Ruth too could not visualise Rossel as a cook or a maid, even though she had never thought of marriage as a job—romantic and young, Ruth had included love as the first criterion for marriage.

Rossel's hard-headed and practical decision shook her but she also could justify Rossel's compromise when she

> tried to imagine Rossel as a short-order cook in a hash house. Rossel was too lovely. She tried to see her as some woman's maid. Rossel was too close to needing a maid herself. Rossel was not meant to be among the wretched of the earth, and Rossel apparently knew it. (192)

Symbolically, Rossel was ready to sell herself (and her soul) to the devil rather than accept a life time of degrading labor and Walt Terrel, pompous as he was, was not after all a devil. Beneath Rossel's supreme confidence and disdain however is a shadow of uncertainty as she, hugging the crying Ruth says: "May be some day we'll both understand why marrying him is supposed to be so much better" (192). Having been close to her father, she had witnessed daily his grief over the loss of his wife, which must have brought home more painfully to her the empty pretension and hypocrisy of her own loveless marriage. With a resolute, calmly set and expressionless face, she had promised Ruth that there would be improvement and progress in the school and the community after she married Walt. Clearly, having secured her own future, she had also envisioned the social work she could persuade her husband to do and try to improve the lot of the poor blacks of the neighbourhood. Perhaps if Rossel had been able to work for the upliftment of the poor and the needy of her community, she could have been redeemed as a person.

The last glimpse of Rossel that Walker offers the reader is when she comes to her father's funeral, leaning within the protection of her husband's arm looking like a "stricken queen" and "apparently" more devoted to him in one year. She is exhibited proudly by her husband like a priceless jewel along with his flashing array of medals. The childish abandon with which Rossel leans on Walt indicates her status as a dependent, and ornamental wife whose job it is to look beautiful and devoted. Cunningly, Walker inserts the word "apparently" to suggest that the devotion that one interpretes/assumes from Rossel's clinging stance is only surface deep. The unsavoury truth remains that her marriage was a job—a burdensome compromise—a contract to be fulfilled.

The Treasure sisters Lucille and Margaret of Meridan are unusual representations in that they were owners of a plantation in Georgia (Southern state) which was extremely racist at that time. Their work was to maintain the farm and the property their father had left them and they lived as owners and workers of their own farm.

The emerging pattern in the changing labor roles of African-American women from Category III to IV shows the only difference in that the latter category has more material comfort and luxury than the former and the prestige of belonging to the upper class, but as dependents, they have no freedom. The choice between limited options available—manual work or ornamental life—is really no choice at all. The latter option, being easier, would be chosen by so many black women when the opportunity became available. It is not surprising in the light of the job advertisements that Ruth reads in the newspapers that indicate clearly the job situation—only untrained, unskilled, low paid jobs were then available to black women. Those who had beauty and the advantage of education would naturally choose marriage to wealthy men, rejecting the distasteful and debasing work of a menial. Not surprisingly, given the choice, most girls in their circumstances would choose to "sell" themselves to acquire the coveted and privileged status of rich housewives. These were women who had seen such poverty and ignominy in the lives of their kith and kin that any choice was better to them than the life of a menial. Women of Category IV achieve material advantage however, not fulfilment. In case of spinsters like Margaret and Lucille, their lack of exposure, suppressed desires, emotional vulnerability or unguardedness render them ripe for betrayal. These rich, black women are self-sufficient as such and can provide for themselves—so they become easy targets for fortune-hunters. Like any rich and unattached woman for that matter, black or white, they can be exploited easily on account of their gullibility and need to forge relationships. So in Naylor's *MD*, Junior Lee practised his charms to influence well-off older women who could cater to his material needs and provide for him. So Margaret was driven to have an ill-advised affair, which she later regretted.

In the Category V(b) are included African-American women who are career women of the middle class holding jobs that are not menial but blue collar: school teachers, lecturers, missionaries, hairdressers, shopkeepers, etc. They are women of modest means who earn their livelihood, can exercise some degree of freedom and are in many ways better off than the women of the first three categories. Walker's African-American women of the second generational cycle are women who have a choice, even if limited. There is however the lurking danger that like Mem, they would fall back into the mire of poverty and degradation. Few African-American women however move up from Category V(b) to V(a), the latter including top ranking executives, models, actresses, managers and administrators, high-class professionals, singers, fashion designers or even belong to that category in real life and as such few such characters are represented in fiction. As Walker has mostly concentrated on the rural South in her novels, it would be unusual to find African-American women of Category V(a) at all in her fictional representations. However, Walker does represent some urban African-American women in her *TMF* which spans several centuries and countries including the modern suburbs of the United States where African-American women like Olivia (Celie's daughter from *TCP*) and Fanny Nzingha, Olivia's daughter live, who are educated and employed—these are women who belong to Category V(b). Also Shug Avery of *TCP* is a performing artist—a profession rooted in black folk culture—a traditionally Negro domain. In Category V(c) are African-American women who work as prostitutes, street walkers, pimps and bar or inn owners who may or may not be married but are not housewives in the traditional sense. These are African-American women whose counterparts in real life have faced great odds in life or out of their broken families, extreme poverty and limited resources of money or pleasure have resorted to the often only way out for them in such circumstances. Faced with the choice of menial labor and sex work, they have chosen the latter—sometimes the easier way out, sometimes out of anger and frustration, sometimes because like Josie in *TLGC* they have frankly enjoyed sex and turned their insatiable enjoyment into a lucrative career and often because after repeated rape or sexual abasement or the extreme degradation of poverty, they have been compelled to take up prostitution as a means of livelihood. Several sociological factors have contributed toward the growth of the image of the African-American prostitute—the "bad" black woman, the temptress—whose supposedly inexhaustible sexual libido, immoral urges and availability have lured white and black men alike and led to the growth in the numbers of black prostitutes in real life. African-American women writers have deliberately countered this distorted and misconceived image of African-American women but unlike black men who wrote in reaction to fashion counter-stereotypes in the images of African-American women as merely helpless victims of excruciating social circumstances and racial prejudices, they created more complex characters in their fictional representations who retained their individualities despite their common sociological background. Black women writers have written about these African-American women representing them as both good and evil, generous and mean who combine positive and negative attributes in themselves to form layered personalities. They are not merely helpless victims, sometimes in their cruelty they become victimizers, they may enjoy sex and love men or they may hate both, they may be calculating bitches or unexpectedly generous, thorough professionals or easy going companions, but they have managed to survive through "grit, shit and mother wit" (*cf.* Introduction). Most of them however, even the hardened ones, yearn for "respectability".

In Category V(b) come Addie Beasley, the school teacher in *TCP*, Nettie and Corrine who are both teachers and missionaries, the former also working sometimes as a drudge (performing menial labor), Olivia and Fannie Nzingha—the former a nurse and later visiting lecturer and the latter being a lecturer in the Womens' Studies Department at an American University. Beginning with Addie Beasley, the focus shifts gradually from the rural South to the urban North where Olivia and Fannie manage both career and home as middle-class but emancipated workers and housewives.

Addie Beasley is the local school teacher in the small Southern county of Georgia where Celie and Nettie live. She is the idol of young and aspiring students like Nettie who "dote" on her and wish fervently to follow her example. She has her job and the freedom that goes with it—a woman who is confident and forthright and who has enough personal concern for her students as to try to persuade their parents not to stop them from attending schools. She is among the few African-American rural women who can speak up to men and express her opinions, which however does not go down well with the men of the community. When Celie gets pregnant by her stepfather, he disallows her going to school and Nettie tries to persuade him not to stop her education because Miss Beasley thinks Celie is "smart". In Nettie's view, Miss Beasley's estimation is the highest of all and she attempts to convince her stepfather as such. He however voices the collective male prejudice against Addie Beasley when he says, "whoever listen to anything Addie Beasley have to say. She run off at the mouth so much no man would have her. That how come she have to teach school" (*TCP*, 19). It is evident from his contempt of the school teacher that her educational qualification and ability to speak up irked him as much as it did other African-American men who felt inadequate intellectually to tackle well-read women like Miss Beasley and turned the table on them in frustration by suggesting that it was out of compulsion that Addie had to take up school teaching as a livelihood because no man "would have her". From an object of admiration on account of her accomplishments and financial independence, she is rendered into an object of pity and contempt by Alphonso's chauvinistic suggestion that she had been rejected by men and having been unable to find a husband and the security of marriage had turned to the unenviable alternative of a job as a school teacher. Walker, through Alphonso's casual comment brings to the fore a prevalent social attitude and the sexist prejudice working against women who do not "stay in their place", who break out of the mould of traditional role assignations and redefine womanhood. Addie Beasley was a spinster who had her own job and could not be confined within the precincts of her home. Nor could her labor be exploited in the form of housekeeping that entailed endless duties. She was therefore to be ignored or ridiculed in private though in public, school teaching was to be condoned as a "respectable" job. The double standards of a patriarchal society operate here and even Miss Beasley herself indirectly supports it when after seeing the pregnant Celie's protruding stomach she withdraws immediately without attempting further persuasion on Celie's behalf, leaving both Nettie and Celie bewildered at her sudden departure. Faced with the consequence of Celie's obvious misdemeanour, Miss Beasley was dumbfounded and the behaviourial norms and codes instilled and rooted/anchored in every woman through years of traditional, social expectations and training come to the fore as she abandons her project of trying to change Alphonso's mind. She fails in that sense, in her role as a teacher and a woman in not realising Celie's innocence and not sensing her bewilderment at the changes in her own body. If she does appreciate it, she withdraws because she is not equipped to fight a battle of such magnitude with the school authorities who forbade admission to a girl of loose morals.

Corrine of *TCP* is a Spelman graduate who is the wife of Rev. Samuel. Corrine works alongside her husband as a missionary and teacher and has adopted Celie's two illegitimate children by her stepfather—Olivia and Adam. She has also accepted Nettie as a close friend and confidant, taking upon herself the task of teaching her all that she knew and offering her shelter in her own home. However, Corrine's superior status as a preacher's wife and educated woman herself does not extend beyond the arena of the African-American community as is forcefully brought out by her encounter with the white shopkeeper who addresses both her and Celie as "girls" and deals with her with the same brisk disregard as he would any African-American woman irrespective of class. A Spelman graduate and an active missionary involved in various charitable and social works, as well as the wife of Reverend Samuel, Corrine is insulted by the white store owner's rough behaviour and the refinement of her diction crumbles in the face of his rudeness. Later, as she awaits her husband's arrival with their wagon, she is close to tears but trying bravely to mask her humiliation at being treated like a maid. When the family left for Africa where Samuel and Corrine would work as missionaries amongst the Olinka tribe, Corrine insisted that Nettie accompany them, trained her and lent her her own clothes. However, even amidst her psychological turmoil and resulting depression, she was a dedicated worker and never failed to perform her share of duties—teaching the Olinka women and children, her share of house and kitchen work and looking after her adopted children whom she loved with a fierce possessiveness. In her role of a dedicated missionary, her sensitive understanding of the Olinka tribe's problems and pecularities, her ingenuity in inventing the Olinka alphabet (mentioned in *TMF* by Olivia) her labor of love and untiring efforts for Tashi, Nettie, Olivia and Adam, Corrine is again a rare fictional representation—a complex woman who has been loved, who has volunteered to take up the hard life of a missionary and believed in a cause firmly enough to have done justice to her job.

Thrown together as young girls and as victims of a tyrannical stepfather, the two sisters Nettie and Celie had drawn close and were bonded in a sisterhood stronger than any blood ties could have naturally forged. Always devoted to learning, with an insatiable urge to read and known more, Nettie was hardworking and sincere as also unfailingly patient. Not only was she the brightest student at school, she also tried her best to impart all that she knew to her sister. In trying to educate her, Nettie attempted to rouse her from the state of apathetic acceptance that she had sunk into. Having left her home at a young age on account of her stepfather's evil intentions, she had enough faith in herself to make a life of her own, alone. Later on in life, she became a missionary and school teacher, travelling with Samuel and his family to Africa and looking after Celie's children Olivia and Adam who had been unknowingly adopted by the couple. When she went to live with Celie for a short period after leaving home, she repulsed Albert's advances determinedly. Thwarted in his attempts, Albert would not allow her to stay in his house. Angry at being rebuffed by the stern girl who believed in fighting back rather than accept victimization, he not only put her out of doors, but also in revenge witheld the letters she wrote to Celie.

From Nettie's long accounts of her life in Africa, one learns about her work there as a school teacher, missionary and even as a menial drudge because she also swept the school room clean and tidied up everything after the service was over, working hard from the early hours of the morning till late into the evening, resting only after dinner. She however mentioned repeatedly about how happy she was with her work and toil and affirmed that she enjoyed her work thoroughly. Nor did she feel like a drudge because the work they did was for a noble cause and the austere life they led taught them the dignity of labor. Nettie had been unable to find a job in town that suited her education. Celie had always wanted her sister's lot to be different from hers and other Southern African-American women like herself who were either trapped in loveless marriages or roles as wives and mothers, married life that thrust unwanted pregnancies upon them year after year, draining them of health, looks, youth and zest for life and reducing them to the level of haggard unpaid domestics who laboured endlessly within their homes or ended up working as maids or cooks in a white lady's house or kitchen. Celie shuddered to think of her pretty, intelligent and dignified sister abased to that state, spending her life hopelessly as an inferior menial. She had envisioned for Nettie brighter prospects and the happy life of a lady where she would have a "respectable" job, material independence and above all freedom to decide the course of her own life without the tryannical interference of her stepfather or partiarchal domination from any male. The sexist exploitation that the two sisters had encountered from their very childhood had left deep scars in their psyche but unlike Celie who had faced repeated sexual abuse and physical violence and therefore hated all men in a detached way, Nettie escaped being permanently embittered against men, perhaps because she had been protected from the worst kind of exploitation by Celie.

bell hooks had written that as an African-American woman living in a family ruled by stern patriarchs, since her very childhood she was accustomed to the supportive relationships and bonding that grew among women. Victims of sexist, racist and classist exploitation, African-American women had traditionally clubbed together to counter male domination, share each others' burdens, labor and problems—tending to each others' children and each others' wounds—both physical and psychological, with the nurturing ties of love and compassion.[13] Celie had, in the same tradition, always tried to take upon herself the hard work and responsibilities that Nettie was initially too young to handle or problems she was not old enough to understand. She had protected with her own body and her own labor her younger sister whom she encouraged to go to school while she herself, pregnant by her stepfather, slogged at home uncomplaining and silent. Samuel and Corrine incorporated her into the Missionary Society and trained her for the missionary work they were entrusted to do in Africa. They took pains to teach her all that they knew and Nettie, with her insatiable thirst for knowledge lapped up all the information she could get from her friendly employers-cum- guides and the books that they lent her. She also, in her turn, taught the children and the process of sharing knowledge gave rise to a strong bond of friendship and love that was to hold them in good stead in the future. The job that Nettie did was liberating for her in spite of the austerity, discomforts and strictures of decorum imposed by a sanctified religious society. She therefore in her long letters to Celie mentioned time and again her own sense of satisfaction and the affirmation of her self-worth at the hard work involved in her job, the cause that she had firm faith in (they wanted to help the downtrodden tribes of Africa and give them medical advice). The school that had been set up with so much labor and dedication was a place that gave Nettie's work a sense of purpose, confidence in herself and conviction in the genuinity of their efforts. Though her job entailed all kinds of work including menial, the sincere pleasure she derived from her work was not marred—not even when she realised that the Olinka men and women eyed her with pity and contempt because she was unmarried and the "Missionaries' drudge". In that tribal African society, a woman was considered extremely unfortunate if she did not have a father, uncle, brother, son or nephew to "protect" her and Nettie, in her unattached state was unprotected and vulnerable, having to work for her livelihood and living the demeaning life of a domestic. A woman named Catherine (Tashi's mother) from the Olinka tribe once told Nettie that she "was not much" and with sad humor Nettie acknowledged that all her accomplishments and her pleasure in her hard work and private little hut, her independence and confidence meant nothing to the Olinka men and women. Like Addie Beasley in a white patriarchal society, Nettie in the tribal society is also regarded with pity and contempt if not ridicule. Walker draws an interesting parallel between the "civilized" white American society and the "savage" African tribal society, pointing out that in their insularity, rigidity of social codes, self-centredness and exploitation of women they were very much alike. The generally accepted fact in America about African tribal societies was that they were predominantly matriarchal. However, as Walker portrays both in *TCP* and *TMF*, historically most tribal societies were patriarchal, though sometimes matrilineal in which case they followed the line of descent from the mother's side, though the power was concentrated in the hands of the males in the family—in this case, the mother's brother. The Olinka's were purely patriarchal however and each man could have as many wives as he wanted. All the work was done by the women—they raised their own crops, cultivated fields, wove their own cloth and dyed them, made mats, rushes, baskets, reared children and fed both husband and family while lavishing them with sweets and wine. The men did nothing but sit together and chat, drink palm wine, gobble sweets and smoke. The several wives of the same man worked together, shared each others' burdens, tended and nursed each others' children and bonded in a friendship that was difficult for a strictly religious man like Samuel to understand who believed firmly in monogamy. Also, the husbands held life and death power over their wives and on accusation of sorcery from him could have the woman killed. No mixing was allowed between the sexes and the concept of a woman having a man for a friend did not exist. Through Nettie's informative letters, the readers are provided with a glimpse of an African tribal society that subtly pointed out the magnitude of sociological misconceptions that have been nurtured by the white society about the Negroes as a race. African-American women in America, much as their African counterparts, had traditionally shouldered the major portion if not the full burden of the labor both outside and inside their homes and like them, they had rarely found support from the male members of the community. The accusation therefore that African-American women were matriarchs of their families by virtue of being strong, confident women—a phenomenon having its roots in African tribal societies is belied by Walker's representation of unenviable reality of the Olinka women thereby shattering the foundation of prejudiced social and anthropological views. The Olinka societal structure operates as a parallel for the African-American society. The situation of African-American women and their roles as labor are compared with African women in their roles as labor in order to provide a broader spectrum for analysis. In *TMF*, Walker presents parallel situations from different countries and civilizations to highlight how everywhere women have been utilised as labor, exploited as mothers and wives and dominated sexually.

Despite the rigorous and hectic schedule that her work as missionary entailed (morning, evening and night classes, prayer sessions, housework) that hardly allowed private time for pleasurable pursuits, Nettie enjoyed her work thoroughly, believing in the noble cause they worked for and learning from the austere life they led, the dignity of labor.

For Nettie, who had witnessed the degrading life of her sister, her job was not only fulfilling but also a movement forward, a step towards new roles and a promising life. Nettie's role as labor led her towards a better life. It is through her work as a missionary that Nettie finally finds happiness in life. After Corrine's death, Samuel and she work together, discuss their problems and eventually, becoming very close friends and then lovers, they marry. When she returns to America with Samuel and the children, Celie is waiting for her in loving anticipation. Having found the joys of life and it's true meaning through years of sincere efforts and hard work/labor, we leave Nettie, at the denouement of the novel as a plump, graying woman crying happy tears in the arms of her sister, surrounded by a loving family.

Celie has employed two seamstresses, Jerene and Darlene who are spinsters, educated and sew very well. While working on garments designed by Celie, Darlene tries to teach Celie how to speak English properly and drop her Negro dialect. Having gained self-confidence and achieved success through her creative work, Celie makes room and allows space for other African-American women—unemployed spinsters like Darlene and Jerene who are capable, skilled and in need of work and opportunities. As Celie and the twins sit working at the factory fashioning clothes out of Celie's innovative designs, they represent an all-women and independent business unit with working partners, chatting with each other as they work, creating pleasure out of labor.

Walker re-introduces Celie's daughter Olivia in *TMF* who as a young girl had lived in Africa with her foster parents and aunt Nettie and had been trained to do missionary work. She was sent to the Spelman college to train as a nurse—her education obviously financed by her now solvent mother and family. She took up nursing as profession and later in life married a doctor named Lance and lived a happy marital life with him until he died. After that she moved back to her mother's house and travelled frequently to Africa to deliver lectures to students in the embassy about her life as a missionary in Africa and her experience there. When, after seperating with her husband, Fanny began to accompany her to Africa, she discovered new dimensions in Olivia's otherwise staid and reserved character (her remarkable clarity of concepts and lucidity of speech that made her a wonderful speaker). As a woman who had lived in America and settled there, working in the only Negro hospital in Atlanta named Harrison Memorial as a nurse, Olivia has been represented in the various roles she handles calmly as the modern urban black woman who had unshakable determination and will to survive. At home (in her mother's house), she had felt superfluous because Celie and Shug and even Nettie were so competent and vibrant, they literally ruled the house and Fanny was brought up amidst the adoration and love they lavished on her so that she hardly needed or missed her mother's presence. In Olivia's conversations with her daughter, she expressed once her determination as a young and single mother to take care of her child: "As soon as I had you, I knew there was no work I would not do to keep you in food and shelter and clothing" (172). Here was another African-American mother who was not demonstrative, was vaguely affectionate and engrossed in her own scholarly pursuits so as to appear "boring" to her own daughter but who loved her with a quiet strength that was belied by her impassive expression. Olivia's roles as daughter, mother, wife, lover and working woman are complimentary. She enjoys doing the work entailed by her job because she had chosen her profession. Also, in her travels abroad to Africa, she brings to the fore her talent as a speaker as she gains an engrossed audience in the embassy. As a senior nurse, she imparts her own clarity of conception (ideas) to her students in the class and is reputedly a very good teacher whose students perform well in their exams. She was an African-American woman of a generation when women, both black and white, were coming forward to break racist and sexist taboos and finding a firm foothold for themselves in a changing society. Sociologically, this was a generation that opened up fresh avenues for determined workers, offered newer options and the scope to study for professions to young African-American women and in spite of subterranean racial undercurrents/forces that operated within every institute of learning or profession, at least made space for the inclusion of a few African-American women to work according to their choice or aptitudes. Olivia was fortunate in that she had not had to worry about Fanny's upbringing—she had had the support of her entire family headed by her mother, who looked after the child while she was away studying. Her family had a typically kinship family structure with everyone staying together, looking after each other's children and a lot of friends always coming in or going out. Amidst the constant activities going on in her house and the chatter and laughter of many voices always circling there, she retreated into the privacy of her room and read quietly—always a self-contained and reclusive person. In the private arena of her home, she had always been a retiring person but the public sphere of her job as nurse and the social arena of her work as a visiting lecturer in the embassy of South Africa brought out her potential as a speaker, her clarity of speech, her simplicity, earnestness and total involvement with her work. In her field of work therefore Olivia's personality flowered and she found fulfilment and a sense of purpose—things that she admitted (without resentment) not to have found at home, where her two mothers and aunt were more than enough to cope with household problems. Olivia is an African-American woman who has been enriched by her ties with Africa and by virtue of belonging to a house where one's spirit was encouraged to find free expression. Olivia therefore has, like her grandfather Simon, determined to achieve through her hard labor and indomitable spirit—independence and identity. It was her firm faith and self-confidence that gave her the conviction that she was capable of taking care of herself and provide for her daughter and her work-role gave her the scope of expanding her horizons and discovering her self-worth. Olivia—an unwed, single mother, a daughter, a wife, a lover and a professional nurse and visiting lecturer found fulfilment in her varied roles, none of which, confined or circumscribed her to curb the free expression of her self and soul.

Miss Winter in *M*, was one of the only three teachers on the faculty at Saxon College, Atlanta. Walker mentions that the other two taught Physical Education and French—a subtle indication of the racial prejudice that prevailed in the academia and the accepted idea that Negroes could only be musical, physical or exotic/foreign. However, it was the organist Miss Winter who was a "misfit" at the college. She was a rebel at heart who took the liberty in her music classes to teach Jazz, spirituals and Blues—

or mothering, read by choice to deepen their knowledge, travel, like Nettie and Corrine to widen their horizons, train for skilled work and explore fresh avenues, immerse oneself in literary pursuits, take up jobs of their choice, work for fulfilment and not merely to earn bread. In this there is a movement forward, a step taken towards progression and work roles that give them a sense of self-worth.

Under Category V(c) comes Josie, the owner of Dew Drop Inn-cum-prostitute in *TLGC* and her daughter Lorene who is also a prostitute. Josie's father was a small town preacher at local church whose moral inflexibility and religious fanaticism made him an object of fear and respect in the eyes of the African-American community. After Josie lost her virginity to her teenaged beau, her father refused to forgive her, and she was turned out of his home. She then turned to the only way she knew how to earn money, uneducated that she was and also because after getting pregnant out of wedlock, she was left with two options—either to work as a domestic—a life of degradation and hard labor and the easier life though that would forever stain her "respectability"—one that had already been shattered by her slip and subsequent "fall". Too young and naive to realise that there could be no redemption for her in his eyes, she tried to win back his affection by plying him with gifts and throwing a party on his birthday. Her rigidly conventional father had no compunction in accepting the gifts that she had bought with her income as a prostitute but he took a cruel and perverse delight in humiliating her publicly for daring to break the rules of morality laid down by him, reinforcing the picture of partiarchal domination in a middle-class family where the father is the head of the household and literally the ruler because not only does he control the purse strings but also through moral, psychological and physical domination he establishes his sexist control over the women of the family as also on younger men. Walker has here (perhaps deliberately again) undermined the sociological myth constructed by white American sociologists that the inevitable dispersal of these families are a direct consequence of the lack of discipline and paternal control that can hold a family together. The presence of the father figure in Josie's family results in cruel sexist control and the banishment of the daughters from the family—Josie who takes up prostitution as a profession and her sister who dies after giving birth to Mem in Josie's house. After her public insult, Josie never returned home, taking up prostitution as a means of livelihood, earning money with ruthlessness and determination to finally become the owner of Dew Drop Inn where she would also employ other streetwalkers and night-club dancers. When her daughter grew up, she too took up the same profession—having been brought up in a place where her mother was working and enjoying sex with shameless abandon. Josie has been described as a "great lusty insatiable cat" (36) whose libido was "devouring" and inexhaustible. She gained weight—a fact that is mentioned repeatedly throughout the text—her corpulence symbolic of her deprave life.

Unlike Morrison's "three merry gargoyles" in *TBE*, Josie did not turn into a man-hater—nor did she charge them their last penny with the calculated venom of those three prostitutes. She rather treated older men with a cynical contempt and pity while regarding her profession as one that had given her material freedom and security. She was neither repentant nor guilty and the innocence and naivete that had once prompted her to seek her father's favour were exorcised permanently on that night when Lorene was almost born beneath his foot. The humiliation, fear and utter helplessness she had experienced continued to torment her through regular nightmarish dreams. In her dreams she saw her father as a witch, riding her on her chest, choking her breath out—the artistic device used by Walker to convey sexist domination—the image of the heavy man also symbolic of the repressed moral guilt that weighed upon Josie's conscience. Proud as she was that she had had the "brains" to turn her shame into a lucrative profession and make the women of her town jealous of her gorgeous dresses and make-up, she went to church regularly and her voice was among the loudest ones raised in prayer to God. However, her professed religious morality was only a weekend hangover that lasted till her Sunday visit to church. After that she was back to her job with a vengeance and a totally amoral enjoyment and gusto. The luxury in which she lived, her independence, the taste of power that money gave her, the 'charity' she could indulge in to buy a good name for herself and advertise her kindness—made her the reigning queen and sex symbol of the town and also made her the proprietor of Dew Drop Inn. Now she could work only when she pleased, titillate her lusty, old admirers by doing a strip tease before them and daring them to touch her, or even provide bed and board to a young, virile boy who was employed to gratify her own sexual desires in exchange of his upkeep. Brownfield Copeland, the son of her erstwhile lover Grange was just such a young and uncorrupted/unsoiled male whom Josie "kept"—ostensibly out of maternal affection and sympathy but actually because he resembled Grange. It was her revenge on her unfaithful lover and also simply because she could afford to keep, like a man of means, her private source of unsoiled sexual enjoyment. In her role as a prostitute and lover—a role that she performed with arrogance, ruthless selfishness, gusto and abandon—Josie, the "fat, yellow *bitch*" (61), was the antithesis of the tragic mulatta who was forced into her profession despite her unwillingness and high moral standards. Initially, Josie's circumstance may have been responsible for her first lapse and subsequent rapes that eventually led to her job as a sex-worker. However, she did not seek to redeem herself in the eyes of the society after that first attempt—flaunting her sexuality in the face of her aged lovers and underscoring their impotence.

The apparent confirmation of the bad, black woman or the black bitch stereotype by Josie in her role as sex-worker and brothel owner is however again inverted when she gives up, without a second thought, her profession and sells her brothel/inn to buy a farm for Grange, who returns to her after years of absence. From a calculating, cynical and often heartless woman, Josie reverts back to her naivete in the total faith she entrusted to Grange who proposed marriage to a now ageing Josie. So she moves from Category V(c) to become, as in Category III—a middle-class housewife, esconced in a house on a lonely farm/estate far removed from the hustle-bustle of the town. Ageing and psychologically insecure, and with her inherent obtuseness and pride in her own sexual prowess as also with pitifully simplistic faith in Grange's love for her, she believed that Grange had sought the loneliness and isolation of such a farm to enjoy her charms in uninterrupted pleasure.

Walker traces the changing pattern of Josie's role as lover, jealous wife and Brownfield's accomplice and mistress as angered by Grange's increasing closeness with his granddaughter Ruth, she turned once again to Brownfield whom she had used and rejected. Josie's profession had given her liberty, financial independence, comfort, sexual enjoyment—everything except respectability and love from one man—craving which she eagerly married Grange only to become confined in the domesticated role of a wife because she was not mentally conditioned for it, nor was she accustomed to housework. Being naturally lazy, she resented the domestic responsibilities like cooking, cleaning, washing, taking care of Ruth, canning, preserving, making wine and plucking cotton as a farmer's wife. Having lived a pampered life as a moneyed woman, she refused to co-operate in such work. Her jealousy at being ignored and neglected by Grange made her team up with Brownfield to reclaim her husband's affections, scheming but ignorant, she was exploited once again in her liaison with Brownfield. Her transition from Grange's wife to Brownfield's mistress forces her to step further down to become a manual laborer in old age. Reversal had not been good for Josie and in the end she perpetrates the death of both Grange and Brownfield. Walker has created an unusually complex woman who, having been a prostitute, has always craved to be Grange's wife while enjoying her job and hating domesticity.

Viewed in the light of her careless and casual cruelty towards her own daughter Lorene, it can be said that Josie was never maternal, nor did she have any motherly affection towards her daughter and niece. In this respect also she is an antithesis of the image of the protective African-American mother whose reputedly fierce and instinctive mother-love has always projected her as the universal earth-mother. Not only did Josie regard her own daughter as a competitor in the profession she shared with her, she had also (she confessed as much to Brownfield) no compunction in planning to "dump" her as soon as Grange came to fetch her for their journey to the North where she had envisioned a new life with him. Josie's existence with Brownfield was fraught with trials and now she took in washing—washing clothes for white and black people to buy their bread. Brownfield had never been one to work for his livelihood and Josie—tired, aged and sad—was compelled to resort to manual labor in order to earn their daily bread. In the end Josie loses both husband and lover and has nothing to fall back upon—not even her profession she was now too old for.

Hateful and vindictive as she is, one cannot but sympathise with the hopeful and eager-to-please young daughter who had craved her father's forgiveness to be allowed to resume a normal teenager's life under his guidance and close to his affections and the bewildered, ageing sex-symbol turned housewife who is desperate to regain her husband's love. Josie had found physical and material fulfilment in her job and emotional fulfilment through her marriage with Grange but she failed to achieve wholeness or peace of mind because she remained till the last, a dissatisfied, pampered, complaining and wheedling woman who had, in her essence, never grown up.

The difference between Grange's two wives is sharply underscored—the first, innocent, abused and degraded, commits suicide as a release from her hellish life, while the second, instinctive survivor that she is, fights tooth and nail and is greedy and resourceful enough to, as she herself claimed, "built up a establishment with my own hands and figured out how to git rich my own brain..." (62). Josie's pride in her professional prowess however constructs a picture of freedom that is inverted later by her repentance and realisation towards the end. A long-forgotten incident brings to the fore the realities of a prostitute's existence that they stoically take as a part of their job—an occupational hazard. Josie's job experience as a whore has not always been pleasant. She has faced physical abuses and psychological insecurities that she has not always revealed. In building a "business" with her own "brains", she could not avoid it's pitfalls. In the end she forfeited her lifetime's savings in her naivete or foolish trust on both Grange and Brownfield. She has been valued by men only for her sexuality and the money she has earned. In the end she loses both, with age and betrayal of trust.

Josie's daughter Lorene has been represented in the image of a tough prostitute who takes everything in her stride. She is free and independent as she is established in her work as a prostitute at a very young age; living a life of sexual degradation, she is plagued by no twinge of conscience. This unusual sexual rivalry between mother and daughter overturns all paradigms of expected/normal behaviour and there is little love lost between them. She is also reputed to be very tough and both she and Josie take pride in their shows of callousness and tough unconcern. She set an example of independence and hard strength that stood her in good stead in her profession—one she had learnt instinctively from her early exposure to it and had become an expert in by the time she was a teenager. Her language was a source of enjoyment for Brownfield as with graphic vigour she narrated her exploits. Her exploits as a prostitute, her dealings with her customers (she has her own regular ones), her expertise in handling the razor was admired by teenagers who frequented Josie's bar. Having been given the option of education, Lorene had refused to go to school, taking up the only profession she was fit for—one that offered the easiest way of making money provided one was tough enough to survive. She was fit for only one profession—one that offered the easiest way of making money provided one was tough enough to survive. Lorene has been represented in her role of a sex worker as a hard-as-nails, calculating, vicious and mean woman who frankly enjoys her position, her money, her sexual hold over her customers and arrogantly admits as much defying the romantic notion that violated virtue or material compulsion only motivated women like her to come to this profession. Unlike Josie who had been given no option, she at least had a mother capable of funding her education had she so desired. In the end when Josie marries Grange after selling Dew Drop Inn, Lorene moves off to greener pastures hoping for better opportunities by migrating to the North.

Category VI of the hypothesis includes African-American women who are political activists. These are women who transcend their social status and background to respond to the call of fighting for a cause. These are again unpaid laborers and in their roles as political workers they have labored for the upliftment of their race. Having shunned the security and comfort of a job, a home, a family life and even sacrificed precious relationships, these women have come forward with a vision and have risked dangers and even death to translate that vision into reality. During the Civil Rights Movement, thousands of young African-American men and women had enrolled as workers to fight for legitimate political and social rights (including the right to vote) and Alice Walker herself, while studying in Saxon College, had been an active Civil Rights worker. Walker's personal experience may have been the inspiration behind her portayal of Meridian Hill in *M* as it is permeated with obvious autobiographical touches. The Civil Rights Movement that had begun as a fight for social and political justice for black men and women later on proved to be a great disappointment to many young volunteers. Rifts developed between black men and women on account of the sexist domination that black women encountered in the course of their activist work. Also, black men often gravitated towards young white women who joined the movement while accusing black women of having liaison with white men—historically, a stand taken by black men against their womenfolk for having supposedly joined hands with the white oppressor. Disillusioned, bewildered and confused, black women who had voluntarily taken the backseat in the movement in spite of great capabilities in order to allow their menfolk to assume the role of leaders (negating their own egos, playing down their contributions to thrust their men to the forefront—to allow them the satisfaction of being leaders and placating their already battered egos and to boost their sagging morale), began to react with hatred, contempt or withdrawal at this betrayal/breach of trust. Having sacrificed a great deal for the cause, they had hoped for great chances. However, whether their labor bore fruit or not (the Movement did succeed in achieving some goals if not to the extent anticipated by the Civil Rights workers) African-American women like Meridian and her friend Anne Marion continued the struggle—albeit in their separate directions and in their seperate ways. These are women of Walker's second generation who have wanted to create space not only for themselves but also others—

so they worked for it with a view to achieving these goals and fought for their legitimate rights. They were activists first, so they, like Meridian in *M* sacrificed personal careers and better options for the sake of the movement and upliftment of others.

Belonging to a small town in the South in a middle-class household, Meridian had been a sensitive child who shied away from her mother in an instinctive understanding of the blame she placed on her for having shackled her in motherhood. Mrs. Hill failed to forge the traditional mother-daughter bondage and failing to provide proper guidance as a mother, placed the blame on Meridian for becoming a teenaged mother while still at school. In her role as a young mother and wife, Meridian experienced an acute dissociation with her 'self'—hating as she did the confinement, the restrictions, housework and the tedium of tending to her new born son. Comparing her life to that of other girls of her age, she began to feel like a slave chained to an unwanted burden. The conflict between motherhood and an alternative life where she could complete her education and acquire a job became a psychological turmoil and finally she decided to give her son away to avail of a coveted scholarship to study at Saxon College in Atlanta. Despite her mother's condemnation of her "monstrous" selfishness in abandoning her child, she went on to graduate from Saxon College. In her role as a divorced woman and single parent, she felt both confined and purposeless. It was as if her 'self' and soul were striving to achieve a freedom that her body could not—due to physical circumstances and responsibilities—grant them.

Meanwhile, she had already become aware of the Civil Rights Movement and her awakening consciousness of political events had jolted her out of an apathy to an awareness of "the past and present of a larger world" (*M*, 67). She enrolled as a volunteer soon after and continued for a year to work for the Movement—attend sit-ins, demonstrations, marches, protests—risking the police baton, tear-gas, arrest and detainment in jail. At seventeen, Meridian was, as Walker puts it: "(a)drop-out from high school, a deserted wife, a mother, a daughter-in-law" (70), and by the time she was eighteen, she had become a social activist and a Civil Rights worker. She had encountered for months now, outside the arena of her home aggression, violence and hatred from white Americans while working in close proximity with white men and women who were fighting for the African-American people's cause. In the chapter titled "Battle Fatigue", Walker describes movingly the tremendous toll (emotional, mental and physical) that the work they were involved in had taken upon them. Most of the workers including Meridian, who were passionately involved with the cause, were weary, blank-eyed or in a tearful state—their bodies trembling, battered, beaten and bruised by the swinging bludgeons of policemen, their eyes swollen and red from tear gas, their minds reeling with exhaustion. During that period of non-violent protest, young women and men like Meridian underwent untold tortures but did not retaliate on principle.

Her repressed guilt at having failed in her role as a mother and proven unworthy of the maternal history of traditionally self-sacrificing African-American mothers in order to better herself always plagued her. At Saxon, she had to leave the hostel on account of her political activism that was prohibited according to campus rules, and was forced to take up part time job as a typist to pay for the rent and other material needs as her scholarship did not cover all expenses. Her job experience reveals the distasteful realities that young black women had to encounter even during the 1950s. Even with her education, academic credentials and an African-American boss from the academia, she still had to put up with sexual harassment and unwelcome attention in return of which she could avail of extra favours.

Meridian's work as an activist later became a lone fight as she parted ways with her more aggressive comrades who were ready to kill for the revolution, to work in her own way for the rights of poor black people of the South. While many of them were later bought off including Truman and Anne Marion, she continued to labor for ten long years as a social activist. She travelled from town to town despite her illness and stayed in austere single-roomed shacks with a minimum of necessary personal belongings. For a short time, Meridian lived in a small town in Alabama, teaching in a Freedom School. At that time she still had a few possessions. Stage by stage, she gave up all that she owned, even burning her poems and lived truly like a hermit. When the reader meets her again, she is in Chicokema—a small, little known town, where she is leading a protest alone, followed by a scattered crowd of unsure black people, against the segregation of an entertainment show in town.

Her social work included approaching poor black families to register for voting, and meeting downtrodden people in the slums, lonely black women and even convicts to help them believe in gradual social reformation and change. In the last scene of the novel, Meridian begins her journey to return to the world she had left behind. She had allowed "an idea to penetrate her life" (227)—she was in that sense an idealistic woman with the courage to live the idea in reality. She had worked for the downtrodden with fearlessness, resolution and calm serenity. Now she left Truman to live the life she had lived, endure the pain she had gone through and struggle with question as she had done. She had emerged out of her experience cleansed, forgiving and pure to begin another journey—alone. As Truman says, Meridian, the idealist social worker would always remain an enigma to people—her "ambivalence" and "unorthodox behaviour" incomprehensible and deplorable to revolutionaries and traditionalists alike.

Meridian has not confined her role to that of a wife and mother only. She, unlike her mother, is aware of an external and larger world and her role in society has not been restricted within the precincts of her family. She has stepped into the larger arena of political/social issues and problems beyond the boundaries of private life.

Anne-Marion Coles, Meridian's revolutionary friend was also a social worker—actively involved in the Atlanta Movement. When Meridian met her at Saxon college, she was like "a blade of sunlight" (89)—sharp, bright and tough. Unlike Meridian, she was articulate and quick-tempered—impatient to move on, act promptly and not willing to agonize over questions that had no easy solutions. Anne-Marion and her acquaintances who had accused Meridian of not being fully committed to the cause of the movement and of being a coward, had been sold out. They had compromised and taken the "capitalist fling" and Meridian had not, in the ten years that she had left them, heard of any revolutionary act on their part. Indeed, Anne-Marion had been a success in the sense of wordly and material achievement while Meridian had hung back, unable to be a part of the "future" that social workers like Anne-Marion had envisioned. Walker therefore, in depicting Anne-Marion as the success and Meridian as the failure in their roles as revolutionaries really represents the former as a failure and the latter as truly victorious in that she had neither compromised her soul nor her ideals. Anne-Marion, the fiery, articulate and assertive political activist had in the end alienated herself from the reality of the African-American masses while the quieter and less dramatic worker Meridian had travelled alone in the path of social change and reformatory work.

There were others like Helen Quincy of *TLGC* who were imperturbably calm in the unshakeable faith they had placed in their activist work and its cause—those that had placed all the stakes in the fight. In various references to the role of black women in the Civil Rights Movement, Walker mentions how Truman thinks that black women were, in comparison to the white women involved in the movement, assertive and not easy to work with. Black women asked too many questions and black men preferred white women who stayed in their places and were content to do clerical work, fashion bands and obey the commands of the men. The unspeakable tortures that were inflicted upon black and white women by the police has been mentioned in one or two seperate incidents. These scattered incidents enmeshed in the tapestry of the novel emerge as flashes of single threads that pattern out the socio-historical truths of the time and are evidences of the sacrifice of thousands of black women who shed their blood along with their men to work for and secure a better future.

Besides providing the black male point of view regarding the work that black women had done during the Movement, Walker envisages the emergence of a new role for African-American women that brought out their stengths, complexities, fighting ability and the capacity to endure stress as well as match their men not only in physical labor roles but also in intellectual, policy-framing, planning roles. The political work role of women like Meridian who had suffered immense internal struggles to culminate in her constructive social work brings out new possibilities for African-American women. Their contribution in the political and social roles can be taken as another step forward towards the recognition of new possibilities and determination of fulfilling, meaningful work through such roles.

Under Category VII are grouped African-American women who defy categorisations. In their roles as labor they may range from Categories I to VIII, but they have transcended their work roles and their roles as mothers, daughters, wives, lovers or mistresses to emerge as women who are engaged in a quest for their "self"s or women who expressed themselves fully and freely through their creative labor. In Walker's novels, we find the representation of five such women—Sofia and Shug in *TCP,* Fanny Nzingha and Lissie Lyles in *TMF* and also from the latter novel, Katherine Degos alias Georgia Smith—a character that has not been fully developed and about whom we know from Arveyda's recollections and Frudier's unkind references. Celie of *TCP* has not been grouped in this category because for a major part in the novel she has remained a poor and victimised black woman who has begun to recognize her own potential only towards the latter half of the novel and through Shug's help. In *TMF*, however, Celie has moved over from Category II through V(b) to VII in her journey of relearning herself, rediscovery of her creative potential and a quest for freedom has culminated in the fullest expression of her free self. In the context of *TCP*, she has been categorized as belonging to Category II and her subsequent change and growth has been discussed.

Sofia has been represented as an extraordinary woman whose independent views about her place in the family often shocks the meek and submissive Celie who has not been able to fight back, oppressed as she is by the men in her life. To Celie, Sofia epitomizes all that she is not and could never hope to be. Celie has often referred to Sofia's gait as the marching of a soldier whose conversation with her would be father-in-law is actually a battle of words and a clash of wills. Albert, who has been portrayed as the ultimate male chauvinist, is taken aback by the girl's forthrightness and lack of concern at his threat that he would not allow Harpo to marry her. Sofia was by then seven or eight months pregnant, unashamed and unworried despite it and contrary to Albert's expectations, not at all anxious to marry Harpo. Coming from a middle-class family, Sofia was yet uninhibited, assertive and headstrong. She was not one to marry for respectability, upkeep or social security. A hard-working girl always, she was more comfortable repairing roofs and chopping wood than doing "little things" around the house. She used to, as a child, roam the woods and hunt game with a bow and arrow. Sofia was the antithesis of the traditional white American idea of frail beauty—she was both good-looking and strong, a good cook, a good housewife, wife and mother as well as a good field hand and a woman who could handle with ease both "man's work" like chopping wood and repairing the house and "woman's work" like quilting, sewing and rearing children. Sofia was a wonderful wife and Harpo and she spent an ideally happy married life for three years, sharing their chores, making love and as equal partners in problems and responsibilities, sorrow and joy. In their household, there was no concept of man's work or woman's work that is division of labor according to gender roles, as Harpo would often feed, bathe and put the children to bed, wash dishes and clean up after supper—tasks that he enjoyed doing. Sofia on the other hand would often don Harpo's old pair of pants to climb up to the roof top and hammer nails on the loosening pieces of wood, chop wood into shingles for hours on end, handle the animals and work in the fields—work that required considerable strength and toughness and that she did with ease. Again Sofia would cook and pattern quilts, take care of her children, sew clothes or curtains while Harpo went out to work in his father's fields. There was no "head" in their family that ran smoothly on the hinges of an unspoken understanding.

However, in an attempt to teach Sofia "her place" and consign her the role of a submissive wife, Harpo made the mistake of beating Sofia. The outcome was against all conceivable notions of traditional power dynamics operating in a family because Sofia fought Harpo back like a man, giving back blow for blow.

Harpo's misguided show of strength and husbandly domination resulted in the deteriorating of their relationship. Sofia pities Celie's helplessness and extends a sympathetic understanding that strengthens into a friendship. When Sofia leaves with her brood to move in with her sister Odessa, ironically Harpo is left brooding and downcast while she leaves cheerfully, having decided to leave her past behind, moving forward, to get on with her life. Sofia was an African-American woman who would not tolerate domination even from the man she loved. She needed the space and freedom for the growth of her personality and the uncurbed expression of her "self". Her spirit was untrammeled and free and could not tolerate constraints or impositions. She would be faithful and committed to relationships as long as the same was reciprocated. Otherwise, she was not one to cling to dying relationships or mourn over a broken one. Her indomitable will was admired by everyone and on one occasion, Nettie recalls how she saw an African-American woman accompanying the mayor's wife as maid, whose strength of character was stamped on her features—a woman who looked totally out of place serving someone who was so inferior to her in every way.

Sofia's life changed on the day of her encounter with the Mayor's wife who, impressed as she was with this woman's healthy good looks offered her a job as her maid. Sofia's point-blank refusal was taken as her "sass" and the Mayor dealt with her as he would any disobedient and blunt African-American woman, only to get knocked down by Sofia. The outcome was terrible for her. She was dragged to prison and subjected to a violent beating that cracked her ribs and skull, tore her nose loose on one side and blinded her in one eye. Celie is aghast at her terrible plight and later, when the family visits her in jail, Sofia is no longer the good humoured, laughing girl. A strange wildness has crept into her eyes and the horrible tortures inflicted upon her in jail have taken their toll upon her.

Her work at the prison laundry, the dirt and squalor of her cell and above all the humiliation of having to obey orders and endure insults ravaged her spirit as also her health deteriorated. When she is finally released from jail and set to work at the Mayor's house as a maid, for the first time in her life, she becomes a menial. Living in the basement room of the Mayor's house for more than ten years, Sofia's degrading experience as labor leaves her a calm, unsmiling woman whose behaviour is no longer rashly impulsive but, who still has very definite views about certain things in life, especially about black-white relationships of which she is skeptical but not bitter.

Despite Sofia's inimitable dash and rebellious spirit, she still had to submit to atrocities of racial cruelity. Though her personality had always been reflected in her martial gait, honest face and outspokenness, the Mayor had recognized her potential only in the capacity of a laborer—how efficient she would be as a maid, how capable a cook—evaluating her worth by her work. Encapsulating the white racist attitude towards African-American women, Miss Millie once reminds Sofia that a black person could sit next to a white person in a car only when they were either driving the car or teaching the latter to do the same. Sofia had expressed in her pithy refusal—"hell, no" (*TCP*, 86) what every black woman must have felt like saying to a white woman in her life. Hating as she did the work she was doing and having to stay at the beck and call of her mistress, Sofia still retained enough fire in her to quell her mistress' incessant complaints by her silence. Sofia therefore is an African-American woman who cannot be confined to any category—she is a woman who has transcended her roles to come through as an unique and wonderfully vibrant person—who has endured enough pain to have destroyed any ordinary human being and who has retained, despite all her suffering, the capacity to love. Years of subjugation has calmed her quick temper but the uncowed spirit and spark of life she retained despite the long years of enforced labor. She, in essence, is a confirmation of the positive aspects of a black woman's challenge and her ability to transcend the denigrating evaluation as a woman of the inferior race as also distinct from her worth as a laborer. The poetic justice of Sofia's life comes when Eleanor Jane (the Mayor's daughter) dissatisfied as she is with her life, begins to work for Sofia, a situation that is unacceptable to her family, cooking for Henrietta and looking after her. Ready as she now is for the uneventful tranquility of a housewife's role, Sofia unhesitatingly volunteers to look after Squeak's daughter Henreitta, as Squeak is all set for the adventure of a career. In the end, working in the roles of a wife and mother, she has not lost the soaring spirit and the sense of self-worth that she had before. So Celie dreams while fashioning a pair of pants for Sofia:

> I'm busy making pants for Sofia now. One leg be purple, one leg be red. I dream Sofia wearing these pants, one day she was jumping over the moon. (194)

Walker introduces Shug Avery in *TCP* as a famous blues singer who makes it to the top of her profession at the peak point of her career (she is a friend of Bessie Smith, the great black singer). She is also Albert's mistress, a thwarted lover, a single mother, an irrepressible lover of men, Celie's lover—in other words a woman in whom is condensed a baffling array of contradictory qualities—a woman capable of great love as well as fierce hatred, and above all, a woman who has never in life allowed her spirit to be suppressed or her "self" confined within the codes of conduct laid out by society or role expectations framed by it. She has therefore defied categorization in every way, delineated as she is with such complexity and fluidity so as to overlap barriers and concentrate in herself the essence of womanhood. Shug's creativity has been expressed through her songs that are throbbingly beautiful, provocative, or poignantly moving—depending upon the mood which seizes her and sets her to sing. She has her own band and personal orchestra with whom she travels from town to town, singing for money—as she is a professional singer. However, Shug has never felt compelled to do anything out of necessity. Earning a livelihood has not been as much of a compulsion as the craving to express the yearning of her soul, so she has channeled out her love for life and all its pleasures through her music. Of course, because her career has been a successful one, bringing her name, fame and enough money to buy material pleasures for herself (she has a beautiful house, an expensive car, stylish clothes and jewels, she sleeps in silks and satins, eats luxuriously—everything that money can buy) she has not needed to worry about financial insecurities, but there have been hard times for her too. It is not as if everything has fallen into her lap without her having worked hard for it. Celie has been a witness (when she begins to live with Shug at her house) of the hard work that has gone in to make her a popular singer. She has travelled extensively, been on the road for months at a stretch, having had very little time for rest or sleep. She has had to eat "junk food" and has survived on beer, to return home with bad breath, bleary eyes and bloated stomach, flabby, sickly and greasy as she has had no place to wash herself properly. Shug refers to her boredom at having to perform certain popular numbers again and again, especially on demand from the white people who made up a major portion of her audience. She tells Celie that she would not be able to act in front of her like she does while performing mindlessly before them. This part of her profession is what she obviously disliked because Shug hated hypocrisy and has always spoken her mind with unscrupulous honesty. Yet, her songs have been a part of her growth and maturity into a gentler woman than she had been before.

Shug is introduced in the novel as Albert's former mistress, a woman of dubious repute, and in theory, fitting the image of the bad, black woman. Celie's first impression on seeing her photograph is that Shug is the most beautiful woman she has ever seen. She is also the most stylish and fashionably dressed woman Celie has ever laid eyes on. When Shug comes to her town to perform at Lucky Star Inn, the posters that advertise her show read: "Come one, come all.... The Queen Honeybee is back in town" (33). People flock to see her perform and Albert is dressed up in his best attire/finery to meet his lady love. The Queen Honeybee however falls sick soon after that and the crowd of admirers surrounding her disappear. No one, including her parents, is ready to offer her bed and board or nurse her back to health. The church-going ladies gloat over her "comedown" and wait for the news of her death. The array of adjectives aimed to chastise Shug and demonstrate the eventual downfall of immorality define an attitude very much like that of the black community of the Bottom in Toni Morrison's *Sula*. In that novel, the target of such criticism is Sula, the protagonist whose untraditional behaviour that defies all standard concepts of morality and goodness, angers the community and she is branded as a pariah and ostracized from the community.

The life of a professional singer like Shug necessitated mobility and along with the name, fame, adoration and wealth it brought her, there was also the stigma and bad name of being a "fast woman", of being attached to several males, and of untraditional behaviour. An object of both admiration and contempt, African-American women of the performing arts had an identity of their own and besides the Conjure women, whose traditional, old-fashioned work role offered them freedom, for the performing artists, their creative work in a more modern work role offered liberty that other women could rarely hope to achieve. The arena of blues and jazz music was a Negro domain traditionally, and rooted in the black folk culture. It offered an opportunity for assertion of their ethnic identity and hence offered great scope for these artists to express their great creativity. The affirmation of that exclusively black experience is found in Shug, a work role that opened up great avenues for African-American women and had immense potential for channelising the rich storehouse of creativity and could offer scope for self-expression and growth, experimenting, innovations and flowering of talent. Paradoxically, there were also the limitations, that Shug expressed as play acting or role-playing—the constant demand for flamboyance and glitter, the stressful routine and the price one had to pay for popularity and attaining celebrity status.

Shug, in attaining independence and liberty for herself and meaningfulness in her work role, has also inspired Celie and Squeak to do the same. She has helped them to redefine their identities and in creating space for others, she has herself grown as a person. Taking both Celie and Squeak with her to Memphis, she has guided the one to express her creativity and establish herself as a small-scale business woman, while helping the other by discovering her talent and promoting her as a singer, thus establishing her career. In helping them to find their own worth through their creative work, she has, in essence, acted not only as their mentors (in being their patron) but also their friend, philosopher and guide. With her support, Celie overthrows her marital bondage and gains the confidence to rebel against sexist oppression. Shug also extends unstinted support to Sofia in whom she has recognised a truly worthy woman. Belonging to the third generational cycle of Walker's women, Shug has redefined her parameters and in achieving all that was inconceivable for African-American women of the earlier two generations, she has also helped other African-American women to achieve the same. She was gradually moving towards a deeper understanding of human relationships and her helping hand would be extended to anyone in need. Her music gradually becomes meditation for her and she begins to withdraw from the glitter and glamour of her profession. Shug confirms the image of a black woman as the performing artist—moody, whimsical, talented, passionate, impulsive and independent—the professional front being a domain where she can reign as a queen, an affirmation of professional achievement and a measure of self-worth. In relearning the true meaning of commitment in relationships, in re-establishing long severed blood-ties by meeting her son, in discovering anew the pleasure of motherhood, Shug has at last evolved into a mature woman whose growing spirituality culminates in the establishment of her own church. Shug therefore has never remained confined within the rigid circumference of any relationship—always moving, changing, developing—allowing space for growth for others as well as for herself. Shug and Celie are not only lovers—they are soulmates.

In her new role as a self-designed preacher, Shug is like Baby Suggs of Morrison's *B*, who however was illiterate and unchurched. The idea of Shug's spirituality is fully developed in *TMF*, where Shug has founded her own religion out of her personal innovative concepts about spirituality and God. She has created her own church in the tradition of renegade black women—which was after all a natural progression from her involvement with musical groups—as such black women formed prayer bands where religion and music were interwoven and musical renditions took the form of meditation. This was a trend sometimes noticed in African-American women of great qualities and great receptiveness, who were ready to enfold in themselves the complex variety of God's creations. So Shug and

Celie encourage the congregation of African-American women and men from all corners of the country in their house—people of great talent—who think differently and innovatively and who have accepted the challenge of living differently without bothering about what others had to say about them. Shug holds "church" six times each year. The "seekers" who come during those sessions share their information and experience of their path, their journey, their God and their concept of spirituality and religion. Shug now hums her songs to attain communion with God. Shug's relegion has been structured on the broad and all-encompassing foundation of a great humanity and she has, lived in essence, the role of a great human being, laboring to convey, in her way, the message of world peace and universal love. The Gospel she has framed defines her own life and her own strivings to attain the freedom of spirit that she advocates.

Engaging in a new work, Shug has opened up avenues of new possibilities, a work that is however connected with the age-old African-American tradition of renegade churches. Her profession as a singer has given her scope to think anew and in the final count, Shug has delighted in her own creativity and revelled in the untrammeled and free play of her spirit and bonded in love with the Universe and the Cosmos.

Like Shug, Arveyda's mother Katherine Degos in *TMF* too had founded her own church and defined her own religion, though she did not write her beatitudes as Shug had done. Born in an urban, middle-class family in Santa Fe, Katherine had, from her very childhood, refused to conform to social expectations and even changed the name her parents had given her. Her flair for stylish clothes, for adventure, for a life different from the kind she saw around her marked her as a rebel. A highly energetic and unconventional woman, she had married by choice, and then begun her tireless charity work after he left to join a job in the neighboring state. Indifferent and aloof as a mother, she was however perpetually engaged in a flurry of activities, always in motion and ever interfering in other people's affairs. Her sudden psychological withdrawal was perhaps due to a heartsickness that she however never revealed. Her soul-rooted weariness at the futility of all the charity work she had done (and thought more important than attending church) left her empty and failed to achieve the fulfilment she had envisioned in it.

She was hated "because she exposed herself to what she wanted. What she didn't want, she made very clear. She took risks. She jumped...at the sun" (394). Like Sofia, whom Celie imagines to be jumping over the moon, taking in her embrace the universe, like Sula who was not afraid of a free "fall", like Shug who had set up a church of her own, Katherine too was dissatisfied with her "limited reality" (394). In her heart, there was a constant craving for an existence beyond what she was living—a quest for self, a wish to transcend the confines of a circumscribed existence. Her ideas of religion were similar to Shug for she believed that doing something for the poor was more religious than going to church. Unlike Shug, Katherine had not written down her beatitudes, nor had she been able to hold together the church she had founded but, in essence, Shug and she were "spiritual kins" (295). However, in living life just as she wanted it, in rejecting social expectations and acknowledging the call of her soul, in refusing to recognize constraints/limitations of the body and mind and in taking the risk of freely expressing her 'self'—she was a creative, unusual woman who defied categorization and refuted role expectations.

In *TMF*, Walker introduces Fanny Nzingha, Celie's granddaughter and Olivia's daughter who had been conceived in Africa, out of wedlock while her mother was still a teenager. Her father was Dahvid, a young man of the Olinka tribe who had joined the militant rebel group called Mbeles. Fanny was a perceptive and extremely sensitive and intelligent child who grew up to be very good in studies. She acquired solid academic credentials and a job at the Women's Studies Department in a college at New York. She got married to a fellow professor Suwelo; who taught American History at the same institution. They were very much in love and a very happy couple who seemed never to tire of each other's company. However, when the reader first meets Suwelo, her husband, he is at that time bewildered and hurt by her decision to end their marriage. To Suwelo, who has always loved her with single-minded devotion (at least, he thinks so) Fanny's insistence on divorce is unreasonable, cruel and also strange. In fact, through Suwelo's reminiscences, one learns time and again of the peculiarities of Fanny's behaviour, her obsession with spirits and the complex inner conflicts that seem to disturb her sanity from time to time so that she has to recede into a world of her own, a defensive shell into which she retreats to ward off the intrusion of outer realities with which she cannot cope. Fanny is yet another woman who cannot be confined in one category. She has been a daughter, a wife, a working woman, an intellectual, an academician, a masseuse, a philosopher, a womanist and above all, a humanist. She is a woman who has embarked unceasingly on an inward voyage of self-discovery to explore the hidden depths of her mind and soul. She is again a woman, who has gone beyond traditional role definitions and expectations. Disgusted with the academia and the overt racism that she has encountered there, she leaves her teaching job to join the college administration—an arena where racial prejudice is more pronounced and painful. As Carlotta (a colleague and later a friend—a Spanish American woman fled from Mexico) humorously describes, Fanny's dalliance with administration left her so shaken that she "walked around with a look of such unmistakable distress, it was almost comical" (292). Finally, Fanny leaves her job at college to enroll at the San Fransico School of Massage. She opened her own parlor near the college where she worked and many of her former colleagues become her clients in order to relieve the unbearable stress and tension that they endure in their jobs, encountering daily the racist hatred of the white Americans. Fanny herself had given up her prestigious job despite her extraordinary academic credentials to avoid the mental stress that it had involved. Most of her colleagues and friends (including Carlotta) could not fathom why she had chosen such a "service-oriented, low-prestige" (293) job when she could have easily moved on to other colleges or universities. For Fanny, however, this job gave her the ability to 'cope' with her inner unrest and turmoil.

Fanny's relationship with her husband Suwelo has gone through different phases. Both were initially very much in love. With the passage of time, Fanny grows restless and impatient with Suwelo's concept of equating lust with love. The more introspective and thoughtful she grows, reading books with passionate involvement, listening to music that moves her to tears, trying to persuade Suwelo to read more thoughtfully and creatively, the more irritated he grows with her complexities and idiosyncrasies. By refusing to sleep with him, Fanny is in effect trying to explain to Suwelo what he, in his sexist egotism and callousness cannot see.

Fanny has encountered divisions and sexism and racism even in the work/professional front. The idea that women taught literature because they were imaginative while imparting information (subjects like History) was a male-dominated domain prevailed in the academia. The attitude corresponds with the expectations of behavioral norms determining work-division norms based on gender construct. Fanny's entire personality including her understated, practical but tasteful clothing of alluring hyperfemininity was appealing to her chauvinistic colleagues. She was not ready to mould herself according to their expectations and consequently, she could not make friends with the men or women of the university. The acute sense of alienation dogged her, compelling her to give up her job to find a work that would allow her the scope of communicating with people at least physically at first and then, through contact with their bodily pain, the turmoil in their psyche.

Developing parallelly with her relation to her work was her relationship with her husband. Her suggestion of getting a divorce and living on separate floors of the same house, unconventional as it was, spoke of a new paradigm in a husband-wife relationship, that could, minus the legal bondage of marriage, be a genuine emotional commitment rather than a merely legal tie that amounted to a joint account, house payments, car or children. She was different and unique in her role as wife as she felt that a connection of the body and spirit and a space for growth and freedom were essential ingredients of a marriage in its true sense. It was Suwelo's embarrassment at having to push a cart which in his mind was associated with women and women's work that started the first subtle change in their relationship. As a masseuse, Fanny has dedicated her entire being to the service she is doing. She has planted flower shrubs flanking the way to the little cottage that is her massage parlor. Inside around the massage table are trailing vines that form a live curtain of greenery, burning incense on woodstove makes the air fragrant and beautiful and strange music plays to soothe her clients' nerves. She concentrates all her energy into identifying, locating and recognizing the pain condensed in the bodies that she is touching, and sets to work like a physician to relax the cramped muscles, relieve the tension, loosen the knotted neck muscles, smoothen the curvature of the spine, and help flex rigid toes and tensed jaws. She has also learned acupressure that helps her in her task of draining out the physical pain and tight tension of the bodies beneath her hand. Applying fragrant oils to make her hands warm and slippery, she touches the bodies of her clients reverently, as if trying to learn their pain and her massages may often go beyond the appointed hour till she has relieved the stress of the particular client. The satisfaction on her face indicates the pleasure she derives in helping them to lessen their pain. When Carlotta asks her why she had rejected the academia to take up a job as a masseuse, Fanny's calm reply frightened her:

> I took it up so that I would be forced to touch people, even those I might not like, in gentleness, and be forced to acknowledge both their bodily reality as people and also their pain. Otherwise...I am afraid I might start murdering them. (293)

Fanny's urge to murder people rises from her deep disgust at the injustice (racist, sexist) she sees around her. Her hatred for white people is so deep rooted in her psyche that she has to visit a therapist to unearth the hidden core of hatred and to trace its origin to a childhood experience. Adding personal touches to her workplace helps her to alleviate the tension of her clients and allows her scope to establish physical and psychic contact with people. An intuitive business woman, she gives her customers incentives in the form of free gift certificates. Her success at her work stems from her ability to identify with her customers' problems and her sensitivity to their pain.

For Carlotta and her other clients (even Suwelo occasionally came to her for a massage), Fanny's parlor was convenient, close by, her services were excellent and available at reasonable prices and had the added attraction of the free gift certificates she handed to her friends and people from the college, and the music that one never heard anywhere except her parlor. Her personal involvement in relieving their pain and her skills as a masseuse made them return to her again and again, addicted as they grew to it. They would never be able to imagine the mental agony and turmoil of Fanny who was plumbing the depths of her soul in search of answers and holding on to her connection with reality and the slender thread of sanity that was threatening to snap under pressure. In Africa, Fanny draws parallels between the situation of women, especially African-American women in America and the African women, relating the sexism she meets there with the sexism encountered at home. The racism she has experienced there is here in the guise of patriarchal politics. Fanny who has always denounced patriarchal institutions, including marriage, finds here more overt and direct manifestations of patriarchal domination and oppression. She compares the situation of African mothers whose sole aim is to work for the education and upbringing of their children and whose lives comprise incessant labor—washing, cooking, fieldwork, minework, in fact, all kinds of work, with that of African-American women whose lives in America have been similar. Her long discussions with her parents, her friendship with her sister, her meeting with Bessie Head, the African historian she so admires and serveral others who impress her, help her to restore her equilibrium. Coming back from Africa she is received by Suwelo who is ready to give her a divorce. They spend idyllic hours of joy, each having discovered their separate spaces and the harmony of co-existence without bondage.

Fanny and Suwelo have no children. The African-American woman has now stepped forward into a new kind of role—a marriage where children may not be central, where individual partners give each other space for growth. Fanny's deep and complex 'self' has, in the end, reclaimed its diversity and achieved unthought of dimensions through her humble work and introspection.

Lissie Lyles of *TMF* is not only a woman who defies categories, she is also a woman whose physical reality is not confined to one body. If Fanny Nzingha is one woman with several spirits—she has been a teacher, a masseuse, a magician and witch, a political-social thinker and several historical figures, Lissie has been a spirit with many bodies—she is several women at once and has lived through an astonishing range of experience. Not only has she been different women in one lifetime, she has looked different too, as if her spirit has found different bodies to manifest the role in which she was then enacting.

Also, Lissie remembers her lives in her previous births clearly, so that she can speak of her past experiences tracing them to the beginning of her story. As J.M. Coetzee has put it, Walker weaves a counter-myth of her story as women conceive it as against the man-invented myth called history in *TMF.*[14] Lissie Lyles, through her gradual revelations, speaks of the different lives she has lived—in all of which, she has encountered racist and sexist oppression or both as a woman. She has, she insists, been a woman in all of her births except two when she was once a lion and once a white man. Through the artistic technique of re-memory, Walker makes Lissie relive her past lives and envision her past experiences as women of different countries, of different ages but always as women who have come across great difficulties and oppression in all forms. In her present life, Lissie Lyles—an African-American woman born to a poor black family on an island in the United States, has run the gamut of diverse roles.

Lissie strikes Suwelo as someone who cannot be defined, understood or interpreted by the narrow logic of cynicism or disbelief. Lissie has been, as Hal puts it, not a girlfriend to Hal and Rafe—she has been their wife. Only after listening to the story of Lissie and Hal's life is Suwelo able to understand much of Fanny's strange behaviour or thoughts that had confused him earlier. Lissie was often distracted by her several personalities and did not dare to tell anyone about her well remembered other lives for fear of being ridiculed or branded as insane. She had been photographed by the man she had married and for the first time, the photographs proved the truth of the different women she had been at different times in her past and present lives. Emboldened by the physical evidence of that truth, Lissie became a model for the photographer from Charleston for more than thirty years and the different portraits were framed and hung in Rafe's house.

Lissie therefore is an extraordinary woman whose roles have ranged from lover, wife, mother, mistress and friend in the lives of the two men she has loved most and has been loved in turn. As the photographer Henry Laytrum discovered, she could not present the same self twice—in spirit she was Lissie while her selfs were different and multiple. With her changing self, her appearance also changed—she was in different photographs, tall, short, dark, light skinned, acrobatic and healthy, crippled, sad or merry. Lissie has testified to being a slave, a prostitute, a fortune teller, a woman confined in a harem, a witch (healer) and her selfs can be categorised accordingly. However, unbelievable as it seems, Lissie is the complex spirit of a woman—an African-American woman who has lived through and felt first-hand the pain of injustice, the suffering and torture inflicted upon women in all countries, in all ages. Rationally, Lissie can be termed as a philosopher, thinker and humanist who has been able to envision the story of women's suffering. Or, as she herself has pretended, she can be called a griot who has travelled to Africa to learn stories of the diaspora from the storytellers and record keepers there. During the sixties, she delivered talks and lectures about her African experiences—all of which she remembered but because the professional way of presenting it required that she admit she had heard it from someone/it had been told to her, she tried not to mention that she remembered it all. For Lissie, "it is the nature of the eye to have seen forever, and the nature of the mind to recall anything that was ever known" (65) as she did not believe in the invincibility of the written word—the way by which man circumscribed knowledge by putting it down on paper.

Lissie here is a spokeswoman for Walker's own views about women's oppression and woman power. Her role is not merely that of an African-American woman within the physical realities of that existence. She is a visionary artist/philosopher/spirit who encapsulates and condenses the essence of humanity. She is the spirit of womanhood who has found numerous selves to express herself. As she says in the tape Hal has sent Suwelo after her death:

> Hal loved me like a sister/mystic/warrior/woman/mother.... Rafe, on the other hand, knowing me to contain everybody and everything, loved me wholeheartedly, as a goddess. Which I was. (372)

Lissie has felt within herself the frustrations of numerous women—the humiliation, absolute degradation and hopelessness of a slave woman, the raw pain of a wife who was forced to become a prostitute because her husband (also her childhood lover) had accused her of adultery, the tremendous power of the Mother Goddess and her subsequent destruction in the hands of man, the sense of betrayal and utter futility of witch healers routed from their homes and burnt at stake. She has lived in all these roles and at one time or other in her life these submerged identities have emerged in her photographs. So Lissie became the intense visionary painter towards the end of her life, having been humbled by the knowledge of the great suffering of womanhood.

The Conjure women represent the traditional role of power of African-American women. They were also called "two-heads" because of their reputed wisdom and their ability to change themselves into whichever form or color they wished to. Basically, these were fortunate tellers, magicians and doctors who prescribed herbal remedies for maladies both physical and psychological. These were powerful women whom people of both the races (white and colored) feared and respected. The black communities especially respected these wise two-heads who, as Grange aptly puts it in *TLGC*, could "look at things in more than one way" (129). However, Conjure women, laments Grange, were hard to come by and sister Madelaine of *TLGC* was the only two-headed lady in town. Grange tells his grand daughter Ruth about the extraordinary things that these strange women could do and how as a boy, he had seen them work and how people believed in their abilities. These women were very sensitive, remembers Grange and also powerful. Sister Madelaine herself, though not believed by Grange to be as accomplished as the conjure women of old, was reputed to be a powerful woman who had it was believed, changed herself from "a white colored woman to a gypsy fortuneteller" to avoid ending up as a cook or maid. Grange's view makes it amply clear that conjure women were unanimously and unquestionably respected by the people of the African-American community which firmly believed in traditional herbal cures and also witchcraft and magic. Walker represents Sister Madelaine from Baker county very interestingly, as a "modern" conjure woman, who operates more like a psychologist than a magician. She has sent her son (Quincy) to study in a college "up North" and the steep fee that she charges for fortune telling and doling out remedies, goes towards financing her son's education and their upkeep. Quincy had as a child been ashamed of his mother's profession, which he had considered old fashioned and based on superstitions that thrived on the ignorance and illiteracy of black folk. However, after he left college to join the Civil Rights Movement, stepping into the arena of the larger world, he began to appreciate his mother's "inventiveness" and ingenuity in taking up the challenge of a profession that was fast disappearing in a world of growing disbelief and learned cynicism. Madelaine had refused to become a domestic in order to bring up her child alone. So she took up the profession of conjuring, using her practical inventiveness and insights to earn money for supporting them. Her son greatly respected her for it and was as proud of her work as his friend was of his surgeon father.

As a Conjure woman of the modern era, Sister Madelainc infused her fortune-telling with psychological insights and approached her profession from a practical angle, seeing it as a means of livelihood and enjoying the power and benefits it gave her. She has been represented not as the traditional conjure woman who was feared and respected for her magical powers but as an innovative and independent African-American woman who chose her area of work. Refusing to labor as a domestic in a white man's kitchen, she took up a profession that gave her scope to utilise her ingenunity and her sharp mind unlike the conjure women of old, her services were not rendered free of charge or at the cost of a few pennies. She charged a hefty sum (her customers gave her that unhesitatingly) because, as she tells Josie, she has her limits and also a son in college meaning that she too has to survive like anyone else and look after her child—and the business of survival required money.

In *TMF*, Lissie Lyle's grandmother Dorcy Hogshead—the woman who was reputedly a "witch" was also an excellent midwife and a genius at delivering babies. She was cantakerous and had a mean temper. The power that the memory of her past lives gave her, she used in interpreting the past (by putting it together in patterns) in the context of the present. So she was widely known as a wise witch, a fortuneteller who could interpret dreams and foretell the future. Dorcy's reputation as a midwife was also widespread. She operated in her own distinctive style. Dorcy who lived alone even at her age, is represented as one of those African-American women who, skilled in their work, have earned respect and also fear because of their "supernatural" powers and extraordinary abilities. Yet, moody and temperamental, she is often unpredictable and as during Lissie's delivery, she could behave sometimes with incredible stubbornness. The all-knowing, wise witch and skilled midwife could be childish and nasty too when the mood caught her and her character has been delineated by Hal with both humour and admiration.

From Category I to VIII in Walker's representation of African-American women in their roles as labor, the pattern of progression and evolution can be traced. Beginning with slave women who were only, but only laborers, to performing artists and blue collar and white collar workers, to conjure women, who were powerful in their traditional and old-fashioned work roles, African-American women of different generations have faced victimization, oppression and alienation in different ways. Yet, from menial drudges of Category II they have determined great distances to emerge as individuals in their own right, despite and because of their roles as labor which have been both confining and liberating at different times.

NOTES AND REFERENCES

1. The term was used by feminist critic Mary Helen Washington in her "An Essay on Alice Walker". She was an apologist, she writes, to mean one who speaks from a position. In *Alice Walker: Critical Perspectives Past and Present*. Eds. Henry Louis Gates Junior and K.A. Appiah, p. 37.

2. 1973 Interview, with critic Mary Helen Washington. In *The Norton Anthology of African American Literature*. Eds. Henry Louis Gates Jr. and Nellie Y. McKay. New York: W.W. Norton and Company Inc., 1997, p. 2375.
3. *Ibid.*, pp. 2377-78.
4. *Op. cit.*, pp. 39-47.
5. Alice Walker, Interview with Mary Helen Washington. Jackson, Mississippi, June 17, 1973, p. 6.
6. bell hooks, *Feminist Theory: From Margin to Center.* Boston: South End Press, 1984, p. 15.
7. Alice Walker, "In Search of Our Mother's Gardens: Womanist Prose", *The Norton Anthology of African American Literature.* Eds. Henry Louis Gates Jr. and K.A. Appiah, p. 2384.
8. Alice Walker, Interview with Mary Helen Washington, 1973, p. 6.
9. Alice Walker, "Writing *The Color Purple*," *Reading Black, Reading Feminist: A Critical Anthology.* Ed. Henry Louis Gates Junior. New York: A Meridian Book, Penguin Group, 1990, p. 453.
10. Ann Petry, *The Street*. Boston: Houghton Mifflin, 1946, p. 206.
11. Barbara Christian, "An Angle of Seeing Motherhood," *Black Feminist Criticism: Perspectives on Black Women Writers.* Berkeley: Pergamon Press, 1985, pp. 245-46.
12. Term used by Walker in her essay "Everyday Use: For Your Grandmama" in *In Love and Trouble: Stories of Black Women.* Barbara Christian in her *Introduction to "Everyday Use". Alice Walker* (pp. 10-11) discusses Walker's concept of heritage and the everyday lives of Black women past and present, encircled by family and culture. Walker's quilt is an emblem of African-American women's culture, an object of communal harmony, a product of bonding—daughter/mother, woman/woman, domestic/aesthetic, and of practical everyday use. Also see, Wilfred L. Guerin, et al. Eds. *A Handbook of Critical Approaches to Literature.* Fourth Edition. Oxford, New York: Oxford University Press, 1999, p. 231.
13. bell hooks, *From Margin to Center*, p. 10.
14. J.M. Coetzee, *The New York Time Book Review on The Temple of My Familiar*, 1989.

    [Quotations from novels have been indicated by abbreviated names of the novels followed by page numbers within parentheses initially. Thereafter, till another novel is alluded to, numbers in bracket indicate page numbers of the same novel.]

Towards New Horizons: African-American Women as Labor in the Novels of Gloria Naylor

4

Gloria Naylor won the American Book Award for *Women of Brewster Place* in 1983. The gripping realism of the novel has placed her in the league of leading contemporary novelists. She has proved her social consciousness and awareness of the exploitation of black women in her representation of their roles as labor in not only her first but also her subsequent novels. Dorothy Wickenden writes in *The New Republic* that "Gloria Naylor's women, much like those of Toni Morrison and Alice Walker, are daunting even in desolation. Most of them find that through laughter and companionship, they can make themselves virtually impregnable".[1] The comparison stands in the light of the hypotheses taken up in the present study. Naylor, like Morrison and Walker, has probed into the realities of everyday existence of the African-American women and through her representation of black women characters in their roles as labor, verified that reality in her novels.

In her four novels, Naylor has, like Morrison, chosen different geographical settings. In *WBP* she has taken up the urban ghetto of Brewster where the underclass and working-class black women and men live cloistered in their poverty and alienation from the affluent sections of the town. Barring a few, most of the black women of this novel belong to Category II. In *Linden Hills*, Naylor presents black, bourgeoisie families where black women, despite their material advantage, have become alienated from not only their cultural roots and identities but have also become dissociated from their own 'self's and souls. A majority of the black women in this novel belong to Category III or IV because they are either middle-class or rich housewives. It is noteworthy that in this novel, only the women who belong to Category II seem to achieve some measure of meaningfulness in their lives. Even career women belonging to Category V(a) fail to find satisfaction in their roles and there is no bonding of sisterhood here as discerned in *WBP.* In *Mama Day*, Naylor shifts focus from urban settings to the semi-rural island of Willow Springs that is politically and geographically not a part of the United States and is an isolated, self-contained world free from the social codes and norms of America. However, the bridge that connects the island with the mainland serves not only as the physical link with the outside world but also as the symbolic link between the two worlds. Willow Springs has its own societal norms and codes framed by the inhabitants who are all black, that preclude social circumstances that have singled out African-American women for a three-fold exploitation. The island is therefore an idyllic haven or paradise and the islanders pride themselves on their indigenous methods of survival, work, diagnosis and treatment of diseases, language, beliefs and superstitions. The island world wings back to the ancient African tribal culture and lore, practices of medicine and network of associated traditions. Encroachment or intrusion from the outer world upon their domain is resisted by these economically and culturally independent islanders even in the name of material progress. In their roles as labor therefore, black women of the island are more independent than the women in the mainland, community solidarity being a strong fortress for them. However, their own social codes are gradually changing with the new generation of islanders going across to the mainland more frequently and imbibing ideas from there. New York acts as a tempting lure—an alternative existence for young women and men who may travel across to settle in the mainland or hold jobs there to come back on vacations. In New York, Charleston or in the other cities in the mainland, black women counter the same oppression and if not overt, at least sub-terranean racism that comes to the fore when they go in search of jobs, the labor market being a highly segregated arena. Bailey's Café is geographically located at Brooklyn in

1942, another urban area where poor and middle-class black people reside, though there is also a white Jewish man living in that area. Black men and women who come to Bailey's Café are not the winners but the losers of the world. Battered and hopeless, they come here, which is symbolically the end of the world. Like in Brewster Place, people come here as the last resort and either survive, die, or go insane. Naylor's portrayal of black women in their roles as labor marks the gradual transition from the hopelessness in the urban ghettoes, squalor, dirt and demoralization to the independence and freedom envisioned in a life sustained by the ties of sisterhood. Individual success and fame seem only to estrange isolated black women from their sisters in neighbourhoods like Linden Hills where emotional reaching out is unknown and unthought of in the stiff formality of relationships that creates distance rather than joins.

In *WBP*, Naylor presents eight black women who came there "because they had no choice and would remain for the same reason" (*WBP*, 4). They have come from different backgrounds, having known middle-class comforts or even the luxury of rich homes to stay in these dingy apartments—poor black women who had been browbeaten by circumstances to flock to Brewster Place. In their roles as labor, they have performed in multiple shifts, having had to work outside their homes to earn bread and within their homes as housewives and mothers—as both breadwinners and homemakers. These women have stood with their backs literally to the wall where they have been pushed by the society (physically and metaphorically the brick barrier that has walled off Brewster Place from the rest of the city, turning it into a dead-end street), they have stood together at bay and have fought the hostile world and society with their weapons of love, humor and undaunted courage. All of them have not succeeded, all have not been strong, but they have, in their strengths and failures been true to human relations (with their men, husbands, lovers, fathers, mothers, brothers, sisters and children) that have often taxed their tolerance or made them suffer, tested their capacity to bear pain or burdens beyond the point of endurance. For the women of Brewster Place, men hardly exist as partners of burden-sharing. It is the women who have to fight it out with fate alone—even married women do not rely on their men, who remain in the background and drift in and out of their lives. In representing them as such, Naylor, apart from "indict(ing) a social structure that could tolerate the under-development of so much of Black America"[2] has explored sensitively the subtleties and complexities of the problems of black womanhood in a white racist, sexist America. She has, in her portrayal of her women characters, exploded the myth of the black matriarch while strengthening the image of sisterhood and solidarity among the downtrodden black women who have jeopardies planted in their face. In spite of the romantically idealistic picture such group solidarity creates, it is essentially true that black women, beaten down by fate and cruel circumstances, link hands and stand shoulder to shoulder to survive. They share laughter and tears, work and leisure and amid their daily labor and tedium try to create as much space for themselves as possible. Work for them is often the only means of survival as they cannot afford to rely on their men and pooling their strength in unspoken understanding of each others' problems, these poor black women fight their lot.

Naylor's awareness of the social/sociological issues that operate behind her representation of poor, black women as labor must be referred to here. Her deliberate design has been to draw attention to social and racial prejudice working against black women who are forced to participate in the labor force out of economic compulsion. In "Stealing B(l)ack voices: The Myth of the Black Matriarchy and The Women of Brewster Place" Celeste Frasier writes that African-American women are farthest first from financial well-being. Symbolically, the image of the black woman serves to legitimise policies with impact beyond that group. She discusses how in a strategy to lay the blame of impoverishment upon the impoverished community itself, sociologists like Murray and Moynihan have tried to locate the cause of poverty within the structure of the Negro family, the absence of the father and the female-headed household (matriarchal set-up). The black woman was made out to be a black beast/monster who shamelessly indulged in illicit sex with countless lovers for the sake of "churn(ing) out" babies for whom they could claim welfare cheques. Not only were these women allegedly immoral and libidinous, they were also calculating, and in their strength, "debilitating".[3] The black woman was branded as the root cause of all evil and her dark skin became a metaphor for dubious morals. This stereotyped image of the black woman was created as a part of a "politically dishonest" agenda to "cut the knot" of tangled welfare measures and social services, which had been initially formed to help impoverished families.[4] Clearly, the agenda of the federal government in the 1980s was to provide "a ready supply of low-wage labor to employers and to ensure that the welfare system does not offer an alternative to jobs at below-poverty wages".[5] In *WBP*, Naylor strikes at the base of such a monolithic and prejudiced image of the black woman by her portrayal of a number of different and distinctive women characters. In *LH*, *MD* and *BC* likewise, Naylor has represented black women as labor belonging to different categories of the hypotheses, but with a fluidity that avoids stereotyping. Women like Mama Day, Mattie Michaels, Eva Turner, Grandma Tilson, Nadine and Eve are both strong and vulnerable and none of them are matriarchs because they have all been, with the exception of Eva Turner and Mama Day, victims of circumstances that have forced them to rely on their own labor in order to survive. Each has functioned differently in their roles as labor, having formed their own perceptions about the work they do, be it confining or liberating, creative or mechanical. Naylor herself has said: "...one character couldn't be *the* black woman in America.... So I had...different women, all in different circumstances, encompassing the complexity of our lives, the richness of our diversity, from skin color on down to religious, political and sexual preference."[6] The internalization of the black woman's complex experience in America and its representation in fiction by Naylor through different characters in their varying roles as labor has allowed the scope of chipping away at the monolithic stereotypes of black women to create in their place diverse images of women who have each their own dreams, frustrations, sufferings and their own way of dealing with it. The one-dimensional image of the black woman, which has forever posed her strength (physical and mental) and great capacity for labor as her greatest weakness and her generosity as her discredit, has been given the lie by Naylor's portrayal of black women in her novels. If in her other novels, the social awareness and concern is clearly discernible in that it forms the basis and backdrop of her representations, in *WBP*, it is overt and intentional. Here, Naylor refutes the charges placed against black women by placing the blame of their situation upon the politicians and businessmen, government and commerce who have indicted black women for their own selfish ends and the motivated agenda of leaving them with no alternative but to work in the lowest paid jobs in order to survive. Female-headed black households were faced with utter impoverishment because they, being the most vulnerable group economically, were the first to suffer the blows of changes in welfare programs and to bear the brunt of economic oppression on account of racist discrimination, which made their dilemma more acute. The power-nexus formed by the government and commerce/economy generated a system of oppression that was responsible for the unrelieved poverty of the Negro masses, that in turn coerced them, especially African-American women, into the labor force. The black women of these Negro ghettoes, however, are represented in the image of "ebony phoenixes" who rise from the ashes of degradation and denigration to dare shape their own world again, to define it in their own voice. The insistent attempts of thesc women to better their lot has been met by ridicule and cruelty, they have been battered, crushed, humiliated, raped and destroyed, only to rise again, undeterred by the blows of life.

The first category of black women in the hypotheses of the present study include slave women—who were imported to America as laborers and regarded as such and gauged in that capacity primarily—a role that reduced them traditionally to the status of beasts of burden. In Naylor's novels, two women—Luwana Packerville of *LH* and Sapphira Wade of *MD*—belong to this category, both however having been able to change their slave status after marriage. There is a gulf of difference though in their situations, as Luwana Packerville became the wife of a wealthy Negro named Luther Needed but remained his slave because he never allowed her manumission, while Sapphira was initially bought and owned by Bascombe Wade—a white,

Norwegian slave owner who later fell in love with her to marry her, give her freedom and be convinced by her to make over the deed of his island to his other Negro slaves, whom he had also given freedom under his wife's persuasion. Luwana Packerville became ostensibly a rich housewife, having exchanged one form of bondage for the other, while Sapphira Wade wrested her freedom through tremendous willpower, wit and intelligence, coercion, manipulation and cunning that transformed her from a slave woman to a towering figure of strength to be reckoned with. In Luwana Packerville, the frustration, hopelessness and especially the sense of bondage is overwhelming, while Sapphira confirmed in every way, the mammy image projected by the black oral tradition, folklore and slave tales.

Luwana Packerville Needed was the first Needed wife to be brought to Linden Hills by her husband who was the first Needed who bought land and established the settlement known as Linden Hills as an exclusive enclave for upwardly mobile African-Americans. He became a rich, ruthlessly ambitious land owner with a vision of social respectability which was followed by his successors, all named Luther. It was rumoured that the first Luther Needed had sold his wife and children in order to get the money with which he bought Linden Hills. When he brought Luwana home, rumours were rife that he had bought back his original wife. However, Luwana was only twenty years of age and an octoroon[8]—a pre-requisite for a Needed wife. Beginning with her, none of the Needed wives featured anywhere in the hundreds of years old history of the Neededs. There were hardly any records about them and very few people could remember them by name or face, because they were addressed even by their own husbands as Mrs. Neededs. They hardly kept company with other black women of the community as they were envied for their "privileged" position as Nedeed wives, and they lived and died anonymously. The untold history of the Nedeed women, their personal tragedies and unspeakable experience were recorded in between pages of a Bible, diaries and albums, written painstakingly and hidden between folds of silk and lace cloth and old dresses inside trunks and is finally, painfully deciphered by the last of the Nedeed women during her imprisonment by her overbearing and jealous husband. Luwana's diary was recorded on the gold-edged tissue paper pages that divided one book of the Bible from another in her personal leather-bound Bible that she had gotten as a wedding gift from her mistress. The first entry was in 1837 when she was married to Luther. Subsequent entries did not have separate dates and they were months, often years apart. She came as the undertaker's wife, took charge of his housekeeping, and bore him a son next winter—a son who was an exact replica of his father and was also named Luther. In the first entry, Luwana expresses her humiliation and sorrow at the painful recognition of the horrible truth that Luther still kept the legal papers of his ownership over her securely locked in his safe, while she had expected him to have destroyed the shameful evidence of her thraldom and subjugation, immediately after marriage. She had in effect, changed owners and the years of fidelity, love and service had been meaningless. Her records, which were initially meant to be hidden from a husband's indulgent but "amused contempt" (*LH*, 117) gradually became the "diary of a slave" (*ibid*). Luwana was obviously well read and could also write expressively. She had been trained by her mistress to be a lady and the freedom that she had given her was ironically taken away by Luwana's husband, who gradually assumed the mantle of her master, though he was unfailingly polite to her. She was, she realized, being systematically erased from the Nedeed household in the form of exclusion from all activities including housekeeping—a role that she desperately tried to cling to, as a reason for survival. For the first few years after the birth of her son, her life was filled with the joys and natural rhythms of motherhood. Her days were full of domestic chores, housekeeping for her husband, cooking, cleaning, gardening and caring for her son like any other housewife and mother. The pride of being Mrs. Nedeed—a new identity, the taste of which was heady—gave her life a new dimension. However, the young mother's elation and sense of fulfillment in her role soon dimmed, as Luther began to spend more and more time with Luther Junior. The two were inseparable and the meticulous training imparted to the latter, soon made him a replica of his father not only in mere physical resemblance but also in behavior, habits, and even thoughts, so that Luwana found herself being hemmed in by the powerful presences of two Luthers. To add to her sense of injured pride and hurt, Luther Junior's manumission was arranged and she asked to prepare a dinner in celebration of her son's freedom that was legally necessary in view of the decree that "a child must follow the condition of its mother" (119) and therefore he would be, unless manumitted, a slave. Luwana was not manumitted however, and her "final humiliation" was to be forced to celebrate "the fact that (she was) now to be owned by (her) own son" (*ibid*).

The patriarchal domination and the power politics operating in the Nedeed family is underscored by the psychological oppression of Luwana who, in spite of being the mistress of the house (in name), was in truth a slave. Her mental agony was unbearable in the light of the fact that she had only this house in the world to call her home, she had put in all her love and labor to make it a home, and after all she had done, she was still held as a slave by her husband who did not trust her enough to free her from bondage, and still believed that she might run away, if given a chance. To ensure his hold over her (legal) he held her in leash much as one would a domestic animal. Having utilized her labor and commodified her motherhood by treating her as a mere vessel/carrier of her own son, he violated her sense of dignity and self-respect, denigrated her self-worth and made her independent spirit rebel at his peremptory dismissal of her very presence and need in the house. By appointing a housekeeper and gardener, Luther cut the source of the last iota of creative satisfaction that Luwana might have got from her role as labor, insisting upon flaunting his status (financial and social) and affronted by her refusal to accept her good fortune or be thankful in that she would no longer be required to slog like a maid. For Luwana, whose spontaneous mother-love had been curbed by her husband (she was not allowed any demonstration of affection towards her son nor was she allowed to cook his favorite dishes) and who was not his wife in any sense, physical (he never came to her after Luther's birth) or legal, her garden was her last resort to hold on to her sanity and sense of purpose and creativity. The unbearable hurt at the realization that not only did her husband mistrust her (after he had read in the newspaper about an incident where a slave woman had poisoned her master's soup) (119), even her son regarded her with the same mistrust, shattered Luwana. For the two Luthers, she only existed as a 'self' less form, to whom they were courteous and distant. Alienated, totally isolated and without a single soul to whom she could confide in, Luwana turned to scribbling between the pages of her Bible, addressing her letters to her "sister" Luwana (herself) and replying to her own queries. Alice Walker's Celie in *TCP* had written to God, but for Luwana, there was no solace in the idea of God, nor was there an living soul who cared for her life or death. The frightening vacuum in which she existed suspended her in a territory of soullessness that threatened to erase her identity and her 'self'. In her erstwhile mistress' (Mrs. Packerville) place, she had been required to work hard but compared to her present situation, ironically, she had had more liberty as a slave than a wife. Mistress Packerville's flaws diminished in her eyes in comparison with the 'evil' she encountered daily in her house. There had been more scope for self-expression in her mistress' house, her opinion was necessary in all the activities that took place there, her active involvement was appreciated, she was in knowledge about everything that happened there and her mistress "consulted" (122) her about all matters. There, her role as labor had not been forced and her work was meaningful and productive. Naylor gives a new dimension to the mistress-slave relationship when Luwana remembers how her mistress had shed tears at parting from her (as a person, not maid or laborer) while her own husband and son had demeaned her role to that of a glorified servant or worse, a puppet on a string. Here female bonding transcends racism and class considerations, while sexist discrimination is foregrounded. While earlier she had the liberty to refuse or deny some chore (she often avoided sewing lessons as she disliked it) and had the freedom of movement (she went for walking in the woods), now she could not even attend Church as Luther had quarreled with the minister. She feared that her growing restlessness and anger at the two Luthers' indifference and overbearance would drive her insane. She had served her purpose and "outlived (her) usefulness" (123) to her husband

and son who were pushing her inexorably out of the house, which had been her home for so many years. Having already left the Needed home in spirit, she was living there now as a moving corpse. The intense loneliness and sense of isolation impinged on her consciousness daily. She could have no friends among black women who hated her "privileged" status as a Nedeed wife and none among white women because of racial prejudice. Left alone to her own devices, she devised her own way of combating her frustration. A victim more of gender than racial or class discrimination, Luwana was entrapped amid stony silence, indifference and utter disregard of her emotions and feeling, and a negation of her personhood. She was a lost soul plagued with the overwhelming loss of "self" and identity—Mrs. Nedeed was only a name in reality—she was not a wife, mother, mistress, servant or even a person. Being rendered a non-person was especially degrading because it had happened in her own home. The bloody record of the exact number of times she had been spoken to and had voiced a reply was carved on her own flesh with a hatpin—her way of examining her own sanity and existence against the daily erasure of her identity and dignity. The last entry of her record was soul-wrenching, as Luwana wrote how she felt about her son's going away to school and how she expected him to address her wrapper and fail to notice that she was not sitting on the rocker as he came to wish a routine goodbye (124-25). The choked voice of a black woman found expression in those hidden records where, buried under the accumulated weight of racial and gender discrimination, it labored to find avenues of self-expression through a recognition of "self" as separate from role identities of wife or mother, that she was denied as she was not allowed freedom or spontaneity even in those roles.

MD has the legendary figure of the mother-goddess Sapphira Wade whose life story lived in that part of folk-memory in Willow Springs that could not be "use(d) to form words" (*MD*, 4). Different versions of the story were believed in by different people—each a little different from the other but the main contents remained the same. Sapphira Wade, a full-blooded African woman had come to Willow Springs as a slave woman, managed to marry Bascombe Wade (her master), bore him seven sons, persuaded him to will the island to his slaves and after his death left her land to her sons and set forth on a journey back to Africa (under unexplained and mysterious circumstances, believed as such by the islanders). Sapphira was believed to have been a conjure woman of repute with a magic healing touch, capable of walking through a lightning storm unscathed, known to grab a bolt of lightning in her palm to set fire to the dry wood under her medicine pot—a superwoman with matchless qualities, extraordinary strength of mind and great knowledge and wisdom. Her sale-deed, however, underscores the reality of her situation as a slave woman who, despite her unusual traits of character, had still been only a beast of burden for her white masters. The conditions of the sale-deed, which must have been a replica of a thousand other sale deeds of slaves sold in those days, indicated Sapphira's age, race, sound physical condition and behavioral traits. She was, like a prize horse or mule, a possession to be evaluated in terms of purity of stock, breed, strength of limbs, teeth and mildness or otherwise of disposition because she was being bought or sold for her labor primarily. The total dehumanization, commodification and decivilization of slaves was evident in every line of the deed. The black woman Sapphira was only a she-animal who happened to have some unusual traits in the eyes of her owners. Sapphira's remarkable traits of character defied stereotyping and the deed brings to the fore her individual characteristics. Her "sullen disposition", "bilious nature", resistance even "under reasonable chastisement the performance of field or domestic labor" and her "extreme mischief" in having "del(ved) in witchcraft" (5) indicate clearly that Sapphira had not been the run-of-the-mill submissive and cowering slave woman, nor was she amicably disposed towards her captors. The "reasonable chastisement" she was subjected to can well be imagined to be an euphemism for the terrible tortures (physical and mental) inflicted upon rebellious and disobedient slaves and Sapphira's stubborn resistance even under the lashings of a whip to submit to the performance of field or domestic labor speaks of her indomitable will and courage. It is needless to reiterate the hardships she must have endured in keeping up her rebellious aggression. Through understatement and scattered references, Naylor gives clues about her slave life. It was also mentioned in the deed that Sapphira was an expert nurse-maid and mid-wife but suspicions were harbored against her regarding her acquaintance with witchcraft and sorcery. As a slave, she had the potential of functioning in multiple labor roles as besides domestic and field labor, she could also serve as mid-wife and nurse. As for her magical powers, they were confirmed by her ability to bewitch her master, whom she poisoned or stabbed, according to folk belief. As a wife, she was more than anyone could wish for, having borne seven sons to him within a span of a thousand days. However, no one knew whether they all were Bascombe Wade's sons as they traced their lineage back to the mother, starting the trend and tradition of matrilineal descendance. Towards the close of the novel, a new and contradictory dimension is given to the accepted relationship between Bascombe Wade and Sapphira when, from the diary unearthed by Miranda from a hidden place in their old house, she gleaned information that proved that they had loved each other. More than the actual facts of Sapphira's life, her remarkable feats and achievements as a slave woman who "*took* her freedom" (111) contributed to the constructing of her image as a superwoman and goddess. The story of Sapphira is told through the voice of the island and the truth or otherwise of the stories is irrelevant because one needs only to keep in mind the circumstances of Sapphira's coming to the island, the odds she had faced and her determination and strength that enabled her to overcome them by outwitting/tricking/coercing or truly loving her master and husband. The word "slave woman" came to acquire a different and new meaning on account of Sapphira who upended the theory of the slave's status as a social "non-person" by setting a new definition to her role. Sapphira was a true matriarch in the sense of the politics of empowerment. This African-American woman was able to reconstruct the image of the African-American slave woman through her fierce pride, independence and ability to impress and influence. She spoke of intelligence and fearlessness, of which the former attribute was rarely, if ever, credited to a black woman. From the status of a slave woman, Sapphira came to acquire, by virtue of her extraordinary capabilities, the status of her master's wife, mistress of the island, mother, reputed conjuress, matriarch, superwoman and finally a goddess in the memory of the island folk who became the guardian angel and guiding spirit of the island—a black slave woman who had transcended through the performance of her multiple labor roles, the very meaning of slavery and enforced work, having achieved independence not only for herself, but also for others. Her multilayered personality lays open the option of several interpretations and labor-role possibilities. She bequeathed her descendants with the heritage of benevolence and power.

Category II, comprising the poor, black women condemned to a life of unremitting toil include most of the women of *WBP*—having come, as already mentioned, to stay at Brewster Place, an urban slum because they had no choice. Brewster Place was the last destination of the black women, many of whom had migrated from the South for better opportunities, or to escape poverty or pain. Mattie Michael was born in the South (Tennessee) and was an only child. Her father had a farm of his own and a modest income. They were lower middle-class (rural) blacks who however did not lack in food or the basic necessities of life—Mattie's father was a typical patriarch, with very strict codes of conduct and propriety. He was a religious, stern, quiet man who would provide his wife and child with the security and stability that most black men could not provide for their families. As the breadwinner and provider, he also expected total obedience and submissiveness and would brook no misdemeanour from either wife or daughter. So when his beloved and adored daughter lost her virginity to Butch Fuller who, in his opinion was a "no count ditch hound" (*WBP*, 9) in spite of the strictures he had imposed, in a violent fury, he subjected Mattie to a vicious beating with a broom stick. He had raised Mattie in such a way that his mind was "conditioned over the years to her unquestioning obedience" (21-22) that precluded any possibility otherwise. In trying to physically wound Mattie, he was actually trying to stamp out the ugly head of blatant disobedience that had reared in the form of her refusal to divulge the name of her lover who had impregnated her. Ironically, Mattie was trying to protect her father from further disillusionment and hurt by letting him know that his daughter had betrayed his trust not with the man he had chosen and deemed fit for her but the man he had always condemned. Mattie's instinctive response was to shield the baby in her womb from harm, and Mattie's mother Fannie reacted instinctively too by intervening to plead with her husband and finally to save her daughter's life by using the shotgun blast to bring Samuel to his senses, who broke down to weep when he saw that he had mindlessly beaten his cherished daughter to a pulp.

The incident marked the beginning of a new phase in Mattie's life. During her pregnancy, she had drawn closer to her mother and away from her father. Now her estrangement with her father pushed her into cutting the knot of parental/familial ties, her roots and her home. Her sole purpose in life was to create a new world for herself and her soon to be born child, whom she had decided to give her own name. Having never cared emotionally for Butch, she did not contact him, as she knew that he was a goodtimer and would never take the responsibility upon himself anyway. Nor did she blame Fuller for any of it because she had succumbed to the pleasure of his caresses, knowing well that he had no normal inhibitions, taking the enjoyment of sex purely for pleasure's sake. Mattie's strict upbringing had only suppressed, not eliminated her natural sexuality and like any young girl (and virgin) she was ripe for the thoroughly sensual pleasure that Butch had promised and given her that fateful afternoon. She had tasted to the full the joy of the life in the rhythms of her body, and for her, it was enough for a lifetime. Never one to cling to relationships, Mattie set forth on her journey to the North, where the war time job market invited labor from all around especially the South. Her pride and independence made her leave the security of her father's house that she had known as home, the fresh country air, good food, the large front yard and mostly, the open spaces she had been accustomed to as a country girl, and that she craved for in the cramped apartments she had to put up in. Her childhood friend Etta Mae Jonson lived in North Carolina and she took her in. In her apartment, Mattie's son Basil was born. The next twenty years of Mattie's life was devoted to the upbringing of her cherished son. Her pride in having been able to create a life and nurture it against all odds made her forget that Basil was not only a part of her own flesh and blood—he was also Butch Fuller's son who, despite his charms and candidness, was irresponsible and reckless. As Etta Mae said to the fascinated mother, who found her new born son to be the most perfect of creatures she had ever seen, and over whom she felt, no one but she had any claim: "That's right, all yours, built-in heartache for the next twenty years" (26). But to Mattie, with a new role identity to live for, these words fell on deaf ears. Motherhood had given a new purpose to her life and she was determined to labor tirelessly for the well-being of a person she had brought into this world. Mattie's pride did not allow her to hide the fact that she was an unwed mother, nor did she ever marry again, the first priority being given to her son always, but always, even when she herself doubted the wisdom of doing so. Etta Mae moved then to New York and Mattie was left to survive with her newborn son in a boarding house apartment, with some supply of food for the baby. Left to her own resources and all alone, she began her fight for survival. The "assembly-line job" (27) that she found at a book bindery required her to stay away for the whole day, and she was forced to employ a baby-sitter for her son with money that she could ill-afford. Mrs. Prell, an old lady living in the same apartments as she, agreed to look after the baby while she was away at work, but she was forgetful and Mattie was petrified as to what harm the baby might come to during the day. Her anxiety drove her to walk the thirty blocks back to her apartment just to see her baby and ensure his safety. In order to save carfare, she rushed back and forth on foot while having her lunch as she rushed through the street. She was like a young mother-bird, trying to shield her son with her own body. Her struggles however had only just begun. The money she earned was barely enough to meet the needs of a growing child. Half of her salary was spent in paying the baby-sitter, the rest went towards paying the rent for the cramped boarding house quarters, buying food and keeping money aside for emergencies and essential purchases. She scrimped on personal expenses, gave up the only source of entertainment (the Saturday night film shows), did not buy clothes or shoes till absolutely necessary. The little money she could save by cutting down her personal requirements went as fees for a specialist and costly medicine when Basil developed stomach ailment. In her role as mother, therefore, Mattie sacrificed everything for her son's sake and all her labor was directed towards a single goal—the comfort and well-being of her adored son. During those hard days, Mattie often thought about her lovely home and longed for the healthy food, fresh country air and open spaces for her son to grow up in. Struggling alone, she felt the acute need of her mother's loving care and support but her fierce pride curbed any desire she had of going back. Her mother was unable to leave her father to come to stay with her for a while as he was now a broken man, and her consideration for his feelings and concern for her made her refuse her mother's offer to send Basil home to her care so that she could earn money without having to worry about child care and child rearing. Basil's unmistakable resemblance to Butch Fuller would be an instrument of psychological torment to her already shattered father. Mattie was too caring a daughter to subject him to this renewed torture in his old age, nor could she lay her son open to insults, young though he was.

So Mattie, despite having a choice, chose the hard way out. Her wish to take courses at a night school (to improve her job prospect), was thwarted by her need to spend at least the evenings with her son as she was already missing out on the little but all-important joys of motherhood like Basil's first step and first words. Her relationship with her son was the only sustaining bond that made life meaningful for her and she could not bear to become a stranger to her own flesh and blood in the process of earning their bread. The status quo would have continued had Basil not been bitten by a rat one Friday night. The weekend found Mattie, her child hoisted on one hip and lugging a heavy suitcase, leaving the boarding house for good, and walking the town from one end to the other in search of a new residence. She was turned away again and again, as most people would not take in children. Her choice being limited, she could not afford to approach white or affluent black neighbourhoods and the latter two in any case insisted on "respectability" and a marital status or at least the name of a father for her child that she could not produce. Shunned, weary, dejected, with blistered hands and heavy feet, she dragged herself through the same block of houses twice. Her options had dwindled, home being the only safe and feasible alternative. It was then that she met Eva Turner, a white-looking black lady who was to change the course of her life yet again, and to become for her the mother, friend and guide she had been in dire need of. This second turning point in her life bought her a new phase of happiness because here she had a generous and kind friend who was also practical and astute enough to lend her advice, though she often disregarded Eva's good counsel to indulge her son. Along with Ciel (Eva's granddaughter) and Eva, she and Basil formed a family and she was at last enfolded in the security and warm embrace of a family. Despite Mattie's insistence, Eva refused to take rent, making her deposit that amount in the bank so that after Eva's death, she could buy the house from her heirs. This beautiful old house was home for her in the true sense of the word and came to mean more than mere security and comfort—it stood for everything Mattie had struggled for and striven to obtain—space, light, warmth and greenery—a place to rest in peace. With Miss Eva taking care of Basil, she could go to her workplace in peace, but she did not have any inclination to have relationships with men—casual or serious, and she avoided contact with them, emotional or physical. She existed only as Basil's mother in spite of Eva's repeated warnings against over-protection and possessiveness that was turning her son into an irresponsible and dependent young man. Perhaps Mattie, once bitten, was too shy to entangle herself with men or lay herself open to more hurt or disillusionment. Instead, she channeled all her capacity for love into nurturing and raising Basil, with all her labor directed towards securing a stable future for her son. She preferred to work for her son and realize her only dream that one day her son would grow into a mature and responsible adult, care for his mother and fill her house with the laughter of grand children. Naylor has set the stage here for the final disillusionment of Mattie's life that would once again bring her back to the same impoverished and homeless state as she was before meeting Eva—the only difference being that now she had neither hopes, nor youth and no burden—only herself to care for. Oblivious to the designs of fate and naturally hopeful and hard-working, Mattie took up an extra job to supplement her income and in order to pay the mortgage on the house she had bought. She worked to give her son "room to grow in, a yard to run in, a decent place to bring in friends" (40), and also labored to create a secure home for herself in her old age: "Her own spirit must one day have a place to rest because the body could not, as it pushed and struggled to make all around them safe and comfortable" (*ibid*).

Over the years, her son had grown into a stranger from the young boy who had clung to her skirts, crying for her company. Now she could not recognize this moody and idle man, did not know his friends and did not dare ask about what company he kept, or his whereabouts. Her son had set the rules of the game much like her husband would have, had she married—she was to earn, cook and clean for him (work that she had thought a part of a mother's duty), maintain the large house, its adjoining garden alone and handle all problems alone. On Sundays, she exhausted herself in sprucing up the house, her tired feet and stiff back protesting against years of unceasing labor. In essence, Mattie had always remained alone in her struggles and all the support she had got, had been from women—her mother, Etta Mae and Eva Turner. Basil would run to her with his problems but disregard her requests because Mattie had, as a mother, only given, and neither expected nor got anything in return. With throbbing poignancy, Naylor portrays the last and final betrayal of Mattie's life and the inexpressible hurt that renders her immune to all future possibilities of disillusionment. So Mattie's dreams were shattered by her son and she lost her home—one that she had made with so much love and labor, never having relaxed, rested or given herself time to pause. Basil was convicted of murder and jailed after a drunken brawl, and in spite of repeated warnings from her lawyer, Mattie risked mortgaging her house to bail him out against her better judgement, her mother's instincts roused to protect her son, this time from the squalor and rough treatment in jail. Placing trust on Basil was the mistake that cost her cherished home, for her son ran away, leaving her to face the consequences. As always, Mattie had given priority to his problems, laying aside her own troubles to sort his out first. Having suppressed her physical and emotional needs to mould herself into an ideal mother, Mattie had erased her 'self' to submerge it in her role identity—an identity that had lately begun to grate on her sense of prudence/rightness, but one that she could not give up because that was all she had existed for. So she was left to fend for herself in her old age, having been rendered homeless for the third time in her life—this time, not by choice.

The final phase in Mattie's life began with her search for a cheap apartment within her means, which brought her to Brewster Place. Here she brought her plants and memories and here, at last, she was free from the tensions of a lifetime of worrying about her son and the bond of a relationship that had entailed only sacrifice and given very little, except the satisfaction of having single handedly procured a livelihood and maintained her son, and the emotional fulfillment she had got out of it. In a way, his betrayal was a release because Basil would have always drained her with his constant need for support (ironically that was what Mattie had prayed for, as a young mother—that her son need her always) (52). Like Plum, Eva's son in Morrison's *Sula,* Basil was dependent, but unlike him, it had not been on account of any trauma—he had never really grown up. Mattie was no Eva, however, and she had cast her last die in an effort to give her son another chance. Paradoxically, Mattie's freedom from responsibility of her son gave her a chance to come into her own. At Brewster Place, she acquired an identity of her own, was a woman to be reckoned with—a woman who was not powerful in the sense of a dominating matriarch, but empowered by her great human compassion and all-embracing love that she turned towards the lonely, battered, hurt women of Brewster Place. Here, Mattie found her 'self' in her new role as labor—here, she labored for the love of

Brewster's women, gave them her good counsel, guidance and support and performed her labor of love to save them from the innumerable hurts of life, salvaged the shattered pieces of their 'self's when they were left broken emotionally or physically. Her profound understanding and deep well of love now found a new channel, her labor, a new creativity in her role of a social messiah. She had begun her journey to Brewster Place alone and homeless, to find among its decaying walls a refuge and haven where, like her plants, she would have to struggle to survive amid the dinginess and squalor, and where, only a weak sunlight (symbolic of hope/optimism/joy) filtered through the grimy window panes.

Mattie's invincible spirit cannot but be applauded as she creates a niche for herself at Brewster with her generosity, ready helpfulness and pithy comments that had the "grinding" precision "of a diamond cutter's drill" (91). In her role as labor, Mattie has encountered upheavals and undergone transitions to emerge as a person whose labor as a sister and mother to women in need of support has been fruitful in forging bonds of sisterhood.

Miss Eva Turner's grand child Ciel's life was enmeshed in the vicious cycle and ever-repeating pattern of appearance and abandonment of her errant husband. Naylor presents Eugene in the image of those ineffectual, cynical and selfish black men who drift in and out of the lives of struggling black women who try to bring some semblance of stability by holding on to their husbands or lovers—a representation that refutes the traditional charges brought against black women that they are responsible for the dispersal of their families and for emasculating black men. In exposing Ciel's vulnerability, Naylor deliberately undercuts the image of the self-sufficient black women, for whom men are dispensable complications while for the most part, the mainstay of their independence is compulsion, not choice.

In *LH*, which is an exclusive African-American neighbourhood, only three women belong to Category II, each different and distinctive and able to deal with her problems through her role as labor. Known as "grandma" or "mama" from her very childhood, Mamie Tilson was nobody's fool-spirited and sharp-tongued woman whose firmness of character could be seen clearly beneath her translucent "oiled cheese-cloth" like complexion (*LH*, 13). She had known the original Luther Nedeed closely and had been his partner in fishing at the pond surrounding his house. The land on which her shack stood had been leased in her name by that Luther, and there was no mention of a husband in the deed as such. When Luther's son asked her to sell, Mamie Tilson did not hesitate to give him a piece of her mind. She could anticipate the Nedeed reaction and even their next move, so she had been astute enough to register the deed and her will in the court, legalizing the documents which would pass down her hard-earned property to her progeny. Asked to recapitulate, her answer was to send a wad of tobacco spit contemptuously near Luther's expensive shoes and immaculate trousers that said everything by way of an answer. Luther in his turn did not pursue the matter, deciding to build houses all around her and bury the ugliness of the run-down shack in the bosom of Linden Hills. Grandma Tilson had also been shrewd enough to realize that the principle she had stuck to all these years of not "selling the mirror in her soul" (59) to the Nedeeds or anyone for that matter in the course of ambitious progress would not be carried forward by her daughter-in-law or granddaughter (Lester's mother and sister Roxanne). So, she willed the house in the name of Lester who was not only a poet but also in some ways, a seer of truth. Grandma Tilson's firm belief was that if one traded the "mirror" in one's "soul", there was nothing left inside one except emptiness. That inner "mirror" reflected only the truth about oneself and when the world outside became too confusing for comprehension one needed only to turn to that inner core to regain one's orientation and realize one's essence (*ibid*). Mamie Tilson may have been an uneducated black woman but she was respected by the Negro community of Linden Hills for her ability to arrive at the truth with unerring accuracy, her ability to speak that in the face of every person including Luther Nedeed, and her independence that was not subject to pressure or influence. What Mamie Tilson had done for a living is not mentioned specifically in the text, but it is amply clear that because she was one of the original inhabitants of Linden Hills, renting one of the shacks built by the first Luther Nedeed, she must have belonged to the poor black underclass and must have paid the rent with the money earned by the sweat of her brow and hard work. The nature of the work, in that day and age, for a black woman could have been only menial and it is not difficult to imagine that she had like other black men and women like her, taken up her share of physical labor and survived on the money earned from it. As Luther Nedeed had envisioned cynically, these were men and women who had in the three hundred years of black history in America, been capable of only certain work and were best at "digging another man's coal, cleaning another man's home, rocking another man's baby"(9). A black woman could be a maid, a mammy or a mule (a work horse) for the white men and women and a co-breadwinner, bearer of children, a mother and housewife all rolled in one, for black men. The work she had done to bring up her children and her trials have not been overstated. One needs only to imagine her personal trials against the backdrop of her social realities. However, Mamie Tilson, with her distinctive personality and emphatic opinions would have been more likely than not, of having been a matriarch with a brood of children. Her daughter-in-law accused her of "corrupt(ing)" (29) both her son and grandson by destroying any ambition they might have had to improve their lot. Mamie Tilson had lived a long, eventful life and during all of it, no one in Linden Hills had had the courage to refute her belief or her logic. She had recognized, long back, the potential seed of destruction that lay buried in the egocentricism of Luther and his progeny. Illiterate she may have been, and sometimes biased in her outburst, Mamie Tilson had never lost the "mirror of (her) soul", the sale of which had made Nedeed pose as God in the pride of his creation of an empire, despite his superior knowledge.

Willie Mason's mother Mrs. Mason is referred to several times in the text (*LH*, 58, 167, 173), especially by Willie who had, as a child and young teenager, witnessed and been a part of the trials that she had undergone to bring up six children, without help from an alchoholic husband. Living in a cramped little apartment in Putney Wayne with six children and a bitter husband left her with very few choices in life. Willie's father brought home a meager pay cheque which could barely support three children that led him to drink in frustration. He died of liver cirrhosis, leaving her widowed and alone to fend for six children. She became a welfare mother because the next step would have been starvation. Mrs. Mason had stayed married to Willie's father despite the regular physical abuse she had to face "because a bruised face and half a pay cheque was better than welfare, and that's the only place she had left to go with no education and six kids" (58).

Mrs. Mason was not a welfare mother in the image of Cora Lee in *WBP* who was not mature enough to handle the responsibility of her children. Here was a black woman who endured physical abuse for the sake of her children and yet tried to give them a life of their own even amidst her own struggles and pain. She was first a mother and then a person who had, in her role as labor, taken untold hardships upon herself to protect and provide for her children. She did not relinquish her role or abandon her responsibilities on account of her staunch loyalty to her family and her ingrained sense of duty and worth. In so doing she had come to be adored by her children who valued her opinion and respected her self-sacrifice.

In *MD*, Naylor represents Carmen Rye as a poor, black woman who had married a shiftless husband. In confirming the image of Carmen Rye as a neglecting mother like Core Lee, Naylor has not condoned the strength of male-headed, patriarchal families because in the same novel, she has also shown the strength of matriarchal households like those of the Days. In adding another shade to the already varied spectrum of black women she has respresented in their roles as labor, Naylor has, like a consummate artist, laid open possibilities of the complex psychological dimensions that defy similarities. So Carmen Rye is both like and unlike Cora because she has problems peculiar to her situation, though to a great extent she herself has failed (on account of her indulgent and careless nature) in her role as labor and as a mother, to improve it.

In *BC*, the proprietor of the Café is the narrator who introduces the different characters. He was born in Brooklyn as the youngest son of Negro parents who served a rich, colored family named Van Morrison. His first impression about himself, his parents and life in general was that "there were rich white people, rich colored people—and us" (*BC*, 5) and that "liveried coachmen, sable wraps, and brownstone mansions meant rich, while getting up at five in the morning to stoke the furnace, start breakfast, and lay out the morning suits for people like that meant you weren't" (4). His mother and father were cook and butler respectively, at the Van Morrison's home and his father was so grateful to Mr. Van Morrison for having hired them that he "would have cut his own throat" (5) for his employer. His parents had lived in the slums of Manhattan with his elder brother and they had desperately wanted to move out of them. The opportunity offered by Mr. Van Morrison was manna from heaven because in the nineteen fifties, colored people were hard put to find jobs as domestics in posh suburbs or in fine houses (where rich white people and rich colored people lived). Occasionally, a black woman would be hired for the most menial jobs as a charwoman or laundress for pay work, a black man as a coachman or gardener, but never as residing staff—cook, housekeeper or valet—jobs that were not available to blacks as they were considered unfit for responsibilities or untrained to handle jobs that required poise, manners and skill. Rich Negroes "held the same attitudes as wealthy white people but even more so, feeling that they had more to prove" (7). Given the situation or job scenario, his father considered himself lucky to have been hired at all while his mother, sensing that Mrs. Van Morrison did not want colored servants because it was a come down in status in the eyes of the neighbors (they lived in a posh, all-white neigborhood in Lafeyette), expressed her cutting contempt of her mistress thus: "—it don't matter what colored hands is peeling these potatoes, none of them neighbors is about to sit down and eat with her" (7). She was a poor black woman who had spent twenty-five years of her life working for the Van Morrisons with her husband, during which she hated her mistress with a slow, consuming passion that she perversely enjoyed. She was the self-righteous, morally upright, hardworking black woman, taking her stand against the pampered, rich black woman of dubious morals who had traded her virtue (in her career as a singer) and her association with a "sizeable pension" (7) and a mention in Mr. Van Morrison's will. Prejudiced as she was against her mistress, like Ondine in Morrison's *TB*, she was also not in a position to voice complaints except in private, when she expressed her opinion to her husband or indulged in kitchen gossip with the other servants (the rest of the staff was white). As a residing cook, she was on duty the whole day and was justifiably angry at her husband's view that families were a nuisance. Class having operated more in this case than race, she felt that Mrs. Van Morrison, as a colored woman herself, was superior to her only in respect of affluence and therefore she had cause to be bitter against this woman of her own race who had assumed the superior stance of a white person, having distinguished herself emphatically from her humble servants.

Jesse Bell of *BC* came from a family of tough long shoremen in Manhattan Island and recalled proudly: "It takes a real strong woman to make a home for men like that,..." (120) and her mother was just such a woman who had brought up a whole brood of children without help from their father or fathers. She had known, first hand, the difficulties of bringing up so many children without any aid and she drilled such a strong sense of responsibility into her sons and daughters that even if the Bell men (titled after their mother) did not marry the women who bore their children, "they sure married them children" (*ibid*). Tough as they were, they respected their mother too much and remembering the struggles she had been through to bring them up, they would apologise if they had "bad-mouth(ed) her" (121). Jesse says that they remembered what their mother had to do to survive—work that drained even men at the dock—in freezing or burning temperatures, exposed to the extremes of climate, seasons and the sea. She would "take no shit from a man" (*ibid*), never put up with misbehaviour, and she carried a huge scar on her belly as testimony to the heroic fight she had put up against one such man. She was the reigning matriarch who had empowered herself through honesty, integrity and hard work. An old woman now, she could still wield power. Jesse's brothers had acknowledged her right to rule in the house not out of pity she says, but because "power (knew) power" (*ibid*). She was proud of being the daughter of such a woman—"women like that (bred) daughters like that" (*ibid*) and Jesse was a full-spirited daughter of the docks—prepared to take up the challenges of life, proud of her upbringing, her toughness and her forthright honesty.

A poor, black woman from the working-class background, Mrs. Bell of *BC* had an inherent sense of self-respect that she retained till the last. When she was invited to her daughter's house for a party, she did not come empty handed—she came with gifts of food and drink and finding that they had been called there deliberately to be insulted, she held court in the pouring rain to have her party any way with her children, keeping a distance from her son-in-law's high society and affluent guests. She caught a cold and died soon after—an African-American woman who had inspired respect and admiration in her sons and daughters alike till the very last and having transcended her poverty through sheer grit and hard work.

Under Category III come middle-class housewives of the hypotheses who are materially better off than poor, black women but are confined within their roles as housewives and mothers, existing in relation to their men, respectable and secure in their marital status and finally, alienated from the realities of the Negro masses, having consciously distanced themselves from their poorer sisters, thus losing in the process the ability to communicate, reach out and forge strong tries of sisterhood and friendship. Naylor's middle-class women are from the urban sector mainly and some of them better off than the others and aspiring to attain Category IV (rich housewives and society ladies) have for appearance's sake employed servants (like the middle-class women of Linden Hills) as status symbols. African-American women from the semi-rural sector are found in *MD*, but because they live in Willow Springs, an island with its individual and ethnic codes of social expectations, they are relatively more independent than their counterparts in Morrison or Walker's novels or Naylor's other novels. However, they are still limited within the confines of their own pretences and prudish assertions of propriety and decorum. In Naylor, one finds black women moving towards new horizons in that her representations are more contemporary and therefore her women are freer and more able to express their individualities, so more diverse within the same category.

In *WBP*, Mrs. Eva Turner and Mrs. Fannie Michael belong to Category III, urban and rural respectively. Mattie Michael's benefactress Miss Eva Turner was a mulatta who owned a big house filled with old and beautiful furniture, bric-à-brac and wonderful plants. She was an astute reader of character and with the experience of having lived with five husbands to enrich her life, she was full of a genuine human kindness and true generosity. Miss Eva was an incorrigible survivor whose homespun philosophy and pert observations were perceptive if humorous. In providing Mattie with a home, she became a second mother to her. Having faced life squarely with her usual spunk, she however was not cynical or bitter. She said that husbands were not worth the pain and trouble they caused and children were as much a source of joy as suffering, warning Mattie of the outcome of devoting too much attention to her son. Eva had mothered several children, none of whom lived with her in her old age. She had taken up the responsibility of bringing up her granddaughter Ciel whose parents had left her behind. Miss Eva had been a housewife and even in her old age she looked after the house, cooked, cleaned and maintained it as always, active and sprightly as she was till the last. She had not allowed Mattie to pay her rent, forcing her to deposit that sum in her own account, not expecting anything in return for her generosity. Miss Eva is again yet another black woman who defies the conventional ideas about fair skinned black women. She had made no attempt to cross the colour line or integrate with the white race, taking husbands according to preference. Also she had reached out in kindness to a woman of her own race providing her with a home and motherly love. Miss Eva is portrayed in the image of a kind, loving but shrewd mother, whose past experience had taught her to embrace and not reject life. She had taken patriarchal domination in her stride (her father locked her up in her room for days, after which she again eloped with the same lover) and had learnt how to handle men. She had never hankered after respectability and had not been ashamed of her own decisions or mistakes. She was not the archetypal matriarch but a wonderfully sane and generous person who could look back without bitterness upon the trials of her past life. Headstrong and impulsive as a young girl, Miss Eva had, even in old age, acted emphatically and only according to her perceptions of life, thus allowing no confinement of role identity to erode her 'self' or soul.

Fannie Michael was Mattie's mother and Samuel Michael's wife, living in the South. She was a middle-class housewife with a husband who was a sharecropper and managed to earn enough to have a house of their own, good food, and clothes on their back. She did not need to work outside her home and her husband perhaps would not have allowed it because he was a stern and old-fashioned man. Fannie was however no submissive doormat of a wife. She had a temper, firm ideas of her own and would not take anything lying down. As a mother, she was not indulgent or possessive towards her only daughter but when Mattie became pregnant, it was Fannie who provided her the emotional and moral support and strength to endure her father's rigid silence. Torn between conflicting loyalties, Fannie had the courage to console her daughter in the face of her husband's simmering rage and it was she who sprang to action to prevent her husband from beating Mattie to death. In saving her daughter's life, she risked taking a step which under normal circumstances, she never would have done. When later, she chose to stay with and support her husband rather than go away to live with her daughter and grandson, we see in her the emergence of a new image of the black woman—one who would give priority to her husband rather than her child, which in itself is unusual in the light of a tradition of possessive mother-love that has put the needs of children first. Fannie Michael therefore was a middle-class housewife but with a difference. She would not unduly indulge her only child, nor was she so rigidly moral as to chastise her daughter for having made a mistake. Motherhood, for Fannnie, was as natural as it was noble and it could not be judged by the standard concept of respectability and conventions. She therefore had an independence of thought and a breadth of mind, unusual in middle-class housewives. Not the breadwinner in her family, she however contributed as much towards the functioning of her home by way of labor as any other housewife and she was not one to be dominated by a tyrant husband. The play of patriarchal dynamics is subtle here and with her steady support of her daughter's rebellion, she inadvertently overturned the equation of relationships. In the end, her husband becomes dependent on her emotionally and true to her character, she faithfully sticks to her commitment as a wife. Being a middle-class housewife therefore does not make Fannie as helpless as Sofia's mother in Walker's *TCP* or as circumscribed in propriety as Helene Wright in Morrison's *Sula*.

Kiswana's mother Mrs. Browne lived in Linden Hills, the posh suburban residential area where affluent blacks had their apartments. Her husband Wilson worked in the real estate and had a "five-figure income" (83) with which they could afford to live there and appoint servants to look after the house. Coming from the upper midle-class background (urban), Mrs. Browne had a natural poise and elegance that her daughter envied. She was "copper-colored" with "streaks of ebony and gold in her complexion" (76 and 85) and dressed expensively, but with quiet good taste. She did not need to work outside her home either to supplement her husband's incomc or as a means of self-expression or creativity because she was a typically contented housewife who kept her own lovely home beautifully, decorating it to her taste. Though she had enough money to spend as she wished, Mrs. Browne was not lavish. She had come from a family of proud, black people (*cf.* Syndey in *TB*—proud, Philadelphia Negroes) and like them, refused to let all the hard work and effort that had gone into achieving their present status go to waste. Unlike Helene Wright of *S*, Mrs. Browne was proud of her ancestry and in her own way, her husband and she did their bit for the large majority of less fortunate and struggling black people [as members of the NAACP—a republican organization that Kiswana sneeringly called the "middle-of-the-road dumping ground for black republicans" (85)]. However, she had a typical, if natural bourgeoisie aversion for the disorder, poverty and squalor that one found in poor slums like Brewster Place. She generalized slum-dwellers indiscriminately as "these people" (83) who could pose a threat to a single girl like her daughter, living alone amidst them. But offended as her sense of propriety is by the statue of the naked Yoruba goddess that Kiswana kept in her living room, concerned that it would invite unwelcome attentions from her male friends, pained and worried as she is by her daughter's decision to live in these "shabby and rundown" (83) quarters and struggling to get a job and unable to afford a telephone, Mrs. Browne was not a mother who would "drive" her daughter's "imagination underground" (*cf.* Ch. 2, Helene Wright in *S*). Her arguments were based on logical and practical considerations when she tried to persuade Kiswana to complete her college education and aim for jobs that would make her influential enough to be of real use to her people. In Mrs. Browne's eyes, Kiswana as a struggling, unemployed black woman, aiming for blue-collar, clerical jobs, living from "hand-to-mouth"(84), could only rave and rant, and organize meetings rather than bring about any meaningful change in their situation. For Mrs. Browne therefore, self-advancement and individual ambition were stepping stones towards a nobler cause—the upliftment of the poor black community—a means that need not be condemned as it justified the end.

In her anger at her mother's attempt to distinguish themselves from the common black people, who like them, were pitted against a racist society, Kiswana accused her of being a "white man's nigger" (85), thus provoking her into a reaction that ultimately elicited Kiswana's apology and grudging respect. Mrs. Browne's impassioned speech about her ancestors who were full-blooded and free blacks, spoke of her pride in everything they had striven for:

> I am alive because of the blood of proud people who never scraped or begged or apologised for what they were.... And I learned through the blood of these people that black isn't beautiful, and isn't ugly—black is! It's not kinky and its not straight hair, it just is. (86)

She had been hurt unbearably when her daughter had changed her given name in a revolutionary zeal—a name she had given her in great love and pride because it had been her grandmother's name—

> a woman who bore nine children and educated them all, who held off six white men with a shotgun when they tried to drag one of her sons to jail for 'not knowing his place'. (86)

Mrs. Browne was no over-ambitious mother like Mrs. Tilson of *LH*, who wanted her children to negate their racial roots or people of their race in order to establish themselves. She had a quiet self-pride, which was as strong in its own way as Kiswana's idealistic rebellion against bourgeoisie education and republicanism. In an age when young black men and women thought it fashionable to rediscover their Africanism and flaunt it by wearing "Afros" and kinky hair, Mrs. Browne, who had come a long way in life, thought of a maturer and more stable and intrinsic revolution in the form of social change that would bring a significant upliftment in the lives of African-American people who lived below the poverty line and dreamed that one day that would save enough out of their "meager...pay checks" (77) to leave slums like Brewster Place. In wanting the best for her children, she was, as she said, "not being white or red or black"—she was just "being a mother" (86). She strikes a chord deep in Kiswana's heart and reaches across barriers of race to remind one that one's skin colour does not influence the primordial and universal instinct of motherhood that seeks, more than anything else, the well-being of her children. In the light of the new understanding that mother and daughter achieve, they move towards an acceptance of each other's opinion. In the final count, Mrs. Browne represents (despite her impressive exterior, dignity of bearing and inherent self-respect) the concerned mother who is portrayed in the delightfully identifiable and familiar mould of a loving, if children-centred mother. This puts her on a different plane than either Helene Wright of *S* or Mrs. Tilson. While Helene Wright had tried to find satisfaction by concentrating on the "outer" realities of life to make up for the long absences of her husband, Mrs. Browne's obvious conjugal happiness was indicated by her acqueisance to her husband's wish by painting her toe-nails—a thing that tickled her daughter because it suggested the humane warmth and sexual intimacy of her parents' relationship. Finally, Mrs. Browne resigned herself to Kiswana's decision of staying at Brewster, though she insisted on helping her on and off. As an upper middle-class housewife she felt she had justified her worth enough to have deserved the comfort and luxury she was now surrounded in and the social standing and privilege she had achieved and still labored to maintain.

In *LH,* even before grandma Tilson's death, Lester's mother, her daughter-in-law, had begun the ambitious project of rebuilding the old shack into a "modest" two-storeyed house. Mrs. Tilson was a petite, pale yellow woman who had refined manners and polished speech cultivated carefully to fit the new social class into which they had graduated. According to her, Lester's father had been a useless "bum" (*LH*, 28) who had been lazy and unambitious. She also hated her shrewd, and in her opinion, scheming mother-in-law for having influenced both Lester's father's and Lester's thoughts so that Lester refused to enroll in an university after finishing school to "make it" (52) in life. Her great ambition was to move down towards Tupelo Drive—the ultimate symbol of success for the blacks of Linden Hills. However, Mrs. Tilson's deceptively dainty manners, soft words and mincing gait hid her pushiness and drive. She had a "right hook worse than any boy at Wayne..." (25), which she was not averse to practicing on her son if necessary as she had used her verbal power to persuade her husband to work two jobs in order to earn more money. Lester's deep disgust and fury at his mother's ruthlessness and pressurization of his father finds expression in an outburst when Willie tries to convince him that his mother "means well" (52).

> Sure she does, Willie. She meant well when she killed my father too. That's one well-meaning woman. It took a crowbar to pry her out of his casket after she had him working two jobs with a heart condition.... I think about him sleeping four hours a day for ten years and want to choke her.... No woman's gonna hound me into the grave so she can weep over it in imported handkerchiefs. (52)

While one does not blame Mrs. Tilson for her motherly concern and efforts to push her children towards a better future (materially), her pretentiousness and hypocrisies cannot be overlooked. Her calculated snobbery was directed towards Willie—her son's friend, of whom she did not approve because he came from a poor family. Her achievement-oriented labor lacked the essential connection between her mind and her soul. She had divorced herself from the inner essence of a self, which could tell her the difference between right and wrong. The surface or 'outer' reality and the paraphernalia of wealth had come to mean everything for her while, in Lester's words, she had "lost touch with what it is to be (her). Because there's not a damned thing inside any more to let (her) know" (59).

Mrs. Tilson's status-consciousness and social etiquettes were all at the expense of a loss of the inner "mirror" of her soul. She could never gauge the loss in terms of self-delusion that she had incurred as a price for moving up on the social scale. Her son refused to trade his inner peace for a highly-placed job (that one could never get, given the social forces, without compromise or manipulation). Mrs. Tilson's shallowness and superficiality however had precluded that insight and her choice of lifestyle had never been motivated by a purely unselfish mother-love. Her untiring labor and efforts were unfailingly directed towards the achievement of material advancement, social status and the glamour and glitter of the rich families of Linden Hills. As a middle-class housewife (having risen through her drive and manipulation to that category from her earlier status of the wife of a poor, black man), her ambition and aspiration had made her overwork her husband. In her soulless quest for advancement and climbing upwards in the social ladder, Mrs. Tilson, more than Mrs. Browne, comes through as an African-American woman who had deliberately distanced herself from black people of a lower class, fawning upon those superior (according to her) in wealth and status while setting her own limits and circumscribing her views to narrow and selfishly motivated concerns. To her therefore, Kiswana Browne was crazy and unfathomable, whose actions and sacrifice were incomprehensible and frightened her. She had bartered the "mirror" in her soul and could not see how self-centred her labor and efforts had been.

Lester's twenty-seven year old sister Roxanne's aim in life was to "marry black, marry well or not at all" (*LH*, 53). She was a graduate from Wellesly and held a job at an advertising agency, which paid her well, but not well enough for her to be able to afford a Linden Hills address. She had taken to heart the practical wisdom of the comment of her colleagues (girls) in office: "you don't get a Park Avenue husband with a Harlem Zip code" (*ibid*). It put in a nutshell the sum total of Roxanne's efforts towards releasing her aim of becoming the mistress of a grand house and the wife of a rich and successful black man. Her six-month course in Black History (towards the personal payment of her debt towards the Civil Rights Movement) had ironically given her statistical evidence of the widening gap between black and white men and doubly convinced her that black women had a tough fight ahead, to choose from the minority's minority of successful black men who were "going somewhere" (*ibid*). So she "groomed her life and body" with a "hawklike determination", so that one of these choicest men would "take her along on that ride" *(ibid)* to success. Though a working woman belonging to Category V(b), Roxanne's life and labor were moulded by her ambition to be a rich housewife and a middle-class mentality of underlining her difference from poor black people. She had little interest in her job that gave her no satisfaction and she was more than ready to give it up as soon as her ambition was realized. Her attempts to cultivate carefully her dress, manners and speech to spell the "class" (as distinct from "mass") bring to the fore her classist snobbery and middle-class prejudice.

Roxanne's affair with Xavier Donnel, the eminently successful black man and eligible bachelor of Linden Hills was a blow hot, blow cold one, where she was compromised and belittled again and again, despite which she thought of him as a "real man" (55). In Roxanne's perception, the ultimate definition of manhood was success and fame and like her mother, she was prepared to trade her self-respect for marrying this man who could give her the lifestyle she craved. So she braved the callousness and insults because the catch would be worth it. Ironically, her much admired "real man" allowed his decision to be influenced by his idol—the super-successful Negro, Maxwell

Smyth (also his boss)—in making the most crucial decision of his life. Roxanne was summarily dismissed by Maxwell as one of those self-opinionated black women, the "climbers" (109) with their hunting instincts and "one foot in the ghetto and the other on a watermelon rind" (116), in marrying whom Xavier would destroy his own chances of reaching the top. Caught in the trap of their own insatiable ambition, middle-class black women like Roxanne clung to their superficial relationships with successful black men whom they used as step ladders to acquire prestige and name.

Laurel's grandmother Roberta Johnson in *LH* comes across as an impressive and astute old woman, much like Eva Turner of *WBP*. An independent woman, she lived in a five-roomed shack in Georgia, never letting circumstances to beat her down. Not dependent on her wealthy son for upkeep or care, she had been a pillar of support to Laurel, whom she had offered to bring up after her mother's death. Roberta had encashed her life insurance—the only security she had left with her—to finance Laurel's education when her son could not afford it due to financial constraints. After that, she witnessed Laurel's steady climb towards success and her gradual psychological decline. The burden of a lifetime of experience sat heavily on Roberta's shoulders, as in the end, she could not, with her philosophy of work as the panacea for pain, prevent Laurel's suicide.

Roberta had the spunk and grim determination to face the trials of life. With her untiring hard work, independence, home made recipes and home spun philosophy, she has been represented as a grandmother-figure in the image of black mammas and grandmammas with their assorted history and heritage of rich experience, memory of community ties and strong, bonding relationships. Roberta Johnson's failure to communicate that solid strength of belief in oneself and one's activities lies not so much with her as with Laurel's inability to connect with it.

Frances is represented in *MD* as a well-off, middle-class and ageing single woman who, late in life, took Junior Lee, the local Casanova, as her lover—a shiftless young man who preferred to live with older women because he could live off them as well. He used his sloppish charms to hook financially solvent women who could support his material needs while he carried on his philanderings under cover of a steady relationship and Frances was thoroughly exploited by him. This middle- aged black woman, suffering from the insecurities of approaching old age, had made the mistake of attaching emotion to their liaison. In her role as a jealous lover, Frances was laboring for the love of a man who did not deserve it. As Miranda foretold, she was used, her money spent and her sanity destroyed in the aftermath of this ill-advised love affair. The middle-class inhibitions usual in ageing spinsters was not evident in Frances. Perhaps because the island of Willow Springs offered more freedom and scope for untraditional behaviour (despite the gossip and the bad mouthing) Frances could gamble her respectability and good name late in life in the name of a reckless passion—a helpless victim in her role of betrayed lover. For a woman, "keeping" a lover had different connotations than a man, as emotional entanglement complicated a relationship already fraught with doubts and insecurities.

Abigail Day was Miranda's younger sister and Cocoa Day's grandmother in *MD*. The unspoken but strong ties of love held the two sisters together and since their childhood they had greeted each other in the same way each day, without fail—"you there, Sister?" asked Miranda and "Uh, uh" (*MD*, 35) replied Abigail. The trauma of losing a baby sister in their childhood had been overlapped by the trauma of losing their mother to insanity and Abigail had turned to Miranda for emotional support, calling her "Little Mama" (88), and placing total faith and trust in her. A mother and a grandmother herself, she still turned to Miranda for guidance.

In the text, Abigail has been represented as the softer and more feminine version of Miranda's personality—a beautiful, graceful, lady-like old woman who could weave magic with herbs and was much admired for her excellent cooking, elaborate recipes and wonderful housekeeping—her house sported laundered curtains, lace and chintz and the spacious, light-filled, airy rooms reflected her personality and taste. She was a natural housewife who, as Miranda put it, "glow(ed)" (178) when there was a man around the house. She was cut out to be a model housewife and mother. Having weathered life's struggles together for more than eighty years, Abigail was closer to Miranda than she could possibly be to anyone else, even her husband, who is, in any case an absent figure (long dead) in the text. Together, these two sisters represented home for Cocoa, Abigail being the more indulgent and soft-hearted of the two. They complimented and completed each other, Abigail being Miranda's positive foil to Ruby's negative one—representing the more mundane and homely side of her personality.

The upbringing that Abigail had given Cocoa had instilled in her an ingrained self-respect and grace. She drilled into her the philosophy that "a real lady never has to get mad—if she knows how to get even" (103). Instinctively and always, Abigail had included Miranda in all her pain and happiness and when Cocoa fell ill under Ruby's evil spell, she came to Miranda after all her efforts to nurse her adored grandchild back to health had failed. She had nursed Cocoa day and night, cradling her like a baby, as she passed through phases of horrifying psychological distortions. Despite her mild temper and appearance of vulnerability, Abigail had an inner strength that could withstand the toughest of trials and as before, she fought once again, valiantly and tirelessly for Cocoa's life. Her battle was long and hard but this old woman would not admit defeat till Miranda gave up hope. Hating as she did any mention of her own mother's madness and the death of her sister Peace, Abigail, at past eighty, was still tough enough to fight another loss. Abigail emerges therefore in the image of a wonderfully loving, compassionate and delightful grandmother whose vulnerability makes her more appealing to George (Cocoa's husband) than Miranda who is the stronger and more aggressive of the two.

Category IV of the hypotheses puts forward African women who are rich housewives and who, amid the luxury and comfort they have achieved through their marriage (compromise) are not able to define their 'self's. The meaningless external rituals that their lives comprise of, the artificiality of their existence and the objectification of their beauty may sometimes make them feel like entrapped birds. On the other hand, others revel in the glamour and the artificiality with remarkable ease, never pausing to think about the hypocrisy of their soulless existence, the operating metaphor in their lives being the loss of the inner mirror of their souls. There are also those like Marie Hollis in *LH*, who has given up her career to marry the man she loves only to be betrayed and disillusioned by his insatiable urge to prove his masculinity and his consequent philandering. Naylor's rich housewives are mostly found in Linden Hills—the posh suburbs where affluent blacks of the locality aspire to lease houses as a mark of their superior social status.

Marie was Reverend Michael Hollis' wife and had been his girlfriend in college and at the university. A doctor's daughter, she was from a wealthy family and was studying to be a psychologist. Michael Hollis had come from a middle-class background and after having been the star player and star student at college was then studying for a theological degree as his aim was to enter the ministry of church. Marie was high spirited, sensitive and sharp. She was also thoroughly in love with Michael and understood his insecurities, strange decisions and frustrations and accepted them. She gave up her own career as a psychologist for him and was prepared to travel with him as he pursued his career as a minister, thankful as she was that Michael had not got himself ordained for Catholic priesthood, which would have sealed her fate. She came to him with the gift of love and did not complain when Michael made it clear that he would prefer to preach in churches that were poor and dilapidated and serve a poor congregation. All the support, physical and emotional, the firm anchor of love and faith, she gave to her then lover and future husband, prepared to go all the way for him, ignore her own sadness in the face of Michael's devastation at having discovered his inability to father children. Marie in fact wrapped her soul around one person—the man she loved, and gave up her own ambitions, career and even dreams for his sake. However, in spite of so much love, consideration and support—even the physical side of their relationship was perfect—Michael could not stop himself from having affair after affair with scores of women. All Marie's efforts could not save the ruining of a relationship that was so pure and true. After twelve years of married life to this man, Marie "crumble(d) inside bit by bit" (161) and unable to tolerate the humiliation and indignity any more, she left Michael one day, after which, he was desolate and inconsolable. He did pick up the threads of his life but turned into an alchoholic and began the slow but sure journey downwards towards an irredeemable hell. As much as he was responsible for his own destruction and his wife's, Michael could always recall her passionate love for him, her selfless devotion—a wife who should have been worshiped and who deserved loyalty of the highest order. Willie put in a nutshell Marie's emotional vulnerability when he said,

> (w)omen were funny.... They could stand up under things you'd expect to keel them over. And then bruise so easily from something that shouldn't matter much. No, it had to be something besides the drinking. To leave a house like that and a man with a job like this, it had to be something else pretty awful—at least, to her. (173)

Marie had "keeled over" not because of the shattering of her treasured dreams or physical abuse or financial difficulties or Michael's drinking but because of an emotional/psychological betrayal by the man she loved which "bruised" and broke her up inside. Michael's pitch black wife shone like a rare gem in his memory for the purity of love that she had offered him—a woman who had come to him with confidence, entrusting her happiness unquestioningly in his hands, only to encounter an inexplicable betrayal.

In her role as a rich housewife, Marie unlike others, had a scope of achieving fulfillment because she had married the man she loved and had no regrets about her career. Their eventual estrangement could have been averted if they had children to give her a purpose in her empty life. Marriage, to Marie had been hell and one does not know where she went after the dismal failure of the most important relationship in her life. Pushed beyond the point of endurance, her spirit rebelled and her 'self' reasserted itself as she shook off the painful bondage that her marriage had become. In that, Marie fought defeat and emerged a winner while Michael gradually sank into the abyss of degradation. Marie had the courage to end an unfulfilling relationship and give up the meaningless role of a sacrificing wife to take a step into a freedom she had long deserved. She had submerged her 'self' in her role as Michael's wife, giving of herself generously and unstintedly, only to be left emotionally drained and exhausted. So, before the trauma of her marriage could drive her to insanity, she forced herself to leave Michael and step into a life without him. In so doing she re-affirmed her faith in life and emerged unscathed from her past experience.

Mrs. Donnel was Xavier Donnel's well-to-do aunt whose beautiful and luxurious house stood on Crescent Drive at Linden Hills. The deed of the house was in her name and would pass down to her nephew Xavier upon her death. As mistress of the house, Mrs. Donnel was a rich black woman who could dictate terms in her house. She was snobbish, artificial and typically class-conscious, and with the customary condescension of the rich she assumed that all poor people were available to do her "dirty work" which she wouldn't soil her hands to do.

Another frustrated upper-class housewife was Cassandra. She became the wife of Winston Alcott, an ambitious young lawyer who lived in Second Crescent Drive and hoped to move gradually towards Tupelo Drive. Winston Alcott was successful, rich and very much in love with his best friend David—he was a homosexual. His decision to get married was a compromise made under pressure. Winston was an up-and-coming lawyer with a promising career in a well-reputed law firm. In the face of a threat of exposure, he was pushed to a corner and agreed to marry Cassandra—a match that ensured the approval and blessing of the patrons of the society, especially Luther Nedeed. Cassandra became the pawn in the hands of a ruthless, patriarchal power game, where her emotions or feelings were not taken into account. Obviously, she was considered good enough and suitable material to be Winston Alcott's wife but apart from being a silent presence in bridal finery who moved as a puppet would on a string, she was given no voice by the author to underscore the message that Cassandra "(did not) count" (76). Her husband dismissed her as only a means to an end—a step ladder to success. Cassandra, after having served her purpose, could not be safely put away on a shelf marked "Mrs. Alcott". When David says:

"...I feel sorry for the girl. She's got some life waiting for her" (*ibid*), he sums up her situation precisely. Winston was a "made man" (80) who had made the painful compromise for a future and a career and used Cassandra to achieve it. She really did not count in the whole scheme of things and was expected to fit into her tailor- made role of an affluent man's stylish wife.

It can be anticipated that Cassandra would be an ornamental wife since her very marriage was founded on compromise and false vows, at least on Winston's side. If she was unaware of Winston's relationship with David, she would be an innocent victim of a demoralizing relationship but, as Jesse Bell in *BC* says, as a poised and unperturbed (at least on the surface) woman of the elite class who was expected to keep up appearances in public, she too would don the façade of artificial gaiety simply because she could not "afford to cry" (*BC*, 122). The set of keys given by Luther Nedeed to the young couple is symbolic of the falseness and insincerity of their business-like marriage that promised nothing but wealth and luxury and was devoid of the true essence of marriage—the union of two souls in a pledge of undying love and commitment. Consciously or unconsciously, Cassandra had acquiesced to the high-society marriage because that was how the game of power was played in a patriarchal, capitalist society. Perhaps she herself knew no better than to find her "happiness" in the role for which she was chosen—a high-society, decorative and ornamental wife—more a possession to be flaunted and a symbol of acquisition than a true soulmate to her partner.

Lycentia Parker of *LH* had been Chester Parker's wife—a wealthy and self-assured woman who was also an active social worker of renown. She was much appreciated in her circle of exclusive, elite class friends who praised her hard work in the interest of the Linden Hills society and quoted her words with pride. Lycentia's activities are reported by others and since the reader is not acquainted with her in her lifetime, it is from the views of the people gathered at her funeral and her husband's frequent references to her that one can surmise about her role in her home and as a social worker. Lycentia Parker had been a forceful and influential woman, a prominent society-lady who had been equally dominating in her house. The equation of her relationship with her husband became amply clear from Chester's nervous and apparently bereaved looks and his quoting his wife's words to indicate how mindful he had been and still was of her wishes. Ironically, however, he had appointed Willie and Lester (local young boys on the lookout for Christmas jobs for extra money) on a secret job of changing the entire wallpaper of his wife's bedroom, getting it thoroughly redone even before her burial. Chester's protestations that she would want it that way and he was merely following his dead wife's instructions could not convince the boys who shrewdly guessed that he wanted to remove all traces of his dead wife before bringing a new one to that bedroom. Lycentia of course had no say now about any matter including her husband's behaviour. The couple had had no children and Lycentia had directed all her time and energy to serve as co-ordinator of the Linden Hills' Beautification Project and Secretary of the Tupelo Realty Neighbourhood Board and at her funeral she was lauded as an outstanding member of the community whose loss however was less regrettable for her husband than the Linden Hills society. She had fought to prevent the encroachment of poor, black people of Putney Wayne into Linden Hills and when, after her death, the housing project for the Putney Wayne people was passed, her neighbours felt that all her good work had come to nothing with the imminent threat of invasion of poor niggers right in their backyard. The society ladies and elite class men of Linden Hills had shared with Lycentia Parker the disgust for the Negro underclass, who were indiscriminately and collectively bracketed as hoodlums, rapists or drug addicts by them, whose proximity spelled danger for their ordered and systematic lives, whose behaviour put a slur on their immaculate manners and speech and without whose labor their houses or cars would not have remained sparkling clean. Lycentia Parker was therefore a wealthy black woman, whose strength and determination were in reality the muscles of power and wealth that she flexed to keep at a distance the threat of the ominous Negro underclass. On the domestic front, her henpecked husband was now doing a reverse or volte face and his plans to marry immediately underscores the empty charade that their marriage had been—a relationship both had honoured only for appearances sake.

In *LH*, the Nedeed wives had all been rich housewives whose personal records of misery were buried in the recesses of trunks in forgotten corners of the basement room, where the last of the Nedeed wives Willa was imprisoned by her husband. Willa unearthed the records of Luwana Packerville, Evelyn Creton and Priscilla Macguire Nedeed, that told her the untold herstories of the gradual erasure of their 'self's beneath the weight of subjugation and domination of their men.

Willa stumbled upon volumes upon volumes of cookbooks and recipe books, in which were printed in a clear, square handwriting, the name of Evelyn Creton. The painstaking precision with which Evelyn had recorded not only the recipes but also the exact dates on which she had bought the ingredients and their measures and the amounts of food prepared each day, made Willa wonder how and why she did it. Gradually, however, the meticulous records began to make a different sense and Willa realized that Evelyn was, in truth, speaking a different story—a horrifying and moving inner story—through them. Evelyn Creton, like her predecessor Luwana, was again fair and beautiful, who initially took elaborate care of her looks in a bid to keep alive her husband's attraction and affection towards her. However, the same pattern was repeated in her life, when, with the birth of the next Luther, her husband drew away from her, and father and son drew closer to shut her out, pushing her inexorably towards insanity and death/suicide.

One could, like Willa, well imagine from her handwriting, what a "proper" and dignified woman Evelyn must have been. The "vision of quiet dignity and immaculate grooming" (*LH*, 187) that was evoked belied the turmoil and desperate longing that smouldered beneath the surface calmness and unruffled poise—a restlessness and primitive urge that drove her to extreme lengths. The changing ingredients of the recipes that she experimented with, traced out her suppressed story of frustration. Willa felt a burning sense of shame at having discovered the lengths to which even a supposedly controlled woman who "never had a curl out of place, a ribbon knotted loosely, a stick of furniture not glowing with lemon oil..." (187) could go to. Here was a woman who was not ordinary or mediocre, whose housekeeping was perfect, whose social etiquettes were above reproach: "She gave the right parties at the right time for the right people" (*ibid*) and must have been admired for her perfection. But the raw, pulsating need that reached out from the endless lists of recipes where the normal ingredients were being gradually replaced by herbs and roots associated with black magic, filled Willa with a disgust for the disgraceful absence of self-respect in her and at the level to which she had stooped to win back Luther's attentions. The records unfolded the "empty cavities that had been living all along between the covers of (the) book" (188) and the bewilderment, confusion and the inexplicable need to be wanted/desired, building up within Evelyn. Willa could, despite her disgust, identify with and draw inevitable parallels with the story of her own life as any woman would understand the need to be loved, needed, and above all, recognized as an individual, not a name.

Evelyn had channelised her creativity in frenzied activity in the kitchen but, with the passing of years, this frantic woman, unable to resist the encroaching insanity had begun the process of a slow and deliberate suicide by her cutting down on nutrition and simultaneous consumption of laxatives. The long drawn out torture and physical and mental agony she must have gone through before succumbing to death becomes synonymous with and a symbol for her poisonous marriage with Luther.

Evelyn Creton—the perfect housewife, excellent cook, dutiful wife and mother, much admired hostess, a proud and beautiful woman—had successfully hidden behind the façade she had erected for the benefit of her social role, an emptiness and aching need that could not be expressed adequately in words. Driven beyond the point of endurance, she had still managed to make her death appear natural, burying deep within the pages of her cook books the disgraceful loss of self-pride and the primeval and untamed sexual/psychological/emotional urges that could never be expressed to the world. Without writing a single word about herself and her troubles, she had "measured (out)" (190) her pain little by little and drunk it as poison to kill herself. Her helplessness to resist the force that had driven her to an ignominy and self-abasement so profound filled Willa with a growing panic and horror, so that she tore at the soul-wrenching records in an attempt to destroy and exorcise the spirit of this repressed Nedeed woman.

The next Mrs. Nedeed's (Priscilla Macguire) story was recorded in the innocuous pages of her albums that were filled with numerous photographs of various phases in her life. In the photographs before her marriage to Luther Nedeed, Priscilla came across as a wonderfully spirited, lively and audacious woman whose bubbling and infectious good humour spilled through the confinement of the lifeless photographs. She was, therefore, destined to be a misfit in a family where women were treated as little better than serfs. Priscilla's wedding photograph symbolized her future married life with Luther in that his dark hand clamped firmly over his bride's shoulder was to become not only the hand of possession, but also the hand that would restrain her freedom (or "flight"—the hand that literally held her down as if her body and spirit were poised for flight). The image of Priscilla as a free bird whose flight had been curbed is reinforced by the posture of careless, reckless abandon in the photo taken before her honeymoon trip and the metaphor of entrapment and then erasure would become clear gradually through the photos that marked the transitions in her life. Priscilla had, in truth, been enchained in marriage to the man she had chosen as husband and who would become a possessor and oppressor. Luther's dark and menacing presence and immobile face, invariably at her side in each photo, marred the fluid rhythm of her energetic body. Luther's hand finally left Priscilla's shoulder once she was "held down" (207) by the one-month-old child in her lap. When Luther Junior, at six years, stood beside his mother, the impression of being hemmed in from both sides grew. Yet, Priscilla's determined insistence in giving a slightly different posture in each photograph emphasized her distinctive personality.

However, even this spirited woman was gradually overshadowed within the precincts of her own home, where the identity and individuality she had achieved as an outstanding member of the society would come to nothing and when she was awarded the "Mother of the Year" title at the club ceremony, which was a public recognition of her exemplary labor in that role—a recognition that brought tears to her eyes in its cruel reminder of her meaningless existence in her home and her growing psychological distance from her son.

The ominous and gloomy presences of her husband and son had begun to overshadow her personality and the import of the twin shadows that eclipsed Priscilla's sunny radiance registered her slow fading out and finally the loss of face and absence from the family photograph, symbolizing the same process taking place in her life. Like Laurel Dumont, Priscilla must have experienced a sense of acute loss of self so that in an act similar to Laurel's suicide and annihilation of her face and self, she obliterated her face from the family photographs, scrawling "me" (249) in place of her face to underscore her impotence and helplessness but also, to proclaim her individuality and rebellion in marking her erasure emphatically.

Willa Prescott Nedeed was the last of the Nedeed wives who had been chosen with deliberate care by the present Luther Nedeed from among a group of college graduates, who had lost the ambitious expectations of youth and were grateful for the first opportunity (by way of marriage proposal) that would liberate them from the growing insecurities of spinsterhood. Unlike the earlier Nedeed wives, Willa was a "dull brown shadow" (*LH*, 18) but had the same "pale", "white" spirit and the essential meekness conditioned to "fade against the whitewashed boards of the Nedeed home after conceiving and giving over a son to the stamp and will of the father" (*ibid*). The purpose for which she was given the privilege of using the Nedeed name was the same and in the hundred and fifty years that had passed in between, there had been no change in the attitudes of the Nedeed men, who continued to exert their quiet but ruthless authority over their wives as well as their community. It was unthinkable therefore that anything untoward could happen to break the sacred cycle of calculations that had given the anticipated result—the birth of a son who was an exact replica of the father. For the first time in the history of the Nedeeds, the impossible happened when

Willa gave birth to a "white" son despite Luther's precautions and painstaking observation of instructions left by his forefathers to the exact detail. The medical report ensuring the normalcy of his own reproductive organs was written proof validating his doubts regarding his wife's fidelity. In spite of the child's striking resemblance to him except his pale complexion, to Luther his "ghostly presence mocked everything his fathers had built" (*ibid*). For this egocentric man, the child was a blatant insult flaunted in his face by his "treacherous" wife who however, innocent as she was, was unfortunate in that she had unknowingly, and through no fault of hers, violated the sacred Nedeed family canon.

In the five years that followed, Luther was convinced that Willa's unforgivable crime (disobedience, daring, betrayal, infidelity, mockery of Nedeed values) must be punished and she be made to pay because he had given her everything she owned, even her identity—that made her a woman of consequence. Her pale, submissive spirit, that was expected to fade away into invisibility began to impinge on his consciousness. Luther's awareness of Willa as a "woman" infuriated him because for five generations, Nedeed men had treated their wives as commodities. He resolved to turn the "whore" he had married into a "wife" (19). So Luther worked himself up into a righteous rage at the "injustice" done to him and decided to punish the ingratitude of the woman who had dared to challenge the institution of patriarchy and male domination by striking at the foundations of a century-old familial structure and violating the sancity of a tradition laid down by his forefathers. He therefore got the basement morgue ready as his wife's penance chamber. How he managed to force Willa into the basement is not mentioned but the reader can surmise that he would have had no compunction in using physical force, violence, cunning and coercion to achieve his wish.

Willa later refers to the psychological pressure and verbal abuse he had used to imprison her on the charges of adultery and betrayal of trust. The terrible humiliation and mental agony she experienced can be appreciated in the light of her innocence and total ignorance of her alleged "crime" that had provoked Luther to inflict such a degrading punishment on her in his blind and unreasonable wrath. As husband and protector, he had been duty bound to care for her well-being but ironically, he himself had violated the sanctity of his marriage vows.

The reader's first acquaintance with Willa takes place through the eerie howl that was carried across Tupelo Drive to rattle at the glass windows of the houses in Linden Hills and Putney Wayne, where it chilled the blood of Norman, Ruth, Willie and Lester because the cry could not be associated with any animal nor was it expressive of any recognizable human emotion. No one knew that it was "a plea for lost time" (60)—a cry not of despair, pain or anger—a cry that pleaded for resurrection of lost opportunities and time for action—a cry that echoes across the frozen lake in Tupelo Drive "to die in the aching throat of a woman who was crouching over the shrunken body of her son" (61). The bitter December cold and lack of food had brought on a high fever that had led to the death of Willia's son whom Luther had never acknowledged as his own. Her psychological turmoil and the acute agony she lived through moment by moment is rendered with such breathtaking poignancy that her torture and self-blame for having failed to protect the child as a mother should have done, is internalized by the reader. Remarkably however, in all of her reminiscences and recapitulations, she never once blamed her son's untimely death on Luther—taking upon herself the responsibility for inaction, foolish trust, for not being able to recognize the potential for danger that lay within the safe precincts of her own "home". In shouldering the burden of her child's death alone, that in itself was an act of rebellion and an assertion of an individual and distinct personality, Willa emerges as a woman whose spirit was not made to "fade away" and that did not merely serve as a foil for the dark and threatening presence of her husband and his patriarchal power. In not asserting her will earlier by choosing to leave Luther and a meaningless marriage, she felt that she had precipitated the death of her own son.

For Luther, his wife's absence "was much more intrusive than her presence had ever been" (66). Her excellent house-keeping had been taken for granted by him because he had expected that service in return for the material benefits he had bestowed. He had brought her to perform the role of a glorified servant, a bearer of and nurse to his son, after which she was to have been content in handing over his legacy in flesh to him and conducting her life and performing her duties as unobtrusively as possible so as not to disturb his plans in any way. Now that all his calculations had gone awry, he sat brooding in his den on Christmas Eve, missing her work as the pile of dirty clothes, cold grate, tasteless food and imperfectly blended drink reminded him of her efficiency. He was convinced at last that she was indispensable for the smooth running of his household as he firmly believed in his father's assessment of woman. Naylor's lancing satire underscores his ingrained chauvinism when he thinks: "(b)reaking in a wife is like breaking in a good pair of slippers. Once you'd gotten used to them, you'd wear them until they fell apart, rather than go to the trouble of buying a new pair" (87). Luther would therefore reuse Willa with whom he was comfortable and she would give birth to the son *he* wanted while she resumed her role as obedient and dutiful wife. In his arrogance, Luther had misjudged the stamina and tenacity of a woman's willpower to underestimate Willa, who emerged from the trauma of her son's death, internalized the herstories of unspoken pain, abnegation and psychological turmoil of three generations of repressed Nedeed women, exorcised the horror of the experience, to finally destroy the root of evil by killing Luther along with herself to cleanse Linden Hills and its society of his evil influence.

The story of the successive Nedeed women as painstakingly recreated by Willa through their distinctive records is one of rich wives whose identities are ground to dust by their callous, power-hungry men folk. Willa's story is that of a woman who is literally imprisoned by her cold-blooded husband for not fulfilling her role as wife and mother. He hopes to slowly starve her into submission but spurred by her discoveries about the similar sufferings of her predecessors and in revenge for her dead son, she revolts. The magnitude of her husband's actions spread itself over generations of oppression of poor people outside their home and the calculated erasure of the spirits of their own wives, whose labor they utilized, productivity they exploited and identity they wiped out. With a resurrection of her submerged selfhood, Willa emerged in the new role of a woman who would now rebuild what she had destroyed through her own submissiveness and reclaim what was rightfully hers.

The long forgotten picture of Willa's personality and individuality submerged in the six years of role-playing at the Nedeed home was pieced out by her bit by bit. Tracing the activities of her own life, she found that she had made her family the centre of her existence and devoted every waking hour to make the Nedeed house a home, never failing in her duties and never complaining. She had been, without doubt, a good mother and a very good wife. Evaluating her services, she was convinced that she had done everything in her power to live up to the name that had become her identity for six years, but now she was left with nothing, as her descent down the steps into the basement symbolized her descent into a space where she had lost her motherhood, identity and dignity. She would now reclaim her identity, that she had worked hard to achieve, by "walk(ing) back up" (280).

As Willa rose from her cot after a rejuvenating and dreamless sleep, she was all set attack to the disorder in her life and scour away all uncleanliness. Refreshed and filled with a purpose, the "nucleus of self-determination" (289) in her brain programmed all her limbs to function accordingly and her symbolic rebirth took place simultaneously, urging her to break out of her physical captivity like the butterfly from its mould. The first thing she instinctively began to do was "keeping house". Meticulously, she cleaned up the basement where she had been held prisoner and having accomplished that, began her journey upstairs—the symbolic ascent that would culminate in her destruction of the one and a half century old Nedeed home and family.

As Willa moved from room to room clasping her dead child in one arm, her relentless cleaning continued as she cleared up and set right the disorder and chaos in each room. For once, Willa had not waited for Luther's approval or consent to shape the course of her life and driven by a will of her own and a determination like that of a lone wingless queen ant who "drag(s) her bloated egg sac as long as at least one egg is left uncrushed" (300) she appeared before Luther, Willie and Lester intent upon her sole purpose—to cleanse the accumulated dirt in her home. Naylor compares Willa to the queen ant (cf. Morrison's queen ant in *TB*) who would die in her role, but not abandon it. So when Luther tried to separate the dead child from her, she rebelled, her free hand shooting out to hold him in a vice-like grip as the three moulded figures careened towards the fireplace and were engulfed in flames. As the Nedeed abode went up in flames, the Linden Hills community watched silently (indicating aloofness, anger and rejection of all that the Nedeeds had stood for) without making a single move to even call the fire department.

Finally, Willa Prescott Nedeed—the "mad woman" in Luther Nedeed's "attic"[9] had broken out of her confinement to reclaim her identity and act in the role of a symbolic torch-bearer to cleanse the Nedeed home of it's weight of sins—purging years of accumulated misery, suffering and oppression of helpless women and poor black folk in the flames of an active revolt—symbolic of the inferno or the hell-fire. From a good wife, a good mother and an ideal housewife, Willa emerged as a "woman", who in asserting the essence of her womanhood and identity, destroyed in her rebellion a patriarchal and capitalist structure founded on century-old exploitation.

The passion for motherhood overwhelming her other roles as rich house wife and also working woman is seen in *MD*, where Naylor creates the character of Bernice Duvall. Cocoa's childhood friend, she had married Ambush Duvall, one of the most eligible bachelors on the island and also her childhood sweetheart. She was considered to be extremely fortunate to have been chosen by Ambush who was not only hardworking, wealthy and well-mannered, but also the gentlest and most considerate husband one could wish for. Bernice however, was not happy even in her privileged position as a woman with a husband who was both loving and rich (a double boon) because of her pre-occupation with her inability to become a mother. A reed thin, nervous and high-strung woman who was trying desperately to conceive a child, Bernice's obsession was to become a mother.

It was as if all the mother-love she had stored up within herself for a baby that refused to come despite all her efforts, were being channeled out in her fidgety movements and restlessness—physical manifestations of her inner discontent. Her appeals to Miranda to use her magical powers had been met with pointed refusal, as Miranda advised her to have patience as one could not possibly work against the forces of nature. Meanwhile, she was under Miranda's care whose herbal medicines and instructions of regular exercise would prepare her body for the task of nurturing a new life. She however lost patience with the slow and steady process of Mama Day's herbal medication because she was in a hurry to prove both to herself and also her acid-tongued mother-in-law that she was capable of motherhood.

Bernice's urgency was provoked to a large extent by her mother-in-law's barbed comments regarding her incapability of giving Ambush the son he deserved to carry forward his name and business. Though she had faith in her husband's considerate patience and love for her, somewhere in her mind the insecurity lurked that if she failed to provide a child, she would not be able to "keep" (*MD*, 43) the man she had won in love. Ambush could afford, with his flourishing business, to build her a "split-level ranch" (257) with central air-conditioning, to buy municipality bonds, run a joint tuition account for their son when he was born, and provide a separate car for his wife's exclusive use, thus not requiring Bernice's income. Bernice worked at the cash register of a medicine store, more for diversion than need. At home, her modern kitchen equipped with the latest gadgets and a refrigerator packed with instant, tinned food indicated not only her affluence but also indifference as a cook and the minimum amount of time she spared for housework. Mama Day therefore understood that Bernice's remedy would have to start in the kitchen, where cooking could be turned into a work of art and pleasure.

However, in spite of all her advice and against her better judgement, Bernice stole a bottle of fertility capsules from the drugstore where she worked, due to which she developed ovarian cysts and false symptoms of pregnancy. Mama Day had to come to her rescue again and upon discovering by accident a fully furnished child's room laid out with touching care and loving anticipation, she decided to take matters into her hands. The raw need that reached out from Bernice, who had risked her own life in trying to get pregnant, made Mama Day curse herself for not having listened to her more carefully. Here was a woman's inner urge to nurture a baby, bestow all the love and care she was capable of upon it, a woman who craved for the fulfillment of motherhood more desperately than luxury, comfort or pleasures that money could buy. Here was a hidden fountain of unrestrained mother love that moved Miranda to use her ultimate knowledge in trying to create life in Bernice's womb by guiding her through a process of physical healing and psychological stability that would lend her the strength to cross over the forbidding line that nature had drawn against manipulation of natural forces.

Bernice co-operated untiringly with Miranda, following her instructions to the last detail, till with the help of Miranda's mysterious, magical ritual she became pregnant and gave birth to a son. Since the confirmation of her pregnancy, she avoided Miranda and shied away from contact with her. Her obsession with and possessiveness over her son became a joke on the island, and people shook their heads over her pre-occupation with her precious child. Bernice was, they said, "rais(ing) a God instead of a child" (162) worshipping the ground he walked on.

The cruel fate that awaited her shook everyone when her son died. His death was one of the most poignant and tragic losses of the island. As Bernice carried her dead son in her arms to Miranda (her last refuge) in an attempt to bring his life back magically, the wildness in her eyes shook George. Yet, when the little coffin was placed in the grave, Bernice summoned up enough courage to bid her son a final goodbye with composure—her quiet words echoing with the vibrations of a grief too deep for tears. Bernice had fought with nature to achieve motherhood but, in the end, she was defeated by death. She is represented not in the image of those fiercely loving but practical black mothers who could take the rod, if necessary, to punish an errant child. Bernice, like Mattie of *WBP* had found in motherhood an anchor, a purpose of life, a meaningfulness that had made her submerge her entire self in that role.

Unlike most African-American families in America where acquisition of wealth seemed to be the outcome of compromise, selfishness and exploitation of others, Ambush had built his business with his hard work and sincerity. Bernice was not like the rich housewives represented by Morrison, Walker, or Naylor in her other novels. She could have avoided her tragedy, had she been content with the loving and steady relationship she had always shared with her husband. Yet, minus the fulfilment of motherhood, Bernice had felt an incompleteness that had threatened to destroy the inner core of her 'self' and also her sense of self-worth. In the final count, though a failure in her role as a mother, Bernice could hope to emerge from her trauma with the emotional and moral support of a loving husband to tide over the worst phase of trial in her life. She would then begin to comprehend her role as a woman in its essence.

Jesse Bell in *BC* had married into the wealthy king family and had been shocked to discover the realities of the king women's existence. These were rich housewives trapped as prisoners in their roles and unable to express their utter unhappiness and desolation. They were anchored helplessly to their rigidly moulded roles—afraid to let go for fear of abandonment by their husbands/men who were successful, rich and powerful. The sexist exploitation of these women was taking place daily within the patriarchal family's confines of decorum, under the guise of sophistication and polished manners. Jesse Bell was aghast to find that this power game was a quicksand that sucked these women towards a death-well—the death of their independence, individualities, freedom, power of speech and their 'self's. The Sugar Hill women,

> Got treated any old way and took it…there are worse things than hitting a woman. Like having husband call you stupid and lazy in front of a whole roomful of people while you stand there and smile and smile…yeah, there are worse things. Like having a girlfriend and the wife at the same dinner table. Like the wife knowing about it all the while, and the husband knowing she knows, and him getting a

> thrill out of it all. Cause the wife's not going to say a word. Cause this son of a bitch is a doctor somebody or a lawyer somebody—or maybe just a man somebody that she feels she's nobody without. Women up there look at other women as nothing unless they are attached to some man's name. And attached they stay, no matter what he does. And personally, I know a few of them who actually got their butts beaten worse than some women on the docks. But they got beaten by stone sober men behind stained glass doors. And with all their money, they couldn't afford to cry. (121-22)

Jesse's account contains in a nutshell the precise situation in which black women of this category find themselves entrapped. Their self-esteem has been systematically eroded so that they have become appendages to their men and unlike poor, but independent African-American women, they are mindless puppets manipulated on the string of marital respectability and polite behaviour by their rich (read powerful) men. Unlike their underprivileged sisters, these women abnegated other women if they were unattached to a male (protector, provider, possessor, master) and in believing that a woman had no identity, personality, selfhood or respectability if she was not branded as personal property of a man, they debased and abnegated themselves. Unable to express their emotions, enjoy life's pleasures, speak up or strike back in anger for fear of being rejected, thrown out, ridiculed or humiliated, they curbed their spontaneity to sport carefully groomed smiles—for smiles they could "afford", tears they could not indulge in. So these women were compelled to live lives of utter compromise. They were unable to forge bonds of friendship with other women and were therefore cut off from the life-giving and sustaining strength of relationships and sisterhoods that could have salvaged their wrecked lives and enabled them to break free of the bondage of imposed roles in a shared companionship and quest for selfhood and inner joy.

Unlike the rich wives who lead idle if usually unhappy lives, are the rich and successful career women, who however have a different problem. Under Category V(a) therefore come Laurel Dumont and Mabel Thompson of *LH*. The former had reached the pinnacle of her career and was the head of a prestigious management firm. The latter was a Cost Analyst at the office of Xavier Donnel's boss Maxwell Smyth, also very good at her job and reputedly tough. Both women represent roles as labor that African-American women have been able to achieve only recently—white collar jobs that required not only excellent qualifications but also a mellowing down of the racial bias. However, in having achieved success in their careers, wealth and fame, these are also women who have been alienated from their roots consciously or unconsciously. Laurel admits that she cannot identify with the realities of poor, black women or relate her psychological distress with the hardships of these women because she has never encountered poverty in her life. Had she been able to reach across barriers to understand their pain, and find an answering echo in her heart, had she been able to forge at least that bond of identification with the experiences of poor, black women, slave women, exploited and downtrodden women that Bessie Smith[10] sang about, she could have bridged the yawning chasm that had filled her soul and eventually destroyed her. In representing these women as successful career women, Naylor has also indicated the frightening loss of their self and soul in the artificiality and glamour of their lifestyles—so much so that they are suspended in an emotional vaccum, unable to breakout of their role identities and unable to connect with the grief of other black women, with their maternal herstories or with their folk roots and culture. Like Jadine in Morrison's *TB*, they may neglect the clamour in their souls or like Laurel they may step over the fine line of sanity into despair and annihilate themselves in the abyss of death.

Laurel Dumont had been, as a child, spirited and passionately in love with music and water. As a motherless child, Laurel yearned desperately for a mother's love that no amount of love from her grandmother could compensate, and till the last, she remained emotionally an orphan, (*cf.* Jadine in *TB*—a cultural orphan) failing to find her true 'home', even in her own soul. Her childhood pleasure in spending her holidays with her grandmother was lost as with every passing year, she drew away from the placid, uneventful life at Georgia till she hardly found time to visit her at all. The strong bond of love that had grown between the old woman and the mischievous child became strained as Laurel gradually made her career, success and ambition the centre of her life.

Graduating from the university with a degree in MBA and impressive academic records, she became, even before she was twenty-five, the head of IBM—one of the leading institutions of management in America. A brilliant careerwomen, her photographs were splashed across newspapers and business magazines. Laurel Dumont became a name that spelled success, fame, power, glamour and drew admiration everywhere. In her dizzying flight to a meteorical success, she threw herself into her work with a frenzy that ensured her ascent. Her marriage to Howard Dumont, "the first black D.A. in Wayne Country, hand-picked to be the next attorney general", was inevitable because she was tailor made for the role of a Dumont wife and the only type of woman his family would have accepted:

> Laurel came with the Dumont's ingrained pre-requisites: she was sepia, stunning, and successful. She walked into a house that was complete, and could think of no major changes she could make. (232)

Laurel was the envy of the neighbourhood and she believed she was happy because people said so. Power, money, talent, a dream marriage, an opulent house, a powerful husband, a brilliant career—apparently Laurel had achieved it all and there was nothing she could want. Laurel had been nicknamed as the "Amazon" (228)—a towering, giant-like presence who had, with her genius and brilliance, dwarfed the host of men at the executive board of IBM, subduing, imposing upon and drawing fear and respect from every man. In her work arena, no one would dare to cross swords with her. She symbolized everything that every black woman, including Willa Nedeed, could dream of and wished to emulate. Yet, this decision-making, confident, powerful woman had a personal life that was a void, a marriage that was turning to shambles and the surface glitter sadly masked the intense loneliness and emptiness that had lodged inside her when she was a child and had grown into a yawning chasm over the years. Looking back, she could visualize her life and all her achievements only as a chain of mistakes: "wrong—she and the career at IBM that she clung to with a desperation mistaken for pride, ambition or contenment: mistaken for everything but what it was—a mistake" (228). Driven by the demons of her personal loneliness, she had launched into a ceaseless upward and forward movement, swathed in appreciation and admiration, travelling from city to city, dazzling everyone, getting photographed, never failing or pulling back or pausing to allow herself time to think. Trapped into an existence that was becoming increasingly meaningless for her, Laurel began to sense a frightening vaccum that threatened to overwhelm her sanity: "...she found herself imprisoned within a chain of photographs and a life that had no point" (228). The two separate staircases that she and Howard had been climbing to the top seemed to have sloped away from each other so that after a decade of giving priority to business meetings over their personal lives, they seemed unable to reach out and touch each other's hand. There had been no time for a child who could have filled the space between them and steadily and inexorably, Laurel sank into an abyss of depression that Howard could not retrieve her from. After providing her mettle to the world, Laurel had found nothing within herself—no inner peace, no long-standing emotion, no role to support her dissolving 'self'. In a last attempt to gather herself and find her moorings, she visited her now eighty year old grandmother in Georgia to recapture the pleasures of youth and grasp back the substance of life in her company. She was disappointed to find that beyond temporary relief, she could hope for no permanent solution to the problems that had accumulated in her life. Returning from Georgia, she isolated herself to shut herself up in her den, her music system issuing a wall of deafening music to rebuff advances, enquiry or approach by friends, relatives and even her husband who left her and sued for divorce. Roberta arrived and was able to reach across the barrier of stony silence and loud music she had erected and in the next few days, tried to set her to strenuous physical work that she had believed could be the panacea for pain. But Laurel was now beyond help. She had no friends in whom she could confide or share her feelings with association with Ruth and Willa could not be pursued because of the former's illness and the latter's unavailability. In the end,

Laurel felt that her salvation lay in her swimming pool and she took her last dive from her thirty feet high diving platform to crash to death on the frozen swimming pool.

In losing her face in her suicide, Laurel's faceless body became a symbol of her lost 'self' and a metaphor for the pointless life and meaningless existence she had led. A black woman who had reached the peak of material achievement, a sensitive individual, she could have soared had her wings not been clipped and her brilliant flight arrested by the absence of an inner core of conviction. In Laurel Dumont, Naylor represents the tragic quest for 'home' and 'self', the failure and destruction of a black woman to connect to her roots, to identify with the pain of common black folk, to find inner peace and a place to roost. Disillusioned, utterly lost, and a bewildered child in reality, this awe-inspiring woman had built an artificial façade around herself, only to discover how lonely it was at the top and that her existence or otherwise meant nothing to herself. Laurel had failed in her role as granddaughter, daughter and wife, had never become a mother, finally to understand and acknowledge that she had forged no meaningful human relationship to provide the emotional support, stability and sustenance necessary to continue with life. Her life and career had become synonymous and she ended both by her plunge to death. In her inability to "connect", Laurel remained an alienated figure—a "crippled bird" (242) who had not found her "nest".

Mabel Thompson was again a brilliant career-woman with high qualifications and was struggling to bring up two younger brothers and provide for their education. She is represented as such through the words of Maxwell Smyth, her boss—a rich, powerful man who was much admired by all aspiring and up-and-coming black men and women as the epitome of success and fame. In representing her from Maxwell's point of view, Naylor subtly underscores that real dilemma of the highly qualified black women who, like their fiercely independent but less privileged counterparts were accused as castrators for undermining the egos of their men.

Mabel had graduated from the accounting school with very high grades, managing to do well despite all her burdens. A born fighter, she was called "a tiger" (110) by Maxwell for having achieved all that against great odds and whose aggression he applauded on the professional front. Mabel was one of those black women who had proven their capabilities and efficiency (according to her boss, she was the most efficient cost analyst in the eastern division of his office) only to be rejected for their toughness and determination. Maxwell Smyth denied her womanhood and ability to love because in championing her strength he undermined her vulnerabilities, her personal need for love and understanding. He appreciated her tenacity, admired her capacity to fight, survive and make way for herself, and wondered at her staunch sibling loyalty—reserving admiration from a safe distance for women like her who would sacrifice their own pleasures to bring up and educate younger brothers and sisters, women who had great reserves of love in them—but failed to understand their vulnerabilities. In essence, black men such as Xavier and Maxwell were conditioned to expect and demand different things from women on the personal and professional levels. So they would promote a Mabel Thompson, but not marry her. In condoning the image of a tigress for independent and successful black women like Mabel, who were able and strong, who apparently needed no support and could whip out their sheathed claws in self-defence, black men denied them their core of womanhood, thus turning their victory into an empty act of soulless ambition or mindless survival instinct. Categorizing her as an emasculator [there was always the danger of getting one's "balls clawed off" (110) if they got personally involved with such women], Maxwell negated her role in the capacity of an ideal wife who must need be docile and submissive. Separating the identity of black women as either career women (home breakers) and homely housewives (home makers)—one self-centred and the other self-giving, black men became accomplices with white men in their oppression of black women like Mabel in overlooking their insecurities, trials and fears.

Theresa is another successful career-women in *WBP*. Naylor represents Theresa as an independent and outspoken girl who worked as a Personnel Director for the Board of Education and earned enough money to afford renting an apartment at Linden

Hills or Park Heights (another expensive residential area) but had given up her homes there because of Lorraine, with whom she shared a lesbian relationship, living with her in Brewster Place. Naylor sets the two girls apart from the other women of Brewster Place by placing them in the chapter titled "The Two", suggesting their isolation from the cloistered black women of Brewster Place not only in terms of their better jobs or affluent background (at least Theresa's) but also due to their psychological alienation as lesbian women. Naylor's presentation of the taboo subject is more psychological then sexual—a relationship that had formed strong ties of love between two women quite different in nature. In exploring the roles of Theresa and Lorraine as labor, Naylor sheds light on the complex relationship that precludes the sexual/gender politics present in a man-woman relationship but nevertheless operates on its own problematic dynamics.

Theresa is portrayed as the more aggressive of the two, very pretty and very confident, whose "lousy attitude" (*WBP*, 133) did not invite friendly overtures or curiosity from her neighbors. She could not care less about what they thought and underscored her wish to keep a distance from them. In her relationship with Lorraine, she was the stronger partner of the two in that she was the decision-maker, the advisor, more articulate, independent and forthright. She made no attempt to be extra-polite to anyone, nor did she encourage the men of Brewster Place, but she made her intentions clear of not moving from this place because she was weary of Lorraine's insecurities and fears that had compelled them to shift residence time and again, in search of undisturbed peace. Brewster, with its dead-end wall and dilapidated buildings in a "God forsaken part of town" and its "bunch of ignorant niggers with the cotton still under their fingernails..." (134) was the last resort for her. Theresa herself had been originally from Georgia (South) but had gone to college in the North and had acquired a sense of her self-worth, unafraid to take the responsibility of the rightness or otherwise of her decisions and unapologetic for being what she was. However, as Lorraine felt, because her job was not threatened by her sexual preferences, she was unafraid of gossip or people's opinion. Theresa had absorbed, confronted and adjusted to the difference of being a lesbian and learned to dismiss people's contempt when they discovered that she was "that way" (131) and accepted it unquestioningly and unashamedly. But in living with Lorraine, she was confronted with the ugliness of it every day because Lorraine wanted to justify herself to others, wanted her neighbors' appreciation, to be with them. In her toughened and hard-headed, practical attitude towards life (a defensive shield erected of necessity for aggression may often indicate a defensive stance), she could not understand Lorraine's sensitiveness, emotional vulnerability and constant need for support. Her job entailed decision-making that demanded intelligence, shrewdness and ability to withstand pressure—a job that no one (except Kiswana) could even think of at Brewster Place and it placed her on a different plane than the other women there—a cut above the rest—a different class altogether because she need not worry about making ends meet. She could not identify with the poor and "ignorant bunch of niggers" whom she despised because of their inability or lack of inclination to work or act to change their situation. She believed in action rather than complaints. Theresa's emphatic differentiation of herself from her neighbours indicates the snobbery and superiority complex that came along with being an educated women with a well-paying job. Having blamed Lorraine for being paranoid and over-sensitive about their neighbours' changing attitudes, she was shaken by the hostility and suspicion she encountered from the mother of a young girl whose scraped knee she had been tending to. True to character, she reacted with a smouldering fury and later uncharacteristic tears, to be consoled and for the first time, by Lorraine.

If one attempts to categorise Theresa and Lorraine into gender roles according to gender constructs, the former would fit the more powerful, masculine, head-of-the-house image while the latter would be recognized as the feminine, weaker and more submissive of the two. Corresponding with the image is the fact that Lorraine was a first grade school teacher, a job that required affection, patience, tolerance and also entailed child care with instruction—categorised traditionally as "woman's work". Theresa on the other hand handled a job that required toughness and decision-making, classified traditionally as "man's work".

However, when Lorraine's personality underwent a change after her friendship with Ben, Theresa was disturbed by the new confidence and firmness she saw in her. Perhaps, as Lorraine accused in a confrontation, she had wanted Lorraine to be independent of other people and look up to her for guidance, thus confirming the possessiveness of her love that had stifled the growth of Lorraine's personality. Their last fight culminated in Lorraine's uncharacteristic decision to attend a lesbian party alone, returning from which she was gang-raped and left to die on the streets. After this, Theresa prepared to move out of Brewster Place, but at Kiswana's block party, she joined hands with the women of Brewster Place to destroy the wall that turned the place into a dead-end alley. In an act of solidarity and sisterhood, Theresa overcame her personal prejudice against these women and stood with them in their rebellion against deprivation and injustice. It was her tribute to Lorraine's memory by way of forging a new and meaningful bond with other black women.

Under Category V(b), i.e. women in middle-class occupation like teaching come Lorraine—a first-grade school teacher in *WBP*, Beth Wilson, the choir woman of the Sinai Baptist Church in *LH*, Reema, the hairdresser, Sue Henry, the receptionist at Dr. Smithfield's place, Selma from Alabama and working in a New York office, and Miss Irene Jackson who ran an orphanage (appointed in-charge) in *MD* and Nadine, the co-proprietor of Bailey's Café in *BC* where there is also a mention of Irene Jackson. Skilled and semi-skilled workers as they are, they earn a modest income and are often too comfortable in the security of their jobs to think of marriage. Some like Reema do marry and work both within and outside their homes while those like Nadine have struck a balance between housework and professional work. Esconced in the respectability of their blue collar jobs, they may stand aloof from the uneducated and ignorant black folk but some like Lorraine may try to reach across barriers and attempt to forge friendships only to be rebuffed. Naylor's representation of black women of this category are varied and multidimensional, each having her individuality in spite of common roles as labor.

Lorraine of *WBP* was the shy but friendly girl who had moved in with her friend Theresa to Brewster Place. Her vulnerability and sensitiveness had appealed to the women there but, later, these same qualities had made her the target of their venom and still later, a victim of gang rape. Lorraine had reminded Theresa of "smoked honey" (*WBP*, 135) when she first met her, and in their relationship, Lorraine had always been the more insecure and eager-to-please of the two. At seventeen, and still at school, Lorraine had been banished from her home by her father, whose disgust at her "unnatural" inclination (as a lesbian) made him burn all her possessions. In all the years after that, he acknowledged no letters from Lorraine, sending back the birthday cards she sent, till she stopped putting the return address on them. Since then Lorraine had fended for herself, working at the local bakery to earn money for school and staying at a friend's place. After completing her studies, she became a school teacher. Her insecurities and fears stemmed from a very practical problem—the possibility of losing the goodwill and healthy reputation that her job demanded because the care of impressionable students was entrusted with her. In a society where behavioral expectations and codes of conduct had condemned homosexuality as taboo, she was striving always to prove and establish her high moral standards. Unlike Theresa, Lorraine cared greatly about her neighbours' opinions, their attitudes and their approval because in an earlier instance, complaints from neighbours and guardians to her school authorities had forced her to resign. To an extent therefore, her insecurities could be justified. So it was Lorraine who was hurt and shaken by their sudden withdrawal and aloofness, by Sophie's various and obscene accusations and by C.C. Baker's (the local gangster) verbal abuse and name-calling—none of which she had provoked. Sophie's verbal attack on Lorraine was motivated by a jealousy (that crystallized a social attitude) because both she and Theresa were on a different plane than these women—beyond the periphery of risk, betrayal, motherhood, pain and care, out of reach of their men (their indifference to whom perversely insulted them). They also represented a threat to their own womanhood because, in the aftermath of their own disillusionment in their relationships with men, they had always fallen back on their closeness with women. As Etta and Mattie both realize, these women felt jeopardized by the fact that they themselves had always forged more abiding and loving relationships with women than men. Targeted by Sophie's crude and indecent accusations, Lorraine stood trembling and crucified before a roomful of people at the block association meeting, her defenceless frailty and valiant struggle for control moving Ben to defend her and offer her fatherly protection and comfort and a friendship that gradually changed Lorraine's personality. Her timidity and dependence were replaced by a quiet determination—a change that Theresa resented. Their last fight drove Lorraine to prove her worth to herself and while returning from the party, she was accosted and gang raped by Baker and his friends. In the aftermath of that rape, in a state of psychological shock, Lorraine murdered Ben, while she herself died of the abuse her body had undergone.

The guilt of Lorraine's rape and subsequent death lay heavily on the collective conscience of the women of Brewster Place. They had separated and alienated her from themselves, thereby leaving her open to the ultimate form of male violence and domination upon a woman—the desecration of her body against her will. Frustrated and misguided young black men like Baker had only one way of proving their strength to themselves in a racist society—through asserting the superior virtue of the phallic power in their "six-feet wide" (170) world—the narrow alleys and streets of black ghettoes like Brewster. Confronted by a woman who was beyond the reach of their physical subjugation, they tore into her with a ferocity born of insecurity.

After Lorraine's death, the women of Brewster Place destroyed the wall stained with her blood in an act reinforcing the solidarity of black sisterhood and symbolic of rebellion against the social forces that had hemmed in and isolated these women, marginalizing them for so long. In joining forces with them, Theresa acknowledged Lorraine's conviction of racial and gender solidarity as the only way towards improving their lot—affirming that her efforts had not been in vain.

Mary Beth Wilson, the choir leader of the Sinai Baptist Church had a remarkable voice but had not been trained at those "fancy" (*LH*, 178) music schools in Paris that taught elite music and Latin. Relying on the spontaneity of her renditions that had been appreciated highly in the South, she was disgruntled by the classist snobbery she encountered here and humiliated by the instructions she had to take from Byron, the music director who had been trained at a posh conservatory. At Sinai Baptist patronized by the elite coterie of Linden Hills, she had to restrain the spontaneity of her voice and render stiff pieces in a language she did not understand. When Reverend Hollis proposed that they give the stiff-lipped folk of Linden Hills a taste of what a moving sermon and real choir rendition could be like, Mary reciprocated with matching enthusiasm. As the priest tried to draw the taken-aback polished congregation into the throbbing current of a truly impassioned sermon, Sister Wilson backed him to the hilt, conducting the choir with spirit and gusto and for once enjoying her job. The failure of their wonderful dual performance lay with the congregation's inability to appreciate the depth of genuinity and raw power they had witnessed in music and speech. So, Mary would continue to serve at the church obeying the orders of her proper and elitist director, a compromise necessary to continue with her job, albeit at the cost of self-respect and despite the lack of creative or job satisfaction.

In *MD*, Reema was a hair dresser who ran the local beauty parlour, while Sue Henry was the receptionist at Dr. Smithfield's clinic at Willow Springs. Belonging to Category V(b), the former supported a large family while the latter was a young girl with a typical arrogance characteristic of confident youth. In the same novel, Cocoa's friend Selma hailed from Alabama and had come to New York at twenty-one years of age with a "bad accent and a bad attitude, knowing she had to lose one and keep the other if those bastards weren't going to get the best of her" (103). Selma's belligerent attitude was a defensive front that she put up to thwart unwanted attention. However, despite her chronically distrustful attitude towards all men, she fell into the trap of a sexual pervert and all her practical sense and cynicism could not give her the readymade happiness she wanted. Like thousands of Southern black girls, Selma had come to the North expecting to "make it" by securing a good job or a rich husband. But she was doomed to spend her life cocooned in a hard shell of defence around her, unable to reach out to forge emotional relationships because of her fear of betrayal. She has been represented in the image of the independent, strongwilled, street smart colored girls who had dreams when they came to New York but managed to kill them in their battle for survival.

Another active woman of the same novel, Mrs. Irene Jackson ran a state funded orphanage where Cocoa's husband George was brought up. She has also been referred to in *BC* (228) where, after the black Jewish girl Mariam gave birth to a bastard child (George), he was handed over to Irene. Known for her total commitment to her job, she was a hard and emotionless woman who in her blunt honesty, did not pose to be other than what she was. Her discipline may have bordered on cruelty, but George acknowledged the formative influence of the list of rules that she enforced with precision and quiet aggression on her wards. Her toughness made her a success at her job and she turned out her wards as responsible citizens. In teaching them practical crafts and the art of fending for themselves, Irene drilled into them the hard facts of life. Her message to each and every inmate was "only the present has potential, Sir" (23). The respect she accorded these orphan boys with, ensured that they developed a sense of self-respect and she formulated her personal code of rules in order to be sure that none of them turned out to be burdens of the state or misfits. In denying them maternal protection, she taught them to rely on themselves and acted in the role of a down-to-earth, hard-headed well-wisher. In the final count, she was indeed the mother of her boys in spirit because she gave them the strength of values and the sense of propriety to face the world, to battle against odds and win. Though she proclaimed that she was only doing her job, she did it as a pledge—a duty to be fulfilled sincerely and with full devotion. Her service was invaluable and as George said, "the world lost a lot when she died" (*MD*, 126).

Another positive but unusual character presented by Naylor is Nadine, wife of the owner of Bailey's Café in the novel of the same name. She is presented thoughout from the point of view of her husband. She was taciturn to the point of rudeness and though a good cook, she would do it only when the mood hit her. The customers of the Café were accustomed to her strange ways and the fact that she neither had a welcoming smile on her face nor a word of greeting. Her quietness enveloped her like a cloak as she silently handled money at the cash register, while her loquacious husband communicated with the customers while cooking for them. She did not like to be disturbed too often and would be reluctant to get up and fetch an order for her customers. Described fondly as an "African goddess" (*BC*, 13) by her husband, she was known never to smile. After her marriage, Nadine and her husband had to struggle to make ends meet as he was only a lift operator. In the 1940s Brooklyn when colored people were struggling to survive, it can be easily surmised that Nadine had to work to supplement her husband's meager income and given the kind of jobs available to black women, she could have been scrubwoman, cook, laundress, maid, or factory worker. After her husband's return from war, they bought Bailey's Café which placed them in a better situation materially. The absence of drama in their lives and their quiet adjustment to each other's ways throw in stark relief the stories of intense suffering that they narrate. Nadine has been represented as an exceptionally reticent black woman with deep perceptions about life.

Nadine is an unconventional woman who does not fit any stereotype. She confounds the stereotype of the free and easy black woman who has a smile for everybody. The essence of her character is self-containedness and self-sufficiency that earns her the respect of all, including her husband. Like Sula in Morrison's *S*, she is not very likeable in that she is not given to casual chatter or idle conversation due to which she cannot strike up easy friendships. Her role is more that of a silent and moody presence in the background who however takes the full share of her responsibility as the co-proprietor of Bailey's Café. The stability of her relationship with her husband is more the outcome of adjustments made in mutual understanding and unlike most black women (poor, middle-class, rich) who would go to any lengths to keep their husbands, Nadine is independent and uncompromising, having the courage to give her husband an ultimatum when he was enjoying his third year in the navy. He got a single line letter from her that said she would marry the butcher if he did not come home immediately and knew better than to take it as a joke (13). Nadine has been able to deliver the message clearly not only to her husband but to everyone when she says, "I'm more than my body" (18).

Under Category V(c) of the hypotheses, the study includes prostitutes, streetwalkers, night club dancers and singers, sex workers and brothel-owners who confirm the stereotype of the bad black woman. Some of them manage to achieve material independence and amoral pleasure while others, unable to recover from the trauma of a choice made out of material compulsion or circumstances are driven to a slow and painful death or insanity. In *BC*, Naylor has presented the stories of a number of women who have all found refuge and shelter in Eve's boardinghouse/ bordello/brothel where they now work as prostitutes. Without exception, each of these women have encountered such horror, pain, degradation, injustice and exploitation that blood curdles in terror or revulsion at the unfair deal meted out to them. These are women who are undoubtedly victims of their circumstances and not one is like Josie of *TLGC* or the hardened and laughingly defiant prostitutes of *TBE*. Without exception, each woman's story wrenches the heart, rendered with such compassion, sensitivity and soul-shaking poignancy.

Sadie of *BC* was an alchoholic and a two-bit prostitute whose journey from the state of innocence to prostitution had not marred the absolute clarity and beauty of the "mirror" in her soul. She is one of the rarest women in fiction on account of the purity of her soul despite the prostitution of her body. Sadie was self-educated in grace and poise and drunk as she always was, one never heard an indelicate word uttered by her. In her presence, even the most crass and insensitive of people became cautious about words they used.

Sadie's life was a long saga of unrelieved suffering and exploitation. Born in the South Side of Chicago where poor, colored folk settled in slums, Sadie was an unwanted child. The sociological backdrop provided by Naylor to Sadie's parents' story indicate the cycle of poverty, demoralization and laziness that had caught them in a vicious grip. South Side of Chicago had a concentration of Negro ghettoes where black men and women struggled to survive amidst poverty and unemployment, waiting for times when out of a low supply and high demand in the labor market, they would get jobs despite their race. Wartimes or union times (when Negroes had to be fought to be kept out of jobs) held racial and gender discrimination at bay and poor Negro women could find employment and save a few pennies—precious savings that went towards the education of the brightest child of the family. Sadie's parents were not among these hardworking and tenacious survivors. They were "easy living folks. Party folks" (41) who would never try for jobs that entailed hard work. Her father took up odd jobs when his gambling was going through a bad phase and her mother would earn a bit of money from the dance halls and could somehow make ends meet. They had married each other upon the understanding that they would not allow their family to extend if they were to survive the way they wanted—irresponsible, free and minus the complication and commitment of children. So Sadie's mother would not have been capable of hard labor even if she tried, as she had been exhausted and drained physically by her numerous abortions. A child would have hindered their mobility as frequently they shifted localities when chased by the Sheriff for not paying room rent and they fled to another place and settled there. Sadie's mother hustled with the grocer and butcher and her father borrowed money from his new set of friends before moving again and somehow managed to pull through. The abortions were accomplished at home by her mother with the help of a friend and crude and dangerous methods [like a little peroxide on a coat-hanger (41)] but she had to fight with her husband for money if the pregnancy was in an advanced stage and she was forced to take professional help. Sadie was "The One the Coat Hanger Missed" (42)—a child whose conception was a curse to her mother in that even before she was born and her mother was seven months pregnant, her father abandoned her—going out on an errand, he never returned. The gist of this woman's attitude towards her newly born child is given by Naylor in her succinct portrayal of this unwilling mother's feelings. Faith and hope had deserted her with her husband's abandonment and all the charity she could summon up for her daughter ("bastard" for her) had amounted to her goodness in not cutting her throat (42). Forced to fend for herself and her unwanted child, Sadie's mother took recourse to the only job she was capable of doing—prostitution. She took to drinking a contraband liquor and night after night of drinking and prostitution took its toll upon her health and looks and filled her with a venomous hatred for the child who had unknowingly perpetrated her ruin and unfortunately resembled her father.

Sadie was accustomed therefore, from her very childhood, to her mother's harshness and believing innocently that the vicious beatings she received was on account of her own badness, she labored ceaselessly to be "very good". In her superhuman efforts to please her mother, Sadie erased her own needs and ironically, all the violence and abuse she endured turned her into a lady. Her teenage dreams of miraculously acquiring education, a respectable job and a trim, white house were soon to be destroyed as her mother engineered her encounter with her first "customer". Locked in the vicious grip of an irredeemable situation that led her down step by step into the abyss of utter degradation, Sadie's pure and innocent soul still strove to soar high. Her dreams changed with her changing situation but in all their variations, a constant factor remained—her craving for her mother's praise and love. Her mother's decision to sterilize her permanently established her future in prostitution as a profession because it demanded her nights and her body, unburdened by the problems of motherhood. This warped mother had, in her zeal to push her daughter into prostitution, destroyed her capacity for motherhood.

After her mother's death, Sadie's fortune underwent frequent changes and she became a maid in a brothel run by two rich white women. Having been a streetwalker, she had already experienced the worst of life's realities and her job in the brothel was more secure than the dangers of night walking. The next phase of her life saw her as the wife of a much older man. In marriage, she achieved for the first time a role she had craved. Her love for Daniel made her strive to do everything in her capacity to please him but her perfect housekeeping and passion for cleanliness perversely irked him. Her life lapsed into another routine where her drunken husband subjected her to physical abuse regularly while she labored painstakingly to lend her stark and dingy shack the stability of a home. The death of her husband brought her back on the streets as she could not, despite working herself to exhaustion, save her precious home by buying it from her husband's daughter.

In the last phase of her life, Sadie resumed her earlier work as a streetwalker but by then had begun to drink steadily. She was, in the end, too far gone to begin another future even when Iceman Jones proposed her marriage, recognizing the beauty of her unspoilt soul. Sadie's story may have condensed in it the untold sufferings of countless women like her, but in representing her as transcending the physical degradation of her role as labor through the unmarred crystal clarity of her inner self and soul, Naylor has lent unusual poignancy to it.

Esther's story is ridden with the symbol of darkness as she herself is pitch-black, ugly and small, with a monkey face. Hers is also a story of violated innocence, destroyed childhood and victimization—similar to that of Ben's daughter Elvira in *WBP*, but different in that Esther had been betrayed by her brother, the one man she had loved most in the world. Having lost her faith in the humanity of all men, Esther was warped psychologically forever and the icy aura of man-hate that surrounded her, chilled Bailey's spine when he laid eyes on her for the first and the last time as she came to the Café at midnight to ask for Eve's boarding house.

At twelve years of age, Esther's adored elder brother who had provided for her so far, traded her services to a rich man who was a sexual pervert. Having been told that she was lucky to be chosen as wife by such a man, instructed by her brother to obey her "husband" without demur, Esther could not understand, despite her innocence and gullibility, why such a man would marry her. At first she was too uninformed and naïve to understand also the sexual exploitation she was being subjected to because the paraphernalia of leather straps and steel "toys" her husband used during their meetings in an underground cellar gave a sadistic pleasure to him and did not match her concept of a sexual relationship. As she endured the unspeakable horrors of sexual perversion year after year, no God came to her rescue and she did not rebel or escape because "she (was) a good sister" (98) and her services ensured that her brother got higher wages each year and peace at home when he met the demands of his complaining wife. She "stay(ed) one year for each year (her) older brother took care of (her) against the shrill protests of the fat wife", and "coun(ted) the days left to repay (her) debt" (98-99).

Esther could never be a wife or a mother. She had been sold by her brother as an object, and used by her buyer as a sub-human toy. Having been reared as the scapegoat, she was sacrificed at the altar of selfishness and necessity. The refrain punctuating Esther's story, "we won't speak about this, Esther" (95-99) may have been her brother's warning or her husband's command. The one sentence draws within itself a well of frightening darkness and secrecy that were to become an inseparable part of Esther's life. As she "count(ed) the many ways in which you (could) hate a man", knowing that her "brother knew" all the while about the tortures she was going through, Esther thought of killing the man who would buy other girls to satisfy his perverted pleasure, "other twelve-year-olds with brothers" but had to admit that there were "too many of them to kill" (99).

When, the brothel keeper Eve looked into her honest face and wounded eyes, she wordlessly offered her the basement room where her sexually perverted callers would have to bring her white roses and call her "little sister" to get her services. In recognition of her unspeakable suffering, Eve called her "sweet Esther" (99) in endearment—a black woman whose role had been that of a victim—like other black girls—of their brothers, fathers or circumstances, her story gathering in it the pent up hatred of all those little black girls whose childhoods had been destroyed forever.

Likewise, Ben's wife Elvira in *WBP* drove their innocent daughter to a degradation, from which there was no redemption. Being poor sharecroppers on the rented land of a white landlord in the south was not the easiest of lives one could wish for. Ben's daughter was not capable of working at the fields because of her lameness and was therefore sent by her mother to the white landlord's house for a cleaning job every weekend where she was forced to stay the night under the pretext of extra work and her inability to walk home from his house after she finished work. The girl had approached her parents to complain of the sexual harassment she was being subjected to but Elvira would not listen and was not prepared to hear any complaint against their benefactor while Ben was helpless to prevent it. The routine continued week after week and Elvira did not turn a hair as she enquired if her daughter had "(done) a good job" (151) for Mr. Clyde.

The victimized girl ended the weekend routine by leaving home to head for Memphis, as she had arrived at the logical conclusion that since her parents needed money which she could not give them without selling her body, she had better go to a place where she would get a higher price for her services. So every month thereafter she sent them an envelope full of money, paying back with interest, like so many young black girls in real life, the debt or being born to parents like Elvira and Ben, themselves victims of demoralizing circumstances—a mother who had unhesitatingly allowed the commodification and degradation of her daughter for material advantage and a father who could not summon enough self-righteousness to prevent the sexual exploitation of his own daughter. She became a victim of the selfishness of one and the impotence (psychological) of the other, one's action and the other's incapability to act.

Another of the inmates of Eve's brothel is Mary, the daughter of a bricklayer, her father's cherished baby, whom he adored for her stunning beauty. She was her father's "gold" (102), pampered and protected like a prized possession by him in the face of disapproval from her mother. The complex psychological urges that gradually led Mary, despite her father's best efforts (his cajolings, beatings, tears, pleadings) towards a journey of gradual self-abasement, self-hatred and degradation that in turn led her to the edge of the world (Bailey's Café) and finally, the healing of her wounds (psychic and emotional) at Eve's boarding house (brothel) is portrayed by Naylor with a deep understanding and enfolding sympathy. Mary's physical beauty had hounded her from her very childhood, evoking the same feeling from all men—young and old—lust. She had been given the best of everything and all the comfort that her father could afford. Her bedroom was filled with an assortment of mirrors that reflected her perfect beauty but were instruments of torment for her with their repeated message that she was a "whore" who was "born to be fucked" (102, 104).

In refusing to recognize the potential of betrayal in herself and the primitive and uncontrollable urge that would eventually make her violate all the virtues of goodness, respectability, commitment and love and break her father's heart, she broke the mirrors that told her the truth. Growing up, she threw herself into all activities in a frenzied attempt to silence the "whore" in her that tempted her to a different lifestyle. She excelled in studies at the academy, sang in the Church choir, joined the Girl Guides, Missionary Circle and other charity works, sang for war relief, rolled bandages for soldiers in Spain, worked part time at the druggist's store—all in an effort to prove her worth to herself and others, to convince both that there was more to her than just good looks. But all this was to no avail as she was haunted by the shadow of lust that drove her from one man to another and then out of her home to cheap, rented rooms, sustaining herself with jobs at the shops which she soon lost due to the mistrust and jealousy of her bosses' wives. In her journey from middle-class respectability to prostitution, from an adored and cherished daughter to a nymphomaniac and then a prostitute, Mary had struggled valiantly to keep her "good self" from merging with her whorish self, but failed.

After betraying numerous men, perversely enjoying their hatred of her because of her infidelity, Mary was imprisoned in a relationship with a crippled gambler who was rich enough to keep her in luxury, loved her with a possessiveness that drove him to travel with her from city to city to put a distance between her and her latest lover but was unable to protect her from the deep self-hatred that made her mutilate her own lovely face with a beer opener. That final step in self-hatred paradoxically released her from the grip of an urge that had destroyed her self-esteem and peace of mind.

At Eve's boarding house, Mary is free to be herself, to exorcise her demons and recuperate her damaged self to be reborn with a sense of inner beauty and self-worth. So her "gentlemen callers" dwindle in number and Eve can promise her broken father that one day, his daughter would be returned to him "whole" (114)—not as the fragmented self that she had been. The wall that Mary's father had erected to ward off her teenage boyfriends had been as ineffective as her crippled lover's strategy of moving from one place to another to discourage her countless lovers. Like a bird in a golden cage, Mary yearned for freedom. She had not yielded her body out of material compulsion, she had been driven from the confines of her respectable, middle-class home and a father's love and vigilance by a psychological need and purely physical urge. Her insatiable craving for sex had made her a "whore" because that was the only way she could avoid commitment and enjoy sex. Hating herself as she did, Mary is a woman who had run from herself in the beginning and then from people who loved her to culminate her journey at Eve's brothel where the customers paid her not in money but with flowers. Here, she could hope to discover her own true self and her own true worth.

Jesse Bell had been a true daughter of the docks in her independent and rebellious spirit and lack of inhibitions. Coming from a family of tough longshoremen and having a mother who was an exemplary figure in her role, Jesse had inherited the ingrained self-respect, strength of character, spunk and pride in her toughness from them. She had not married the eldest son of the rich King family in her ambition. She had married him for love contrary to the assumptions of his class-conscious family. Refusing to be cast in the mould of artificial decorum of the other King wives, Jesse Bell remained till the last, a rebel at heart. Her husband's uncle Eli had resented her from the moment she entered the premises of the King household because Jesse was an embodiment of all that he despised as a chauvinistic and snobbish man. The open challenge she threw in his face by conducting her household affairs according to her own wishes was an insult that he would avenge with calculated malice. Uneducated though she was, Jesse was too spirited to allow uncle Eli to dominate her and aware that her working class background made her a butt of ridicule in the King family, she avoided their elaborate parties. Her people made an honest living through hard work and Jesse was justifiably proud of her heritage and the tradition of independence and forthrightness that her mother had instilled in her. So she scorned the well-groomed King women who hid the truth of their subjugation and ill treatment behind a façade of poise. Jesse was never one to feel ashamed of a demonstration of affection, strong emotions or passion.

In her battle against the systematic undercutting of her marital relationship by uncle Eli, Jesse had to admit defeat. Over the years, her son was estranged from her as he was trained by uncle Eli and convinced of his mother's crudeness and ashamed of her connections. As Eli's long-drawn-out and cold-blooded plan to oust her from her house began to bear fruit, her plea for understanding was lost on her husband. Having taught him the joys of a married life with her inimitable flair for humour and open passion, having truly cared for her family as a wife and mother, Jesse felt that she had been a good mother and a good wife. Her uncomplicated approach to life had not taught her tact and wiliness and Jesse's defeat was a demonstration of how male power or authority could be wielded in cunning if unable to subdue by force. So Jesse was "killed...in (her) own home" (130) by Eli. When she turned to drugs and her "special friend" (125) (a woman) in desperation, he used his influence to defame her in the newspapers, thus destroying her good name irreparably. After that, Jesse began her steadily downhill journey to end up as a drug-addict in a prison cell from where Eve brought her to her boarding house. When Jesse says, "...it's all about who's in charge of keeping the records" (118) she means the distortion of her story by the superimposition of history—Eli's deliberate projection of her in the image of a faithless "slut" despite her attempts to defend her actions. After nineteen years of married life, Jesse became a prostitute at Eve's brothel, earning her livelihood, creating a space for herself and living independently.

Losing her battle despite her labor of love, she at last made a heaven out of her private hell.

Eve was the proprietor of a boarding house for single women that was called a brothel by Sister Carrie and a "whorehouse convent" (116) by Jesse Bell. Eve herself was called a pimp by jealous neighbours and a land lady by her friends. As a moneyed woman, she was her own mistress, living her life according to her own perceptions. Like Nadine, Eve never smiled but unlike her, she had no sense of humour and no inner laughter, having lost that capacity in her symbolic journey across "the delta" (82) that took her a lifetime and during which she aged by a "thousand years" (*ibid*).

Eve's childhood was dominated by the frightening figure of her Godfather who had rescued her out of a patch of ragweed to bring her up, thus vindicating his claim to have "made" her. He was a powerful man in the small town of Pilottown where his temporal and ecclesiastical authority reigned supreme as the preacher, teacher of the school and owner of the cotton gin. Brought up under his hawk-eyed vigilance, Eve was a repressed child who longed for physical contact with a human being her Godfather held her destiny in his hands—he, the all-powerful male, and she, the cowering girl-child. Using a biblical allegory, Naylor presents Eve's banishment from her father's home in a totally naked and defenceless state for having dared to enjoy the physical sensation of the earth's vibrations beneath her burgeoning body as a teenager. Stripping her of everything he had given her, he banished her in the same state he had found her—"naked and hungry" (88). She was forced to steal a sack that served as clothing as she traveled across the delta, from Pilottown to Arabi, walking mile upon mile of rough terrain and blessing the hard way in which Godfather had brought her up, a life that had strengthened her for this ordeal. When she reached New Orleans finally, she was a creature born of the earth, caked in mud and "delta dust" (82) and genderless. Penniless and destitute then, Eve rose out of sheer will power and determination to a position where she had amassed enough wealth to keep her in comfort for the rest of her life. An astute business women, she had an unerring business sense that served her in good stead.

Eve had created through her efforts her own world where she called the tune. She was not given to charity but was not devoid of human compassion. Instead of being embittered, she used her strengths to her own advantage—uncaring about what people said about her. She gave refuge to women who needed her support but they and also their callers had to obey the rules laid down by her. The men had to buy flowers that she grew in her garden as payment of the services they received. In a magnificent inversion of Godfather's world, she created a world where women reigned as queens, men stood in line outside the doors of her female tenants and Stanley Carver (who was the embodiment of true manhood) served as her housekeeper, whom she renamed Miss Maple and who wore women's dresses. Inverting the traditionally expected roles of masculine and feminine, Eve presented a startling vision of female empowerment. Represented as the symbol of the earth, Eve was also the nurturer and nourisher in that she reached out in understanding to forge bonds with broken women, whose damaged 'self's she helped resurrect. Like the earth, she had grown stronger and tougher with the increase of stress on her. So she survived the delta journey but having lost her laughter, she also cried for the innocent Mariam who was unaware even of the violation of her body. In that sense, Eve was also a mother-figure.

Mariam was referred to in *MD* as George's mother. The impression that George carried about his mother being a prostitute was however refuted in *BC* where she comes across as an innocent, unspoilt and victimized child.

Category VI of the hypotheses includes African-American women who are social or political activists—workers who have left their homes shunning the affluence and personal comforts, to work in their own way for the upliftment of their downtrodden brethren. Kiswana of *WBP* has come to stay at Brewster Place to experience firsthand and be a part of the hard life of poor African-Americans. Moving away from the 'elite' or the 'respectable', she has embraced the hardships of the underprivileged class and attempted to forge ties with them to fight against oppression and exploitation. In creating awareness among the apathetic black underclass, she tries to achieve a new definition for her 'self' and move towards an increased appreciation of their realities by teaching them to assert their rights.

Kiswana Browne alias Melanie hailed from an upper middle-class family in Linden Hills and was living at Brewster's ghetto by choice. A young and idealistic activist, she had dropped out from college because she had felt that she could be in day-to-day contact with poor black folk there and experiencing their poverty herself would give her the impetus and sense of purpose necessary for bringing about social changes in a racist society that deprived African-Americans of their rights. Though her youthful ardour and impulsiveness are rendered with delightful humour, her sacrifice in choosing a difficult lifestyle, genuine wish to help the residents of the slum by organizing meetings and forming associations, her personal involvement in improving their lot and raising their awareness, her concern about the welfare mother Cora Lee and her friendly overtures to Lorraine and defence of her in the face of C.C. Baker's ugly taunts, are admirable if ineffective. If on many lonely nights, she misses her parents' love and care and the comforts of her lovely home, she does not admit it even to herself. If her idealistic zeal and attempts to appear grown up before her sophisticated and poised mother are treated with Naylor's urbane humor, beneath it there is also the grim reminder that young black women like Kiswana had opted out of a bright future for themselves because they felt that their rise in class was directly proportional to their alienation from their cultural, racial roots and that in aiming for material success, they were moving away from the larger and oppressive reality of a poor black-America towards the privileged, white, racist, classist society. The flaunting of their Africanism in the face of a disapproving white America by wearing Afros, changing straight hair to kinky hair, changing names and renouncing bourgeoisie background may have achieved little, but were outward expressions of genuine feelings that ran very deep. So Kiswana had expressed her identification and oneness with her struggling community by refusing to fit into the middle-class mould of ambition and upward mobility. She held her mother's love and concern at an arm's length while vehemently accusing the educated blacks of Linden Hills as afflicted with a "terminal case of middle-class amnesia" and her mother of being a "white man's nigger" (85). Her mother's passionate repudiation of her prejudiced assumptions makes her realize that she had been wrong to bracket her as lacking in racial pride. In understanding Mrs. Browne's mature and contained approach to the social issues she was so passionate about, Kiswana was able to form a new bond of understanding with her mother by accepting her natural concern for her daughter's well-being. Unlike Jadine of *TB* and Roxanne of *LH*, Kiswana has had enough faith in her cause to continue with her social activities.

Category VII presents African-American women who defy categories as they cannot be categorized in their roles as labor. These are women who have transcended their circumstances and achieved the fullest and freest expression of self, who have thought unconventionally, who have been independent, have emerged as mature women after encountering pain, loss and death and who have been untrammelled in their roles as *women.* Ruth Anderson of *LH*, Ophelia (Cocoa) Day of *MD* and Etta Mae Johnson of *WBP* are women who defy categories or categorizations.

Born in Rock Vale, Tennessee, Etta was Mattie's childhood friend who had migrated North much before Mattie had even thought of a life apart from her parents. Etta's rebellious spirit would not accept lying down rules defined by others. The white people of Rock Vale were faced with her overt challenge when she "looked them straight in the face...when she reserved her sirs and mams for those she thought deserving, and when she smiled only if pleased, and regardless of whose presence she was in" (*WBP*, 59-60). Her teenage years saw her constantly in trouble as she was willful and very much her own mistress. When she left her home town to elude her white lover Johnny Brick, his men burnt down her father's farm in fury. Etta's only regret was that she had not killed the "horny white bastard" (60). Etta has been described as a woman who "built her own roads" (68).

Etta's life was a journey that had begun from Rock Vale to wind up in Brewster Place. Memphis, Detroit, Chicago, New York and a succession of cities beckoned to Etta one after the other to make a wonderful living. She was tireless, ever young, insatiable and inexhaustible as she moved in her quest from city to city to find each of them unprepared for her "blooming independence" (60). Like Morrison's Sula who was a dangerous artist with no art form to express her tremendous potential, like Walker's Shug Avery who set and broke her own limits, Etta Mae in her restlessness of spirit and wish to give so much to the world, with her boundless energy that she could not channelise, was always on the move—propelled forward by an unstoppable inertia of motion. However, with all her independence, she could not fashion a way for herself to survive alone. So she had a string of men friends—all wealthy, all with enough money to "invest" (26) in her and keep her in style. In all these years, she had found no abiding, stable relationship, nor any one who would promise the commitment and security of marriage. She therefore could not transcend the objectification of her physical and sexual attributes. She was constantly waging a war against old age and slipping youth, having no time for introspection and not caring as long as she traveled first class and lived "top drawer" (69). Her recklessness and headstrong denial of the need for emotional support by way of home and family hid the growing insecurities that came with old age. Admittedly incapable of hard work, she could not now opt for a permanent job so late in life. So her defiance and arrogance were cultivated postures to conceal her weariness of the incessant game of love she was involved in.

In a bid to win quick respectability (she had always been misunderstood and branded as a fast woman), Etta tried to hook Reverend More, the visiting preacher of Brewster Place's church who was dashing and rich enough to attract her attention. Ironically, he categorized her as one of those "worldly women" (73) who enjoyed a one night stand without attaching any emotional complication to it. His treatment of her put in a nutshell Etta's lifetime's experience with men. The sameness of the experience told Etta of her foolishness in expecting the permanence of marriage from this relationship. Her unspoken regrets had crystallized into the vision of a future she had woven with uncharacteristic naivette and usual high ambition, only to be faced with betrayal and despair. As she returned to Brewster Place in utter dejection and hopelessness, she saw the light in Mattie's window and with a lift in her spirits and lightness in her heart she began her ascent up the steps towards the warmth of love and understanding that awaited her there. In acknowledging the bond of Mattie's friendship and sisterhood, who she knew had waited to gather her broken pieces and give her back to herself, she was filled with a new happiness of having arrived home at last.

Another woman who stands out as unusual is Ruth Anderson of *LH* who had come from an affluent background and married into one. Living for six months as the wife of a wealthy person and the mistress of a grand house in Linden Hills had filled her with a deep disgust for the hypocrisy and emptiness she found there. Her journey had been exactly the opposite one to that of Roxanne Tilson's, who had started on the first lap of the upward climb and hoped to make a conquest that would ensure her social position on the class ladder. One was so thoroughly disillusioned with the upper-class lifestyle that she forbade her present husband to even contemplate about applying for a house in Linden Hills, while the other was hopeful of achieving what Ruth had shunned by choice.

Having married Norman Anderson of Wayne Avenue, Ruth had earned the disapproval of her rich family including her mother. The Andersons' poverty was a standing joke in the neighbourhood and when Norman invited Willie and Lester for a cup of coffee, the latter reacted with exaggerated amazement because it was rare to find two cups in their house. Willie, who was particularly enchanted with and awestruck by Ruth's golden beauty felt that Norman did not deserve the love he got from Ruth, but in all his poverty, Norman tried to fill up with his love all the gaps in their lives and all that he could not give her. Ruth appeared to radiate such contentment that no one would guess the heroic struggle she had had to undertake to achieve this state of mind and perfect harmony with her husband.

The Anderson home was a bare, three-roomed apartment with hardly any furniture, but filled with an air of warmth and welcome, giving the impression of such well-being, care and mutual love that it was a "home" in the true sense. The spare furniture and wooden floor were dusted and polished with loving care. Even the disposable Styrofoam cups were made to last as they were washed and put away for re-use. Ruth worked as a waitress at a hotel and Norman worked different jobs according to their availability. However, their idyllic life was overshadowed by a strange malady, which afflicted Norman periodically. The psychological disorder named "the pinks" (35) came upon him every alternative spring, during which the habitually gentle and loving man was transformed into a hair-tearing maniac who rushed about the streets trying to claw off the imaginary pink slime that was consuming him with his nails, teeth and every untried and jagged, hard surface he found. So Ruth disposed of all their wooden furniture, crockery, cutlery and hard plastic—surfaces that could be used by him to hurt himself. For three months after that he would exist in a "twilight" (35) in a mental asylum to return defeated and broken. Ruth would then restart another phase of peaceful, joyous life and rebuilding her shattered household, that would last till the next attack of the pinks.

Norman could keep a job only for eighteen months while Ruth had to tide over alone in the times of his illness. She could not afford to give up her steady job as a waitress where she was required to lift heavy trays and be on her feet all day (her swollen and tired feet—a recurring motif in Walker and Morrison too, underscoring black women's life of labor). After four years of marriage to Norman, Ruth had been "bone tired" of being torn "between her hatred and love for this man" (*ibid*). Pushed beyond the point of endurance, seriously ill due to the inflammation of her ovaries, all her money drained in Norman's treatment, and having lost her job as she was unable to handle heavy manual tasks, she had decided to go home, ending her marriage with Norman. As she got ready to leave, Norman returned from work with red rimmed eyes that indicated the commencement of the pinks. Seeing Ruth doubled up in pain on the bed made him ward off the disease forcibly, and he held on to his sanity desperately to tend to Ruth. After that she never attempted to leave him because she had exorcised the hate and lived with only her all-encompassing love.

Ruth and Norman lived now in a bare house, not replacing the destroyed furniture, saving money for Norman's medication, hospital bills and therapy sessions. Returning after each trauma, he found Ruth waiting in welcome—a safe shore for him to come home to. The couple dreamed of adopting a baby, window shopped for their dream home, filled the empty spaces with companionship, and the people of Wayne Avenue laughed affectionately, if enviously at them, saying: "if Norman brought home air, Ruth would make gravy, pour it over it, and tell him not to bring so much the next time" (32). Ruth had also wanted, like any woman, the "anchor of security that comes with the weight of accumulated things" (35) but denied that stability and permanence, she created permanence out of those eighteen months of peaceful interludes. Her quiet acceptance and heroic struggle for the man she loved gave her an inner glow that no material achievement could have given and for Willie, she remained a Goddess of his dreams—to be admired and worshipped.

Ruth had condensed in herself the essence of womanhood. She was materially poor, not by compulsion but by choice, and she had had to pay the full price of having chosen a hard life for herself. Yet, in her role as labor, she had achieved a completeness and contentment unknown to most women. Naylor has championed in Ruth's struggle, not the collective strength of sisterhood, but an innate individual strength that had however paradoxically not hardened, but mellowed her. The richness of her soul had allowed her to transcend poverty and material lack.

Though *MD* has Miranda at its center, the central action of the novel pivots round Cocoa Day who is Abigail's granddaughter and Mama Day's grandniece. Cocoa is a young woman, living and working in New York. A major part of the text is composed of Cocoa's "voice" and her supposed conversation with George, her boyfriend and their exchange of feelings, emotions and thoughts. When the action shifts to Willow Springs, which is

Cocoa's "home, home" (*MD*, 22), Abigail and Miranda are found preparing for Cocoa's yearly visit, talking and worrying about her and hoping for her marriage and children. Coming from a place like Willow Springs, so rich in the heritage of its past, so full of mystery and beauty, Cocoa carried with her an aura of the South, a part of "home" that did not allow her to become like the hard-as-nails Selma or the countless "too bright, too jaded" colored city girls with "polished iron webbing around their hearts" (32) that George had initially thought her to be. The old-fashioned values and lady-like grace that had been inculcated in her since her childhood restrained her fiery temper and city-bred cynicism that came inevitably after living in New York for seven years. She had gone beyond the bridge to a world which was fast paced and jet-setting from a world which had a magical charm and where progress had been lulled to a standstill. Cocoa combined the positive aspects of both worlds in herself and in doing so, she becomes the protagonist of the novel.

It would be an understatement to say that Cocoa was the apple of Abigail and Miranda's eyes. Their world revolved round her and it was Miranda's cherished wish to be able to die surrounded by the loving attention of Cocoa's children. Cocoa had a "butter nut" complexion that she herself despised but was much admired in the city for its rich golden glow. Her name had been given to "put color on her somewhere" (39-40) and to give her a defence weapon against the teasing of her schoolmates who called her "Lulu the Leper" (199). Spirited as she was, she was still hurt by the taunt and on one occasion had come home distraught, ready to chop off her finger (reminiscent of Sula in *Sula* by Morrison) to prove that her blood was as red as the darkest of children. George praised Cocoa for her "spunk" (31) that made her meet situations head on and unflinchingly take the consequences of her actions. Miranda and Abigail remember how she had come fighting and kicking into the world—a "little ball of pale fire", who, denied her mother's milk, had still survived because she was a born fighter. "Pulling Mother's knick-knacks off the curio before she could barely crawl, running before she could walk—she was *the* baby girl" (39) and therefore named as such. The two old women had fought tooth and nail to keep her alive, resolving never to allow her to escape them in death. So she had her two grandmothers, a wonderful childhood, a host of memories and firm roots in the island of Willow Springs to call her own—together, they meant "home" for her. She had inherited more than the original house and acres of land as a legacy of the days—she was the true heir of the ancestress Sapphira after Miranda in having inherited the same strong will, headstrong attitude, independence, courage to take up challenge, ability to take burdens and responsibilities and the capacity to bear pain. Combining in herself the values of the island world and the practical sense and spirit of achievement of modern America, Cocoa stood poised at the threshold of the century as *the* African-American woman, a powerhouse of strength, light, emotion and positive values: "and now she strides so proud, a sunflower...long strides flashing light between the blur of strong legs...it's only an ancient mother of pure black that one day spits out this kind a gold" (47-48).

Finishing high school with good grades, she had been put through two years of business school where she graduated at the top of the class. Seven years of job experience as an Office Manager at an insurance farm, steady promotion over the years for her efficiency and a pay rise of over fifty per cent had made her financially secure till she lost her job when the company closed down. Upon the reader's first encounter with Cocoa she is out of job, living in an in-city New York apartment which was both cramped and expensive, hunting desperately for employment. In between her appearing for countless interviews, she took short breaks to rest her sore feet, swollen from long walks on high heeled sandals. In her prolonged search for employment, she formed her own conclusions about segregation and racism, having encountered New York's particular brand of subterranean racism that was more of an inconvenience than a frankly racist city would have been. Summing up the city job scenario she said:

> Mama day and Grandma had told me that there was a time when the want ads and housing listings in newspapers—even up north—were clearly marked colored or white. It must have been wonderfully easy to go job hunting then. You were spared a lot of legwork and headwork. And how I

> longed for those times, when I was busting my butt up and down the streets.... One of (Selma's) certain people was so upset his voice shook: "you mean, you want to bring back segregation?" I looked at him like he was a fool—Where had it gone? I just wanted to bring the clarity about it back—it would save me a whole lot of subway tokens. What I was left to deal with were the ads labeled *Equal Opportunity Employer,* or nothing—which might as well have been labeled *Colored apply* or *Take your chances.* And if I want to limit myself to the sure bets, then I was an equal opportunity to be what, or earn what? That's where the headwork came in. (18-19)

It was in the course of her job hunt that Cocoa met George whom she later married. He discovered that her independence, sharp tongue and confidence hid a vulnerability and honesty that appealed to him. In trying to reconcile the duality of her experience at home and in the city, to overcome her insecurity at the fast pace and fast changing city life, her psychological defence mechanism worked overtime to produce the characteristically bizarre expressions and descriptions she used to define people. In appreciating her forthrightness and accepting her faults, George stuck up a relationship with her that was one of the rarest kind found among black men and women—in which Naylor has been able to create a new paradigm.

Whenever Cocoa came home, she was "herself"—a place where she could express her fullest and freest self. Three years after their marriage, she convinced George to go to Willow Springs with her and he discovered why this place symbolized home to her more than the city would ever become. Tragically, Cocoa lost her husband at Willow Springs when he died in saving her life. The period of mourning, overcoming the intense grief over such a loss, coming to terms with his death and accepting a future without him exhausted Cocoa. However, a true daughter of Miranda in spirit, she recovered from this trauma to emerge as a mature and contained woman. She settled in Charleston that was nearer to Willow Springs than New York with her second husband and children. She came home often to visit George's grave to spend hours with him in silent communion. At the close of the novel, she is a middle-aged woman whose face has been "given the meaning of peace. A face ready to go in search of answers, so at last there ain't no need for words as they lock eyes over the distance" (312). Cocoa had at last amalgamated and reconciled within herself the conflicting values of an ancient world loaded with history embodied by Willow Springs and the fast changing values of a modern America. In that she has indeed looked forward towards new horizons.

Category VIII which includes conjure women is also represented in Naylor's novels. These are the wise old "witches" who represented the accumulated weight of hoary traditions (*cf.* Morrison's *Sula*), the richness of folk culture and beliefs, the knowledge of herbal remedies and the magical and supernatural powers that made them objects of both admiration and fear. Naylor's *MD* is named after the greatest conjure women on the island of Willow Springs—Miranda Day who was called as such by the islanders. In *Mama Day*, Naylor presents a combination of wit, humour, practical wisdom, strength of mind, knowledge of medicinal plants and homely remedies that she had acquired with her great intelligence and superb sensitivity that she inherited from her ancestress Sapphira Wade. It has been observed time and again in the course of the study that of all African-American women, the highest degree of freedom in the role of labor (in the form of an independent, traditional and powerful profession) was available to conjure women. Neither Sapphira, nor Miranda nor most of these benevolent witches expected money in return of their services. These were doctors who had graduated from the school of life and had the knowledge and experience to mix and match potent herbs to ensure a cure, a speedy recovery, lessening of pain or even perform an operation if need be. Added to their knowledge of medicinal plants was their thorough knowledge of the human body, especially a woman's physiology, which made them excellent midwives. These were wise women and brusque, their ready wit and humour making their task lighter. They rendered social service through their medical help, wise counseling and good advice and in return they were widely respected and admired. They were loved and trusted by the black community and whenever there was trouble, men and women approached them for guidance, help and advice. There was also a tinge of fear regarding their magical powers.

Their service was returned with gifts of gratitude that acknowledged their care and concern. Money had no significance for these women for whom their abilities were a gift from God. Unlike Walker's Sister Madelaine who was a modern witch, Naylor has represented Mama Day in the image of these traditionally strong and determined women capable of dealing with every circumstance, come what may. In *MD*, Naylor also presents Ruby, the evil conjure woman who misused her knowledge of black magic for her own selfish ends. Ruby serves as a foil to Miranda in that the former is an avenging ruthless witch while the latter is a witch in the sense of a healer and a wise woman.

Miranda Day of Willow Springs was a captivating figure, whose physical ordinariness belied her toughness and inner strength. She was the gifted daughter of John Paul who was the seventh son of a seventh son. She was the most respected, loved and feared person on the island—a woman who would heal, tend, nurse, deliver and extend a helping hand to anyone in need. Yet, if she was crossed or she saw injustice done, she would also punish in her own way—it was her judgment that ruled on the island. The legends and hearsays surrounding Miranda and her healing hand in a shroud of mystery and impression of power were many and varied but the unshakeable faith in her abilities and belief in her power esconced her firmly in the hearts of the people. Miranda is represented in her social role of empowerment and as Larry Andrews writes: "Miranda's woman power is... presented as an expression of natural forces (note her gardening ability) and as an inheritance from the legendary ur-mother of the community."[11] The degree of freedom and independence exercised by Miranda is reminiscent of the African tribal culture where the powerful witch was adored for her extraordinary capacities. Sapphira had initiated a tradition of female power, which Miranda continued. As Willis says, "for black women history is a bridge defined along motherliness"[12] and Miranda carried forward the legacy that had come to her from Sapphira. She served as doctor and midwife for the people of her island, her instinctive knowledge of the woods and herbs serving her in good stead. Throughout the text there are numerous references to her doctoral abilities and also detailed descriptions of her performance in the role of a healer.

Mama Day who had never been married, nor had any children of her own had become everyone's "Mama" by virtue of her maternal role. She was still a child when the insanity of her mother and withdrawal of her father made her Abigail's "Little Mama" (88) as she took upon herself the responsibility of the entire household. Since then, the mantle of motherhood remained with her and sometimes, during particularly nostalgic moments when she was weighed down by the burden of wisdom and foreknowledge that she carried in her mind, she wished that she had had a life and family of her own making. Her youth had passed in her involvement with the problems of her parents and sister—tending to a sick mother and a younger sister, managing house for an aloof and preoccupied father, so that there had been no time to think about herself. As a young girl she had also fallen in love but could not abandon the responsibilities of an entire family that needed her support for the promise of a new life that beckoned in the boy's offer to take her away with him. There was no choice because she could never think of leaving her loved ones:

> The cooking, the cleaning, the mending, the gardening for the woman who sat in the porch rocker, twisting, twisting on pieces of thread. Peace was gone. *But I was your child, too*.... Being there for mama and child. Being there to catch so many babies that dropped into her hands. Gifted hands, folks said. You have a gift, Little Mama...we need you Little Mama. Mama and child. Mama and sister. Too heavy a load to take away...Everybody's mama. (88-89)

Her role as everyone's mother in the family gradually extended to include the entire island as she delivered, tended to and nursed to health hundreds of babies, serving as midwife and doctor countless times. Now, Abigail's family was her own and to Cocoa, she and Abigail together made a whole mother figure—unable as she was to distinguish between their love. From Cocoa's talk about home and her great aunt, George had gathered the impression that she would be a towering figure of strength. He was taken aback to find a small, fine-boned lady, earth-brown in color and with a flawless skin, but no teeth (*cf.* Ajax's mother in *Sula*). However, the apparent impression of vulnerability and youthfulness was broken when upon a closer look when one discovered the "steel" (176) beneath the smooth skin that compelled one to regard her with wary respect. As George said, her "straightforward honesty" would "cheapen anyone returning less than the same" (*ibid*). At ninety, she had the strength to walk miles, though ironically, she had had "no time to be young" (88). The onus of a life time of caring, pain, struggles, decision-making, work and more work and playing the role of a nurturer, healer and mother had settled on her shoulders but had not been able to bring a slump to them.

Miranda was a wonderful cook, an excellent seamstress, a good fisher woman, a midwife par excellence and an efficient surgeon whose operations were as neat as a trained doctor and the superior skill of her deft fingers was admired by her professional rival Dr. Smithfield. The magical quality of her powers was however highlighted when she manipulated the forces of nature to impregnate Bernice, called up a thunder storm to teach a rude, white boy the lesson of his life and when, delivering the final judgment on Ruby who had dared provoke her fury by harming "what was (hers)" (271), she made the lightning strike her house twice. She had mastered the science of magic and the art of logic—a potent combination that made her an invincible figure.

Towards the climax of the novel, Miranda is represented as a weary old woman who had lost her magical powers and was unable to cure Cocoa of her fatal illness (the result of Ruby's evil spell). Withdrawing to her old house—"the other place" (91) she meditated to get back her lost power wondering whether God had punished her for having played "God" (262). It was only after her encounter (in her dreams) with her ancestress Sapphira that her magical powers were rejuvenated. With the establishment of this vital link with the ur-mother Sapphira, Miranda emerges as the link between the past and future (Cocoa). She therefore plays the pivotal role of a guide and guardian to her strong-willed grandniece who would carry forward this legacy of female empowerment.

In presenting Ruby as a foil to Miranda, Naylor has portrayed her in stark contrast, even in physical appearance. Ruby was a massive, mountain-like woman with an immobile face and immense figure. Her proportions underlined forcefully the difference in the quality of her power with Miranda's subtle strength. Ruby was feared by the islanders on account of her voodoo powers that she had acquired over the years. She had learnt the practice of evil magic and unlike Miranda, who very rarely practiced magic, Ruby misused it, to harm people. She was a woman of few words who went about her work with a single-minded, one-track determination and ruthlessness that could not be reasoned with. Represented as the evil sorceress, she used hate as her weapon and harmed rather than healed. She emerged as an evil force to be reckoned with after her liaison with Junior Lee. She was a rich widow who had reputedly murdered her husband and lived alone in an isolated house that was surrounded by the grounds she owned. In this, she was the fearsome figure whose isolation served to enhance the aura of mystery surrounding black magic. After her marriage to Junior Lee, she came across as the over-possessive wife, but on account of her vindictiveness, she became a dark and menacing presence who would destroy every woman who crossed her husband's path in her mindless and irrational jealousy. She was no ordinary jealous wife however, and the victims of her hatred had to face terrible consequences. It was her misfortune to cross swords with Miranda when she targeted her beloved grandniece and overstepped the line of her tolerance. In provoking her fury, she had to pay with her life.

Ruby was ignorant and motivated by base emotions—the social role she played was that of a mischief maker, an evil witch whom no one dared to meddle with. Like a malevolent and blindly destructive force of nature, she could not be diverted from her purpose of eradicating all potential contenders (imaginary or otherwise) for Junior Lee's affections. While Miranda dealt in life, using the knowledge she had gleaned for the benefit of people and with a total lack of self-interest,

Ruby used her powers for exactly the opposite reasons. It was in the justice of things that she faced retribution for her misdeeds.

Naylor's novels clearly indicate the emerging trend of labor roles of African-American women as progression corresponding with changing times and changing job market scenario. The transition of African-American women from social non-persons and only work horses (as laborers) through improving job opportunities to an affirmation of the traditionally powerful role of the conjure women to the black woman of the modern era who stands on the threshold of a new beginning, marks the process of social change and development that is taking place gradually. If there are still African-American women who act in fear of losing their jobs, there are others who would give their private lives preference over their professional existence. They now have the courage to quit jobs and look for new work as more choices/options are available to them. The job market scenario is more promising and work roles more fulfilling for them. African-American women, as perceived by Naylor, may now look forward to a better future and new work roles that however would inevitably demand new adjustments and attitudes.

NOTES AND REFERENCES

1. Dorothy Wickenden, *The New York Republic.* September 6, 1982 (Book Review).
2. Henry Louis Gates Jr., "Preface", *Gloria Naylor, Critical Perspectives Past and Present.* Eds. Henry Louis Gates Jr. and K.A. Appiah, Amistad, New York: 1993, p. ix.
3. Daniel Patrick Moynihan, *The Negro Family: The Case for National Action.* (Westport, Conn.: Greenwood Press, Publishers Reprint, 1981, p. 30). Quoted in Celeste Frasier. "Stealing B(l)ack Voices: The Myth of the Black Matriarchy and the Women of Brewster Place". *Gloria Naylor: Critical Perspectives Past and Present.* Eds. Henry Louis Gates Jr. and K.A. Appiah, p. 94.
4. Frasier. *Ibid.*, pp. 91-95.
5. *Ibid.*, p. 92.
6. Gloria Naylor, "The Women of Brewster Place", *Ebony*, 41, March 1989, I, p. 123, quoted in 3. *op cit.*, p. 92.
7. Gloria Naylor, *The Women of Brewster Place.* London and Sidney: Sphere Books Ltd., 1980, p. 5. Quoted by Celeste Frazier in 3. *op cit.*, p. 96.

8. An Octoroon is an offspring of a quadroon and a white, person of one-eighth Negro blood.
9. See Sandra M. Gilbert, and Susan Gubar. *Madwoman in the Attic: The Woman Writer and the Nineteenth-Century Literary Imagination.* New Haven: Yale University Press, 1979.
10. Bessie Smith (*LH*, 235) was a famous Blues Singer, also referred to in Walker's *The Color Purple* (New York: Pocket Books, Washington Square Press, 1983, p. 74) as a close friend of Shug Avery. Also see Appendix, p. vii.
11. Larry R. Andrews, "Black Sisterhood in Naylor's Novels", *Gloria Naylor: Critical Perspectives Past and Present*, p. 296.
12. Susan Willis, *Specifying: Black Women Writing, the American Experience.* Madison: University of Wisconsin Press, 1987, p. 6.

[Quotations from novels have been indicated by abbreviated names of the novels followed by page numbers within parentheses initially. Thereafter, till another novel is alluded to, numbers in bracket indicate page numbers of the same novel.]

5

African-American Women as Labor in the Novels of Toni Morrison, Alice Walker and Gloria Naylor: A Comparative Analysis

The present study has attempted to examine and analyse the representation of the roles of African-American women as labor in the selected novels of Toni Morrison, Alice Walker and Gloria Naylor. In the course of applying the stated hypotheses, certain similarities have emerged in the representations rendered by these three authors, as was anticipated in the Introduction, as also distinctive qualities and treatment that make each of their work unique and individual. In grounding their work in the tradition of black women authors, whose heightened perceptions and awareness about the marginalisation and exploitation of black women stem from their personal encounter with racism, sexism and classism in America—the interlocking factors that have made black women sufferers of a three-fold discrimination—the study has acknowledged and recognized the solidarity of sisterhood that has functioned as the *tour de force* of their fictional works. In bringing together and comparing the respective treatment of women as labor theme in their role representations of black women, the study has identified an emerging paradigm—the affirmation of faith in the positive values of life, a collective consciousness and shared understanding of the existing problems and situations, a re-inforcing of the bonds of sisterhood with a view to strengthening not only racist but also gender solidarity and finally, the new horizons and the new roles of fulfilment that black women in the novels of Toni Morrison, Alice Walker and Gloria Naylor envision in their changing roles as labor. As work is and has always been, the central metaphor in the lives of black women, with changing times and changing work roles, their roles as labor at home has also undergone remarkable changes. If in role-representation, the author allows the fictional character's action to determine what the character is, then, through the work roles of the African-American women, Toni Morrison, Alice Walker and Gloria Naylor have manifested their multilayered personalities, their typical traits, their individual 'self's and the growth, change or otherwise of their personalities. As artists they have represented black women's victimization, rebellion, expressions of creativity, achievement of material success or inner joy and fulfillment and completeness as individuals or as organic units of close knit black communities and their individual advancement or collective growth. They have also shown African-American women's empowerment through identification, sharing, enhanced understanding and appreciation and relieving of each others' pain and finally, through creating space both for themselves and for their sisters in oppression in their novels.

From slavery to freedom, the trajectory of African-American women's experience as labor can be traced in the novels of Toni Morrison, Alice Walker and Gloria Naylor. The awareness of slavery and the knowledge of the 'herstory' of pain have shaped their imagination, colored their interpretation of sociological and cultural realities and defined their aesthetic representations of African-American women who have, since the times of slavery, tried to achieve selfhood in spite of and paradoxically also through their labor roles. In *Beloved*, Toni Morrison represents through intricate detail and repeated references, the horrors and tortures of slave life. Unafraid as an artist to reveal through the technique of rememory that throws up sudden and vivid flashes of a past consciously suppressed by the protagonist who is a victim of terrible abuses of slavery, Morrison has made a bold statement of her standpoint regarding the dehumanization and exploitation of slaves, especially black women, regarded as they were as labor and property that could multiply itself without cost. Underscoring the sum total of a slave woman's life in *B*, Morrison made Baby Suggs say that slave life had "busted her legs, back, head, eyes, kidneys, womb and tongue" (*B*, 217). Morrison has shown how, as Christian writes, black women were valued not as mothers but as breeders who "produced" workers and for their ability to nurture them till they became "producers" for the society—as laborers and breeders in their turn.[1] So Sethe in *B* felt that she could not love her children fully because she had no claim over them as their bodies and their labor belonged to the slave master. Again, Sethe's mother, like other slave women in that era, was not allowed time to nurse her baby for more than a week as children were separated from their mothers and put in charge of wet nurses (usually black women like Nan of *B* who were unable to handle other strenuous tasks) and were looked after collectively. Finally, she died in a faceless anonymity that was the lot of must slaves (tried as she had to show her daughter the brand that distinguished her from other slaves) treated as they were as units of labor.

Walker's concern about these brutalized slave women has been expressed in her interview with Mary Helen Washington,[2] where she speaks about their "work-worn" and abused bodies and benumbed state of mind, existing they did in a "suspended" state and only in the capacity of laborers, their crushed creativity chanelled out through the medium of their work. In her novels, Walker represents slave women through scattered references to some black women in *M* and *TMF.* Louvinie of *M* had her tongue uprooted for narrating a tale to her master's children, one of whom died in shock. The tongue was symbolic of the slave woman's power of speech or her speaking voice and creativity that was ground under her master's heels. Like True Belle in Morrison's *J*, she had a flair for storytelling—the only outlet for her rich imagination. Meridian Hill's great grandmother, also a slave, expressed her creative potential through her wonderfully innovative paintings. Living in an era where their worth was gauged only as laborers/work horses, these were slave women who yet tried to find outlets for self-expression amidst their daily toil. In *TMF*, the historical perspective of the slave experience is rendered in detail by Walker through Miss Lissie's memory of her past life as a slave woman bought from Africa, who was herded, sold, branded, overworked, beaten and finally driven to death. Walker's Lissie "rememories" her past lives, through which technique the author makes her recount, griot-like, the overwhelming tortures she had undergone as a teenaged girl, along with her mother who died before she could be shipped and her siblings whom she never saw again. Her narrations are rendered with a starkness and unrelenting power with the deliberate intention of shocking the readers into an awareness of the slave woman's terrible plight.

In Naylor's novels, there are no vivid or graphic details of slave experience and their roles as labor but oblique references and subtle statements are introduced (*cf.* the sale deed of Sapphira Wade of *MD*) to evoke the vision of the tortures these women were subjected to or the work they had to do as slaves—chastisement in the form of vicious whippings being a common punishment for laziness, sickness or unwillingness to work.

The role of poor, black women as laborers both in the rural South and the urban ghettoes has been represented by Toni Morrison, Alice Walker and Gloria Naylor in their novels. While Morrison concentrates more on semi-rural townships and urban ghettoes, Walker chooses to explore the rural settings, Naylor's poor women are mostly urban. They have therefore their peculiar as also similar problems. From slave women to poor free women—the transition has not been easy for these black women. Owning now their labor, they still are burdened with the responsibility of their families and children and more often than not, they cannot afford to rely on their men for support. The absconding/errant/absent father/male is a recurring motif in all the three authors and even if the men are shown to be present, they often become perpetrators of sexist domination, transferring their frustration and rage at racist victimization upon their women (*cf.* Margaret and Mem of *TLGC*, Eva of *S*, Pauline of *TBE*, Sadie's mother and Sadie of *BC*, Ciel and Cora Lee of *WBP*) or simply abandon their responsibility to take off for greener pastures (Jude and Boy Boy of *S*, Solomon of *SOS*, Grange of *TLGC*, Eugene and Sammy's father of *WBP*, Sadie's father of *BC* and a host of others). As field laborers, domestic workers, charwomen, chamber maids, washerwomen, maids, factory workers and cleaning ladies, these women get the worst choice of jobs as unskilled workers. Occupying the lowest rung of the labor market, they are the lowest paid and worst exploited. The job scenario has been authentically presented by Toni Morrison, Alice Walker and Gloria Naylor in their representation of working women of Category II and in *SOS*, Morrison presents the dilemma of a college educated woman Corinthians who, in the course of her job-hunt, discovers the unpalatable truth that in a white-dominated work world, colored girls were required for only certain kinds of work—that of a maid or prostitute, even as late as 1960. Walker's poor, black women of the South (rural) are faced with crushing poverty and caught in the grip of sharecropping along with their husbands, their lives becoming a chain of "unrelenting misery" (*TLGC*, 86) from which either death or insanity could grant them respite.

A similar picture emerges in Naylor's portrayal in the urban black ghettoes of Brewster Place or Southside Chicago, where black women struggle to fight for survival. If as welfare mothers (Cora Lee of *WBP* and Mrs. Mason of *LH*) they manage to make ends meet from the welfare cheques, they are also victims of politically motivated laws framed by the state in order to coerce more and more black women into the labor force and lowest paid jobs so as to generate cheap labor. Poor, black women therefore have to function in multiple roles both within and outside their homes in order to keep afloat themselves and their families. The recurring motif of weary and aching feet of overworked black women can be traced in the novels of all the three authors (Ondine in *TB*, Mem in *TLGC* and Ruth in *LH*). Yet, all the three authors have shown how, despite the unremitting toil, these women retain their capacity for laughter and love in the face of surmounting problems and demoralizing circumstances. Their labor therefore attains a dignity that the society has consistently denied them.

The prevailing social myths and prejudice about the poor and working-class black women is put succinctly by Patrick Bryce Bjork when he writes:

> The "good" woman was pure, sexually repressed and physically fragile; she was married, a mother, or a spinster

who was dependent on and therefore non-threatening to man. The "bad" woman was dirty, promiscuous, physically and mentally strong: she was a prostitute, a laborer, a single mother who paid her own way in spite of her social and political invisibility.[3]

So, black women, who were compelled to work for survival and who "paid their way" despite their invisibility were always seen by the American society paradoxically as "dominant non-entities."[4] On the other hand, Doreatha Mbalia Drummond has expressed concern about the "wildness" in African-American women—wildness that signifies defiance, aggression, rebellion, selfishness, silence—all caused by the triple exploitation of race, class and gender. Walker's Wild Child in *M* and Morrison's Wild in *J* show the outcome of such oppressive social forces and the authors' anxiety and concern about these women because, as cultivators and nurturers of the family unit, the eruption of such a destructive wildness in them is both disturbing and alarming.[5]

Middle-class and rich women represented by Morrison, Walker and Naylor, though better off materially and free from the back-breaking sequence of drudgery are however victims of sexist domination within their homes and racist oppression outside the arena of their communities, where irrespective of their background, class or upbringing, they are "nigger" women whose worth is evaluated through their role as laborers. Cut off from the women of their own community on account of their classist snobbery, they are alienated and isolated, having achieved the respectability of marriage and having emulated the tenets of white middle-class society. Walker's rural middle-class women are servants in their husband's houses, existing in routine domesticity, unable to assert their opinion, subjugated and submissive. In some like Mrs. Hill in *M*, the conflict between motherhood and work comes to the fore and they bear the burden of children and their responsibilities resentfully and bitterly. In Morrison, these are color-conscious, artificial and prudish, decorous women who have tried to find meaning in the meaningless rituals and external realities of their existence while avoiding or refusing to acknowledge the emptiness that lies beneath the surface glamour of their lives. Naylor's middle-class women are ambitious and her rich women confined as prisoners in the golden cages of material wealth and affluence.

Of Category V(a), Morrison and Naylor represent successful and brilliant career women Jadine of *TB* and Laurel of *LH* respectively who are both orphans, literally and culturally and who have failed to find fulfillment in their work roles despite the glamour of their jobs. Morrison presents through Jadine's psychological conflict and subsequent choice, the attitude of modern black women who, having the privilege of education and training, logically choose to opt out of the confining and traditional roles expected of them as black women. In so doing however, they risk making materialism, ambition and the acquisition of fame, wealth and recognition the centre of their existence, negating on the one hand their racial identity and denying on the other their cultural roles. In failing to identify with their race women, they fail to find sustaining emotional and psychological links with their past and a corresponding richness or stability in themselves. In substituting emotional burdens and responsibilities with intellectual freedom, they have found a measure of self-worth but paradoxically lost the essence of their womanhood to be haunted by repressed guilt. Morrison's Jadine chooses to ignore the clamour in her soul to reclaim her elevated lifestyle after a short period of contact with Son (symbolic of the Negro underclass) while Naylor's Laurel Dumont rejects all that she has achieved by dint of hard labor—the empire she has built, the fame and glamour of her position—to succumb to the frightening well of emptiness within herself and commit suicide. It is noteworthy that both authors apparently suggest that material success does not seem to suit black women who, if they have achieved singular and phenomenal success, always seem to be plagued by the guilt of having pursued their personal ambitions and having labored for self-advancement. Even if what they have achieved is well-deserved and the compromises they have made only natural, given the tough fight against odds, they have had to cope with alienation, isolation and pay with a loss of their peace of mind. Also, Jadine's fear in recognizing another dimension of her personality (the potential for mothering or nurturing) stems from her belief that in choosing the maternal role like the night women (who haunt her dreams), she will fall into the quagmire of socio-political stagnation and regress. She thinks that these women had chosen their roles out of a personal weakness and in that she fails to understand their strength. Betrayal of community therefore becomes a motif in the representation of successful black women by Morrison and Naylor. None of the black women in Walker's novels fall in this category and the conflict of personal advancement versus racial loyalty comes in when she represents political activists like Meridian and Anne Marion in *M*, where the former chooses to pursue a humble lifestyle and work in her own way for the upliftment of poor, black people by fighting for their rights while the latter, initially more fiery and action-oriented than the former, finally "sells out" to become a rich poetess, owning her own lake and grounds. Meridian determined a reverse journey in respect of social position when she, from being a teacher, is said to have hired herself out as a gardener, waitress, even a dishwasher and cook (*M*, 19)—work roles that became increasingly humble and that she took up, like Fanny Nzingha of *TMF*, to atone for past actions that she felt had been selfishly motivated. It was her way of penance and soul-searching.

Walker's personal involvement in the Civil Rights Movement has inspired her to portray black women activists' fight for social and political rights, their bitter disillusionment and then the final resolution or coming to terms with their own conflicts, the clash of ideology and practical considerations that often caused a profound psychological turmoil in them and the emotional and psychic toll that the work they had done as political activists had on them, through her representation of Meridian and Helen in *TLGC*. Naylor moves forward in time to represent Kiswana Browne in *WBP*, an idealistic social activist, in an era after the Civil Rights Movement. In Kiswana, she portrays the enthusiasm and zeal of young black women who, in attempting to identify with and experience firsthand the rigours of poverty, had given up their affluent homes and privileged social set ups. In Morrison's novels, there are no black women activists, though the essential conflict remains, to haunt successful women like Jadine.

The traditionally powerful African-American women in their labor roles were conjure women who have been represented by all the three authors differently. Morrison's conjure women functioned as evil magicians as well as doctors and were widely respected and feared by the African-American community. Walker's conjure woman Madelaine in *TLGC* was interestingly a modern witch who operated more as a psychologist than a magician, making a profession of this traditional role. Naylor's portrayal of Mama Day in *MD* is a full-fledged representation of a black woman in this role where Miranda performed not only as a witch doctor but also as a wise healer, a surgeon, a midwife, a magician, a root worker, a social messiah and a benevolent "two headed" (*TLGC*, 129) conjure woman. She however did not take any payment in return of her services that were motivated by kindness and a genuine wish to help the people of her island. As her negative foil, Naylor represents Ruby, the evil conjuress, who is motivated by selfish concerns. However, all the three authors represent conjure women as embodiments of female empowerment who could and had always, acted unconventionally, exercised freedom, drawn admiration and even fear, relied on their ingenuinity, intuition, inventiveness and knowledge of African tribal medicine, myths and lore, practiced magic and functioned as wise healers.

Morrison, Walker and Naylor have represented black women of Category VII as individuals who are able to transcend their racial identities, gender constrictions and class inhibitions to express themselves to the fullest extent. The quest for their self and soul has made them rebels, outcastes and pariahs. They have set their own parameters and defined their roles. Yet, the individualized quests of these extraordinary women have ended in enhanced appreciation of community ties. Their labor roles have not restricted or confined them—rather they have been able to lend new meaning, dimension and worth to their work through their fine perceptions, sensibilities and deep human compassion. If Sula in *S* has shunned the community and communitarian values, if Katherine Degos of *TMF* has withdrawn from society into a self-imposed isolation, then they have been misunderstood, berated and condemned. Lack of communication has always been depicted as negative by black women writers. In Morrison's *B*, Sethe who had withdrawn after the community's refusal to warn her of the approach of slave catchers and is later reclaimed after eighteen years of alienation, Sula who is not "put away" (*S*, 172) after death, Violet's (in *J*) divided self and double consciousness—her alienation in the city and the condemnation of her action of violating the dead body of her husband's girlfriend are consequences of a failure to communicate. Walker's Katherine Degos who abandons her charity work, rejects all forms of communication to die alone, Fanny Nzingha also of *TMF* who tries to communicate with other people's pain through her job as a masseuse, giving up her prestigious job in the academia that had alienated her from her own colleagues, Naylor's Laurel Dumont and the Nedeed wives in *LH* who fail to communicate with the women of their community which finally leads to their death, are instances of the same collapse of human relationships, lack of contact and inability to reach out to others. All these women, at a particular point in their lives have begun to feel a dissatisfaction with their work and the overwhelming sense of a loss of purpose has made them withdraw into themselves. This phenomenon can be related to their work experience and said to be the product of the tension and dilemmas they have been confronted with at particular junctures of their labor history where they have been called upon to resolve the conflict within themselves. As Morrison, Walker and Naylor's characters are individuals, not stereotypical representations, so the problems of emerging individuality against the community chained to traditional concepts of woman's role as the self-less mother gives rise to problems that defy easy solutions. On the other hand, women like Pilate (*SOS*), Shug and Sofia (*TCP*), Lissie (*TMF*), Ruth (*LH*) and Cocoa have affirmed positive values, have created space for others and in searching for self-expression and a true measure of self-worth, they have helped others to launch on the same quest, inspiring them to change, grow and lead an unafraid, free and untrammeled existence with their heads held high.

While analyzing representations of the roles of African-American women as labor by Toni Morrison, Alice Walker and Gloria Naylor, the study has been able to trace their major concerns and also the similarities and unique or distinctive qualities of their treatment of such themes. Morrison's obvious concerns are predominantly racist and classist, sexist concerns being submerged but strong. She represents in the roles that African-American women perform, their actual dilemma and the complexity of their roles, class being a very important factor that shapes/determines the reality of the African-American laborer's existence, along with racial discrimination. Sexist exploitation is brought out clearly in her novels, though in interviews,[6] she has denied pronounced or overt feminist concerns. Her novels show her sensitive exploration of African-American women's dilemma in the multiple labor roles they perform and that are expected of them. Walker's predominant concerns are racist and sexist while classist issues take a backseat in her novels. Most of her characters move from one category to the other and back, thus crossing the class barriers again and again. Also, material solvency does not mean the possession of "class", that requires respectability, which black women always seem to strive for but are rarely able to attain. Naylor's novels on the other hand exhibit pronounced classist and sexist concerns while racism is submerged issue varying from novel to novel and coming to the fore occasionally, especially during the portrayal of job hunts and work world scenarios.

Walker boldly represents characters in role stereotypes to create strongly individual and complex characters that flout the very stereotypes they are supposed to project—an artistic technique used with consummate ease by Morrison and Naylor too. An admirer of Toni Morrison, her influence is clearly discernible in Naylor's work while that of black feminist tradition can also be traced in her novels. In *WBP* especially, Naylor has represented the poor, black working woman's problems, drawing parallels with the sociological realities and refuting the image of the calculating, debilitating black woman who is a burden of the state economy, drawing attention to her circumstances that force her to work as cheap labor.

In Morrison's novels, black women represented in their roles as labor resist categorical divisions as there are overlappings and merging of work roles. However, the flexible mould of the hypothesis has accomodated a spectrum, allowed space for change and has accommodated differences and contradictions within the same category. So Corinthians of *SOS*, a rich man's daughter, has become a maid while Pilate of the same novel has transcended poverty to come through as an extraordinary figure of strength. In Walker's novels, the representation of African-American women in their roles as labor is very flexible as they often shift from one category to another and may even belong to two or more categories at once. To some African-American women in her novels, even labor may acquire a spiritual dimension and creativity is often expressed through work by many of them. Even in excruciating circumstances and amid total degradation and hopelessness, poor black women like Mem in *TLGC* have, like Walker's own mother, planted flowers in front of the broken shacks they lived in, while others like Shug of *TCP* and Fanny of *TMF* have given up professional singing careers or jobs in the academia to found their own church or tried to learn the reality of others people's pain. There are those again like Celie of *TCP* who has broken and overthrown the shackles of gender oppression to establish her identity and make an emphatic statement of her own worth, evolving from a drudge into a self-developed dress designer, asserting herself and creating art out of her labor. There is also the visionary philosopher Lissie who has run the gamut of African-American women's experience, living several lives and encountering the evolution and change that African-American women have undergone through the ages from slavery to freedom to modern age.

In the novels of all the three authors, sisterhood among black women is a strong working bond that brings together women who labor side by side, cover for each other at work, share each other's burdens and responsibilities and pool their strengths to combat gender oppression, classist exploitation and racist discrimination. The nurturing and sustaining role of sisterhood is acknowledged by these authors who explore the complexities of this bonding that may sometimes develop into sexually charged lesbian relationships (*cf.* Celie and Shug in Walker's *TCP*, references to developing feminist consciousness as tied with awareness of homosexual attractions in *TMF*, Lorraine and Theresa in *WBP* by Naylor). In *Jazz*, Morrison presents the unlikely friendship between Violet and Alice Manfred to suggest a new possibility of the unity of women as a solution to gender oppression as also the relationships between Ruth and Pilate, Magdelene and Corinthians in *SOS* that show female bonding against sexist domination by husband/father and brother. Morrison's *S* has at its centre the relationship between two young black girls Sula and Nel in the 1920s, who hold on to each other as emotional anchor in a world which shackled black females, forbidding them every "freedom" and "triumph" (*S*, 52). Naylor's *WBP* has eight single women who come together to tear down the wall of Brewster Place in a symbolic act of rebellion against hostile social forces that have pushed them to a corner and made them sufferers of poverty and degradation. All the three authors explore the ties of sisterhood and show how a perceived failure to reach out and embrace their fellow sufferers and sisters of the race have destroyed African-American women like Laurel Dumont and the Nedeed women in *LH* and have rendered futile/barren the lives of rich and isolated women like Jadine of *TB* and Corinthians, Lena and Ruth of *SOS*, who had no emotional support structure of women friends that they could fall back upon. In contrast, such bonds have sustained communities of impoverished and downtrodden black women, both urban and rural as the women of Brewster Place represented by Naylor in *WBP*, the Georgia women in *TBE* and Violet and Alice in *J* as represented by Morrison and Celie, Shug, Sofia and Squeak and a host of other women as represented by Walker in *TCP*.

The fiction of Walker and Naylor represent a continuum, characters reappear in several novels. Their novels are looser in structure, episodic and even documentary like Naylor's *WBP*. Morrison's novels are more tightly knit with a distinct framework. Sequential characters repeated in more than one novel are found in Walker and Naylor, in progression from one to the other, developed fully by Walker in *TMF*. In Morrison's novels, there are no sequential characters, although there are similarities in the circumstances and work roles between different characters of different novels. In Naylor's representation of African-American women as labor, sequential characters like Walker's Celie, Olivia and Shug of *TCP* who are reintroduced in *TMF* are also found in progression (Miranda in *LH* and *MD*, Willa of *LH* spoken of in *MD*, Kiswana Browne of *WBP* referred to in *LH* and Irene Jackson and George are mentioned in *BC* and developed in *MD* and vice versa with Mariam, George's teenaged mother in *BC* who is also spoken of by George in *MD*). Linking up the incidents of different novels and portraying African-American women who change their roles as labor, find scope for self-expression, and make room for others.

Different approaches to race relations are found in the three novelists and the level of interaction between the two races varies in scope and nature. In Morrison's novels, there are representations of black working women as degraded menials who envy the lot of white women. They had, as Sojourner Truth says, never ever been "carried over ditches,"[7] have been compelled to do the dirtiest work, devalued as women and forced to accept their "ugliness" (*cf. TBE*, 34) where Pecola is convinced of her ugliness, Pauline tries to imitate the actress Jean Harlow (*TBE*, 96) to measure up to of white standards of beauty. Morrison's black women are not always proud of their work. They often try to imitate white women in behaviour, action, manners and even looks. In *TBE* and *S* especially, African-American women have a pronounced envy and admiration for white women (their mistresses) and a fascination for white skin and blue eyes—as Claudia of *TBE* feels when she is presented by adults with white dolls to admire and treasure (*TBE*, 13). There is also a contempt for the slovenliness of white women as Pauline Breedlove of *TBE* and Circe of *SOS* feel, both of whom have been maids in white houses. There is again of course a reverse snobbery and the attitudinal difference gradually becomes marked as African-American women emerge from their roles as maids to gain confidence and poise to affirm their own sense of beauty and self-worth as in *TB*—where Jadine is a famous model whose beauty is gauged by fashion model standards while the tar black African woman is described as the "unphotographable beauty" (*TB*, 43).

In Walker's novels, black women, even the maids and menials, are not jealous of white women. Rather, they are proud of their ability to handle tough and strenuous work and their efficiency, regarding white women as useless and ornamental "baby machines" (*M*, 105) who are insipid and unable to assert themselves. In all her novels, the idea/concept of black womanhood as inclusive of toughness, strength, efficiency, endurance of pain and stress, capacity to work hard and a fierce racial pride is reinforced through her representation of black women as labor. So Sofia in *TCP* is an unlikely maid for the unimpressive Miss Millie who cuts a sorry figure beside her ruddy good looks and Mrs. Hill's mother-in-law, a former maid, is of the opinion that minus maids, white women would live in pigsties (*M*, 105). Walker celebrates the unique quality of African-American womanhood when she writes in *M*:

> ...black women were always imitating Harriet Tubman—escaping to become something unheard of. Outrageous... black women struck out for the unknown.... They commanded attention. They deserved admiration.... It thrilled (Meridian) to think that she belonged to the people who produced Harriet Tubman, the only American woman who'd led troops in a battle. (105-06)

In Naylor's novels, which focus on exclusively black neighbourhoods and where the interaction between black and white people is minimum, black women exist in their own world, having little or no contact with white people and comparison therefore is not always possible. However, black women's ingrained pride in their ability to work hard is pronounced and women like Miranda and Abigail in *MD*, the Nedeed wives, Roberta Johnson and Mammy Tilson in *LH*, Mattie Michaels in *WBP*, Mrs. Bell in *BC*, all excel in their roles as labor as housewives, mothers and working women. There are those like Laurel Dumont of *LH* who are brilliant career women, confirming the emergence of a new breed of modern black women who can handle decision-making, administrative jobs, flaunt their superior capabilities in the face of chauvinistic assumptions and take admiration as well as criticism in their stride. Most black women as perceived by the author now do not take their work as degrading and a wide range of labor roles offer possibilities and provide scope for self-satisfaction and advancement through work. Contemporary characters include executives and career women—women who are good workers and have confidence and power. Yet, there is also the consciousness of subterranean racism and discrimination as Cocoa of *MD* encounters in New York, Miss Maple of *BC* in the cities and Roxanne Tilson of *LH* in her office while Mabel Thompson of the same novel is regarded as an ambitious work machine shorn of womanhood. Similarly, Laurel Dumont (also of *LH*) is shown as an Amazon in the work arena only to be humiliated by the rich property developer Luther Nedeed, himself a black man, reminding one that gender oppression still existed and often power in the work arena did not extend into the family and society where patriarchal domination still reigned supreme and female empowerment was illusory.

Morrison's African-American women are very color conscious, taking pride in their pale skin and the darker complexioned ones often wanting to lighten their skin color. Yellow is prized and black berated as color operates as a symbol of class. Again there is the instance of Lady Denver who is contemptuously referred to as the "white nigger" (*B*, 304). For Walker's women, skin color is mostly accepted as a natural physical pigmentation that cannot be helped—as Mem in *TLGC* believes, color is what the ground does to its flowers (58). Naylor presents a new concept of color consciousness in *MD* where Cocoa is teased in Willow Springs because of her golden complexion which is coveted however and much admired in New York. The reverse racial prejudice of the independent black community of the island is that the blacker the skin, the more beautiful the person. The gradual change from envy to pride as perceived by the three authors marks the transition in attitude and indicates the acquisition of confidence and poise by contemporary black women who have begun to set their own standards of beauty (*cf.* Appendix, pp. iv-vi).

Both Walker and Naylor present in their novels parallel situations of black women in their roles as labor from Africa (Ethiopia, Egypt) South America and other parts of the world to bring to the fore the situation of African-American women in America. The sociological perspective is introduced and inevitable comparisons are drawn between black women in different continents. The sexist exploitation that is very much a part of their lives along with the racist exploitation is found in South Africa, Africa and America. Thus, Nettie in *TCP* is shown to recount her experience in Africa among the Olinka women and *TMF* is permeated with historical allusions to the African experience not only of Miss Lissie but other characters like Fanny Nzingha and Olivia. Morrison in *TB* presents in a comparative perspective the black woman's situation and her role as a laborer in the Carribean island named Isles des Chevaliers as a parallel of the African-American women's situation in Georgia in *TBE*, Eloe in Alabama and also in the ghettoes of New York city in *TB*.

Thematically and structurally, Morrison has used the technique of Jazz music in her novels, especially in *Jazz* where like a true jazz artist she uses improvisations or solo flights, where changing scenes are painted like the successive canvas of a painter. A consummate artist, she blends skillfully theme and structure to represent the African-American woman's experience in the city of New York. Similarly, Naylor uses the structure of jazz music in her novel *Bailey's Café* to represent the stories of a range of characters as the throbbing, vibrant and unique notes of the same composition. Jazz music being an inseparable part of the African-American experience, had expressed in its essence, the vibrancy and fast pace of city life that had beckoned black men and women from the country to the cities. The rocking of the train/locomotive that carried them away from the land of slavery and suffering of their ancestors (the country South) towards the burgeoning promise of the great cities formed an integral part of this music and both authors have used the technique of Jazz music to render powerfully the poignant chords, the muffled strains, the undertones, keynotes and sub- notes and the layered rhythms/ textures of the varied range of African-American experience.

All the three authors have put forward in their novels communities of African-American women who are economically and sexually independent of men as also communities where they are not able to do so. Morrison's women of Medallion in *Sula* are restricted within the strict/rigid tenets of societal codes and behavioural norms and unable to break free from their confined, spider-like existence, suspended as they are from the webs of their own making (*S*, 120). On the other hand, the women of Alabama in *SOS* have been shown as independent, hard working and free of inhibitions. The women of Eloe in *TB* are equally hardworking and efficient but cater to the chauvinistic assumptions of their men in accepting their definition of their womanhood and traditional roles. Morrison's Georgia women of *TBE* come together in celebration and sorrow to share their experience of suffering in a racist, sexist society. Walker's women of *TCP* gradually club together in their recognition of sexist domination and exploitation by and from their men. Unlike Margaret and Mem of *TLGC* who have suffered terribly but are isolated figures in their similar tragedies, the African-American women of *TCP*—Squeak and Celie, led by Shug and Sofia along with her strong and emphatic sisters came forward to help each other in mutual understanding and sympathy with each others' problems and to overthrow sexist domination. In Shug's house in Memphis and later in Celie's own house, men (even Samuel, Nettie's husband) have little role to play, as everything (including household affairs to earning a livelihood) is managed and conducted by the women with confidence and efficiency. Both authors have courageously flaunted in the face of traditional accusations against black women as castraters, images of independent black women who are nevertheless sensitive and capable of great love—women who forge not only sexual but meaningful, asexual friendships with men (cf. Stamp Paid and Baby Suggs and Stamp Paid and Ella of *B*, Celie and Albert in the latter part of *TCP*, Samuel and Nettie before marriage in *TCP*, Shug, Celie and their talented and creative men friends in *TMF* and Eva and her men friends in *S*).

Naylor's *WBP*, *MD* and *BC* all represent communities of women who are independent both sexually and economically and who take lovers or husbands according to their will and wish. They come together to resist society's exploitation of black women. Yet, emotionally, the women of Brewster Place are still attached to their men despite their irresponsibilities, the non-existent role they play in the family and their repeated betrayal of trust and disappearances. Only Theresa and Lorraine, the lesbian couple in *WBP* are totally independent of men for which however they are kept at a distance by the other women. Black women in *MD*, living on the island of Willow Springs have been shown as relatively free from the societal codes of America as the island has its autonomous culture, values and ideology. Worshipping Mother Goddess Sapphira as the ancestress who had founded the Day family and wrested freedom for her people, the island's present reigning mother-figure is Miranda Day who is widely respected and esteemed. In *BC*, Naylor presents Eve's brothel as the alternative version of a male world—a magnificent queendom where the women call the cards while the men wait in line outside, awaiting their turn of favour. This inverted picture of the true state of society represents Naylor's subversive strategy and vision of female empowerment and the strength of all-woman communities in combating racist, sexist, classist exploitation.

Traditionally and historically, the relationships of black men and women have been fraught with misunderstanding and complex psychological problems stemming from their harrowing experience as slaves, and non-persons. Often black men's anger and bitterness have been encouraged intentionally by the white society's portrayal of black women as emasculators and castrators. Again, motivated by envy and an inferiority complex (as historically, black women have been superior workers, capable, intelligent and confident) black men have placed the blame of their own inability to cope with debilitating circumstances upon their women. While resenting the black woman's importance in the family, angered and frustrated by their own inability to prevent their sexual exploitation and degradation by white men, they were urged, by a psychological need to exorcise their own sense of impotence, to brutalise black women. All the three authors have represented the relationships of African-American men and women in the light of the reality they themselves have witnessed or experienced in their lives. Morrison's men—Cholly Breedlove in *TBE*, Jude Greene in *S*, Solomon, Macon Dead and Milkman in *SOS*, Paul D in *B*, Son in *TB* and Joe in *J* have, in one way or another misunderstood their women and been the cause of their pain and emotional and physical suffering. Morrison's Sethe in *B* therefore feels, like her mother-in-law Baby Suggs that men fail to "measure up" over the "long haul" (158) and accepts the situation stoically. Walker's black men are represented more negatively—men who turn viciously upon their women, torture, beat and dominate and even drive them to death as Grange and Brownfield do in *TLGC*, Alfonso and Albert do and Harpo tries to do in *TCP*. In *M*, she presents the chauvinistic Truman and Tommy Odds who as activists are irritated by inquisitive and thinking black women activists who are not content to merely confine themselves as badge makers and slogan writers. Criticised for her deliberately negative portrayal of black men[8] Walker nevertheless has also represented Sofia and Jack and Nettie and Samuel in *TCP* and Miss Lissie and Hal in *TMF* as couples who have perfect mutual understanding and wonderful empathy—a relationship they have achieved after coming to terms with each others' faults and virtues and having accepted it. Fanny and Suwelo and Carlotta and Arveyda in *TMF* are also shown in the process of achieving a better understanding of their relationship and Fanny insists on the need for space and growth of each individual partner within the commitment of a marital relationship that should not be confined to merely stability and security. Similarly, Morrison creates a new paradigm in her representation of the relationship of Sixo and the thirty-mile-woman in *B*, the former finding the latter to be a "friend of his mind" (335). When Paul D in *B* is able to understand Sethe's actions, he feels that this woman has "left him his manhood" (335) which is a new beginning for both of them. Naylor's Eugene and Cora Lee's husband in *WBP*, Luther Nedeed in *LH*, the rich men of Sugar Hill in *BC* are all African-American men who brutalise or take for granted their wives or lovers. Naylor too, like Walker, consciously represents black men as perpetrators of physical and psychological abuse on their women—the kind of torture varying with their elevation in class. So if Cora Lee of *WBP* knows that a burnt pot of rice would be rewarded with a fractured jaw (113), Willa Nedeed is locked in a basement and starved to teach her a lesson for her supposed infidelity and the Sugar Hill women who are the wives of affluent men of the so-called elite class are ridiculed in public and beaten/abused behind closed doors. Morrison's Cholly and Boy Boy, Walker's Grange and Brownfield, Naylor's Eugene, all belong to the Negro underclass and are angry, frustrated and irresponsible men who transfer the rage of their thwarted need for space and freedom from burdens upon their women, subjecting them to violence and brutalisation. The bestial image of a caged animal used by Naylor to describe Eugene, forcefully conveys the idea of recklessness, banked anger and suppressed frustration and violence. In Naylor's *WBP* a group of young Negro boys (C.C. Baker and Gang) channel their need to prove their own manhood into raping a helpless Lorraine who, as a lesbian, is beyond the purview of their sexual domination. However, Naylor presents too an alternative possibility in the relationship between African-American men and women when she represents Cocoa and George in *MD* and Nadine and Bailey in *BC* as couples who have achieved a rare harmony in their relationship. The former have been shown as going through a long phase of courtship that culminates in marriage, during which they have come to accept each other's idiosyncracies, likes and dislikes and weaknesses and strengths through wonderful exchange of dialogues full of wit, humour and passion. On the other hand, Nadine and Bailey hardly speak to each other, nor do they need to as each knows the unspoken needs of the other and their calm, uneventful married life speaks for their long years of harmonious co-existence. Bailey's admiration for his "African Goddess" (13) and her quiet love for him make their relationship one that is unusual among African-American women and men, suggesting new possibilities for the resolution of conflicts between them in future.

Lesbianism as a theme is explored by both Walker and Naylor. While in Walker, the representation of lesbian relationships is psychological and sexual, as in case of Shug and Celie who live together as lovers and Walker's references to lesbianism as a developing alternative chosen by black women/feminists in *TMF* (243), Naylor represents lesbianism more as a psychological drawing together of women as "The Two" Lorraine and Theresa in *WBP* and Jesse and her "special friend" in *BC* (125). All these women, especially Lorraine and Jesse, unlike Walker's women, have to pay for their choice as their rejection of men and psychological difference or need is interpreted differently in their different societies and they become victims of black male violence and patriarchal politics respectively. Toni Morrison on the other hand does not bring in overt sexual overtones in her presentation of Nel and Sula's relationship in *S*, which she mentions in an interview with Claudia Tate to be deliberate on her part:

> Friendship between women is special, different and has never been depicted as the major focus of a novel before *Sula*. Nobody ever talked about friendship between women unless it was homosexual, and there is no homosexuality in *Sula*.... It seemed to me that black women have friends in the old fashioned sense of the word....[9]

Jacqueline Jones in her book *Labor of Love, Labor of Sorrow* discusses the various reasons for the African-American woman's migration to the North. She writes how "(s)ignificantly, black men mentioned the degraded status of their womenfolk as one of the prime incentives to migrate, along with low wages and poor educational opportunities for their children. Husbands told of sexual harassment of wives and daughtes by white men and of other forms of indignities woven into the fabric of southern society."[10] Sexual harassment and violence faced by African-American women at the hands of white men is explored by all the three authors. Morrison probes into it in *TBE*, *B* and *J*, Alice Walker writes about it in *TLGC* (the white boss Shipley who sexually harasses Margaret) and refers generally to it in *TMF* and also in the context of Lissie's slave experience in the same novel. Naylor writes about it in *BC* where Stanley Carver's mother is raped and killed by white men and in *WBP* where Mr. Clyde, the white boss sexually harasses Ben's young daughter.

Motherhood is another theme explored by the three authors in its different and loaded connotations. Morrison represents slave mother Sethe's love as "too thick" (202) and possessive enough to kill in order to protect in *B*, Eva Peace's dominating mother love that makes her an awesome figure of power in that she deals death to her son just as she cuts off her leg to provide for her children, Pauline Breedlove's bitterness towards her children for being her burdens and her failure to provide protection to her daughter Pecola, Ruth of *SOS* who valiantly rises to her role as mother to fight for her son's life, Jadine of *TB* who refuses to stagnate in the role of a nurturer, shows African-American mothers as varied as the concept is problematic. Walker has presented another angle of motherhood through the character of Mrs. Hill in *M* who resents bitterly her role and its burdens. Her daughter Meridian feels that she has failed in her role as a mother by giving away her son, her guilt at having let down the age-old tradition of her maternal ancestors haunting her for a long time. On the other hand, Walker's women of an earlier era—Margaret and especially Mem, found in motherhood the only role that could give them dignity as laborers and a noble purpose for doing work that was harsh and degrading. Motherhood therefore becomes a conflicting and paradoxical role for African-American women as represented by Walker in her novels as she seems to suggest that enforced acquiescence to the society's standard expectations from a mother could lead to confinement instead of the fulfillment that such a role could actually give. Naylor on the other hand represents Mattie Michael in *WBP* and Bernice Duvall in *MD* as mothers besotted with their only sons, though each belongs to a different class and social setting. For the unwed mother Mattie, motherhood was the only reason for her struggle for existence while for Bernice (a rich man's wife), motherhood was an obsessive all-encompassing passion. Naylor seems to suggest through her representation of rich African-American women that motherhood could have provided the emotional anchor and psychological mooring that could have saved their marriage and lives—a cohesive factor that could have prevented the disintegration of women like Laurel, Mary Hollis, the Nedeed wives and others in *LH* and Jesse Bell in *BC*.

There is however the emerging paradigm in the novels of all the three authors that suggest the changing labor roles of African-American women that have made possible their passage from despair to fulfillment and towards the opening up of new horizons. In tracing their transition from existence merely and solely as laborers to women and persons, which has determined their worth from the times of slavery to freedom through to contemporary times, Toni Morrison, Alice Walker and Gloria Naylor have attempted to find solutions to problematic questions like the confining and liberating possibilities of their work roles, the conflict of motherhood and work, role as labor in relation to traditional feminine roles of mother, wife and daughter, the conflict and resolution of multiple roles, the sociological situation of and social expectations from Negro women, the labor of love versus the labor of compulsion and the new problems that emerge in the new situations and new work roles. African-American women in their novels are no longer content to function in the traditional roles of mammies or fiercely protective and sacrificing mothers and consequently refuse to be shackled by the responsibilities and burdens of maternal roles. On the other hand, natural feminine and maternal instincts cannot be ignored or neglected, leading to complexities in the labor role situation as also a psychologically traumatic state as in Bernice of *MD* or Violet of *J*. The modern African-American woman today, as perceived by these authors, has however left behind the trauma of slavery, taken racism in her stride and has attempted to explore possibilities and take up challenges of emerging opportunities. So Alice Walker has made Nzingha Anne in *TMF* speak of woman power substituting manpower, "matriot" (*TMF*, 258) instead of patriot and herstory rewriting history, Naylor has posited the new woman Cocoa Day of *MD* who combines the positive values of the past and present and Morrison has presented Pilate of *SOS* as the bearer of African racial-cultural heritage who leads the African-American man towards a recognition of his past heritage and acknowledgement of ancestral roots. These are women who have been able to discover their worth despite and because of their work roles and have transcended the limitations imposed upon them by history and society.

NOTES AND REFERENCES

1. Barbara Christian, *Black Feminist Criticism: Perspectives on Black Women Writers*. New York: Pergamon Press, 1985, p. 219.
2. Alice Walker, "Interview with Mary Helen Washington", Jackson, Mississippi. June 17, 1973, p. 6.
3. Patrick Bryce Bjork, *The Novels of Toni Morrison: The Search for Place Within the Community*. New York: Peter Lang Publishing, 1992, p. 19.

4. *Ibid.*
5. Doreatha Mbalia Drummond, "Women Who Run with Wild, The Need for Sisterhoods in *Jazz*", *Modern Fiction Studies*. Vol. 39. Nos. 3 & 4, Fall/Winter 1993, @ Purdue Research Foundation, pp. 623-42.
6. Interview on radio in 1983 where Morrison claimed at first to write without gender focus but backtracked to affirm that being a woman made her valuable as a writer. Quoted in Linden Peach's *Toni Morrison*. New York: St. Martin's Press, 1995, p. 14.
7. From Sojourner Truth's famous speech at the Women's Rights Convention at Akron, Ohio titled "Ar'n't I a Woman?" Quoted in *The Norton Anthology of African American Literature*. Eds. Henry Louis Gates Jr. and Nellie Y. McKay. New York: W.W. Norton and Company Inc., 1997, p. 198.
8. From Walker's biography in *The Norton Anthology*, p. 2377.
9. Toni Morrison, Interview with Claudia Tate. *Black Women Writers at Work*. Ed. Claudia Tate. New York: Continuum, 1983, p. 118.
10. Jacqueline Jones, *Labor of Love, Labor of Sorrow: Black Women, Work and the Family, From Slavery to the Present*. New York: Vintage, 1985, p. 157.

Conclusion

6

The present study has analysed the representation of the roles of African-American women as labor in the novels of Toni Morrison, Alice Walker and Gloria Naylor and has arrived at some conclusions briefly summarized here.

Morrison's novels have yielded a clear picture of the roles of African-American women as labor and the changing work roles of black women from the times of slavery to the present that have given them the scope to achieve dignity and selfhood (where earlier they had been solely laborers in the eyes of the white society). Tracking the developing trend from Category I to Category VIII of labor roles, it can be said that the representations suggest a transition from enforced labor to work out of choice for African-American women and points towards the availability of better scope and opportunities. The gradually changing work roles indicated in Morrison's novels show the changing social attitudes and job market scenario that seem to have enabled African-American women to evaluate their own worth and gain a measure of self-confidence.

From Category I to II, African-American women of Morrison's novels have been represented as struggling, operating in their roles as labor by compulsion—economic and sociological. As slaves, they have not been owners of their own bodies or labor and were unable to reap the fruits of their toil. As poor, black women of rural areas in Category II, they have been slaves of poverty and multiple responsibilities, having therefore to operate in their roles as labor as menials, doing work that was strenuous and degrading, living for their men and children and obeying orders of their white masters and mistresses.

If most rural women like Pauline Breedlove of *TBE* or Violet of *J* have migrated to the North with their husbands to urban areas in search of brighter prospects, they have again had the choice of the lowest paid and worst jobs. They have occupied therefore the lowest rung of the labor market, struggling to make ends meet and working both at home and outside their homes in multiple shifts. If, like Mrs. Macteer of *TBE* they do not work outside, they have had to scrimp on expenses, and have labored to save every penny, dogged by the fear of being "put outdoors" (11), and tried to supplement their husband's income by putting in extra work (like taking in a paying guest). As maids and chamber-women they have often been required to work at night as Janey in *B* and Malvonne in *J*, as in the former occupation, their duties have extended beyond appointed hours and in the latter, the cleaning of office buildings had to be completed before daybreak. Like Nel in *S*, they may be promoted to be chambermaids in place of cleaning women but their pay was still much lower than that of their men as is testified by Nel whose husband had earned more as a waiter even in the 1930s. If like Ondine in *TB* they have left behind their past occupations at butcher shops or as field laborers, they still have had to slog at the white man's kitchen as his housekeeper or cook, as Ondine has served Valerian Street for years, though this situation was a marked improvement on the previous one. They are then constantly plagued by job insecurities and the fear of falling back into the same pit of poverty and denigrating labor as before. If Violet in *J* has left behind the harsh and grueling field labor and the memory of whipping with the nightmare of sharecropping, she still has had to brave inclement weather, icy winds and snowfall, depend on the whimsicalities of her customers, as a houseworker and unlicensed, freelance hairdresser—reflecting the truth that very few African-American women have had the privilege and training of skilled work. As slaves in Category I, they have hankered for the sustaining ties of relationships—a husband, family and the dignity of motherhood while as poor, black women in Category II, their men have betrayed trust again and again and their children have become burdens whom they have borne with long-suffering patience and with the righteous satisfaction of having been ideal mothers, "real women" (*TB*, 283) and staunch race-women as their real life counterparts have done. In the rural, semi-rural and semi-urban communities as in the backwoods of Georgia or Ohio, Medallion or Alabama, they have been shown to form supportive relationships with other women—fellow-sufferers in the triple-fold oppression that they have faced, generating sisterhoods that have sustained them through thick and thin, testifying to the formation of such bonds by black women in life. Traditionally, from the times of slavery, black women have been known to stand by each other in times of trouble and community solidarity has lent them the strength to fight against racial injustice and Morrison has shown the same community solidarity in her representation of such groups of black women. Unlike Walker however, Morrison's communities of women have stood more with racial than gender solidarity and only in isolated instances have they come together to fight sexist/gender domination/exploitation (*cf.* Pilate helping Ruth and Magdalene fighting for Corinthians in *SOS*). As urban proletariats or rather as laborers in the urban sector (Violet has no job security, so not a true proletariat), Morrison's African-American women have faced alienation and an acute sense of dissociation from self and consequent disorientation because estranged from their roots (that truly lay in the country), these women have been shown to find themselves adrift in citics that offcred them job opportunities and the promise of a better life, only to leave them disillusioned, emotionally anchorless, psychologically insecure and economically deprived (as Pauline Breedlove of *TBE* who yearns for the sights and sounds of nature that she had loved in the country South). In defence, black women of the cities as Morrison represents in *J*, may have therefore become aggressive or resigned, have attached themselves to armed and powerful men, or like Violet and Alice, have forged unlikely friendships, having broken class barriers to draw together in empathy and identification with similar psychological alienation.

African-American women of Category III have been represented by Morrison as artificial and self-conscious, who have traded their freedom for economic stability, emotional predictability, marital respectability and security, social propriety and stiff-lipped decorum and sobriety. These are women who have been houseworkers primarily, laboring to create perfection and neatness in their own homes and holding themselves off from any association with Negroes of the lower class. In Morrison's novels, middle-class African-American women are mostly urban, barring exceptions, due to which they have not been required to work as hard as rural middle-class housewives of Walker's novels. Also these women have chosen to hold themselves aloof from their sisters as they are equally, if not more, class-conscious than their men, motivated as they are by the pervasive fear of being sucked back into the quagmire of a degrading and impoverished lifestyle they had worked hard to rise from. Remarkably, almost all of Morrison's middle-class women are light-complexioned mulattas, underscoring their difference with the common "darkies"—a difference that they have wished to maintain by eliminating all traces of their racial heritage in behaviour and appearance. The author seems to suggest that the improvement in their situation and the economic stability they have gained is in truth a confinement they have imposed upon themselves and in denying their emotions a freedom of expression by forcibly curbing them, they have buried their "me-ness" (*S*, 29) and individuality like Nel and Helene of *SOS* and Geraldine of *TBE*.

There are few housewives and rich men's daughters belonging to Category IV in Morrison's novels as in real life and their limited and circumscribed existence is shown to be shorn of even the dubious satisfaction of laboring to produce order, neatness and perfection in their house or work. More than the women of Category III, they have been dominated by their men, flaunted as possessions but chided like children and insulted like prostitutes by their own husbands, fathers and brothers. Economically and materially, they are the privileged and envied ladies. Nevertheless, it is clear that their privilege has given them no satisfaction. Some like Ruth in *SOS* may have tried to rediscover their worth through mothering, some like Magdalene (*SOS*) have kept their hands engaged in mechanical and meaningless tasks to hold on to their sanity and those like Corinthians in the same novel, have rebelled against this ornamental and dependent existence by discovering their self-worth through their work (though Morrison writes in the context of Corinthians' job hunt that work options still involved manual labor for African-American women even as late as 1960s, which indicates her awareness of the real life scenario of the job market that she has represented fictionally through Corinthians' experience as an educated maid).

African-American women of Category V(a), (b), (c) in Morrison's novels earn their living through work of varied nature. Only Jadine of *TB* as represented by the author belongs to Category V(a)—a modern, educated, well-bred, beautiful African-American woman who has used her privileged upbringing to her own advantage—achieving singular success in her modeling career and choosing to accept the challenge of a demanding profession despite its inherent pitfalls, shunning the traditional roles that African-American women have been compelled to function in and their pride in their great sacrifice and greater labor. As a woman of the present times, Jadine's attitude is a marked change from that of African-American women of earlier categories (and earlier eras) or to that of blue-collar workers. The African-American women of this category in the novels of Walker [only Shug Avery, the performing artist in Walkers *TCP* belongs to Category V(a) but has been included in Category VII as a woman who defies categorizations. None of Walker's African-American women besides Shug belong to V(a)] and in Naylor's novels, though still few in number, have the advantage of education and also alternative options of work. The inner turmoil and loneliness and the feeling of inauthenticity that haunts Jadine, overshadowing her success is the pointer used by the author to show that despite this new found freedom of choice in the occupational arena, successful black women somehow seem to be unable to resolve material success with racial-cultural loyalty or their modern, work and career-oriented roles to that of the traditional roles of African-American women as mothers and nurturers. The clash that drains them emotionally is inherent in their situation and often irresoluble because they are also unable to identify with or connect with other African-American women, being essentially alienated and alone. The author does not condemn Jadine for the final selfish choice she has made while suggesting that she could have, had she not been afraid, given another dimension to her role as a woman had she accepted the challenge of emotional relationships and the risk of hurt and betrayal.

As blue-collar workers of Category V(b) African-American women of Morrison's novels have achieved some amount of economic stability through their work that is not degrading and is better paid, as semi-skilled in nature. Morrison's representation of such African-American women both in the urban and rural sectors, in their work as school teachers, hairdressers and seamstresses indicates that their jobs have given them a relative independence and improved their standard of living—a progression and change in labor roles from the work they have hitherto been allowed to do.

In Morrison's novels, African-American women of Category V(c) represent the outcome of sociological and economic forces that have left them with few choices so that many have taken up prostitution in preference to hard labor. Morrison's prostitutes are however not represented sentimentally, as they are hardened women who derive cynical pleasure from their degrading work, are proud of their sexual prowess and above all, are independent and free of inhibitions. The only exception is Sweet from *SOS*, who is generous and warmly giving, confirming a black woman's ability to derive pleasure out of sex, which they have considered as natural and joyous. For women such as Sweet, Hannah of *S*, or Reba of *SOS*, sex is spontaneous and enjoyable as all these women have been shown to be not immoral or promiscuous but generous and open minded. These women vindicate Morrison's artistic stand point by defying social codes of morality and subverting the myth of the loose black women and the stigma attached to them. By delinking morality from sex and sexuality, Morrison demystifies the myth of the bad black woman.

None of the African-American women of Morrison's novels belong to (Category VI of the hypothesis (political and social activists) but in *J* Morrison has written movingly about the "frozen…faces" (75) of the grim and silent Civil Rights protest marchers who struck deep chords in the souls of the onlookers with their songs of faith. The political, historical scenario and the upheavals in the society during those times as shown in the novel provides the backdrop against which the story of the novel unfolds and its characters develop. Morrison has represented in her novels African-American women who belong to Category VII as those who have transcended their material status to achieve recognition of self and freedom of soul that makes them defy categorizations. They therefore are not bound within the limitations of their labor roles or the problems inherent in those roles. These are women who have set their own standards and have chosen not to remain circumscribed within the definitions imposed upon them by society. As aesthetic representations, women of this category manifest or articulate more than the others, the author's artistic stance. In the fullness of their characterization, depth and dimension, they represent the author's perception about the scope of freedom and quest of self-worth for black women. So Pilate in *SOS*, though a poor black woman, works only when she chooses to, having established her own bootlegging business. Sula on the other hand is educated and has always shunned hard work. Given the day and age she lived in, she may have therefore been, like Etta Mae of Naylor's *WBP*, a mistress to rich men in exchange of a luxurious upkeep, abandoning however the fruitless game of love to return home and die a glorious but lonely death.

Category VIII includes conjure women who have been shown as powerful in their traditional roles and exercised considerable freedom in their roles as labor. So Ajax's mother and M'Dear are both respected and held in esteem—the latter operating more in the capacity of a diagnostician. The former did not believe in being possessive about her children while the latter was not married at all—both unusual situations in the African-American context where women were, apart from a few rare cases, almost always surrounded by family and children. As in real life, the unusual degree of freedom exercised by conjure women of Morrison's novels placed them beyond the purview of societal norms and codes. They were regarded not only as wise but also feared for their supernatural powers and knowledge of black magic, which nevertheless also implied that they were not ordinary or normal women—they were thought and expected to be strange, their eccentricities were tolerated as a part of their profession—that put them on a different plane altogether from other African-American women. The author's representations affirm the image of the wise conjure women who were held in high esteem by the African-American society.

Morrison's representation of women as labor in her novels therefore confirm the emergent paradigm of the changing roles of African-American women as labor as a progression towards an affirmation of self-worth and the opening up of more promising work roles.

In Walker's novels, representation of African-American women as labor indicate again the emerging paradigm as optimistic and open-ended. She has shown how, where slave women and poor black women of the rural South had existed primarily as laborers, the latter so even in their own homes, they had even so tried and often succeeded to express their creativity through the work medium available to them. The real life counterparts of these women had existed in an age where besides being considered as work horses or "mules of the world" they were also recipients of abuse and physical violence not only from the white masters but also their own men folk. Difficult as it was to break out from the cycle of unremitting and ceaseless toil, these women still had a vision for their children as Walker movingly writes in her poem "Women". These were also women who had to fight tooth and nail to keep their children with them, and Walker represents as a conscious artistic strategy the saga of prolonged suffering of these women and their heroic struggles that she has admitted to have inspired her as a writer (*cf*. Chapter 1, pp. 51-56). Meridian Hill's maternal ancestress in *M* bore inhuman tortures as a slave woman, to die out of overwork and starvation, only to keep her children with her. Meridian's great grandmother was able to buy freedom for her husband and herself out of the money she earned as a wonderfully creative painter who drew figures on barns and Meridian's grandmother undertook extra work despite being already overburdened, to earn the fees necessary for sending her daughter to school. Again Mem in *TLGC*, caught in the grip of crushing poverty and misery, tried to express her love for beauty by planting flowers all around the broken shacks where she lived (like Walker's own mother Minnie), trying to make out of these hovels a home for herself and her children. Walker writes how in this era, even with the advantage of education, black women like Mem fell back into the pit of unrelenting misery and impoverishment due to the chain of sociological events that pressed them down even if they attempted to rise (*TLGC*, 56). Progression therefore from Category I and II in Walker's novels has achieved little for her black women, who in effect exchanged one form of slavery with another. The picture corresponds with the demoralizing situation in which black women in real life were trapped in that era. However from amidst such women, Walker has shown the emergence of Celie (*TCP*) who, having been a submissive wife and menial drudge in her husband's house, discovered her self-worth and with the help of her husband's former mistress, established her own small business as a dress designer and seamstress, creating art out of labor and improving herself in every way. There is also Shug's aunt in *TCP* who is a roadhouse cook and who, despite being poor, has lived a life of her own choice and liking, combining hard work with uninhibited pleasure and enjoyment of sex. Through these separate stories of achievement, recognition of self-worth and long deserved rewards, Walker has vindicated the need for poetic justice in any given situation to construct an encouraging picture of possibility and optimism for suffering or demoralized African-American women in real life.

The representations of African-American women of Category III in Walker's novels were mostly rural who lived confined lives at home as glorified domestics and docile housewives, who did not dare to rebel for fear of being thrown out by their husbands on whom they depended for upkeep and also the respectability of marital status. However, Mrs. Hill in *Meridian* was an educated middle-class woman who had given up her job to restrict herself in the domestic arena, had begun to resent the burdensome responsibility that motherhood entailed. Countering the traditional expectations regarding black women in their maternal roles, Walker has imaged the conflict of motherhood versus work in her representation of the character of Mrs. Hill. Motherhood is shown to have taken on a new dimension for

African-American women as it had always been loaded with complex emotions and implications for them. Where as slave mothers and poor, struggling women, their sole focus had been the privilege of proximity with their children for whom they were willing to lay down their lives and undergo any amount of pain, now, with the choice of an unmarried and calm life of a woman earning a modest income, motherhood became an unwanted role. Where earlier, the only way a black woman's labor could attain dignity was through her efforts as a mother, now, the author envisages how women like Mrs. Hill felt themselves circumscribed in that role. Interestingly, however, Mrs. Hill would not relinquish her maternal role or fall short in her duties as a mother because she wanted to be worthy of her maternal ancestors whose tradition of sacrifice for their children, she admired. For her daughter Meridian, it was impossible to suffer this lifelong imprisonment and she gave away her son rather than bring him up with the simmering and suppressed anger at being forced to cater to the society's expectations from a mother. The difference in attitude has been used as a pointer towards the fact that African-American women in Walker's fiction as in real life, were now trying to find a measure of self-worth not through the equation of motherhood that had been the only role accessible to them that had a semblance of human dignity, but through work roles that entailed creative as well as intellectual involvement. The material advantage that women of Category III have achieved in Walker's novels is shown to be unfulfilling and dissatisfying because, in restricting themselves within the circle of societal codes of decorum, they have circumscribed their existence and lost their sense of self-worth.

The same stands true for African-American women of Category IV in Walker's novels. The emerging pattern in the representations of the changing labor roles of African-American women from Category III to IV shows the only difference in that the latter category has achieved more material comfort and luxury than the former and the prestige of belonging to the upper class, but as dependants, they have gained no freedom. Walker has, through her portrayal of Rossel in *TLGC*, pointed out that the choice between limited options available—manual work or ornamental life—is really no choice at all. The latter option, being easier, would logically be chosen by so many black women in real life as in fiction when the opportunity became available. They can hardly be blamed and it is not surprising in the light of the job advertisements that Ruth in *TLGC* reads in the newspapers that indicate clearly the job situation—only untrained, unskilled, low paid jobs were then available to black women and Walker's graphic and authentic detailing of the socio-economic scenario projects her awareness of the situation and deliberate representation of the same. So black women who had beauty and the advantage of education would therefore naturally choose marriage to wealthy men, rejecting the distasteful and debasing option of working as menials as Rossel has done. Not surprisingly, given the choice, most girls in their circumstances would choose to "sell" themselves to acquire the coveted and privileged status of rich housewives. African-American women had seen such poverty and ignominy in the lives of their kith and kin in real life that any choice was better to them than the life of a menial and the fictional representation therefore corresponds with the true picture. Women of Category IV have achieved material advantage however, not fulfillment. In case of spinsters like Margaret and Lucille in *M*, their lack of exposure, suppressed desires, emotional vulnerability or unguardedness has rendered them ripe for betrayal. These rich, black women are self-sufficient as such and can provide for themselves—so they become easy targets for fortune-hunters. Like any rich and unattached woman for that matter, black or white, they can be exploited easily on account of their gullibility, need for sexual fulfillment or emotional vulnerability. So in Naylor's *MD*, Junior Lee practised his charms to influence well-off older women like Frances and Ruby who could cater to his material needs and provide for him. So Margaret was driven to have an ill-advised affair with a much younger working-class man, which she later regretted.

Walker's blue-collar workers of Category V(b) have been shown to have achieved at least a relative degree of advantage in comparison with the women of the earlier categories. Though they have to be very cautious in their work roles so as not to violate the decorum that is expected of them and also limit themselves to a biased interpretation of the social realities, they are still better off than women like Margaret or Mem in that they have leisure and money to call their own and their economic independence does give them a freedom that is however subject to the degree of their compromise. These women may sometimes have an inflated sense of self-worth (*cf*. Mrs. Grayson of *TLGC*) that they emphasize by distancing themselves from the Negro underclass, but there are among them women like Corrine, Nettie and Olivia (belonging to different generations) who have a quiet confidence that is expressed through the excellent work they do in their professional arena. They have also now a choice of education, vocational training and gradually opening up avenues or job options that are no longer demeaning, though still segregated. Walker has shown these women to have in the later generations, found a degree of fulfillment through their work roles. The emerging picture of African-American women as labor hints at the possibility of a better life for them. From having to fight and batter down doors for their children in the representations in Category I and II, African-American women in Walker's novels have moved towards acquiring education but have been shown as still leading confined lives with narrow perspectives and few choices like Mrs. Hill of Category III does. Now, as Olivia does in Category V(b), they could choose a career, spend time in reading unhindered by the pressing burdens of housework or mothering, read by choice to deepen their knowledge, travel, like Nettie and Corrine to broaden their horizons, train for skilled work and explore fresh avenues, immerse themselves in literary pursuits, take up jobs of their choice, work for fulfillment and not merely to earn bread. In this the fictional rendering of African-American women as labor suggests a movement forward, a step taken towards progression and work roles that have given them a sense of self-worth.

On the other hand, African-American women of Category V(c) in Walker's novels have taken up prostitution as their profession—one that was open for them as the only other option besides working as domestics, maids or menials and to one many a young African-American girl was lured or was forced to turn to on account of their early exposure to sex and violence in the Negro slums in the towns and rural areas alike. Often after their first slip, they were inexorably led towards it like Josie of *TLGC* who made a lucrative business out of her sexual prowess, while others like her daughter Lorene were brought up in the brothels run by their mothers and could only aim to become sex workers when they grew up, enjoying as they did the independence, toughness and sexual freedom that such work guaranteed. The other side of the story comes to the fore through Josie's sad musings later in life when she recalls the violent beating she had received from a customer whom she had refused to give extra time. For women in this trade, much hazards and insecurities haunting their lives were common and with slipping youth, their wish to gain respectability sometimes overwhelmed them. Walker's representation of women of this category is complex as she does away with stereotypical images of bad, black women by paradoxically showing up their selfishness, meanness or aggressiveness that are an outcome of their circumstances. In refusing to be apologetic by trying to project too-good women who turn to prostitution out of absolute compulsion, Walker, like Morrison, refuses to create positive stereotypes of African-American women in this trade by absolving their personal guilt totally while showing the practical advantage of running a flourishing juke joint or brothel.

Political activists like Meridian Hill of *M* are included in Category VI. Besides providing the black male point of view regarding the work that black women had done during the Movement, Walker envisages the emergence of a new role for African-American women that brought out their strengths, complexities, fighting ability and the capacity to endure stress as well as match their men not only in physical labor roles but also in intellectual, policy-framing, planning roles. The political work role of black women like Meridian who had suffered immense internal struggles as presented by the author, culminates in her constructive social work and their contribution in such roles can be taken as another step forward towards the recognition of new possibilities and the determination of doing fulfilling, meaningful work through such service. The situation of black women activists in real life is brought to the fore by Walker's representation of the tremendous psychological and physical toll that such roles had taken on them. While fighting shoulder to shoulder with their men, these women were condemned for asking too many questions and being aggressive and decisive. Their dilemma is represented in *M* where Walker constructs a picture corresponding with the unpalatable realities and problems encountered by black women during the movement which however they rarely voiced for fear of hurting their men's egos (see Chapter 1, pp. 31-32). Earlier, despite her college education, Meridian had to face sexual harassment at her job as a typist, though her boss was an old African-American professor, much respected in the academia. Women have always had to fight such occupational hazards in life and for the African-American woman, the problem has been acute from the very beginning as her sexuality was always considered available and was taken for granted as inseparable from her role as labor. So African-American women had, over the ages, countered advances from white men, and borne the humiliation of being regarded as sex objects by men half their age (*cf*. Mrs. Hill of *Meridian* when she worked as a domestic to earn extra money). African-American women of Meridian's generation learnt to counter or manipulate such attentions from even African-American men and Walker shows Meridian as having to tolerate the old professor's lust because she needed the job desperately to continue her college education.

African-American women of Category VII and VIII as represented by Walker confirm the movement forward towards an achievement of the fullest expression of self and the traditional role of female empowerment for them respectively. While Shug of *TCP* has achieved freedom and power through her work role, Sofia of the same novel has transcended her role to achieve dignity and a full measure of her self-worth. If a brilliant academician like Fanny Nzingha of *TMF* has opted out of her prestigious job to open a massage parlour and become a masseuse in an effort to recognize and internalize the magnitude of other people's pain, an unconventional and ambitious Katherine Degos has changed her name, and lived life just the way she wanted, founded her own church and worked to alleviate others' troubles in the tradition of real life renegade black women.

As a performing artist, Shug Avery's work role has given her the scope of expressing her talent and spontaneous creativity as a singer. A traditionally Negro domain, the field of blues and jazz music has enabled African-American women to establish their identities in this arena where their prowess has drawn admiration and ensured them success, fame and wealth. The ethnic quality of black music has gained it increasing popularity and despite the moral stigma attached to the names of such traveling, performing artists, they achieved freedom from constraints and material advantage along with creative satisfaction that few other work roles could offer. Shug Avery is the representation of such a travelling, performing artist who has however also created a mark as a truly compassionate human being.

However, Shug Avery withdraws from the glamour of public singing to found a church—a trend that was often seen among renegade black women who founded prayer bands or musical bands to sing and pray and formed their own distinctive ideas of spirituality, religion and God as different from the mainstream ones (*cf.* Baby Suggs of Morrison's *Beloved*). From the head of a musical band, Shug gradually moves towards meditative and spiritual music and finally evolves her own church, writes her own beatitudes and holds prayer meetings at her house, where like-minded people congregate periodically. Having achieved the fullest creative satisfaction and a free space for herself, Shug has created space for others like Celie and Squeak, encouraging them to establish independent careers, to discover their self-worth and has also given them unstinted help and support to make that possible. In doing so, Shug has emerged as a sensitive human being who could identify with others' pain and suffering and is capable of forging truly bonding sisterhoods with other black women.

Lissie Lyles on the other hand has run the gamut of female experience and in passing through the trajectory of African-American women's experience as labor from slavery to the present, Lissie has emerged as a person with an all-encompassing and humane vision. Her progression (though in several lives) from a slave woman to a creative and whimsical painter, a deeply compassionate person, a perceptive artist and a philosopher with a broad vision, encapsulates the journey of the black woman from her existence solely in the capacity of a laborer to a person with a world-view.

Walker's representations of conjure women, like Morrison's, are powerful in their traditional roles of wise fortune tellers, which again is an exclusively African-American domain, having its roots in tribal culture and belief, herbal medicine and magic. However, Walker's Madelaine in *TLGC* is a modern conjure woman who has infused her fortune telling with psycho-analytical insights, approaching her profession from a practical angle and charging a hefty sum for it. She has seen her profession as a means of livelihood and enjoyed the power and benefits it has given her—an innovative and independent conjure woman who has chosen her area of work and has become successful in it, shunning the other distasteful option of becoming a domestic. On the other hand, Walker has also presented Dorcy Hogshead of *TMF* as the moody, temperamental and old-fashioned witch figure who is also an excellent midwife, respected widely for her ability of interpreting dreams. The two women in Category VIII confirm and reinforce the hypothetical inference that conjuring—modern or old-fashioned, offered African-American women the scope of experimenting with innovative ideas and indigenous methods of diagnosis and medication. Along with this, they could also learn and practice the occult as well as suggest indigenous remedies for maladies both physical and psychological. Walker's conjure women therefore affirm the image of independent and assertive African-American women who have been able to exercise a degree of freedom and achieve economic stability as well as enjoy the power and respect that this profession granted them. However, the other side of the story is also hinted at in *TMF* where Walker writes about the Egyptian witches who were burnt at stake for their extraordinary powers though they, as wise women and healers had never harmed anyone. African-American witches were kept at an arm's length and rarely meddled with by white people because they either believed and feared them as evil sorceresses or disbelieved and dismissed their abilities in the later ages.

It is Walker's artistic triumph in having been able to represent African-American women in their roles as labor as journeying from despair to fulfillment despite the disadvantages and manifold oppressions they have faced in their historic journey from social non-persons to a realization, recognition and establishment of their self-worth and self-esteem.

Gloria Naylor's novels offer a more contemporary picture of African-American women in their roles as labor, though she has shown how the sociological realities have changed very slowly for African-Americans and the memory of a collective suffering and traumatic past has haunted and still haunts most black women. In *WBP*, she represents these women therefore, at work and at home, as women who have been conditioned to pool their strengths in community and gender solidarity. In Naylor's novels, which focus on exclusively black enclaves and neighbourhoods, African-American women come together more on the basis of class loyalty because contact with the white race is comparatively less. An established Negro elite and middle-class have now made their presence felt and Naylor presents such an up-and-coming black upper-class or elite coterie in *Linden Hills*, while the black underclass of Putney Wayne in the same novel is shown as largely resentful of these ambitious and successful, privileged people of their own race who have distanced themselves pointedly from their less fortunate brethren. Needless to say that African-American women of different classes in Naylor's novels reflect the same attitudes and now their work roles (labor roles) can be distinguished more emphatically as they are divided along class lines. This barrier often makes communication impossible between black women of different classes and even among women of the same class in case of rich housewives and career women of Category V(a) who are confronted with a wall of reverse snobbery, wariness from other black women, alienation and emotional barrenness in themselves that robs the satisfaction of their success in their work roles or the privilege of being attached to rich men (as their wives or daughters). On the other hand, there are the poor, struggling black women of Brewster Place who can come together in an identification and empathy with their common problems.

Analysing the representation of African-American women in their roles as labor in Naylor's novels, one can identify the change and gradual evolution of the black woman from her status of slave woman to a modern American woman who combines in herself the values of the past, and a vision for the future, turning her face towards new horizons and new possibilities, embodied in the fictional representation of Cocoa Day of *Mama Day.*

The transition for African-American women from Category I to II in Naylor's novels is again one that has brought little difference in their lives. Naylor's poor women are mostly urban and the crushing poverty and squalor amidst which they live, struggling to make ends meet and still without the help of their men who drift in and out of their lives, entrap them in a different kind of bondage. In the job market, they work in the lowest paid jobs as they are uneducated and unskilled. African-American women from the Southern counties often flock to slums like Brewster with a hope to find employment and relief from the gruelling labor involved in sharecropping. However, here too they have to work as menials and with their growing families and growing needs, they try to find a stability that has always been elusive to them. Their meager pay cheques have allowed them to put up in the dingy apartments of these all-black slums in impoverished neighbourhoods where cut-off from the main town, they carry on their lives' struggles amidst work, responsibilities, tears and laughter. As mentioned earlier, the mainstay of their independence is compulsion and that their rebellion, undaunted spirit and capacity to withstand the blows of life as well as the sustaining bonds of sisterhood and mutual understanding, help them to recover from their personal suffering and traumas. It is also this solidarity that helps them to stand shoulder to shoulder against the injustice done against them and the exploitations they have had to endure. In *WBP*, the women of Brewster Place tear down the brick wall that turned Brewster into a dead-end alley in a symbolic act of repudiation of victimizing social forces that have subjected them to a triple-fold oppression. There are also poor, black women like Mamie Tilson of *LH* and Mrs. Bell of

BC who are fiercely proud of their hard work that has brought them a degree of material solvency. Their independence, emphatic concepts of right and wrong, ingrained pride in their racial heritage, confidence and belief in their work, a comprehension of their self-worth and self-esteem that have not been eroded by the demoralizing poverty they have endured, make them figures of strength who project the positive values of life.

African-American women of Category III in Nayor's novels (Mrs. Tilson and Roxanne Tilson of *LH*) have been portrayed as ambitious go-getters, whose sole aim is to continue their single-minded upward climb along the social ladder of status, wealth and recognition. Class distinctions having become more pronounced with the emergence of a new black bourgeoisie (the urban middle-class) who are proud of the hard work that has gone into their achievement and material advantage and justifies the manipulation and compromise that has also been instrumental in their success. Unlike them, there is Mrs. Browne of *WBP* who is a balanced and mature person and content in her role as a middle-class housewife, who does not hanker after money and power and has her own ideas about social change and development of the situation of poor Negroes. There is also Fanny Michael of the same novel who could assert herself and take her own decisions, Eva Turner (*WBP*) who lived life to the full, outliving her husbands to stay alone in her own house, Roberta Johnson of Alabama in *LH*, who believed work to be the antidote for pain and was even at eighty, independent and forthright and Abigail Day of *MD* who was a wonderful housewife and a lady in the true sense of the word. Naylor's middle-class women therefore are more confident and poised and not as insecure or confined as Morrison's Helene and Geraldine or Walker's Mrs. Hill because with a movement forward in time and a lessening of the passion for integration and emulation of while middle-class values to prove their worth, they had taken a step forward towards the achievement of a balanced perspective and attitude that precluded the inflated sense of self-worth that middle-class black women of the earlier generations had. As Naylor represents them, not all of them are ambitious and ruthless and they can be content now in their roles as home makers that vindicated, not negated their self-esteem and they are no longer haunted by the constant need to prove themselves.

In contrast, Naylor's rich women live dissatisfied and pretentious lives and the feeling of entrapment that they have experienced in their ornamental roles have undermined their efforts towards a recognition of their worth, identity and labor. As Jesse Bell of *BC* says, these women attached themselves to their men in an effort to hold on to their respectability and social status tolerating all the while, humiliation and insults behind closed doors, that they carefully shielded with a façade of artificial poise. In considering all women worthless if they were not attached to men, they debased their own worth—their predicament encapsulated by Jesse when she says that they could not afford to cry.

Most of Naylor's rich housewives and career women either have no children or if they have, are unable to forge close bonds with them (*cf.* Marie Hollis, Laurel, Lycentia, Mrs. Donnel, the Nedeed wives of *LH* and even Jesse Bell *BC* who was formerly a rich housewife and whose son had been, with calculated malice, weaned away from her by the male father-figure of the King family). The emotional anchor that a child could have provided is absent in their lives, which makes their existence unbearable. So like Priscilla Macguire of *LH* who cried when she got the "Mother of the Year" award, these women watch in helpless grief, the gradual estrangement of their children from them, which they are unable to prevent.

Only Willa Nedeed of *LH* and Bernice Duvall of *MD* are close to their sons, but both lose them to death, the former rejected and neglected by his own father and the latter dies due to unknown reasons. In Bernice Duvall, Naylor presents the yearning for motherhood and a desperate craving for a fulfillment that neither her role as wife nor her work role can give her. Naylor seems to suggest through her portrayal of rich housewives that motherhood, or fulfillment in the role of a mother (an instinctive role for women) could be a panacea for the restlessness and lack of purpose in the lives of rich women and wives. However, when it became an obsession, as it did with Bernice, the outcome could be devastating emotionally.

African-American women of Category V(a) are presented by Naylor as brilliant, efficient and confident in their work roles. Though the number of real life black women at the top is still a mere handful statistically, yet the slowly rising number of such women is suggested by the changing pattern of work roles that are shown to be now available for black women along with the widening options and job prospects. Due to the material advantage gained by black women of this era in Naylor's novels, they have transcended demoralizing poverty but are faced with new problems inherent in the nature of their jobs. With their history of social disadvantage and the resultant prejudice they have suffered in a racist, class-conscious and patriarchal society, African-American women have much more to prove than their men or white women and have to work twice as hard to stay at the top. So when Laurel Dumont, the head of IBM and the "Amazon" (*LH*, 228) who struck fear in the hearts of her business associates through her competence and hardheaded, brilliant and ruthless decision-making, withdrew behind a wall of self-created aloofness and silence, her husband reminded her that even she could be replaced, despite her erstwhile track records. The success she has achieved is at the cost of inner peace, meaningful relationships and emotional fruition for which she has not been able to spare time. So Mabel Thompson has had to fight tooth and nail to prove her efficiency and reach where she was today and in doing so, she has come to be admired as a tigress but rejected as a woman.

In Category V(c), Naylor has presented case studies of a number of prostitutes, all of whom have come to Eve's brothel in *BC* as the last refuge—their poignant stories confound stereotypes—their individual traumas confirming the truth of sociological records of the horrifying atrocities that black women have suffered, not only from the white society but also their own men. Esther of *BC*, and Ben's daughter of *WBP* have been sacrificed at the altar of necessity by their closest relations, Jesse (*BC*) has been a target of patriarchal politics, Sadie (*BC*), a victim of circumstances that shaped her destiny even before she was born and Marie (*BC*) who is the nurturer who embraces these battered women, having created her own "queendom" where she, in subverting through inversion her tyrant Godfather's world, has given a new dimension to the vision of female empowerment.

Kiswana Browne of Category VI is represented in *WBP* as the bright, enthusiastic, and truly committed social worker/activist of the present era—a movement forward from the soul-searching political activist of the Civil Rights phase in Walker's *M*. Her well-meaning sacrifice in leaving her privileged social set-up to live among the African-American underclass in an impoverished slum may achieve little, but her efforts stem out of deep concern for the need for social change that has motivated young, college-going African-American women like her. The heartening commitment of such hopeful social activists sets a progressive trend as against the hardened, insulated and selfish ambition of women like Roxanne Tilson. Kiswana has pitted her strength against individual achievement and towards a fight for the upliftment of the underprivileged people of her race.

In Category VII Naylor has represented three exceptional women: Etta (*WBP*), Ruth (*LH*), and Cocoa (*MD*), who are each strong individuals, unconventional and headstrong persons who have transcended their disadvantages to emerge as figures of resilience and strength. Cocoa Day especially confirms the image of the new/modern black woman, who has stepped into a new world of unfurling possibilities. Naylor's portrayal of African-American women of this age show them as confident individuals who now know how to deal with job hazards and unwanted attention in their work roles. Cocoa has dealt with her over-interested boss in her inimitable style and her boyfriend George feels that in recommending her for that job, he has turned up the "lamb" (her boss Hopewell) to the "wolves" (Cocoa)—thus acknowledging her spunk, aggression, toughness, ability to protect herself and take occupational hazard in her stride.

Naylor's conjure women are represented through two contrasting figures—one good and the other evil—Miranda Day and Ruby of *MD*. The former is portrayed not only as the embodiment of female empowerment in her role of traditionally powerful witch/healer/wise woman/matriarch but also in a wonderfully humane way, though the compassionate services she rendered were not only as a powerful conjure woman, but from an instinctive maternal and protective affection for a helpless mother and a younger sister dependent on her emotionally and a father who needed her loyalty. When Cocoa, her beloved grandniece, falls sick, she again functions out of emotional involvement and not as a detached and all-powerful witch-doctor. Her personal involvement with Bernice too projects her as a compassionate and concerned, if undemonstrative human being. Ruby on the other hand is presented as the dark foil to Miranda, as the negative manifestation of this powerful role.

Increasingly, in the novels of Toni Morrison, Alice Walker and Gloria Naylor, black women have been shown to have begun to transcend their roles as labor. Though their job experiences do affect them as persons, modern black women are represented to be no longer as engrossed with their work roles as with their emerging personalities and individualities. All the three authors have underscored the fact that unlike white women who have learned to find their individual identities through the equation of meaningful work only recently and for whom, work has a different connotation than for black women who have traditionally been forced and co-erced into their roles as labor that has compelled them to be assertive, independent and aggressive, black women now need to prove another point. In the novels of all the three authors, they have come of age and are now ready to combine a knowledge of and identification with the trauma of their ancestors with the hope of a better future for themselves. Also, like their authors and as they have been portrayed, they are faced with the task of reconciling the conflicting values of the past and present, resolving the clash of personal ambition versus collective/communitarian concerns, maternal and feminine roles versus career-oriented roles, so that they can surge ahead towards new horizons with rejuvenated determination and strength, fashioning work roles for themselves that are meaningful and fulfilling and defining their worth with confidence.

The central idea of Toni Morrison's critical work *Playing in the Dark, Whiteness and Literary Imagination*—that the reader must be able to learn the truth or interpret the truth of a fictional representation for oneself—can be said to be the operative and persuasive force behind the writings of black women writers. In the same vein, Toni Morrison, Alice Walker and Gloria Naylor have, through their wide range of representation of African-American women in their roles as labor, attempted to encourage readers to read and see differently as well as independently from the "traditional" way of approaching literature that is based on European standards. The stereotypes of African tribal cultures, the Africans and the African-Americans that have been assimilated in the consciousness of the European critics and writers need to be done away with, if one must approach literature from a new perspective. Black women critics and writers have been struggling to evolve a new scholarship that does not use the measuring rod of a European heirachy or hegemony to gauge the worth of a work of art. A common female impulse to struggle free from social and literary confinement was made more acute by the added constraints of race and class that had made the situation of black women more problematic and motivated black women writers to voice the herstory of their collective struggle and achievement. As already stressed in Chapter 1, the present study has grounded its analysis within the developing tradition of African-American women writers and against the backdrop of an African-American women writers' literary movement where, as artists, creative writers and critics, they have tried to undercut the negative stereotypical images of black women that have been fashioned by history, society and culture of a dominant society making their already harrowed situation worse. They have also countered, with equal courage and innovation, the positive stereotypes of black women that have been fashioned by black men as a reaction to the denigrating images churned out by the racist prejudice of white Americans. The post-colonial women writers, especially those who belong to the ethnic minorities, have been involved in asserting their right to speak for themselves, in trying to evolve new forms and language to express their experiences and have also had to redefine themselves in order to subvert and shatter the myths constructed by a male cultural hegemony and tradition of writing. Writing from within the identifiable and distinct counter-tradition created by black women writers, Toni Morrison, Alice Walker and Gloria Naylor have rendered their fictional representation of African-American women characters in their roles as labor which has traditionally been the most loaded, complex and paradoxical role for them. Dehumanized as laborers, decivilized as members of an 'inferior' race and exploited sexually as women, these women have both lost and found their personhood in their work roles. In representing these real life black women for whom labor has been an inseparable part of their existence in America, Toni Morrison, Alice Walker and Gloria Naylor have created fictional counterparts in their novels that correspond on the one hand with the socio-economic scenario of the times (as each novel has a time frame and geographical setting) and the job market realities, while on the other they refute typified and one dimensional characterisations to emerge as complex individuals and fluid or nuanced characters. In Chapter 5, where the three writers' representations of black women as labor have been analysed in comparison to each other, each of them have established their artistic standpoints in that each have, in their distinctive treatment of the theme of black women as labor, also proved their allegiance to their common backgrounds as black women in white America and testified to the development of a distinct female literary tradition. In Chapter 1, the study had put forward a few questions on the basis of which the selected novels of the three authors where examined and analysed. In the course of attempting to find answers to the questions, the study arrived at conclusions already enlisted above. In determining the importance of work roles and in defining new images of black women as against the stereotypes fashioned by media and literature, the new dimensions of selfhood and developing personality of black women as recognized and represented by Toni Morrison, Alice Walker and Gloria Naylor have been discovered. The hypothetical framework (categorisations) that was adopted to facilitate the systematic analysis of the wide range of characters represented in their novel accommodates the gamut of black women's roles as labor and brings out the kaleidoscopic range of their experience in their labor roles. From Category I to VIII, the African-American women represented by Toni Morrison, Alice Walker and Gloria Naylor have been seen to move towards a recognition of their worth. From compulsion to choice, from oppression to self-expression, from helpless victims to rebelling individuals, from confinement to liberation, from mechanical, degrading and harsh menial labor to creative, fulfilling work, the process of change in the work roles of black women has been shown to be gradual, fraught with strife but positive nevertheless.

In tracing the trajectory of African-American women's experience as labor as represented in the novels of three authors, the changing roles of black women as envisioned by them have been foregrounded. Probing the fictional representations of African-American women as labor by these three representative authors of the black women's literary tradition, one can clearly identify their common aesthetic, thematic, stylistic and conceptual approaches due to the social, political, cultural and economic experience that they have been bound to share. Each author has conceived, in her own way, artistic methods of representing this change. Each has, like a Jazz artist (a traditionally Negro domain, *cf.* Appendix, p. vii) in that they have been able to define/project through their representation of the work experience of black women in America, the evolution of a new identity for the modern black woman. The definition of that identity, to borrow what Ralph Ellison says in *Shadow and Act* about the jazz artist, is three-fold—as an individual, as a member of the community and as a connection or link in the chain of tradition.

As literary artists, Toni Morrison, Alice Walker and Gloria Naylor have represented African-American women in their roles as labor to build an alternative picture or to create another reality in order to refute the prejudiced distortion of the reality of black women laborers fashioned by dominant groups—white men, white women and black men. As African-American women themselves, their heightened consciousness of the dilemma of black women in white America has made them adopt a clear standpoint. They refuse to eulogise or romanticize the struggles of African-American women, while giving them their due share of dignity and respect as individuals. In their representations therefore, black women have emerged not as superhuman, larger than life, towering figures of strength, not as matriarchs who are debilitating and castrating figures of power, not as submissive, self-sacrificing, obedient, maternal, all-embracing, nurturing women but as individuals who are complex, sometimes whimsical and erratic and often full of contradictions. The fictional representations of African-American women in the novels of these three authors defy labeling and narrow definitions. In using the strategy or artistic device of apparently affirming certain stereotypes, these authors have subverted the myths surrounding black women by creating three dimensional and paradoxical characters. For instance, Morrison has created the three prostitutes of *TBE* against all notions of romantic stereotyping by representing them as "whores in whores' clothing" (*TBE*, 43)—as calculating, hardheaded sex-workers who have no compassion for men and no regrets for lost innocence. Walker has represented Josie in *TLGC* as a mean, lusty and avaricious brothel owner who enjoys her sexual prowess as much as she does her economic independence. Yet, these women cannot be dismissed as totally devoid of human emotions like love, charity or generosity as "bad" black women were supposed to be because they are individuals whose personalities have been influenced by their circumstances and they have each their own insecurities, doubts, struggles and the personal/individual ways of dealing with them. So a cynical Josie has given up her flourishing business prompted by a naïve trust and blind faith on the one man she has always loved, to become his wife, while Morrison's "three merry gargoyles" (*TBE*, 42) have a tender concern for a young Pecola and compassion for all upright and "good Christian colored women" (43). Naylor on the other hand presents the stories of black women from varied backgrounds in *BC* who are now residents of a brothel in the manner of case studies or solo flights of Jazz music. Her prostitutes are different and unique, each with a traumatic past that has changed them and shaped their destiny. So a rich housewife Jesse Bell, a beautiful and adored daughter from a middle-class background Marie, an innocent Esther who becomes a sacrificial lamb at the altar of poverty to be 'sold' by her brother, have come to Eve's brothel to find refuge and peace of mind, while a truly beautiful soul Sadie, haunted by poverty and circumstances has turned to streetwalking. Each of these women have poignant and soul wrenching stories to tell and cannot be confined within any stereotypical pattern or image.

In representing black women of Category VII who defy categorizations, Toni Morrison, Alice Walker and Gloria Naylor have each presented their vision of the extraordinary black woman and their perception of the possibilities that have opened up before them. If Morrison's Sula in *S* has defied all societal norms and codes in an era where black women had little or no choice but to become a maid/menial or a housewife, ageing prematurely and confined within the narrow circle of morality, virtue and duty, Naylor represents Etta Mae in *WBP* who, as early as 1937, looks white people in the eyes, refusing to address them as Sirs or Mams and as a reckless teenager who builds her own roads. If Walker's Shug Avery in *TCP* has, as a performing artist, lived a life of her own making and created space for other black women like Celie and Marie Agnes, there is also her Sofia in *TCP* from a middle-class background who has fought all her life against male domination and established her worth. If Morrison's Pilate of *SOS* has transcended poverty and circumstances to emerge as the true bearer of African cultural heritage, Walker's Lissie in *TMF* has run the gamut of black women's experience in America to emerge as a seer and visionary painter. Walker's Fanny Nzingha in *TMF* has rejected the academia to take up the humble job of a masseuse while Naylor's Cocoa Day in *MD* has been represented as the modern black woman of the present era who has combined in herself the values of the past and present.

All the three writers have therefore been able to redefine the image of the African-American woman in America. Morrison has deliberately killed the "angel in the house"—the mammy image, as well as the "monster"—the evil black woman of great strength, as a conscious artistic design, just as Walker has represented her generational cycles of black women and Naylor has used the technique of presenting different stories of eight black women in *WBP*, a number of black women in *LH* and *BC* in order to show the multiplicity of their roles and the richness and variety of their personalities and experiences, which could never be described by a monolithic image of the black woman. In representing African-American women in their novels as responding to the changing times and changing labor roles, Toni Morrison, Alice Walker and Gloria Naylor have made a laudable attempt of bringing forth new parameters in defining black women and have also proven their artistic standpoint and worth. While acknowledging their allegiance to a common socio-cultural backdrop, one cannot however understate their authentic triumph as literary artists of genuine talent and powerful vision as they have been able to combine socio-historical authenticity with artistic freedom, the consciousness of a past heritage of pain and loss with the vision of a better future. Through their fictional representations of African-American women in their roles as labor in their novels, they have been able to render not only the long saga of unrelenting misery, suffering, victimization and struggle of black women in the US but also their journey from despair towards changing roles of fulfillment, recognition of self-worth and the opening up of new horizons and possibilities. In backing their literary representations with the sociological perspective, they have been able to capture (as Margaret L. Anderson stresses in her "Foreword" to *Race, Class and Gender: Common Bonds, Different Voices* that artists must be able to do if multicultural studies are to become meaningful) the underlying social structure of oppression that are more than shifting cultural images. Valuing their descendance and heritage from maternal ancestors (both familial and literary) and having the courage to owe the shaping of their imagination to their encounter with the realities of African-American women's existence in America, Toni Morrison, Alice Walker and Gloria Naylor have shown their black women to have transcended, like them, the hardships and toil to emerge as persons in their own right. In doing so, they have like true artists, been able to aesthetically transform the unrecorded experience of black women in America into wonderful representations that foreground their perceptions and profound appreciation and understanding of the reigning/overriding debates of the present critical discourse such as the politics of the human situation, the interrelation of slavery and freedom, the possibility of creating a literature that is both politically engaged and aesthetically beautiful and satisfying, about the interlocking relations of racism, sexism and classism and the degree of free will African-American women might experience in their ongoing struggles for achievement of self-worth, fulfillment in work roles and their quest for rediscovering their identities from within a capitalist, post-colonial society as that of the United States. As pointed out in Chapter 1, the representation of African-American women in their roles as labor in the novels of Toni Morrison, Alice Walker and Gloria Naylor has lent their art the power and purpose, social relevance, authenticity, the willingness to face the challenge of contemporary and problematic debates, the courage to debunk myths and deconstruct received concepts and images and above all, the motive force and dynamic power that serious fiction entails.

The age-old concept of the universality of a work of art to gauge its true merit has come to be questioned today as marginalized and colonized groups have articulated their experiences to break the conspiracy of silence and to overthrow the cultural hegemony constructed by a dominant critical discourse that has suppressed the voice of the groups. With the gaps/spaces left in the narratives in history being investigated with a view to giving voice to untold stories (history being the edited record maintained by the dominant and powerful groups), writers of the oppressed groups like women and ethnic minority groups have come forward to tell their stories in their language. As a doubly oppressed and thrice marginalised group therefore black women have sought to break away from the traditional notions of authorhood by defying confinement and refusing to be reduced to mere properties, characters and images.

Because of their sympathy and empathy and with black women whose suffering they have witnessed and struggles they have been a part of, black women writers are faced with the task of proving their merit as literary artists who can transmute aesthetically the painful memory of a heritage of injustice and exploitation. There is always the risk of being accused as propagandists and bringing in the politics of racism, sexism and classism in their writings, these being their genuine concerns. Unafraid as artists, Toni Morrison, Alice Walker and Gloria Naylor have not conformed to male formulated concepts of feminine virtue or fragility as they have represented African-American women as labor against the idea of angel-monster poles of femininity to create remarkable characters in their novels that are uniquely crafted works of art.

Appendix

Terms and Concepts

It would be prudent to include and explicate certain terms and concepts that had come up during the analysis of the texts as standard references. An understanding of these terms and concepts is felt to be essential in the context of the study.

From the time when African people of different tribes were imported to America, they were designated by names that signified their inferior status in a society where values, ideologies, laws and ideals were determined by the dominant white race. The assorted system of prejudices nurtured and harboured against Africans for characteristics that were external and physical and that differentiated them markedly from the white-skinned Caucasians, gave rise to a number of belittling names, which expressed the collective contempt of a so-called "superior" white race for the "inferior" black race. Any man of color was termed as a "Negro" because he was branded as a member of the "Negroid origin" with physical traits such as curled or kinky hair, broad/flat nose, thick lips and dark skin. The denigrating epithet "nigger" was a distortion of the term "Negro" ("Negro" at least had an anthropological coinage)—a term used as a prerogative by the master to convey not only contempt but also ownership and possession. A "nigger" may be a male or a female just as a beast of burden may be either. A peremptory command conveyed through the address was a cue for the slave to appear in all humility before the master—head bowed, cap in hand, a foolish/supplicating grin on the lips. "Nigger" therefore conjured up the image of a head-scratching, irresponsible and carefree "Sambo" or an "enduring", obedient "mammy" in its plantation culture connotations. The denigrating quality suggested by the name continued even after the days of slavery and continued to have a host of connotations. The name suggested not a single meaning but an entire network of negative and degrading interpretations integrated into the culture of both the black and white societies. For the blacks of course, "nigger" was not nasty, dirty or abominable—an inherent sense of humor allowed them to turn the joke on its head or on the master who so humiliated them by inverting the deprecatory term into a compliment, an affectionate address or even an intimate endearment with sexual overtones (suggesting the intimacy of a shared experience).

For the rising middle-class, the term "colored" denoted gentility and respectability as against the vulgar and obnoxious connotations summoned by names like "nigger" or "darky". They separated themselves from the large majority of poor, illiterate, working-class "niggers" who for them symbolized everything that they wanted to deny, shun and wash away. Cultivating the values of the white society, these genteel, educated, well-off, successful "colored" men and women were affronted and bitterly hurt at the "injustice" of being labeled as common "niggers" by the people of the white race whom they so carefully simulated and like whom they aspired to become in every way, even physically.

During the Black Power Movement of the 1960s and 1970s, African-Americans were made aware of their African roots, their native culture and traditions and "Black" became the symbol of beauty, authenticity, originality and power. The African-Americans referred to themselves proudly as "Blacks" or "Black Americans" as distinct and separate from white Americans—the middle-class, bourgeoisie assimilationist attitude was rejected and aggressive, militant, black nationalism replaced it with a vengeance. It was then the triumph of black arts/ aesthetics (the Black Arts Movement that reached its peak in the 1970s celebrated the originality and vibrancy of indigenous black aesthetics) and black music (Jazz and Blues), the Harlem Renaissance and fierce pride in racial heritage. Because it was the new slogan that "the blacker the berry, the sweeter the juice" [ironically presented in Wallace Thurman's *The Blacker the Berry* (1970)] the negroes now chose to be called "black". A significant shift had occurred—they could at least voice their approvals and disapprovals—protest against "nigger" and be proud to be called "black".

In the following ages, in the wake of Amiri Baraka's *Back to Africa* movement, the Civil Rights Movement, the funding of the NAACP and other pioneering events in the history of United States the terms "Afro-American" and then "African-American" came to be accepted as the usual name to denote members of the Negro race. After Emancipation, the rise of the Talented Tenth and the black middle-class saw a continuation of the obnoxious and denigrating qualities associated with the term "nigger". A denial of one's ethnicity and the rush to overcome race, the break from one's own roots, assimilationism and "mainstreaming" were characteristic features of this period when being a Negro was a curse and the privileged ones would move as far away as possible from such humiliating epithets. As distinct from Euro-Americans or white Americans, members of the African-American race had now established their separate identities—had emerged as a race with a rich cultural past and had claimed and wrested their dignity from the racist white society. The terms Negro, black, Afro-American and African-American are now used interchangeably and hence, in the present study, these terms have been used as and when convenient/at random in referring to the members of the said race. It is to be noted however that "black" may belong to any nation (viz. Carribean, French, South African, African, etc.) while an African-American belonged only to America thus specifying the nationality of the members of the said race.

The North: The northern states of United States of America which were primarily urban and offered varied and new job opportunity to African-American people, lured them from the rural Southern states. During Civil War (1861), the Northern states fought for the Emancipation of the slaves. During the Great Migration of the early 20th century, there was an unprecedented exodus of African-Americans from the South to the North that promised a new future for them. The North therefore symbolized freedom and new possibilities where dreams could be translated into reality.

The South: The Southern states, primarily rural, were the seats of slavery as an institution. They fought in the Civil War to retain their way of life, the slave necessary as cheap labor to work on the huge cotton and sugar plantations that were the backbone of their economy. Capitalist, patriarchal, racist and the centre of segregation and torture, the South symbolized the land of cruelty and subjugation which the African-Americans were glad to leave behind while paradoxically craving its beauty. [*Sources*: *The Norton Anthology of African American Literature, Down Home* by Robert Bone and *Native Sons* by Edward Margolies.]

The Color Black: Skin Color as a Social, Ethical and Aesthetic Sign: Throughout the history of African-Americans, skin color has been the physical manifestation and indicator of their racial identity—on the basis of which they have faced racial discrimination. The color consciousness or sensitiveness to skin color therefore is a natural outcome of years of racial oppression. In African-American literature, skin color has been an obsessive motif and it has stood for not only racist but also classist definition of a person. Miscegenation and the mixing of the African, white American and Indian blood has resulted in an African-American population of multicolored hue and the concept of beauty, superiority, virtue, purity/chastity, cleanliness or otherwise have pivoted on the skin color of these people. In Zora Neale Hurston's *Spunk* (a collection of short stories), a humorous 'Glossary of Harlem Slang' contained words and phrases denoting different colors and shades of 'high yaller', 'high brown', 'vaseline brown', 'seal brown', 'low brown', and 'dark black'. There are variants of black: 'dark black' refers to a casually black person and there are, with increasing blackness, 'low black', 'lam black', and 'damn black'. The latter shade indicates a very black person and it is said that 'lightning bugs follow him till 12 o'clock in the day, thinking it's midnight'. Likewise 'inky dink' refers to a very black person. [*Source*: Brita Lindberg-Seyersted's "The Color Black: Skin Color as Social, Ethical, and Aesthetic Sign in Writings by Black American

Women", *English Studies.* 1992, Vol. I, Swets and Zeitlinger, University of Oslo. 1992. 51-67.]

The insistent reference to skin color in African-American fiction has several functions. Not only does it operate as the external indicator of the race, it also introduces the socio-cultural dimension of the gradual assimilation/integration/ amalgamation of the races. The aesthetic evaluation of skin color is crucial to a person's self-image and to the way he or she is judged by others (both blacks and whites). Skin color may be the physical parameter of defining superior/inferior social standards, of beauty/ugliness, of virtue/vice, of class—elite or proletariat, of refinement or vulgarity. It has already been mentioned that mulattos emerged out of the miscegenation and illicit physical relations between the master and the black female slaves. These lighter skinned offsprings were then distinguishable from their darker kins and eventually being the offsprings of the master lent them certain advantages (as also burdened them with complex psychological problems and moral dilemma). They learnt to read and write and were trained in certain skilled crafts. Often they lived in the Big House which set them apart from the other slaves. Living in close proximity with the "refined" and "well-bred" white gentry, they internalized their values and ideals and gradually started to hold themselves aloof from the very dark field hands—the "dirty niggers". These mulattos now tried to attain "whiteness" in every way, including physical, and their obsession with skin color (the external trait of the fact of blackness) propelled them further away from the darker skinned majority. Their obsessive goal was to "pass", to cross the barrier or color line, to wipe every trace of negro-ness from their being. "Passing" the color line therefore became a major theme and preoccupation in African-American literature whereby the newly emerging black Bourgeoisie middle class tried to eliminate their "blackness" by removing the external evidence that branded them as such.

In *Black Skin, White Masks*, Frantz Fanon said that the economic reality of being a Negro was that the Negro had to constantly strive to achieve a material status that could elevate him above the constraints of his skin color. Jean-Paul Sartre in

Orphee Noir quoted Senghor who said that for Aime Cesaire, the white man was a symbol of *capital* as the Negro was the symbol of *labor* (emphasis mine). As Fanon says, reaching a certain class—being *that* rich makes one white. For the Negro therefore, skin color could only be transcended if one could reach the pinnacle of success.

The issue of skin color interweaves racism, classism, and above all encompasses gender because feminine beauty as a gender construct affects black women more than black men. The physical appeal of a black woman was determined by her skin color as the lighter she was, the more desirable she became and the color scale was repeatedly used to gauge her beauty in terms of the white society's definition, standard and color prejudice. Within the precincts of African-American society, the standard of beauty was deliberately and consciously inverted by an emerging and rapidly enlarging group of fiercely Nationalist blacks who proudly professed the beauty of the black skin. In this context, the darkness of one's skin was a proud reminder of his/her African ancestry and the slogan of "black is beautiful" gained momentum. The era of black women who bleached their skin and straightened their hair was swept away in the tumultuous rush of a burgeoning black racial pride, an awakened consciousness of noble African heritage and the onslaught of a new tide of wearing "Afros", allowing the skin to darken and to force straight hair into tight curls and the advent of a new era.

The psychological and moral significance of skin color has been changing too over the ages. Where earlier "sin (was) negro as virtue (was) white" (Fanon. *Black Skin, White Masks*, p. 96) now black is the symbol of concentration of all the positive energies of the world, the color that has absorbed all the rays of the sun and all the colors in itself unlike the pale and shadowy whiteness that has only been able to reflect. Blackness is now the essence of richness of the universe. The psychological burden of double identity and double consciousness manifest in their ambiguous coloring is no longer a hindrance—the awareness of a unique identity now challenges the African-American person and artist.

Jazz: This music emerged in the first decades of the twentieth century and developed primarily as a city phenomenon, attempting to capture in music the cadences, voices, and even the rising skylines of new, urban America. It was particularly influenced by the tremendousness, velocity and the music-in-motion of the modern train that represented the power and promise of moving away from the land where one's parents and grand parents had been slaves during the period of the Great Migration of the early twentieth century.

The sound of Jazz is that of the African-American voice scored as band music, with all of black talk's flair for story telling, the dirty dozens, understatements, braggadocio, whispery romance, loud talk menance, eloquence and spare dry poetry. Jazz is collaborative music where one hears the instruments and the singers in conversation with each other in patterns often called call and response or call and recall (cf. Morrison's *Beloved—Baby* Suggs' preaching and structure of *Jazz*). Jazz music fingers the jagged grain of experience and knows that despite all efforts and hopes, things might not work out for the best—thus becoming a metaphor for the African-American experience in America. Jazz is the music of the dispossessed. Yet, Jazz is also the music of rejuvenation, motivated by a strong sense of possibility and humour urged by the wish to celebrate human experience—however tragic. [*The Norton Anthology of African-American Literature,* pp. 55-57.]

Blues: At the beginning of the twentieth century, a new kind of music emerged in the South that unlike work songs and spirituals was usually sung by a single voice accompanied by one or more instruments. This music came to be known as blues and involved a compellingly rhythmical sound that relied on patterns of call/response between singer and audience, and at times between singer and instrument. Ralph Ellison penned the following compelling definition of the form:

> The blues is an impulse to keep the painful detail and episodes of a brutal existence alive in one's aching consciousness, to finger its jagged grain, and to transcend it, not by the consolation of philosophy but by squeezing from it a near-tragic, near-comic lyricism. As a form, the blues is an autobiographical chronicle of personal catastrophe expressed lyrically. [*The Norton Anthology of African-American Literature*, pp. 22-23.]

Bibliography

Primary Sources

Morrison, Toni. *The Bluest Eye*. London: Picador, 1993.

——. *Sula*. London: Picador, 1993.

——. *Song of Solomon*. London: Picador, 1993.

——. *Tar Baby*. London: Picador, 1993.

——. *Beloved*. New York: Signet, Penguin Group, 1991.

——. *Jazz*. Signet, New York: Penguin Group, 1992.

Naylor, Gloria. *The Women of Brewster Place*. London and Sidney: Sphere Book Ltd., 1980.

——. *Linden Hills*. New York: Ticknor and Fields, 1985.

——. *Mama Day*. New York: Vintage Books, 1989.

——. *Bailey's Café*. New York: Harcourt Brace Jovanovich, 1992.

Walker, Alice. *The Third Life of Grange Copeland*. New York: Harcourt Brace Jovanovich, 1992.

——. *Meridian*. New York: Harcourt Brace Jovanovich, 1976.

——. *The Color Purple*. New York: Pocket Books, Washington Square Press, 1983.

——. *The Temple of My Familiar*. New York: Pocket Books, Washington Square Press, 1990.

Interviews and Talks

Bakerman, Jane. "The Seams Can't Show: An Interview with Toni Morrison." *Black American Literature Forum*. 7 (Summer 1978): 60.

Lester, Rosemarie K. "An Interview with Toni Morrison". Hessian Radio Network Frankfurt, West Germany, 1988.

Morrison, Toni and Gloria Naylor. "A Conversation: Gloria Naylor and Toni Morrison." Taylor-Gurthrie 188-217. *Southern Review*, 21 (1985): 567-93.

——. "Nobel Lecture 1993." *World Literature Today*, 68 (1994): 5-8.

——. "The Pain of Being Black: An Interview with Toni Morrison." With Bonnie Angelo. Taylor-Guthrie 255-61 [1989 Interview for *Time* 22nd May, pp. 48-50].

——. "Unspeakable Things Unspoken: The Afro-American Presence in American Literature." *Michigan Quarterly Review* 28(1989): 1-34.

Naylor, Gloria. "Black Women Writers: Speaking in Tongues." Lecture at the University of Pennsylvania, Quoted in "Reconstructing History in *Linden Hills*" by Teresa Goddu. *Gloria Naylor: Critical Perspectives Past and Present* Ed. Henry Louis Gates Jr. and K.A. Appaiah, New York: Amistad Press, 1993.

——. "The Women of Brewster Place", *Ebony*, 41 March 1989] I.

Stepto, Robert B. "Intimate Things in Place: A Conversation with Toni Morrison." *Massachusetts Review.* (Sept. 1977): 473-89.

Tate, Claudia. "Conversation with Toni Morrison". *Black Women Writers at Work*. New York: Continuum, 1983. 117-31.

Taylor-Guthrie, Danille. Ed. *Conversations with Toni Morrison.* Jackson: University Press of Mississippi, 1994.

Walker, Alice. "Alice Walker Talks About Black Women". *Encore.* April 1973, pp. 41-42.

——. "Interview with Alice Walker", *Interviews with Black Writers*. Ed. John O'Brien. New York: Liveright, 1973.

——. "Interview with Mary Helen Washington", Jackson: Mississippi, June 17, 1973.

——. *The Originals: Alice Walker: A Portrait in the First Person/ Interview with Jim Hanley.* Produced by Jim Hanley and David Lee. Chicago, ILL: PMI/Films Inc., 1994.

Wilson, Sharon. "A Conversation with Alice Walker". *Alice Walker: Critical Perspectives Past and Present.* Eds. Henry Louis Gates Jr. and K.A. Appaiah, New York: Amistad Press, 1993, pp. 319-25.

Secondary Sources

Allen, Walter. "Family Roles, Occupational Statuses and Achievement Orientation Among Black Women in the United States." *Signs*, 4 (Summer 1979): 672-79.

Anderson, Deborah and David Shapiro. "Racial Differences in Access to High-Paying Jobs and the Wage Gap Between Black and White Women". *Industrial and Labor Relations Review.* Vol. 49, No. 2 (January, 1996). Cornell University, 273-86.

Awkward, Michael. *Inspiring Influences: Tradition, Revision and Afro-American Women's Novels.* New York: Columbia University Press, 1989.

Baker, Houston A. Jr. *Workings of the Spirit: The Poetics of Afro-American Women's Writing*. Chicago: University of Chicago Press, 1991.

——. *Long Black Song: Essays in Black American Literature and Culture*. Charlottesville: University Press of Virginia, 1972.

Bambara, Toni Cade. *The Black Women.* New York: New American Library, 1970.

Barrett, Michele. *Women's Oppression Today: Problems in Marxist Feminist Analysis.* London: Verso Editions, 1980.

Bauer, Raymond and Alice Bauer. "Day to Day Resistance to Slavery." *Journal of Negro History*, 27 (October 1942): 415-17.

Beale, Frances. "Double Jeopardy: To Be Black and Female", *The Black Women.* Ed. Toni Cade Bambara. New York: New American Library, 1970.

——. "Slave of a Slave No More." *The Black Scholar*, 6 (March 1975): 2-10.

Beauvoir, Simone de. *The Second Sex*. New York: Vintage Press, 1974.

Bell, Roseann, Bettye Parker and Beverly Guy-Sheftall. Eds. *Sturdy Black Bridges.* New York: Anchor Press/Doubleday, 1979.

Benhabib, Seyla and Drucillia Cornell. Eds. *Feminism as Critique: Essays on the Politics of Gender in Late Capitalist Societies.* Cambridge: Polity Press, 1987.

Bernard, Jessie. *Women, Wives and Mothers: Values and Options.* Pennsylvania State University, Chicago: Aldine Publishing Co., 1975.

Bethel, Lorraine. *All the Women are White, All the Blacks are Men, But Some of Us are Brave.* Eds. Gloria T. Hull, Patricia Bell Scott, and Barbara Smith. Old Westbury, New York: The Feminist Press, 1982.

Blake, Susan. *Dictionary of Literary Biography: African American Fiction Writers After 1955.* Vol. 33. Eds. Thadius Davies and Trudier Harris. Detroit: Gale, 1984.

Bloom, Harold. "Introduction", *Toni Morrison.* Ed. Harold Bloom. New York: Chelsea House, 1990. 1-5.

Bone, Robert. *The Negro Novel in America.* New Haven and London: Yale University Press, 1958.

Bosrup, Ester. *Women's Role in Economic Development.* London: George Allen Unwin, 1970.

Brown, Sterling. *The Negro in American Fiction.* 1937: Reprint, New York: Athenewn, 1969.

Bryce Bjork, Patrick. *The Novels of Toni Morrison: The Search for Place Within the Community.* New York: Peter Lang Publishing, 1992.

Butler Evans, Eliot. *Race, Gender and Desire: Narrative Strategies in the Fiction of Toni Cade Bambara, Toni Morrison and Alice Walker.* Philadelpha: Temple University Press, 1989.

Byerman, Keith E. *Fingering the Jagged Grain: Tradition and Form in Recent Black Fiction.* Athens: University of Georgia Press, 1985.

Cade, Toni. Ed. *The Black Woman.* New York: New American Library, 1970.

Callahan, John F. *In the African-American Grain.* Middletown, Conn: Wesleyan University Press, 1990.

Carby, Hazel V. *Reconstructing Womanhood.* New York: Oxford University Press, 1987.

Chisholm, Shirley. *Unbought and Unbossed.* Boston: Houghton Mifflin, 1970.

Chopra, P.N. "Factors of Production". *Principles of Economics.* New Delhi: Kalyani Publishers, 1996.

Chow, Esther Ngangling et. al. Eds. *Race, Class and Gender: Common Bonds, Different Voices.* Thousand Oaks, London: Sage Publication, 1996.

Christian, Barbara. "Somebody Forgot to Tell Somebody Something: African-American Women's Historical Novels." *Wild Women of the Whirlwind: Afra-American Culture and Contemporary Literary Renaissance.* Ed. Joanne Braxton and Andre Maclaughlin. New Brunswick: Rutgers University Press, 1990. 326-41.

——. "Shadows Uplifted." *Black Women Novelists.* Westport: Greenwood, 1980. 3-34.

——. *Black Feminist Criticism: Perspectives on Black Women Writers.* New York: Pergamon Press, 1985.

——. *Black Women Novelists: The Development of a Tradition, 1892-1976.* Westport Ct: Greenwood, 1980.

——. Ed. "*Everyday Use*": *Alice Walker.* New Brunswick, NJ: Rutgers University Press, 1994.

Collins, Patricia Hill. *Black Feminist Thought: Knowledge, Consciousness and the Politics of Empowerment.* New York: Routledge, 1991.

Connel, R.W. *Gender Power: Society, the Person and Sexual Politics.* Cambridge: Polity Press, 1987.

Contemporary Literary Criticism Vols. 4, 10, 22 and 55 Whiteplains, New York: Longmifs, 1986.

Cook, Michael G. *Afro-American Literature in the Twentieth Century.* New Haven: Yale University Press, 1984.

Davis, Angela. *Women, Race and Class.* New York: Random House, 1981.

Davis, Charles T. *Black is the Color of the Cosmos*. New York: Garland Publishers, 1982.

De Weever, Jacqueline. *Mythmaking and Metaphor in Black Women's Fiction*. New York: St. Martin's Press, 1992.

Eisentein, Zilla. *Capitalist Patriarchy and the Case for Socialist Feminism*. New York: Monthly Review Press, 1979.

Ellison, Ralph. *Shadow and Act*. New York: Random House, 1953.

Evans, Marie. Ed. *Black Women Writers (1950-1980): A Critical Evaluation*. New York: Anchor Doubleday, 1984.

Fanon, Frantz. *Black Skin, White Masks*. London: Paladin. Granada Publishing Ltd., 1970.

Firestone, Shulamith. *The Dialectic of Sex: The Case for Feminist Revolution*. New York: William Marrow, 1970.

Foner, Philip S., Ronald Lewis and Robert Cvornyak. Eds. *The Black Workers Since the AFL-CIO Merger 1955-1969*. Philadelphia: Temple University Press, 1978.

Foner, Philip S. *Women and the American Labor Movement*. New York: Free Press, 1980.

Foster, Frances. "Changing Concepts of the Black Women". *Journal of Black Studies,* June 1973, 433-52.

Franklin, John Hope. *From Slavery to Freedom*. New York: Random House, 1969.

Frazier, E. Franklin. *The Negro Family in the United States*. New York: Dryden, 1948.

Friedan, Betty. *The Feminine Mystique*. New York: W.W. Norton, 1963.

Friere, Paulo. *Pedagogy of the Oppressed*. England: Pelican Books, 1972.

Fullbrook, Kate. "*Free Women: Ethics and Aesthetics in Twentieth Century Women's Fiction*." Philadelphia: Temple University Press, 1990.

Fusfield, Daniel R. and Timothy Bates. *The Political Economy of the Urban Ghetto*. Carbondale: Southern Illinois University Press, 1984.

Gates Jr., Henry Louis and K.A. Appiah. Eds. *Alice Walker: Critical Perspectives Past and Present*. New York: Amistad Press, 1993.

——. Eds. *Toni Morrison: Critical Perspectives Past and Present*. New York: Amistad Press, 1993.

——. Eds. *Gloria Naylor: Critical Perspectives Past and Present*. New York: Amistad Press, 1993.

Gates Jr., Henry Louis and Nellie Y. McKay Eds. *The Norton Anthology of African American Literature*. New York: W.W. Norton and Company Inc., 1997.

Gates Jr., Henry Louis. Ed. *Reading Black, Reading Feminist: A Critical Anthology*. New York: A Meridian Book. Penguin Group, 1990.

——. *The Signifying Monkey*. New York: Oxford University Press, 1988.

Gayles, Gloria Wayde. *No Crystal Stair-Visions of Race and Sex in Black Women's Fiction*. New York: The Pilgrim Press, 1984.

Giddings, Paula. *When and Where I Enter*. New York: Morrow, 1984.

Gilbert, Sandra M. and Susan Gubar. *Madwoman in the Attic: The Woman Writer and the Nineteenth-Century Literary Imagination*. New Haven: Yale University Press, 1979.

Glazer, Nathan and Daniel P. Moynihan. Eds. *Ethnicity, Theory and Experience*. Cambridge, Mass: Harvard University Press, 1975.

Gray, Janet. "Alice Walker". *American Writers: A Collection of Literary Biographies*. Supp. III, Pt. 2. Ed. Lea Baechler and A. Walton Litz. New York: Scribner's, 1991.

Greer, Germaine. *The Female Eunuch*. London: Paladin, 1971.

Guerin, Wilfred L. et. al. Eds. *A Handbook of Critical Approaches to Literature*. Fourth Edition. Oxford, New York: Oxford University Press, 1999.

Hansen, Karen, and Ilene J. Philipson. Eds. *Women, Class and the Feminist Imagination: A Socialist-Feminist Reader*. Philadelphia: Temple University Press, 1990.

Harris, Trudier. *Fiction and Folklore: The Novels of Toni Morrison.* Knoxville: University of Tennessee Press, 1991.

Hartmann, Heidi. "The Unhappy Marriage of Marxism and Feminism: Towards a More Progressive Union," *Capital and Class*, 8 (Summer 1979).

Healey, Joseph F. *Race, Ethnicity and Gender in the United States—Inequality, Group Conflict and Power.* Thousand Oaks, California: Pine Forge Press, 1997.

Hecht, Michael L., M.J. Collier and S.A. Ribeau. *African-American Communication.* Newbury Park: Sage Publications, 1993.

Heinze, Denise. *The Dilemma of "Double-Consciousness": Toni Morrison's Novels.* Athens: University of Georgia Press, 1993.

Hernton, Calvin. *Sex and Racism in America.* New York: Grove Press, 1965.

——. *The Sexual Mountain and Black Women Writers.* New York: Anchor-Doubleday, 1987.

Herring, Cedric and Karen Rose Wilson-Sandberry. "Preference or Necessity? Changing Work Roles of Black and White Women, 1970-1990". *Journal of Marriage and the Family* 55 (May 1993): 314-25.

Hill Collins, Patricia. *Black Feminist Thought: Knowledge, Consciousness and the Politics of Empowerment.* Boston: Unwin Hyman, 1990.

Hirsch, Marianne. *The Mother-Daughter Plot: Narrative, Psychoanalysis, Feminism.* Bloomington: Indiana University Press, 1989.

Holloway, Karla F.C. *Moorings and Metaphors: Figures of Culture and Gender in Black Women's Literature.* New Brunswick, N.J.: Rutgers University Press, 1992.

hooks, bell. *Feminist Theory: From Margin to Center.* Boston: Sound End Press, 1984.

——. *Ain't I a Woman: Black Women and Feminism.* Boston: South End Press, 1984.

——. *Yearning: Race, Gender and Cultural Politics*. Boston: South End Press, 1990.

Hurston, Zora Neale. *Mules and Men*. 1935. Reprint, Bloomington: Indiana University Press, 1978.

——. *Their Eyes Were Watching God*. New York: Fawcett Publishers, 1965.

Jaynes, Gerald D. "The Labor Market Status of Black Americans: 1939-1985". *Journal of Economic Perspectives*. Vol. 4, No. 4 (Fall), 1990, 9-24.

Jones, Jacqueline. *Labor of Love, Labor of Sorrow: Black Women, Work and the Family, From Slavery to the Present*. New York: Vintage, 1985.

King, Mary, C. "Occupational Segregation by Race and Sex, 1940-1988." *Industrial Relations*. Vol. 33, No. 2 (April), 1994, 168-83.

Kinney, James. *Amalgamations*. Westport, Conn: Greenwood Press, 1985.

Krishnaraj, Maithreyi. Ed. *Feminist Concepts*. Part I and II Series-7, Research Centre for Women's Studies. SNDT Women's University, Bombay.

Krumholz, Linda. "The Ghosts of Slavery: Historical Recovery in Toni Morrison's *Beloved*". *Studies in American Fiction* 17 (1989), 157-67.

Kuhn, Annette and Anne Marie Wolpe. Eds. *Feminism and Materialism, Women and Media of Production*. Boston: Routledge and Kegan Paul, 1978.

Ladner, Joyce. *Tomorrow's Tomorrow.* Garden City, New York: Vintage Press, 1972.

Layton, Horace and St. Clairs Drake, *Black Metropolis,* Vols. 1 and 2, New York: Harcourt, Brace and World, 1945.

Lee, Don. "Blackwoman," *Don't Cry, Scream*. Detroit: Broadside Press, 1969.

Lerner, Gerda. *Black Women in White America: A Documentary History.* New York: Vintage Press, 1972.

——. *The Creation of Patriarchy.* New York: Oxford University Press, 1986.

Lindberg-Seyersted, Brita. "The Color Black: Skin Color as Social, Ethical, and Aesthetic Sign in Writings by Black American Women", *English Studies.* 1992, Vol. I, Swets and Zeitlinger, University of Oslo. 1992, 51-67.

Lodge, David. *Twentieth Century Literary Criticism.* New York: Longman, 1972.

Lubiano, Wahneema. "Toni Morrison". *African-American Writers.* Ed. Valerie Smith. New York: Scribner's, 1991. 321-33.

Mainardi, Pat. "The Politics of Housework," .*Sisterhood is Powerful.* Ed. Robin Morgan. New York: Random House, 1970. 23-26.

Margolies, Edward. *Native Sons: A Critical Study of Twentieth Century Black American Authors.* New York: J.B. Lippincott Company, 1968.

Mbalia, Doreatha D. *Toni Morrison's Developing Class Consciousness.* Selinsgrove: Susequehanna University Press, 1991.

Mbite, John. *African Religions and Philosophy.* New York: Doubleday Anchor, 1970.

McKay, Nellie Y. Ed. *Critical Essays on Toni Morrison.* Boston: G.K. Hall and Co., 1988.

McCray, Carrie. "The Black Woman and Family Roles, "*The Black Woman.* Ed. LaFrances Rodgers-Rose. Beverly Hills, Cal.: Sage Publications, 1980.

Mies, Maria. *Patriarchy and Accumulation on a World Scale, Women in the International Division of Labor.* New Jersey, USA: Zed Books Ltd., 1986.

Millet, Kate. *Sexual Politics.* London: Sphere Books Ltd., 1972.

Mobley, Marilyn Sanders. *Folk Roots and Mythic Wings. The Cultural Function of Narrative.* Baton Rouge: Louisiana State University Press, 1991.

Mobley, Marilyn E. "Narrative Dilemma: Jadine as Cultural Orphan in Toni Morrison's *Tar Baby.*" *The Southern Review*, 23 (Autumn 1989).

Moore, Henrietta. "The Cultural Constitutions of Gender." *The Polity Reader in Gender Studies.* Cambridge: Polity Press, 1994.

Morgan, Robin. Ed. *Sisterhood is Powerful.* New York: Random House, 1970.

Morrison, Toni. "Rootedness: The Ancestor as Foundation." *Black Women Writers 1950-1980.* Ed. Mari Evans. New York: Anchor: Doubleday, 1984. 339-45.

——. *Playing in the Dark: Whiteness and Literary Imagination.* Cambridge, Mass.: Harvard University Press, 1992.

Murray, Pauli. "The Liberation of Black Women." *Voices of the New Feminism.* Ed. Mary Lou Thompson. Boston: Beacon Press, 1970. 87-102.

Myrdal, Gunnar. *An America Dilemma.* New York: Harper, 1944.

Noble, Jeanne. *Beautiful, Also, Are the Souls of My Black Sisters.* Englewood, N.J.: Prentice Hall, 1978.

O'Donnell, Patrick. Eds. *Modern Fiction Studies: Toni Morrison Double Issue.* Volume 39, Numbers 3 and 4, Purdue University, West Lafayette: Fall/Winter 1993.

Omvedt, Gail. "Patriarchy and Matriarchy." *Feminist Concepts.* Part I: Contribution to Women Studies. Series 7. Research Centre for Women's Studies. SNDT Women's University, Vithaldas Vidyavihar, Santacruz West. Bombay.

Ortner, Sherry. "Is Female to Male as Nature is to Culture?" *Women, Culture and Society.* Ed. M. Rosaldo and L. Lamphere. Stanford, California: Standford University Press, 1974.

Otten, Terry. *The Crime of Innocence in the Fiction of Toni Morrison.* Columbia: University of Missouri Press, 1989.

Palmer, Phyllis Marynick. "White Women/Black Women: The Dualism of Female Identity and Experience in the United States." *Feminist Studies* 9 (Spring 1983), 151-70.

Peach, Linden. *Toni Morrison.* New York: St. Martin's Press, 1995.

Petry, Ann. *The Street.* Boston: Houghton Mifflin, 1964.

Pryse, Marjorie and Hortense J. Spillers. Eds. *Conjuring: Black Women, Fiction, and Literary Tradition.* Bloomington: Indiana University Press, 1985.

Reiter, Raina. Ed. *Toward an Anthropology of Women.* New York: Monthly Review Press, 1975.

Rich, Adrienne. *Of Woman Born.* New York: Bantam Books, 1976.

Rigney, Barbara. *The Voices of Toni Morrison.* Columbus: Ohio State University Press, 1991.

Russel, Sandi. *Render Me My Song: African-American Women Writers from the Slavery to the Present.* New York: St. Martin's Press, 1991.

Sherman, Charlotte Watson. Ed. *Sisterfire: Black Womanist Fiction and Poetry.* New York, NY: Harper Perennial, 1994.

Showalter, Elaine. *A Literature of Their Own: British Women Novelists from Bronte to Lessing.* New Jersey: Princeton University Press, 1977.

Sizemore, Barbara. "Sexism and the Black Male." *The Black Scholar*, 4 (March/April 1973), 2-11.

Smith, Barbara. "Introduction". *Home Girls: A Black Feminist Anthology.* New York: Kitchen Table, Women of Color Press, 1983. xix-lvi.

——. "Toward a Black Feminist Criticism". 1977. *The New Feminist Criticism: Essays on Women, Literature and Theory.* Ed. Elaine Showalter. New York: Pantheon, 1985.

——. "Doing Research on Black American Women," *Women's Studies Newsletter*, 4 (Spring 1976), 4-5, 7.

Smith, Valerie. *Self Discovery and Authority in Afro-American Narrative.* Cambridge, Massachussets: Harvard University Press, 1987.

Sochen, June. *Her Story: A Woman's View of American History.* Vol. 2 New York: Alfred Publishing, 1974.

Springer, Marlene. Ed. *What Manner of Woman, Essays on English and American Life and Literature*. New York University 1977. Oxford: Basil Blackwell, 1978.

Staples, Robert. *The Black Woman in America*. Chicago: Nelson Hall Inc., 1973.

Steinem, Gloria. "Do You Know This Woman? She Knows You—A Profile of Alice Walker", *Ms. X*, No. 12 (June 1982).

Stone, Louis D. "What It's Like to Be a Colored Woman," *Washington Post*. Nov. 13, 1966 quoted in *Black Women in White America*, Ed. Gerda Lerner.

Stowe, Harriet Beecher. *Uncle Tom's Cabin*. 1852. New York: New American Library, 1981.

Thompson, Daniel. *Sociology of the Black Experience*. Westport, Conn.: Greenwood Press, 1974.

Thurman, Wallace. *The Blacker the Berry*. New York: Macmillan, 1970.

U.S. Department of Labor, *Handbook of Labor Statistics*, 1978; Bulletin 3000, Washington D.C.: Government Printing Office, 1979. 75-79.

Van Deburg, William L. *Slavery and Race in American Popular Culture*. Madison, Wisconsin: University of Wisconsin Press, 1984.

Walker, Alice. Ed. *I Love Myself When I Am Laughing. And Then Again When I Am Looking Mean and Impressive: A Zora Neale Hurston Reader*. New York: The Feminist Press, 1979. 152-55.

——. *In Search of Our Mothers' Gardens: Womanist Prose*. San Diego: Harcourt Brace Jovanovich, 1983.

——. *In Love and Trouble: Stories of Black Women*. New York: Harcourt Brace Jovanovich, 1973.

Walker Melissa. *Down from the Mountaintop, Black Women's Novels in the Wake of Civil Rights Movement*. New Haven: Yale University Press, 1992.

Wallace, Michelle, *Black Macho and the Myth of the Superwoman* New York: Dial Press, 1978.

Walter, Allen. "Family Roles, Occupational Statuses and Achievement Orientation Among Black Women in the United States." *Signs*, 4 (Summer 1979).

Watson, Carole McAlpine. *Prologue—The Novels of Black American Women.* Westport, Connecticut: Greenwood Press, 1985.

West, Cornel. *Race Matters.* Boston: Beacon Press, 1993.

White, Deborah Gray. *Aren't I a Woman? Female Slaves in the Plantation South.* New York: W.W. Norton and Company, 1985.

White, Vernessa C. *Afro-American and East German Fiction—A Comparative Study.* New York: Peter Lang Publication, 1983.

Williams, C. Glyn. *Labor Economics.* New York: John Willey and Sons, 1970.

Willis, Susan. "Eruptions of Funk: Historicizing Toni Morrison." *Specifying: Black Women Writing and American Experience.* Madison: University of Wisconsin Press, 1987, 83-109.

——. "Eruptions of Funk: Historicizing Toni Morrison". *Black American Literature Forum*, 16 (Spr 1982), 34-42.

Winchell, Donna Haisty. *Alice Walker.* New York: Twayne Publishers; Maxwell McMillian International, 1992.

Woolf, Virginia. *A Room of One's Own.* New York: Harcourt Brace, 1929.

Wright, Richard. *Twelve Million Black Voices.* New York: Thunder's Mouth Press, 1988.

Young, Donald. *American Minority Peoples.* New York: Harper, 1932.

Zalokar, Nadja. *The Economic Status of Black Women: An Exploratory Investigation.* Washington, D.C.: U.S. Commission on Civil Rights, 1990.

Reviews and Newspaper Articles

The New York Times Book Review, November 1, 1970 on *The Bluest Eye* by Haskel Frankel.

The New York Times Book Review, December 30, 1973 on *Sula* by Sarah Blackburn.

The New Yorker, November 7, 1977 on *Song of Solomon* by Susan Lardner.

The New Republic, March 21, 1981 on *Tar Baby* by Maureen Howard.

The New York Times Book Review, August 22, 1982 on *Women of Brewster Place* by Annie Gottlieb.

The New Republic, September 6, 1982 on *Women of Brewster Place* by Dorothy Wickenden.

The New York Times Book Review, March 3, 1985 on *Linden Hills* by Mel Watkins.

Ms., *June 1985 on Linden Hills by Sherley Anne Williams.*

The New York Times Book Review, September 13, 1987 on *Beloved* by Margaret Atwood.

The Los Angeles Times, March 6, 1988 on *Mama Day* by Rita Mae Brown.

The New York Times Book Review, February 21, 1988 on *Mama Day* by Bharati Mukherjee.

The New York Times Book Review, 1989 on *The Temple of My Familiar* by J.M. Coetzee.

The San Fransisco Review of Books, Summer 1989 on *The Temple of My Familiar* by Ursula K. Le Guin.

The Nation, May 25, 1992 on *Jazz* by John Leonard.

Johnson, Daniel. *"Prize and Prejudice"*, *The Times,* London. October 1993.

Gupta, Suchanda. "Profile: Black Beauties", *Sunday Statesman* June 17, 2001.